FLORENTINE HISTORY

• THE BARNES & NOBLE LIBRARY OF ESSENTIAL READING •

FLORENTINE HISTORY

By

Niccolò Machiavelli

Translated by
W. K. Marriott
F. R. Hist. S.

Introduction by John Lotherington

BARNES & NOBLE BOOKS
NEW YORK

THE BARNES & NOBLE
LIBRARY OF ESSENTIAL READING

Introduction and Suggested Reading Copyright © 2004 by Barnes & Noble Books

Originally published in 1525

This edition published by Barnes & Noble Publishing, Inc.

Cover Design by Pronto Design, Inc.

2004 Barnes & Noble Publishing, Inc.

ISBN 0-7607-5601-5

Printed and bound in the United States of America

3 5 7 9 10 8 6 4 2

CONTENTS

INTRODUCTION

IN *Florentine History* Machiavelli wrote about his native city, which he loved with a passion — more than his soul, he said — and by which he was exasperated. He was not just the famously cold, ironic analyst of ruthless power politics, evident in much of his most famous work, *The Prince;* he had a fervent sense of the common good and how that might be achieved in a republic. For him, Florence had the potential to be one of the greatest of republics, a match for ancient Rome itself, but that potential had never been fulfilled. In the *Florentine History* Machiavelli explores why not and in the process reveals the dynamic and danger of republican politics — his thinking here, as in all his works, resonating powerfully for us today. The *Florentine History* is a series of eight essays (known as 'books') on the city and its Italian context during the Middle Ages and the Renaissance. They do not follow all the rules of what we see today as professional historical writing — Machiavelli could be as cavalier with the facts as an unscrupulous modern journalist — but they are the fruit of one of the most original minds ever to have been brought to bear on politics.

Niccolò Machiavelli was born in Florence in 1469. At the young age of twenty-nine in 1498, he entered government service in the city state of Florence as Second Chancellor, a senior post, with responsibilities for relations between Florence and its subject territories in Tuscany and more broadly for foreign affairs. His time as an active policy maker came to an end in 1512 when the Medici overthrew the republic and took control of the city. But the period of his greatest influence was to come not as a functionary but as a writer. Along with various treatises, plays and poems, he wrote *The Prince* (1513), the *Discourses* (c.1514-1519), the *Art of War* (1521), and the *Florentine History* (1520-1525). He died in 1527.

Niccolò was the son of a lawyer, Bernardo Machiavelli, whose earnings were meager and whose family fortune had declined over the previous generations. Machiavelli referred in later years to the poverty in which he had grown up, and as a consequence he seems to have regarded himself as an outsider among the Florentine elite. Nonetheless, Bernardo ensured that his son had an excellent classical education. Machiavelli grew up under the benign, behind-the-scenes despotism of Lorenzo de Medici, 'The Magnificent.' He witnessed, at the age of nine, the disastrous conspiracy led by the Pazzi family, heads of a rival faction to the Medici. Sixteen years later, following the fateful incursion into Italy by the armies of the French King in 1494, he saw the overthrow of Lorenzo's successor, Piero, and his replacement as leader of Florence by Savonarola, the apocalyptic friar, who sought to purify the decadent city and piled Renaissance art onto bonfires of vanities. In 1498 Savonarola lost power and was himself burnt on the Piazza della Signoria; the republic was re-born. At that point Machiavelli, through well-placed family connections, secured his job in government service, and was determined to see the republic thrive anew.

During his time in office Machiavelli was sent on a number of diplomatic missions to France, to the Emperor in Germany, to the Papal court in Rome and, most significantly, to Cesare Borgia, the great model of strengths and weaknesses of political leadership portrayed in *The Prince*. In 1506 Machiavelli achieved one of his most abiding goals—the establishment of a citizen militia to replace the unreliable mercenaries on which Florence had previously depended—and in 1509 he reached the zenith of his career in government when his military planning led to the re-conquest of Pisa. But Italy was now the battleground of Europe's great powers, France and Spain, and the fate of Florence was not in the hands of its militia. At the behest of the Spanish, the Medici were restored to power in 1512 and the renewed republican experiment was brought to an end. Machiavelli lost his position and was wrongly implicated in a conspiracy against the new government in 1513, leading to his arrest and torture. Released as part of an amnesty on the election of the Medici pope, Leo X, Machiavelli retired to his farm outside Florence with his wife, Marietta, and six children. There he began to write. He told his friend, Francesco Vettori, how he would spend the first part of his day on business, haggling over wood-cutting, then would read classical love poetry and recall his own amorous exploits, before settling himself in a tavern to play games and gossip with the locals. Then, in the evening, he would return home, change out of his mud-spattered clothes into robes of state, and commune with the great historians and political thinkers of classical Rome. For Machiavelli this life of the mind was both a substitute for power and a preparation for his return to it.

The first major work Machiavelli wrote after his release from prison in 1513 was *The Prince*, a handbook on how to establish a new state and bring order out of chaos. He intended that this work should bring him to the attention of the Medici and back into government service. Although this did not work, his writing continued. Eventually, in 1519, Machiavelli's political luck changed, when Cardinal Giulio Medici became the dominant political influence in Florence. The Cardinal wished to appear favorable to some of the forms of republicanism, and he was also close to Lorenzo Strozzi, a friend of Machiavelli's. In November 1520, Machiavelli received a commission from the Cardinal to write the *Florentine History*, which he was to complete in 1525. Machiavelli's death, two years later, followed shortly after the Sack of Rome, when his patron, who had become Pope Clement VII, fell under the control of Emperor Charles V, and Machiavelli's last hopes for a resurgent Italy finally expired.

Machiavelli's theme in the *Florentine History* is discord. He criticized his great humanist predecessors, Leonardo Bruni and Poggio Bracciolini, as historians of Florence for focussing on external affairs and neglecting the disputes which animated political life in the city. They no doubt saw such politics as disreputable, inimical to the glory of Florence. In contrast, Machiavelli, who was a unique combination of pessimist and idealist, thought that glory and domestic discord were intimately and beneficially associated, so long as the energies unleashed in political strife were appropriately channelled. His main reference point was the golden, classical age of republican Rome, when there had been continual tensions between the aristocrats and the plebeians, but these tensions were contained within republican institutions and the laws. Consequently the Roman aristocracy were never able to impose servitude on the plebs, and the plebs lived in liberty rather than degenerating into their natural state of anarchy. Machiavelli had a dim view of human nature in reaction to the neo-Platonic thinkers of his time, who emphasized the creative, divine spark in Man. Machiavelli thought humankind to be naturally grasping and short-sightedly self-destructive, unable to see that the good life is one lived as citizens in, through, and for the community. Only creative tension, such as in Rome, would constrain baser impulses and allow the common good to flourish.

Instead of this balance of classes, Florence was dominated by *sette*, sects or factions. One group, often speaking for the aristocracy or the people but usually a mixture of the two, would overthrow another, leading to bloodshed and exile, and would in turn be overthrown. This discord resulted in recurrent civil violence rather than in law; it was politics which served private interests rather than the common good. For Machiavelli, the solution to such corruption was domination by an individual whose *virtù* enabled him to humble factions and act as a law-giver. This key concept of *virtù* was most definitely not Christian virtue, but a decisiveness in doing whatever it takes to seize control, to subdue Fortune, depicted, in the gender metaphor of the time, as an unruly woman who could be brought to obedience only by a commanding man. The fact that the exercise of *virtù* would sometimes override conventional morality, as depicted most notoriously in

The Prince, disturbed Machiavelli not at all—he argued it was simply a recognition of necessity and the way the world worked—but it outraged contemporaries then and many commentators today. Others, starting with Francis Bacon in the seventeenth century, are "much beholden to Machiavel and others, that write what men do, and not what they ought to do." For Machiavelli, in writing the *Florentine History*, the immediate problem was that the commanding individuals in fifteenth century Florence, Cosimo de Medici and his grandson, Lorenzo the Magnificent, were the forebears of his patron, Cardinal Giulio de Medici, and they had failed to re-establish republican institutions and laws, and had continued to govern in their private, rather than the public, interest.

Machiavelli wrote to his friend, Vettori, that he wished he had been by Machiavelli's side to advise him as to whether he had exaggerated some things or underrated others in the *Florentine History*. In deference to his Medici patron, Machiavelli poured what praise he could on Cosimo and Lorenzo the Magnificent. He depicted Cosimo's intelligence, as well as his generosity and magnificent building projects, in contrast with his modest way of life— characteristics which attracted friendship but not envy—and his clever financial and diplomatic manipulation of other Florentine powers which maintained the city's security. But Machiavelli also hinted at his shortcomings. The reputation he ascribed to Cosimo was of the highest for someone unarmed; for Machiavelli the only durable power in an unstable world was armed power, and all else was papering over the cracks. Cosimo's *virtù* and control of Fortune were sufficient to exalt his friends and destroy his enemies, but there was no mention of the public interest and, near his end, Cosimo was shown to lament that the city was being ruined by its citizens and his own supporters. Machiavelli acknowledged in a letter that what he could not state directly he could put in the mouth of a defeated rival to Cosimo. (Machiavelli took full advantage of the practice of historians from the classical age through to the seventeenth century of inventing speeches to flesh out the bare chronicle of facts.) Rinaldo degli Albizzi, himself banished when Cosimo returned from exile in 1434, observed in the *Florentine History* that he preferred not to live in a city governed by men and shifting favor rather than by laws. Likewise, Machiavelli's praise for Lorenzo the Magnificent was subtly ambiguous. His achievement had been considerable in maintaining Florence's greatness until his death in 1492 — most spectacularly accomplished by his diplomatic mission, at risk of great personal danger, to the court of King of Naples, through which he obtained that king's alliance at the hour of Florence's direst need. But Lorenzo had never adhered to the advice Machiavelli put in the mouth of his brother, Giuliano de Medici, who was assassinated in 1478, that he should beware taking all power to himself. So the *Florentine History* concluded that on Lorenzo's death the seeds which were to ruin Italy, which only he had known how to eliminate, began to grow.

Because of the constraints of his commission, Machiavelli moderated other elements of his views more boldly stated elsewhere. For instance, he regarded the influence of Christianity in Florence, which was not a factor in classical Rome, as catastrophic when expressed in the public sphere, as it made renunciation of the world, rather than *virtù* and engagement in it, the highest goal of life. In the *Florentine History*, he was careful to make conventional references to divine providence, if not many of them. However, he could not refrain from attacking popes in general, whose misuse of spiritual powers and the instability of whose rule, having neither the institutions of a republic nor the roots of a hereditary monarchy, had led again and again to the intervention of foreign powers in Italian affairs. Machiavelli's most barbed comments were reserved for individual popes, such as Sixtus IV, a great enemy of Florence who died five days after he had made peace, because, Machiavelli suggested, he was such an enemy to peace he could not outlive it.

The humanist form of history writing, which Machiavelli adopted, allowed him to offer a more explicit and developed analysis at certain points. The speeches he invented were often couched in that most sophisticated Renaissance form for exploring political ideas, the dialogue. So, as the mercenary soldier, the Duke of Athens, began his brief tyrannical reign over Florence in the mid-fourteenth century, a delegation of citizens warned him that no amount of force would crush a city used to liberty because its citizens would never give up their resistance and even his supporters would eventually become his rivals. The Duke responded that he offered unity and an end to *sette*, the factions which enfeebled the city. The two speeches taken together posed the key dilemma for Florence—the Florentines could not live with liberty (because of the factions), nor could they live without it. The Duke's rule lasted a disastrous ten months before he was driven out. Machiavelli allowed himself the joke that because the Duke was small, dark, and had a terrible beard, he had deserved to be hated.

As well as the set speeches, each of the eight books comprising the *Florentine History* began with general reflections, for instance, on the comparison between Florence and classical Rome, the need to avoid both servitude and anarchy, the benevolent effects of political divisions which were not factions, the virtues of acquiring reputation through serving the public good rather than private interest, and the way in which conspiracies so often rebounded on their authors. Machiavelli also discussed Florence's relations with neighboring territories in these general reflections. He did not doubt the need for a successful state to dominate its neighbors, but he argued that rather than conquest, which would store up troubles and resistance, domination should develop out of a system of mutually beneficial but dependent alliances. Machiavelli was of course no pacifist—he considered it true commitment in battle when a thousand died, and he poured scorn on battles fought by mercenaries in which, in the complete absence of valour, the casualties might only be a few men accidentally falling off their horses. But he saw no value in what he called the disordered wars which had become the norm in late medieval Italy and brought neither wealth nor security even to the victors. These comments echoed the laments at Italian powers gradually losing their liberty, unable to hold their own in the real wars fought by France and Spain that had raged across Italy since 1494.

A thread running through all these observations was Machiavelli's hope that what he wrote could provide the inspiration and insight necessary for the defense of true liberty. The genre of the *Florentine History*, therefore, is rhetoric, rather than history as we would see it. While the broad sweep of the narrative was generally true, the point was not to present the past with scientific attention to accurate detail, but to instruct and persuade. Machiavelli, like his humanist predecessors, did no archival research, instead relying on a small number of sources, choosing them not on the grounds of their reliability but with regard to their fruitfulness for his theme. His subject was politics, through and through. The cultural achievement of Renaissance Florence was discussed not in itself, but with reference to the prestige of the Medici or criticized as a sign of that political decadence that, Machiavelli argued, accompanies the dominance of refined, leisurely pursuits. Social change or economic developments were of concern only insofar as they led to political upheaval. Florence was Machiavelli's subject not in itself but for a very particular purpose. In his view, the virtue of writing the history of one's own republic, rather than a theoretical overview of republics in general, was that, "if every example of a republic is moving, those which one reads concerning one's own are much more so and much more useful." Machiavelli wrote to move his readers to what he saw as right action; not to emulate great deeds, as was traditional in humanist history writing, but to avoid the error and self-defeat which had, he argued, for so long prevented his beloved native city and Italy in general from securing liberty and achieving greatness.

Machiavelli wrote in the 1520s for a Medici cardinal, for his fellow citizens of Florence and for Italians in general. But the power of the *Florentine History* to provoke reflection is not confined to that time or those readers. Machiavelli argued that, although circumstances change, human passions remain the same, and so conversations about political ideas and experience can traverse time and space. Whatever the philosophical debates about that view, a conversation based on the *Florentine History* has continued. In his *Social Contract* Rousseau cited Machiavelli's portrait of faction in the *Florentine History* to show what could frustrate the expression of the general will. Marx drew on Machiavelli's account of the 1378 Revolt of the Ciompi (workers in the wool trade), which showed the rebels not as immoral thugs or the dupes of demagogues, but as a group responding to economic pressures and pursuing rational interests. Today we can reflect on the *Florentine History* when we talk about creative or destructive political competition among political parties or interest groups, and about the nature and precariousness of liberty in a world where it is still being fought over.

John Lotherington is the director of the 21st Century Trust in London. He is the editor and author of several books on European history.

FIRST BOOK

GENERAL SURVEY OF ITALY

THE people who inhabited the northern regions beyond the rivers Rhine and Danube, living in teeming and healthy countries, very often increased in such vast numbers that part were compelled to abandon the lands in which they were born and seek new countries in which to live. The following method was adopted when one of such territories wished to unburden itself of inhabitants. The population divided itself into three parts, so arranged that each part alike had some noblemen and some low-born, some rich and some poor, amongst them. Afterwards that part to which the lot fell set forth to seek its fortune, and the other two, rid of the third, remained to enjoy the fatherland. Such were the races who, having their opportunity given them by the emperors, destroyed the Roman Empire, for these emperors, by abandoning Rome, the ancient seat of empire, and degrading themselves by residing at Constantinople, had weakened the Western Empire by relaxing their vigilance and leaving it exposed to the rapacity of their servants and enemies. And truly the ruin of such an empire, founded upon the blood of so many brave men, could never have come to pass had there been less sloth on the part of its princes, or less treachery in their ministers, or less effort and persistency in the assailants; for those who contributed to that ruin were not of one race, but of many.

The first of those who came against the empire from the north, after the Cimbrians had been conquered by Marius, were the Visigoths, as their name was in their own language, but in ours the Western Goths. These, after many battles fought on the confines of the empire, remained for a time, by concessions of the emperors, in their own territory on the far bank of the river Danube; and although, at various times, and for various causes, they raided the Roman provinces, the power of the empire was always sufficient to curb them. In the end they were gloriously subdued by Theodosius, and being brought under his yoke did not re-elect any king, but remained content with their subsidy, and lived and fought under his command and banners. But Theodosius dying, and leaving his sons, Arcadius and Honorius, heirs to his empire, but not to his valour and fortune, times changed with the change of sovereign. To the three parts of the empire Theodosius had appointed three prefects, Ruffinus to the eastern part, Stilico to the western, and Gildo to the African Empire. These prefects, after the death of Theodosius, intended to rule not as governors, but as potentates. Gildo and Ruffinus were promptly taken prisoners, but Stilico, knowing better how to conceal his intentions, sought to gain the confidence of the new emperors, and at the same time to throw the empire into such disorder that it would be easier afterwards to seize it. In order to provoke the Visigoths, the enemies of the empire, he advised the emperors that the subsidy should no longer be paid to them; moreover, it did not appear to Stilico that the Visigoths were sufficiently powerful to throw the empire into disorder, so he contrived that the Burgundians, Franks, Vandals, and Alans, northerners, who were already moving in search of new lands, should assail the Roman provinces. Being deprived of their subsidy, the Visigoths made Alaric their king, in order to better revenge their wrongs, and at once attacked the empire; and after many battles invaded Italy, laid it waste, took Rome and sacked it. Alaric died after these victories, and was succeeded by Ataulphus, who took to wife Placida, the sister of the emperors, and by virtue of this relationship he agreed to go to the relief of Gaul and Spain, which provinces were being attacked by the Vandals, Burgundians, Alans, and Franks. The Vandals, who had seized that part of Spain known as Boetica, being hardly pressed by the Visigoths, and having no chance of escape, were invited by Boniface, who governed Africa for the emperor, to cross over and occupy that part of the empire, because, Boniface having himself rebelled, feared his treachery would not be concealed from the emperor. The Vandals willingly entered into this scheme, and, under their king Genseric, became masters of Africa. In due time Theodosius, the son of Arcadius, succeeded to the empire, but he, giving but slight attention to affairs in the west, encouraged usurpers to believe they could hold that which they had seized. And thus the Vandals ruled in Africa, the Alans and Visigoths in Spain, and the Franks and Burgundians not only took Gaul but seized other lands as well, which came to be called after their names, one part being called France and the other Burgundy.

The success of these invaders stirred others to attempt the destruction of the empire, and another nation called Huns seized Pannonia, a province situated on this side of the Danube and called to-day Hungary. As these disorders increased the emperor found himself beset on every side, and in the hope of pacification began to come to terms with the invaders, at one time with the Vandals and at another with the Franks; in this manner the power and authority of the barbarians increased, whilst that of the emperor diminished.

Nor was the island of Britain, which to-day we call England, secure from invasion; because the Britons, fearing the people who had seized France, and finding that the emperor was no longer able to defend them, called over the Angles, a German tribe. The Angles took up this enterprise under their king Vortigern, and from protecting the island they proceeded to seize it, settling themselves there as inhabitants and calling it after their own name Anglia. But the native people being despoiled of their country, and becoming desperate through starvation, and being unable to defend their own land, proposed to seize another. They therefore crossed the sea with their families, and seized a tract of country on the opposite shore, and called it Brittany after their own name.

The Huns, who, as we have already seen, had seized Pannonia, joining with other tribes called Zepides, Berules, Thuringians, and Ostrogoths, or as they are called in our language Eastern Goths, were impelled to seek other countries, and not being able to enter France, which was defended by savage tribes, they descended upon Italy, under their king Attila, who a short time before had killed his brother Bleda in order that he might rule alone. By these means Attila had become so powerful that Andarico, king of the Zepides, and Velamir, the king of the Ostrogoths, were subject to him. Attila having reached Italy lay siege to Aquileia, where he remained for two years without interference, and whilst besieging that city he laid waste all the country around and dispersed the inhabitants. This, as we shall see in its place, was the beginning of the city of Venice. After taking and destroying Aquileia and many other cities, he turned towards Rome, but was moved by the prayers of the pontiff not to destroy it. The pontiff was held in such reverence by Attila that he left Italy and returned to Austria, where he died. After his death, Velamir, the king of the Ostrogoths, and the leaders of other tribes, took up arms against Tenric and Euric, the sons of Attila, and having killed the one, they compelled the other, with his Huns, to repass the Danube and return to his own country, whilst the Ostrogoths and the Zepides held Pannonia and the Erules and Thuringians remained on the far banks of the Danube. After the departure of Attila from Italy, Valentinian, the Eastern Emperor, thinking to restore it and defend it more effectively from the barbarians, abandoned Rome and established the seat of Empire at Ravenna. Those adversities which befell the Western Empire were caused by the Emperor residing at Constantinople, and often handing over the government of the Empire to others, as a possession that was full of danger and expense. The Romans, also, frequently without the permission of the Emperor, had in self defence elected an Emperor, or else someone on his own authority had usurped the Empire, as happened when Maximus Romanus seized upon it after the death of Valentinian, and forced Eudosia, the Emperor's widow, to accept him for her husband. She desiring to be revenged for this indignity—because being born in the purple she could not endure marriage with a private citizen—conspired secretly with Genseric, the king of the Vandals and master of Africa, and let him know the ease and advantage with which Rome could be seized. Allured by the prospect of plunder, Genseric quickly crossed over to Italy. He found Rome abandoned, sacked it, and remained there fourteen days; he also took and sacked many other towns in Italy, and himself and his army, loaded with plunder, went back to Africa. The Romans thereupon returned to their city, and on the death of Maximus created Anitus Romanus Emperor. After many events in Italy and abroad, and after the death of many emperors, the throne of Constantinople fell to Zenonus and that of Rome to Orestes and to his son Augustolus. These men had seized the empire by fraud and intended to hold it by force. Whilst this happened the Erules and Thuringians, who, as before said, had settled on the further bank of the Danube, agreed between themselves, after the death of Attila, to invade Italy under Odoacer, their captain. Into the lands vacated by these tribes entered the Lombards, led by their king Godoglio. These were the last of the plagues of Italy, as in due time will be shown. Odoacer then passed into Italy, conquered and slew Orestes near to Pavia, and put Augustolus to flight. After this victory Odoacer had himself proclaimed King of Rome, and ceased to use the title of emperor, desiring Rome to change the title with the change of holder. He was the first leader of those tribes who at that time were scouring the world to settle himself in Italy; because the others, either out of fear at not being able to hold it, as it was within easy reach of assistance from the eastern emperors, or for other hidden reasons, had plundered it and afterwards sought other lands wherein to settle.

It was in this way that the ancient Roman Empire came under the sway of these sovereigns:—Zeno ruled from Constantinople the whole of the Eastern Empire; the Ostrogoths were masters of

Mœsia and Pannonia; the Visigoths, Suevians, and Alans held Gascony and Spain; the Vandals, Africa; the Franks and Burgundians, France; and the Erulians and Thuringians, Italy. The kingdom of the Ostrogoths had descended to Theodoric, a nephew of Velamir, who being on terms of friendship with Zeno, the eastern emperor, wrote that it appeared to him an injustice that his people, who were superior in valour to all other nations, should be wanting in territory, and that it was impossible for him to keep them within the boundaries of Pannonia; so that, seeing he was compelled to allow them to take up arms and seek new lands, he wished first to come to an understanding with Zeno that, by his good grace, he might meet the wishes of his people by conceding to them such a country wherein they might more commodiously reside. Hence Zeno, partly from fear and partly from the desire to drive Odoacer out of Italy, allowed Theodoric to invade Italy and take possession of it. He at once set out from Pannonia, where he left his allies the Zepides, and entered Italy. He killed Odoacer and his son and, following their example, assumed the title of King of Italy, and took up his residence at Ravenna, being influenced by the same reasons which had impelled Valentinian to reside there. Theodoric became preeminent both in war and peace: always victorious in the one and the greatest benefactor to his people and cities in the other. He distributed the Ostrogoths throughout the land under chiefs, who in war might command and in peace govern them. He improved Ravenna; he rebuilt Rome, and conferred on the Romans every honour but that of military service; he controlled by his personal authority all those barbarian kings who had assisted him to usurp the empire, and that without any tumult of war; he built towns and fortresses between the Adriatic Sea and the Alps, in order to more easily prevent the passage of fresh barbarians wishing to attack Italy. If these great virtues had not towards the end of his life been tarnished by cruelties, caused by distrust of his rule, such as the murders of Simmacus and Boetius, most saintly men, his memory would have been held revered in all honour, not only in Italy but in every other part of the Western Empire, where his valour and capacity had freed the people from attacks which they had endured for many years from immense hordes of barbarians, and had pacified them and successfully restored their affairs to good order. And truly if any times were miserable in Italy, or in other countries overrun by barbarians, it was when they were ravaged by Honorius and Arcadius until Theodoric came upon the scene. Because if one considers what loss may be occasioned to a kingdom or a republic by a change of dynasty or government, not from outside but merely through internal discord—wherein one sees how small commotions will ruin the most powerful kingdom or republic—one can easily imagine what Italy and the Roman dependencies must have suffered in those troublous times, in which not only the government changed, but the laws, customs, ways of living, religion, language, dress, and even names: such vicissitudes—or even any one of them singly, endured in imagination, without witnessing or suffering it—are enough to terrify the strongest and most constant soul. From these changes there arose the foundation and growth of many cities, and also the destruction of many. Among those which were ruined were Aquileia, Luni, Chiusi, Popolonia, Fiesole, Aquila, and many other towns and fortresses that are omitted for sake of brevity. Those which arose from being small towns to be great cities were Florence, Genoa, Pisa, Milan, Naples, and Bologna. To these may be added the destruction and rebuilding of Rome, and many other towns that were destroyed and rebuilt. Amid these troubles and changes of population there arose a new language, as is evident from the speech now prevailing in Italy and France, or in Spain, caused by the native tongue of the new population mingling with that of the ancient Romans. Moreover the names were changed, not only of the provinces and countries, but of the lakes, rivers, and seas, and also of the men themselves, for Italy and France and Spain were full of new names, and all the ancient ones were altered; for example—to mention no others—the Po, the Garda, the Archipelago, are called by names differing from the ancient ones. The men also, from Cæsars and Pompeys, have become Pieri, Giovanni, and Mattei. But among so many changes that of religion was not of the least importance, because the strife between the customs of the ancient faith and the miracles of the new caused the greatest tumults and discords among men. And if the Christian religion had been united fewer disorders would have occurred; but the Greek, the Roman, and the Ravenna Churches fighting each other, and further heretical sects with the Catholic, in many ways afflicted the world. Of this Africa bears witness, for more trouble was endured there from Arianism, which was adopted by the Vandals, than arose from their natural lust and cruelty. Thus it came to pass that men living among so many persecutions began at last to carry written in their very looks the terror of their souls. To add to the infinite evils which they endured, many could not seek a refuge in that God, in whom the miserable are accustomed to trust, because being for the most part uncertain to which they should turn, they failed to find hope or help and perished miserably. Thus Theodoric deserved no small praise for being the first to put a stop to these desolations, which he did during the thirty-eight years in which he reigned over Italy, by restoring it to such greatness that traces of the former ruin could not be found. But when he died the kingdom descended to Atalaric, the son of his daughter Amalasciunta, and in a short time, through the reverse of fortune, all the old troubles returned, for Atalaric dying shortly after his grandfather, and the kingdom remaining to his mother, she was betrayed by Theodatus, who had been called in to assist her in governing. Having murdered her and become king, Theodatus made himself hateful to the Ostrogoths, so that the Emperor Justinian was led to hope that he might drive him out of Italy. He chose as captain for this undertaking Belisarius, who had already conquered Africa and reclaimed it for the emperor by driving out the Vandals. Belisarius therefore seized Sicily, and thence passed into Italy, occupying Naples and Rome. The Goths, suffering under this disaster, killed Theodatus their king as the cause of it and chose in his place Vitigetes, who after some battles was besieged in Ravenna and taken prisoner by Belisarius. But Belisarius, neglecting to follow up this victory, was recalled by Justinian, and Giovanni and Vitalis, men totally unlike him in valour and conduct, were sent in his place. Upon this happening the Goths took courage and made Ildovadus, who had been the governor of Verona, their king. After this man was killed Totila became king, and he dispersed the forces of the emperor, and recovered Tuscany, and re-established his governors in almost all the states which Belisarius had recovered. Thereupon Justinian determined to send him back to Italy, and Belisarius returning thence with but a small force lost the reputation gained by him in his first actions rather than acquired fresh glory. Totila, finding Belisarius with his army at Ostia, took Rome under his eyes, and, finding that he would neither be permitted, nor was he in a position, to hold it, laid the greater part in ruins, drove out the inhabitants, and carried away the senate with him; and, esteeming Belisarius slightly, led his army into Calabria to meet the forces which were coming from Greece to the assistance of Belisarius. Belisarius finding Rome deserted, turned to an honourable undertaking, penetrated into the ruins and very soon succeeded in rebuilding the walls of the city, he then recalled the inhabitants. But fortune, however, frowned on this praiseworthy act, for Justinian, being attacked by the Parthians at this juncture, recalled Belisarius, and he, in obedience to his lord, left Italy. The whole country remained therefore at the mercy of Totila, who re-captured Rome, but treated it with less cruelty than previously, for, at the prayers of St. Benedict, whom he held in the highest sanctity, he endeavoured rather to restore it. Justinian by this time had made peace with the Parthians and contemplated sending a fresh army into Italy, but was diverted from this by the Sclavs, a new people from the northern regions, who had crossed the Danube and attacked Illyria and Thrace. Totila was therefore left unmolested; but Justinian having overcome the Sclavs, sent an army into Italy under Narsetes the Eunuch, a man well practised in war, who defeated and killed Totila, whereupon the Goths who escaped assembled at Pavia and elected Teia their king. Narsetes, on his part, after his victory took Rome, and finally attacking Teia near to Nocera, defeated and killed him. By this victory the name of Goth was completely wiped out, after seventy years' occupation from Theodoric to Teia.

But before Italy had been freed from the Goths, Justinian died and was succeeded by Justin his son. He, by the advice of his mother Sophia, recalled Narsetes from Italy and sent Longinus to take over his command. Longinus, like his predecessors, resided at Ravenna, but he established in Italy a new system of government, appointing governors of provinces as the Goths did, but in every city and town of any size he also appointed captains, to whom he gave the title of dukes. In this distribution of titles he did not honour Rome more than any other city, for he abolished the consuls and the senate, offices which had endured even to that time, and put the city under the rule of a duke whom he sent every year from Ravenna, and called it the Roman duchy. And on the official who governed the whole of Italy from Ravenna he conferred the title of exarch. These divisions gave the Lombards their opportunity to seize Italy, and to bring about its ruin far more easily and swiftly. Narsetes was indignant with the emperor for having taken from him the government of the country which he had won by his own valour and blood, and, as though it were not enough injury to have recalled him, Sophia added words still more shameful, saying that she would set him to spin among the other eunuchs. So Narsetes, full of rage, persuaded Alboinus, the king of the Lombards, who now reigned in Pannonia, to invade Italy. The Lombards, as already shown, were dwelling in those parts contiguous to the Danube which had been abandoned by the Erulians and Thuringians when they were led by their king Odoacer into Italy. Here the Lombards had remained for some time, and afterwards under the command of their king Alboinus, a fierce and bold fighter, they crossed the Danube and attacked Commodus, king of the Zepedians, who held Pannonia, and conquered him. Alboinus, finding among the spoils the daughter of Commodus, Rosamund, took her to wife, and became sovereign of Pannonia. After the savage fashion of his race he made a cup from the skull of Commodus, from which to drink in memory of his victories. Being invited into Italy by Narsetes, with whom he had been on terms of friendship during his wars with the Goths, Alboinus left Pannonia to the Huns (who, after the death of Attila, as we have said, had returned to their own country) and went into Italy, where, finding it divided into so many parts, he seized in a trice Pavia, Milan, Verona, Vincenzo, all Tuscany, and the greater part of Flaminia, which is called to-day Romagna. Thus thinking that he had quickly and completely achieved the conquest of Italy, he celebrated it with a banquet at Verona, and becoming hilarious after much wine filled the skull of Commodus and presented it to Rosamund the queen, who was at table with him, saying with a loud voice so that all could hear it, that he desired her at such a time of rejoicing to drink with her father. These words struck the heart of the lady like a knife, and she determined to be revenged. She was aware that Almachidus, a young and bold Lombardian noble, loved one of her maids, whom she persuaded to contrive secretly that Almachidus should meet the mistress at night in place of the maid. Almachidus arriving as arranged, and finding the lady in a dark place, stayed with her, believing that he was with the maid; afterwards the queen revealed herself, and offered to Almachidus the alternative of killing Alboinus and enjoying her and the kingdom, or of being put to death himself for having violated the king's consort. Almachidus consented to kill Alboinus, but having murdered him he failed to secure the kingdom, and also fearing that the Lombards, out of their love for Alboinus, should put him to death, he fled with Rosamund and all the royal treasure to Longinus at Ravenna, where they were honourably received. In the midst of these disturbances Justinus died and Tiberius reigned in his stead; he, however, occupied with the war against the Parthians, could not send any assistance to Italy. Hence Longinus conceived this to be his opportunity to become by means of Rosamund and her treasure king over the Lombards, and communicating his design to Rosamund, he urged her to murder Almachidus and accept him for her husband. Rosamund agreed, and prepared a cup of poisoned wine, which she took in her hand to Almachidus as he came thirsty from his bath. He had but taken half when he began to feel it affect him, and divining what it was, forced Rosamund to drink the rest. Thus in a very short time both were dead, and Longinus lost all hope of becoming king. The Lombards had assembled at Pavia, which had become the seat of their government, and had elected Clefus their king. He rebuilt Imola, which had been destroyed by Narsetes; seized Rimini and other places as far as Rome, but died in the course of his victories. This Clefus was so cruel, not only to foreigners, but also to his Lombards, that, terrified by the regal power, they would create no more kings, but elected from among themselves thirty dukes who governed the rest. This is one of the reasons why the Lombards never occupied the whole of Italy, and why their kingdom never reached further than Benevento, and why Rome, Ravenna, Cremona, Mantua, Parma, Bologna, Faenza, Furli, Cesena, and many other places were never occupied by the Lombards, these cities either successfully defending themselves or never being attacked. The Lombards having now no king became less ready for war, and when they did undertake it they were less obedient, having been allowed their liberty for so long, and were also addicted to internal discord. These tendencies deprived them of all chance of victory, and finally they were driven from Italy. The Lombards agreeing to confine themselves to the territories they then occupied, Longinus came to terms with them, both parties agreeing to lay down their arms and enjoy what they already possessed.

It was during these times that the popes began to rise higher in authority than they had ever been before, because the early successors of St. Peter had been reverenced for the sanctity of their lives and for their miracles, and their example and repute so spread the Christian religion that sovereigns were compelled, in order to allay as far as possible the confusion which then reigned in the world, to submit to it. When therefore the emperor became a Christian and left Rome for Constantinople, there ensued, as we said in the beginning, the overthrow of the Roman Empire and the aggrandisement of the Roman Church. Nevertheless, until the coming of the Lombards, all Italy being subject either to the emperor or to the king, the popes of those days never assumed any authority but that which men rendered as reverence to their characters or their doctrine. In other things either the emperor or the king was obeyed, and sometimes even the popes, as subjects, suffered death due to their misdeeds. But the time when they became preponderant in Italian affairs was when Theodoric, the king of the Goths, removed the seat of government to Ravenna, and thus Rome being left without a ruler, the Romans paid more obedience to the popes for the sake of protection. Nevertheless, their authority did not increase much, and the Church of Rome only succeeded in securing preference over that of Ravenna. But when the Lombards came and split Italy into divisions, then the pope became more of an active force, because the emperor from Constantinople and the Lombards paid respect to him, as in a sense the head of the city of Rome, so that the Romans by the mediation of the pontiffs made treaties with the Lombards and Longinus, not as their subjects, but as their equals. Hence it followed that the popes, siding at one time with the Lombards and at another with the Greeks, found their importance increasing. And now occurred the ruin of the Eastern Empire under the Emperor Hercules. This was brought about by the Sclavs, of whom mention has already been made, and who now again invaded Illyria and seized it, calling it Sclavonia after their own name. Other parts of the empire were also attacked, first by the Parthians, next by the Saracens, who under Mahomet first came out of Arabia, and finally by the Turks, who invaded Syria, Africa, and Egypt. Thus through the feebleness of the empire there no longer remained to the pope any shield against his oppressors, and on the other hand the increasing power of the Lombards necessitating his seeking new protectors, he had recourse to France. Hence it arose that of the many wars waged in Italy by the barbarians almost all were caused by the popes, as it was by them that the barbarians who inundated Italy were called in, and this state of things has lasted down to our times, and has kept Italy disunited, and still keeps her weak. Therefore in writing of the events which followed from those times down to our own, we shall no longer treat of the downfall of the empire, seeing that it is utterly ruined, but we shall treat of the growth of the pontificate, and of the other principalities, which ruled Italy down to the advent of Charles VIII. of France. And we shall see how popes, first by excommunication, afterwards by that combined with the force of arms, and indulgences, made themselves at once feared and respected; and how they abused both these characters alike, so that their respectability has been lost and their formidableness stands at the mercy of others. But— to return to our subject—after Gregory III. had succeeded to the papacy, and Aistolf to the kingdom of Lombardy, the latter in violation of treaties seized Ravenna and made war on the pope. Whereupon Gregory, for the reasons given above, relying no longer on the emperor at Constantinople, and unwilling to trust in the faith of the Lombards, which had so often been broken, had recourse to Pepin II. of France, who from being lord of Austrasia in Brabant had become the King of France, not so much by his own valour as by that of his father, Charles Martel, and of his grandfather Pepin. Because Charles Martel, when he was governor of France, had inflicted a memorable defeat upon the Saracens near to Torsi on the river Loire, in which there were more than 200,000 men slain; and hence his son Pepin, through the reputation and valour of his father, afterwards became king of that realm. To him Gregory sent for aid against the Lombards, and Pepin promised to send assistance to Gregory, but desired to see him first and to be honoured by his presence. Therefore Gregory went into France, and passed without hindrance through the lands of his enemies the Lombards, so great was the reverence in which religion was held. On his arrival in France, Gregory was honoured by the king, and sent back into Italy with an army, where he besieged the Lombards in Pavia. Then Aistolf was forced by necessity to come to terms with the French, to which they consented at the prayers of the pope, who desired, not the death of his enemies, but rather that they should be converted and live. In this treaty Aistolfus agreed to restore to the pope all the towns which had been seized, but when the army of Pepin had returned to France Aistolfus failed to fulfil the treaty, and the pope had recourse again to Pepin, who sent a new army into Italy, conquered the Lombards, captured Ravenna, and against the will of the Greek emperor gave it to the pope, with all the other towns of the exarchate, and added to them the districts of Urbino and La Marca. But Aistolf died when handing over these towns, and Desiderius Lombardus, Duke of Tuscany, took up arms to seize the kingdom, and asked aid of the pope, to whom he promised an alliance. This assistance Gregory granted, and the other princes were compelled to yield. Desiderius kept faith in the beginning, and confirmed the restoration of the towns to the pope, according to the convention made with Pepin. There came no more exarchs from Constantinople to Ravenna, but it was governed according to the wishes of the pope. After the death of Pepin, his son Charles succeeded to the throne, the same who from the magnitude of his deeds was called the Great. To the papacy at this time succeeded Theodore I. He quarrelled with Desiderius, who besieged him in Rome, and thus it was that the pope applied to Charles for assistance. He crossed the Alps, besieged Desiderius in Pavia, and taking him and his sons captive sent them to France. Charles next visited the pope at Rome, where he decreed that the pope, being the Vicar of God, could not be judged by men, whereupon the pope and the Roman people created Charles Emperor. Thus Rome once more became the seat of the Western Empire, and, whereas the custom had been for the pope to be confirmed in his office by the emperor, a new custom sprang up whereby the pope performed a like office for the emperor. Thus the Empire came to lose power and the popes to acquire it; and by such means the temporal power kept ever growing beyond that of princes.

The Lombards had been in Italy two hundred and twenty-two years and retained nothing of the foreigner about them but their name; and now, during the pontificate of Leo III., Charles being desirous of restoring order throughout the land, consented to allow the Lombards to possess the territories in which they were born, and called the province Lombardy after their name. The Roman name was held in such great respect by many that Charles decided to call all that part of Italy near to Rome, which was formerly under the Exarch of Ravenna, Romagna. Further he created his son Pepin King of Rome, and extended his jurisdiction as far as Benevento, leaving the remainder under the rule of the Greek emperor, with whom he had concluded a treaty. At this time when Pascal I. was pope, the parish priests of the churches in Rome, owing to their proximity to the pope and with a view to controlling his election, began to call themselves cardinals, thus decorating their power with a splendid title; and they arrogated to themselves so much authority, chiefly by excluding the people of Rome from electing the pope, that only very seldom was one chosen except from their own number. Hence on the death of Pascal I., one with the title of Sancta Sabina was created. Later on Italy came much under the influence of France, and changed many of her ways and customs, and the pope usurped much authority in temporal matters. The titles of counts and marquises were introduced from France, as formerly Longinus, the Exarch of Ravenna, had brought in the title of duke. Shortly after this the Roman Osporco came to the pontificate, and because of the brutishness of his name took that of Sergius, thus beginning that change of name which is now always made by a pontiff on his creation.

The Emperor Charles was now dead and succeeded by his son Louis; after his death great discord arose among his children, and in the time of his nephews the empire was wrested from the house of France and given to Germany, and the first emperor was named Arnulf. By these discords the family of Charles lost, not only the empire, but also the kingdom of Italy, for the Lombards, recovering their strength, threatened the pope and the Romans, forcing the latter who knew not where to turn for help to elect Berengarius, the Duke of Friuli, King of Italy. These events encouraged the Huns, who were settled in Pannonia, to attack Italy, but they were met by Berengarius and driven back into Pannonia, or rather Hungary, as that province was now called. Romanus was at this time the emperor in Greece, having wrested the empire from Constantine, whose naval prefect he had been. Puglia and Calabria, which had been in subjection to the empire, as we have seen, now made an attempt at rebellion, and so incensed Romanus that he allowed the Saracens to invade them. This they did and took some provinces and laid siege to Rome. The Romans, however, owing to Berengarius being occupied in fighting the Huns, made Alberigus, Duke of Tuscany, the captain of their forces, and he by his valour saved Rome from the Saracens, who raised the siege. The Saracens then fortified the mountain of Gargano, and lorded it over Puglia and Calabria, whilst harassing the rest of Italy. Thus Italy was sorely afflicted in those days, being devastated by the Huns from the Alps and by the Saracens towards Naples, and she suffered these horrors for many years under three Berengarii in succession. During that time the pope and the Church were greatly harassed, having nowhere to turn for help owing to the disunion among the western princes and the weakness of the eastern. The city of Genoa and all the coasts round were laid waste by the Saracens, and from this cause arose the greatness of Pisa, to which city all who were driven out of their own countries had recourse. These events occurred in the year A.D. 931. But when Otto, a wise man of great reputation, the son of Henry and Matilda, and Duke of Saxony, was chosen emperor, Agabitus the pope prayed him to come to Italy and deliver it from the tyranny of the Berengarii.

The Italian states were at this time governed as follows. Lombardy was under the third Berengarius and his son Albert. Tuscany and the Romagna were ruled by a minister of the eastern emperor. Puglia and Calabria were under the sway of the Grecian emperor, but at this time in the hands of the Saracens.

In Rome two consuls were nominated each year from the nobility, and they governed according to the ancient customs, and added to them was a prefect, who was responsible to the people. They also had a Council of Twelve who appointed magistrates annually to each of the towns under their control. The pope had in Rome and in Italy more or less authority, according as he enjoyed the favour of the emperor or of the ruling power. The Emperor Otto, therefore, came into Italy, and took Lombardy from the Berengarii, who had reigned there fifty-five years, and he also restored the pope to his dignities. This emperor had a son and a nephew also called Otto, who in turn succeeded him in the empire. Now in the time of Otto III., Pope Gregory V. was driven out of Rome and reinstated by Otto, and the pope in revenge took from the Romans the power of nominating emperors and gave it to the six princes of Germany, viz., to the three bishops of Mentz, of Treves, and of Cologne; the three princes of Brandenberg, of the Palatine, and of Saxony. This happened in the year 1011. After the death of Otto III., Henry, Duke of Bavaria, was elected emperor, and after twelve years was crowned by Stephen VIII. Henry and his wife Simionda lived most holy lives, as may be seen from the many churches endowed and built by them, conspicuous among them being the church of San Miniato near the city of Florence. Henry died in 1024, and was succeeded by Conrad the Suabian, and after Conrad, Henry II. He came to Rome owing to the schism in the Church, deposed the three popes, and caused the election of Clement II., by whom he was crowned emperor.

At this time Italy was partly under popular rule and partly under princes, some of whom were sent by the emperor, the chief prince of these, entitled chancellor, kept the others under his control. Among the princes of the greatest authority were Gottfried and his wife Matilda, descended from Beatrice the sister of Henry II. This prince and his wife possessed Lucca, Parma, Reggio, and Mantua, in fact all that part of the country which we now call the patrimony of St. Peter. During this period the popes were at continual strife with the Roman people, who at first had bowed to their authority in order to extricate themselves from the yoke of the emperor. As soon as the people had obtained control of the city, and had reformed it in accordance with their wishes, they showed their hostility to the popes, who suffered far more injuries from citizens than they had from Christian princes. Yet at this very time, when the Roman people were in rebellion against them, the popes could make all the west tremble with their excommunications. Notwithstanding this, the popes and people still strove to wrest from each other all honours and authority. Therefore, when Nicholas II. became pope he deprived the people of all share in the election of the popes and put it solely in the hands of the cardinals, in the same way as Gregory V. had taken from the Roman people the election of emperor. Not content with this, Nicholas covenanted with the princes who governed Puglia and Calabria, for reasons which we shall shortly explain, and further he compelled the officers sent by the Roman people to their several jurisdictions to render obedience to him, and in some cases he even deprived them of their offices. After the death of Nicholas there occurred a schism in the Church, because the Lombardian clergy would not acknowledge Alexander II. who had been elected at Rome, and made Cadolo from Parma the anti-pope. Thereupon Henry, to whom the papal authority was hateful, gave Pope Alexander to understand that he must renounce the pontificate, and he informed the cardinals that they must come into Germany for the election of a new pope. For this action he was made to feel the anger of the Church, being the first prince of any importance to suffer in this way, for the pope called a council at Rome and deprived him of the empire and kingdom. Some of the Italian people sided with the pope and some with Henry, and from this division sprang the Guelf and Ghibelline parties, so that Italy, freed from the barbarian eruptions, was now to be torn with internal wars. Henry, being excommunicate, was forced by his people to cross into Italy, and barefooted sue on his knees for the pardon of the pope; this was in the year 1080. Nevertheless, in spite of this, there again arose discord between the pope and Henry, so that the pope again excommunicated him. This time the emperor sent his son, also called Henry, with an army to Rome, and he with the aid of the disaffected citizens besieged the pope in the castle. Robert Guiscard then came to the pope's assistance from Puglia, but Henry without waiting returned to Germany alone. The citizens, however, were obdurate, and once more Rome was sacked and reduced to its former ruin, from which so many popes had laboured to uplift it. As from Robert Guiscard arose in due course the dynasty of Naples, it may not be out of place for me to relate his descent and deeds.

When, as already said, dissensions arose among the heirs of Charles the Great, an opportunity of attacking France offered itself to a new northern race called Normans, and they seized the country which to-day is known as Normandy. Some of these invaders advanced into Italy at the time when it was beset by the Berengarii, the Saracens, and the Huns, and occupied some towns in Romagna, where they valiantly maintained themselves amid all those troubles. Tancred, one of these Norman chiefs, had many sons, among whom was William, called Ferebac, and Robert, called Guiscard. Their lands had descended to William, and the troubles in Italy had in some measure ceased. Nevertheless the Saracens still held Sicily and constantly harassed the shores of Italy. William, therefore, agreed with the Princes of Capua and Salerno, and with Melorco the Greek, who was ruling Calabria and Puglia for the emperor, to attack Sicily; and it was decided between them that, if success attended their efforts, each of them should have a fourth part of the spoils and the territory. The enterprise proved successful—they drove out the Saracens and occupied Sicily—but after the victory Melorco introduced further forces from Greece unknown to his allies and took possession of the island in the name of the emperor and divided the spoils only. William was highly indignant, but concealed his feelings until a fitter time for showing them should offer itself, and left Sicily together with the Princes of Capua and Salerno. They parted from him and returned home; but William did not go back to the Romagna, but turning aside with his men towards Puglia suddenly seized Malfi, and advancing from thence against the forces of the Greek emperor soon made himself master of almost the whole of Puglia and Salerno, provinces of which, in the time of Pope Nicholas II., his brother Robert had been lord. As Robert had had considerable differences with his nephews concerning the succession to those states, he had availed himself of the authority of the pope to settle them — an authority willingly exercised as the pope desired to conciliate Robert, in order that he might defend the papal prerogative against the German emperors and the insolence of the Roman people; and this service Robert had actually performed when, as already said, at the instance of Gregory VII. he drove Henry out of Rome and tamed the Roman people. Robert was succeeded by his sons Roger and William, to whose territories was now added Naples and all the country between Naples and Rome, of which Roger had made himself master. For on the departure of William to Constantinople to marry the daughter of the emperor, Roger seized upon his share of the state to himself. Elated with this acquisition Roger proclaimed himself, in the first instance, King of Italy, but afterwards contenting himself with the title of King of Puglia and Sicily he was the first who gave a name and title to that kingdom — a title which, with its ancient boundaries, it maintains to this day, although it has seen many changes both in nationality and dynasty. As the Norman race diminished the kingdom fell first to the Germans, then to the French, after them to the Aragons, and to-day it is held by the Flemings.

About this time Urban II. came to the pontificate, and conceiving that, by reason of the hostility of the Romans and the disunion of Italy, he could not retain his position, he resolved upon a great enterprise, and accompanied by all his clergy went into France. At Antwerp he assembled a concourse of people to whom he made an oration against the infidels, rousing their courage to such a pitch that they resolved to make war upon the Saracens in Asia. This and the many similar enterprises which followed was called a crusade, because all those who took part in it had their arms and clothing marked with a red cross. At the head of this undertaking were Godfrey, Eustace, and Aldwyn of Boulogne, the Count of Bologna, and Peter the Hermit, celebrated for his holiness and wisdom; many kings and people contributed money, and many fought without pay. Thus can religion, aided by the example of their leaders, move the hearts of men. In the beginning the enterprise was very glorious, for all Asia Minor, Syria, and a part of Egypt were recovered by the Christians, and hence arose the Order of the Knights of Jerusalem, who to this day occupy and rule the Island of Rhodes, the one remaining barrier against the power of the Mahomedans. Hence, too, arose the Order of the Templars, who after a short time were dissolved owing to their wickedness, and many exploits ensued from time to time in which not a few nations and individuals distinguished themselves. The Kings of France and of England, the Venetians, the Pisans, and the Genoese all took part in the venture, and gained great renown, while their fortunes alternated till Saladin the Saracen entered the field. The valour of this great soldier, and the quarrels among the Christians, deprived them of all the renown which they had won in the beginning, and in the end, after ninety years, they were driven out of every position which they had gained with such glorious success.

After the death of Urban, Pascal II. was chosen pope, and Henry IV. became emperor. Henry came to Rome under the guise of friendship to the pope, but shortly after his arrival threw him and his clergy into prison, and refused to liberate them until they had conceded to him the right of dealing as he thought fit with the Church of Germany. At this time the Countess Matilda died, bequeathing all her estates to the Church. After the deaths of Pascal and of Henry IV. there followed more popes and more emperors, until the papacy fell to Alexander III. and the imperial crown to Frederic the Suabian, called Barbarossa. The pope had many difficulties with the Roman people and with the emperors, which troubles were much increased on the accession of

Barbarossa. Frederic was a fine soldier and too proud to yield submission to the pope, but nevertheless he came to Rome on his election to receive the crown, and returned peaceably to Germany. He remained thus but a short time, however, and then returned to Italy to subdue certain towns in Lombardy that had revolted against him. Now it was at this time that the Cardinal of San Clemente, a Roman, seceded from the pope and was himself elected pope by certain of the cardinals. The Emperor Frederic was then encamped at Cremona, and to him Alexander appealed against the anti-pope; Frederic answered that both should come before him and he would then judge who should be the pope. This answer displeased Alexander, because he saw in it a disposition to favour the anti-pope, therefore he excommunicated Frederic and fled to Philip, King of France. Frederic at once proceeded with the war in Lombardy, took and destroyed Milan, an event which caused Verona, Padua, and Venice to unite against him for common defence. In the midst of this turmoil the anti-pope died and Frederic nominated Guido of Cremona pope in his stead. Owing to the absence of the pope and the difficulties with which Frederic was meeting in Lombardy, the Roman citizens had usurped all authority in Rome, and were reclaiming obedience from those towns which were formerly subject to the city. The Tuscans resisting these claims, the Romans sought to compel them; but the Tuscans were supported by Frederic, and they defeated the Romans with such great slaughter that Rome was never again so populous or so rich. In the midst of this, Pope Alexander returned to Rome, fancying that he would be safe because of the hatred which the Romans had for Frederic, and because of the number of enemies which the emperor had in Lombardy. Frederic, however, putting aside every consideration, took the field against Rome; nor did Alexander await him, but fled at once to William, King of Sicily, who had succeeded to that kingdom after the death of Roger. Frederic, however, being much troubled with the plague, raised the siege and returned to Germany, and the towns of Lombardy that had revolted against him succeeded in defeating

Pavia and Tortona, which were held by the imperial party. These rebels also built a city which became the seat of war against Pavia and Tortona, and called it Alexandra, in honour of Pope Alexander and in scorn of Frederic. Guido, the anti-pope, dying at this time, Giovanni of Fermo was appointed in his place, and by the help of the imperial party maintained himself in Montefiasconi. Meanwhile Pope Alexander had gone into Tuscany at the invitation of the people, who hoped that his authority would protect them against the Romans. Thither came to him envoys from Henry II., King of England, who affirmed that the death of St. Thomas, Archbishop of Canterbury, could not truly be laid, as rumour had openly laid it, to the charge of their king. The pope, therefore, sent two cardinals to England to seek out the truth of the matter, and although they could not find the king manifestly to blame, yet for the infamy of the murder, and because Henry had not honoured the saint as he deserved, they ordered the king by way of penance to call together all the barons of the kingdom, justify himself under oath in their presence, and, further, to send at once to Jerusalem two hundred soldiers with one year's pay and to bind himself to go there in person, before three years should elapse, with the greatest army he could raise; to cancel everything that he had enacted against the liberty of the ecclesiastics, and to allow any of his subjects who wished to appeal to Rome — all of which terms were agreed by Henry; thus a king submitted to a judgment which to-day a private person would repudiate. Nevertheless, whilst the pope had such immense power over remote princes he could not obtain obedience from the Romans, or even by entreaty permission to reside in Rome, although he promised not to interfere in any matters excepting ecclesiastical ones. Thus things that are seen afar off are more dreaded than those which are nearer.

Meanwhile Frederic had returned to Italy, and was preparing to make war upon the pope again, but his barons and prelates, one and all, gave him to understand that they would abandon him if he did not become reconciled to the Church; whereupon he was compelled to go and pay homage at Venice, where the two powers were reconciled. In accordance with this the pope deprived the emperor of all authority over Rome, and nominated William, King of Sicily, as his associate. Frederic, unable to exist without war, went into Asia to satiate against the Mahomedans the ambition he had failed to satisfy on the Vicar of Christ, but, arriving at the river Cydnus, he was tempted by the clearness of its waters to bathe and, catching some disorder, died. Thus these waters were of more help to the Mahomedans than excommunications had been to the Christians, for whilst these latter only curbed his pride, the former killed him. Frederic, being now dead, it only remained for the pope to tame the contumacy of the Romans; and, after many disputes over the nomination of consuls, it was agreed that the Romans should elect them according to custom, but that they should not be allowed to take upon themselves the magisterial office unless they took an oath to observe loyalty to the Church. This compact compelled Giovanni the anti-pope to flee to the Albanian mountains, where he died. There died also at this time William, King of Naples, whose kingdom the pope was desirous to seize, because the king had only left as issue a natural son named Tancred. The barons, however, would not consent, but desired that Tancred should be their king. The pope at this time was Celestine III., and he desiring to wrest the kingdom from Tancred, contrived that Henry, the son of Frederic, should be declared emperor, with the promise that the kingdom of Naples should be his if he restored to the Church all the lands which belonged to it. To facilitate the affair, the pope released from her vows Constanza, the now elderly daughter of William, and gave her to Henry for wife. Thus the kingdom of Naples passed from the Normans, by whom it had been founded, to the Germans. As soon as the Emperor Henry had arranged his affairs in Germany, he came into Italy with his wife Constanza, and a son aged four years named Frederic, and without much difficulty took possession of the kingdom, Tancred being already dead, and having left only a little son named Roger. Some time after this Henry died in Sicily and his son Frederic succeeded to the throne of Naples, whilst Otto, Duke of Saxony, was created emperor. This title was bestowed upon him for the favour he had shown to Pope Innocent III., but when Otto had been crowned, contrary to all expectations he declared against the pontiff, seized Romagna, and prepared to invade the kingdom. For this the pope excommunicated him, and he was consequently abandoned by every one, and Frederic, King of Naples, chosen as emperor by the electors. Frederic came to Rome for the crown, but the pope, fearing his power, was unwilling to crown him, and sought to drive him, as he had driven Otto before him, out of Italy. Therefore Frederic in great indignation went back to Germany, made war upon Otto and conquered him. In the meanwhile died Innocent III., who besides other noble works had built the Hospital of San Spirito in Rome. He was followed by Honorius III. in whose time were founded the orders of San Dominic and of San Francisco, about the year 1218. This pontiff crowned Frederic, to whom John, descended from Baldwin, King of Jerusalem, gave one of his daughters to wife. John, who still held that title and resided there with the remnant of Christians in Asia, made over the title with the dowry. Hence it arises that he who is King of Naples bears also the title of King of Jerusalem.

In Italy the position of affairs at this time was as follows: — the Romans no longer appointed consuls, but in their place they appointed one or more senators, wielding the same authority as consuls; they maintained also the league against Frederic Barbarossa which they had made with the cities of Lombardy, viz., Milan, Brescia, Mantua, most of the cities of Romagna, also Verona, Vicenzo, Padua, and Trevigi. On the emperor's side were Cremona, Bergamo, Parma, Reggio, Modena, and Trente. The other cities and fortresses of Lombardy, Romagna and La Marca Trevigiana, favoured one side or the other, according to their needs. Now there came to Italy in the time of Otto III. one Ezelin, who settled in the country and begat a son, and the son again a third Ezelin. This man being rich and powerful addressed himself to Frederic; and Frederic, as we have shown above, having become the enemy of the pope, entered Italy at the instance and with the support of Ezelin, took Verona and Mantua, destroyed Vincenza, seized Padua, defeated the armies of the confederate towns, and drew near to Tuscany. Ezelin meanwhile had subdued the whole of La Marca Trivigiana, but failed to take Ferrara, it being defended by Azone da Esti and by the Lombardian forces of the pope. Ezelin therefore raised the siege, and the pope gave the city in fief to Azone da Este, from whom are descended those who hold the lordship over it to-day. Frederic desiring the conquest of Tuscany remained at Pisa, and in distinguishing between his friends and foes in that province sowed the seeds of that quarrel which proved the ruin of all Italy, because the numbers of the Guelf and Ghibelline factions multiplied, the partisans of the Church calling themselves Guelfs, and those of the emperor Ghibellines, and it was at Pistoia that these names were first heard. Frederic leaving Pisa now attacked and laid waste the lands of the Church in many quarters, and the pope, having no other resource, proclaimed a crusade against him, as his predecessors had done against the Saracens. But Frederic, who was not abandoned by his men as Frederic Barbarossa and others of his ancestors had been, took into his pay many Saracens, and to bind them to him, and to establish within the borders of Italy a standing antagonist to the Church that would not fear papal maledictions, he gave them Nocera in the kingdom, in order that, having a stronghold of their own, they would serve him in greater security. Innocent IV. not yet having mounted the papal throne, in fear of Frederic, had betaken himself to Genoa and thence to Lyons in France, where he called a council, which Frederic decided to attend. But Frederic was delayed by a rebellion in Parma, and, being repulsed in his attempts on that city, withdrew into Tuscany, and thence into Sicily, where he died, leaving a son Conrad in Suabia, and Manfred, a natural son, whom he had made Duke of Beneventum in Puglia. Conrad having come into possession of the kingdom arrived at Naples, where he died, leaving but one infant son, Conradine, in Germany. Thereupon Conrad seized the state, first as the guardian of Conradine, and afterwards, giving out that the child was dead, made himself king in despite of the pope and the Neapolitans, whom he compelled to assent.

Whilst these events were occurring in Naples great changes were in progress in Lombardy between the Guelfs and Ghibellines. The Guelfs were supported by a legate of the pope, and the Ghibellines by Ezelin, to whom belonged almost the whole of Lombardy as far as the river Po. He it was who, because Padua had rebelled in the course of the war, put to death 12,000 of her citizens. Before the war closed Ezelin died in the eightieth year of his age, and on his death all the lands possessed by him became free. Manfred, King of Naples, after the way of his ancestors, pursued the quarrel with the Church, and kept the Pope Urban IV. in such continual trouble that the pontiff, to bring him to order, summoned a crusade against him, and retired to Perugia to await the army there. When he found, however, that those who joined him were very few in number, poor, and slow in coming in, he realised that to conquer Manfred he must have powerful aid; he turned therefore for assistance to France, and creating Charles of Anjou, the brother of King Louis, King of Naples, urged him to come into Italy and take possession of that kingdom, but before Charles could reach Rome the pope was dead, and Clement IV. reigned in his place. In due time Charles reached Ostia with thirty galleys, having arranged for the remainder of his troops to follow by land. During his residence in Rome the citizens, to gratify him, nominated him senator, and the pope invested him with the kingdom, stipulating that he should pay to the Church every year 50,000 florins. The pope also made a decree that in future neither Charles nor any other occupant of the kingdom should be eligible for the empire. Charles now took the field against Manfred, defeated and slew him near to Beneventum. But Conradine, to whom by his father's will this kingdom belonged, assembled a large army in Germany, advanced into Italy against Charles, and fought him at Tagliacozzo. There Conradine was routed, and in his flight was recognised, taken, and killed.

After this Italy remained at rest until Adrian V. succeeded to the pontificate. He, finding the rule of Charles intolerable — for Charles still remained in residence at Rome, which, as senator, he continued to govern — retired to Viterbo and besought the Emperor Rodolph to come with an armed force into Italy to attack Charles. Thus the pontiffs, now in their zeal for the faith, at another time for their own ambitious ends, have never ceased inviting new warriors into Italy and kindling new wars; and having once raised a prince to power, they repent, and seek to compass his downfall; nor can they suffer that province which they are too feeble to hold themselves to be held by others. Princes have ever dreaded them, because, whether fighting or fleeing, they have always prevailed; unless indeed they were caught by some stratagem, as were Boniface VIII. and some others, who under the pretence of friendship, were taken prisoners by the emperors. Rodolph, however, did not come into Italy, being detained in Germany by a war with the King of Bohemia. In the meantime Adrian died, and Nicholas III. was created pontiff. He was a bold and ambitious man of the house of the Orsini, who wished by every method under his control to reduce the power of Charles. So he contrived that the Emperor Rodolph should complain that Charles kept a governor in Tuscany to support the Guelf party, which after the death of Manfred had been restored. Charles yielded to the emperor and withdrew his governor, and the pope sent his nephew, a cardinal, as a governor for the Empire. For this honour the emperor restored to the Church the Romagna which his predecessors had seized, and the pope made Bertoldo Orsini Duke of Romagna. And now, thinking that he had become powerful enough to look Charles in the face, the pope deprived him of his office of senator, and passed a decree that no one of royal blood should ever again be a senator of Rome. Being minded also to take Sicily from Charles, he entered with Peter, King of Aragon, into a secret arrangement which, after the pope's death, his successor carried into effect. He designed also to make two members of his own family princes, the one in Lombardy, the other in Tuscany, to serve in defending the Church against the Germans, who wished to get a footing in Italy, and against the French who were there. But in the midst of these great designs he died. He was the first of the popes who openly showed his ambition, and who designed, under cover of advancing the interests of the Church, to aggrandise and enrich his family. And whereas up to these times no mention has been made of nephews and other relatives of the pontiffs, in the future my narrative will be full of them; we shall even encounter their children. Nor is there anything else that pontiffs might not attempt, unless indeed, as in our days they have left their sons princes, so in future they might attempt to make the papacy hereditary. It is very true that the principalities founded by them have had but a short life, because for the most part the pontiffs have been so short-lived themselves, or have omitted to plant their offshoots on a solid foundation, or having set them up, have left them with such slender roots that, lacking the virtue to sustain them, the first wind has overturned them.

To Nicholas III. succeeded Martin IV. who, being a Frenchman, favoured the party of Charles. Charles therefore sent an army into Romagna where there was a rebellion; but while it was encamped at Forli, Guido Bonatti, an astrologer, foretold that at a certain time, named by him, the French should be attacked; this fell out as he had foretold, the French being all taken or slain. At this time the scheme mooted between Pope Nicholas and Peter, King of Aragon, took effect, with the result that the Sicilians massacred all the French whom they found in the island, and Peter made himself lord of it, saying that it belonged to him through his wife Constanza, the daughter of Manfred. But Charles died whilst preparing for war to recover the island, and was succeeded by Charles II., who in the war which followed was taken prisoner in Sicily, but was liberated on the promise of returning to captivity if within three years he should have failed to persuade the pope that the royal house of Aragon ought to be invested with the kingdom of Sicily.

The Emperor Rodolph, instead of coming to Italy, sent his envoy to maintain the imperial authority there, and gave him the power to enfranchise all cities that wished to redeem their liberties. Thus many cities purchased their freedom, and on obtaining it completely changed their habits of life. Adolphus the Saxon had succeeded to the empire, and Piero del Murone to the pontificate, as Pope Celestine. He was a hermit and a most saintly man; after six months he renounced the pontificate, and was followed by Boniface VIII. But Providence, knowing the times and seasons when the French and Germans should spread themselves over Italy, and when Italy should be delivered wholly back again into the hands of her own people, to the end that the pope, when his defenders from beyond the Alps should fail him, might neither establish nor enjoy his dominion, caused to arise in Rome two most powerful families, the Colonnesi and the Orsini, whose power and vicinity to the pope might keep the pontificate in check. Hence Pope Boniface, who was well aware of this source of danger, resolved to destroy the Colonnesi, and having excommunicated them, he proclaimed a crusade against them. But this policy, if it hurt the Colonnesi, hurt the Church still more; for the weapons which have worked bravely for love of the faith, when turned against the faithful for private ends are apt to lose their edge. Thus an inordinate desire to satisfy their ambitions has caused the popes little by little to lose their influence. Again, Boniface deprived of office two of the family who were cardinals and Sciarra, the head of the house, taking to flight before the pope could hear of it, was captured by Catalonian corsairs and sent to the galleys; but he was afterwards recognised at Marseilles and despatched to Philip, King of France, who had been excommunicated by Boniface and deprived of the kingdom of Naples. Philip, bearing in mind that in war with the papacy you must either suffer loss or at best incur many perils, had recourse to craft. He feigned a wish to come to terms with the pope, and sent Sciarra secretly into Italy; and Sciarra coming to Anagni, where the pope then was, summoned his friends by night and took the pope prisoner. And although the pope was shortly afterwards set at liberty by the people of Anagia, yet he died within a short time raving mad owing to his capture. Boniface was the founder of the jubilee in 1300, and decreed that it should be celebrated every hundred years. During these times there occurred many troubles between the Guelf and Ghibelline factions, and since Italy had been abandoned by the emperor many towns had become free, and many had passed into the hands of tyrants. Pope Benedict XI. restored the hat to the Colonnesi cardinals, and removed the ban from Philip, King of France. Benedict's successor, Clement V., being a Frenchman, removed the papal court to France in the year 1305.

About this time Charles II. of Naples died and was succeeded by his son Robert. Henry of Luxemburg had been elected emperor, and went to Rome to be crowned, notwithstanding that the pope was no longer there. Upon his coming to Italy great disturbances arose in Lombardy, because he recalled all the exiles, whether Guelf or Ghibelline, to their homes. Hence it followed that each party, endeavouring to drive the other out, filled the whole province with fighting, which the emperor with all his forces could not prevent. He left Lombardy, by way of Genoa, for Pisa, from whence he planned the invasion of King Ruberto's kingdom of Tuscany, but making no progress in this enterprise he passed on to Rome. Here he stayed but a few days, because the Orsini, with the help of King Ruberto, drove him out, and he returned to Pisa. And now with the view of carrying on the war against Tuscany with greater prospect of success, and of wresting the government from King Ruberto, he incited Federigo, the King of Sicily, to attack it, but just as he was hoping to occupy Tuscany, and deprive King Ruberto of his kingdom, he died, and was succeeded in the empire by Louis of Bavaria. Whilst this was going on John XXII. came to the papacy, and during his time the emperor did not cease from persecuting the Guelfs and the Church, which were defended in a great measure by the Florentines and King Ruberto. Hence arose many wars, those in Lombardy being waged by the Visconti against the Guelfs, and those in Tuscany by Castruccio Castracani da Lucca against the Florentines. Since the family of the Visconti founded the duchy of Milan, one of the five principalities which afterwards governed Italy, its importance appears to me to demand a somewhat more extended treatment.

As there still continued in Lombardy the League of Cities, named some way back, for defence against Frederic Barbarossa, Milan, now restored from ruin, and wishing to avenge the wrongs she had suffered, joined the league which had kept Barbarossa in check, and now kept alive the Church party in Lombardy. In the troubles of this strife which followed, the family of de la Torre became very powerful in Milan, and its renown steadily grew, whilst that of the emperor declined. But when Frederic II. came into Italy, and the Ghibelline party recovered its power by the aid of Ezelin, Ghibelline factions sprang up in every city; thus in Milan, amongst the adherents of the Ghibelline party, there was the family of Visconti, which drove out that of de la Torre. These latter, however, remained but a short time in exile, being restored to their country by the terms of the treaty between the pope and the emperor. When the pope removed the court to France and Henry of Luxemburg came to Italy to receive the crown, he was received in Milan by Maffeo Visconti and Guido de la Torre, who were now the heads of their several families. Maffeo, however, was minded to drive out Guido with the help of the emperor, and judged the matter easy because Guido belonged to the faction opposed to the emperor. He seized the opportunity of the complaint which the people made of the overbearing rule of the Germans to incite them secretly, one by one, to take up arms and lift from their backs the yoke of the barbarians, and when he considered his plans to be ripe, caused some of his confidants to raise a tumult, upon which the people took up arms against the Germans. No sooner was the uproar begun than Maffeo with his sons and partisans took up arms and ran to Henry, telling him that the tumult was caused by the de la Torre, who, not content with remaining in Milan as private citizens, had taken the opportunity of attempting to put it to the sack, with the idea of pleasing the Italian Guelfs and thus rising to be princes in Milan. "But be of good courage," they said, "for we and our party are willing to defend and protect you in every way." Henry believed all that was told him by Maffeo, and, joining his forces with those of the Visconti, attacked the men of the de la Torre, who were engaged in many parts of the city in quelling the tumults; these were killed and the remainder were stripped of their property and sent into exile. Maffeo Visconti thus became a prince in Milan, and was followed by Galeazzo and Azo, and afterwards by Luchino and Giovanni. Giovanni became the Archbishop of Milan, and to Luchino, who died before him, succeeded Bernabo and Galeazzo, but Galeazzo, dying soon after, was succeeded by his son, Giovanni Galeazzo, called Count di Virtu. This man, after the death of the archbishop, privily made away with his uncle Bernabo, and thus became the sole Prince of Milan, and was the first who bore the title of duke. After him came Filippo and Giovanni Maria Angelo, and then, Giovanni being killed by the people of Milan, the government descended to Filippo, who died without male issue. Thus the state passed from the house of Visconti to that of Sforza, in the way and for the reasons that will be narrated in their place.

But to return to the point whence I digressed. The Emperor Louis, to win renown and to receive the crown, came into Italy, and visiting Milan, because he must needs raise some money from the Milanese, he made some show of giving them freedom and threw the Visconti into prison. Afterwards, by the intervention of Castruccio da Lucca, he set them free, and went on to Rome, and there to disturb more easily the peace of Italy he created Piero della Covara the anti-pope, intending by his authority, in conjunction with the forces of the Visconti, to keep in check the opposing parties in Tuscany and Lombardy. But Castruccio died, and out of his death arose the beginning of the ruin of Louis, because Pisa and Lucca rebelled against him, and the Pisans sent the anti-pope as prisoner to the pope in France, whilst the emperor despairing of affairs in Italy returned to Germany. No sooner was he gone than John, King of Bohemia, came into Italy at the invitation of the Ghibellines of Brescia and made himself master of that city and of Bergamo. The pope, albeit feigning the contrary, consented to his coming, and therefore the legate of Bologna countenanced him, thinking that he would serve as a bar to the emperor's return to Italy. Affairs in Italy were thus totally changed, for the Florentines and King Ruberto, seeing that the legate approved the doings of the Ghibellines, became at once hostile to all those with whom the legate and the King of Bohemia were friendly, and many princes, without regard to the distinction of Guelf and Ghibellines, united with them, amongst whom were the Visconti, the della Scala, Filippo Gonzaga of Mantua, the da Carrara, and the da Este. The pope excommunicated them all, and the king, alarmed at this league, went home to collect a larger force. Although he returned with additional troops, he did not succeed in his difficult undertaking; but, losing courage, he went back again to Bohemia to the displeasure of the legate, leaving garrisons in Reggio and Modena only, and handing over Parma to the care of Marsilio and Piero de Rossi, the most powerful men in that city. On his departure Bologna joined the league, and the confederates divided among themselves the four cities which were left to the Church party, and agreed that Parma should belong to the della Scala, Reggio to Gonzaga, Modena to the da Este, and Lucca to the Florentines. In taking over these territories, however, much strife ensued, which was eventually settled in a great measure by the Venetians. To some it may perhaps appear unbefitting that in so extended a series of events in Italy we have so long delayed to speak of the Venetians, who were a republic that ought to be celebrated for wealth and power beyond all other principalities in Italy. But—to put an end to such surprise by making my reasons known—I shall go back a long period, so that all may know the beginnings of the Venetians, and why it happened that their intervention in the affairs of Italy was so long delayed.

When Attila, king of the Huns, was besieging Aquileia, the inhabitants, despairing, after many defeats, of their safety, took refuge as best they could with their movables among the uninhabited sand banks which stood at the head of the Adriatic sea. The Paduans, also, seeing the names close to them, and fearing now that Aquileia was destroyed, Attila would seek them out, carried all their most precious possessions down to the same sea, to a place called the Rivo Alto, whither they deported their women, children, and old folk, retaining the young men in Padua for the defence of the city. Moreover the men of Monfelice and the inhabitants of the surrounding hills, actuated by the same fears, betook themselves to the sand dunes of the same sea. After the taking of Aquileia, and the sacking of Padua, Monfelice, Vicenza, and Verona, the Paduans and the stronger refugees still continued to inhabit the marshes that were around the Rivo Alto. Likewise all the people driven out by the same occurrences from the districts round about the town called in ancient times Venezia, had recourse to the same marshes. Thus, driven by necessity, they forsook their most lovely and fertile lands to live in a spot unfruitful, unsightly, and lacking all the conveniences of life. But the confluence of so many people at once speedily made those places not only habitable but delightful, and they lived quite securely, founding among themselves laws and customs, and rapidly increasing in reputation and strength, whilst ruin and devastation was wrought in Italy. Besides the above-named inhabitants, many from the cities of Lombardy took refuge there when driven out by the cruelties of Clefus, King of Lombardy, which increased the new city not a little. In the time of Pepin, King of France, when at the supplication of the pope he passed into Italy to drive the Lombards out, in the conventions which ensued between him and the Emperor of the Greeks, neither the Duke of Beneventum nor the Venetians would yield obedience to either the one or the other, but maintained their liberties against both. Moreover the Venetians, being compelled by force of circumstances to dwell in the midst of waters, were driven to devise some honest means of living independently of the land, and thus, faring with ships over the whole world, they filled their city with the merchandise which other men need, and for which men found it necessary to have recourse to Venice. For many years the Venetians desired no other dominion than that which would enable them to pursue their trade to the greatest advantage; they, therefore, acquired many ports in Greece and Syria, and for placing their fleets at the disposal of the French in the expeditions which they made into Asia, the island of Candia was granted to them as a reward. Whilst they lived in this way their name became dreaded at sea and respected within the confines of Italy, to such an extent that in disputes which arose they were often the arbitrators, notably in the affair between the confederates over the lands which they had divided up amongst themselves, when, the case being referred to the Venetians, Bergamo and Brescia were assigned to the Visconti. As time went on the Venetians, impelled by the lust of dominion, seized Padua, Vicenza, Trevigi, and, later on, Verona, Brescia, and Bergamo, besides many cities in Romagna and the kingdom of Naples, and their renown increased so greatly that not only to the princes of Italy but to the sovereigns beyond the Alps they became objects of fear. Hence a conspiracy was formed against them, and in one day they lost that dominion which with infinite pains they had built up during many years. Although in recent years they have regained some part of it, they have never recovered their former renown or power, and they live at the discretion of others, as do all other Italian principalities.

Benedict XII. had now risen to the pontificate, and seeing that he had no hold upon Italy, and fearing that the Emperor Louis would become paramount there, decided to make friends with all such as had usurped territories that were formerly under the sway of the emperor, to the end that they, having reason to fear the empire, might join with him for the defence of Italy, and he issued a decree that all the tyrants of Lombardy should hold by a legal title those possessions which they had usurped. Benedict, however, died in the act of making this decree, which Clement VI. afterwards confirmed; and the emperor, seeing how liberally the popes had dispensed the imperial domains, resolved to be no less open-handed than their Holinesses with the property of others, and to every despot within the papal provinces he made a present of his lordship, to have and to hold by the imperial authority. In this way Galeotto Malatesti and his brothers became the lords of Rimini, of Pesaro, and of Fano; Antonio da Montefeltro of Marca and Urbino; Gentile da Varano of Camerino; Guido di Potento of Ravenna; Sinibaldo Ordelaffi of Furli and Cesena; Giovanni Manfredi of Faenza; Lodovico Alidosi of Imola; and besides these many others in other towns. Over and above these, out of the many other domains of the Church there were few that escaped without a despot — a circumstance which kept the Church in impotence until the accession of Alexander VI., who restored its power in our days by overthrowing the descendants of those men. At this time died Robert, King of Naples, leaving behind him two granddaughters only, the children of his son Charles who had died shortly before him. In his will he directed that the elder, by name Giovanna, should succeed to the throne, and that she should take for her consort his nephew Andrea, the son of the King of Hungary. Andrea did not live with her very long, for she caused him to be murdered, and married another cousin Lodovico, Prince of Taranto. But Lodovico, King of Hungary, the brother of Andrea, coming with an army into Italy to avenge his brother's death, drove Queen Giovanna and her consort out of the kingdom.

About this time a memorable event happened in Rome. Nicolo di Lorenzo, Chancellor of the Capital, drove the senators out of Rome, and placing himself, with the title of tribune, at the head of affairs, restored the Roman Republic in all its ancient forms, earning withal so much renown for valour and justice that not only the towns near to Rome but all Italy sent ambassadors to him. The ancient provinces, seeing that Rome was born again, followed her lead, and showed honour to her, some moved by fear and some by hope. Nicolo, however, at the very height of his fame, of his own accord, abandoned the work he had begun; for, losing heart under the weight of his responsibilities, he fled secretly, without pressure from any quarter, and sought refuge with Charles, King of Bohemia, who had been elected emperor by order of the pope in spite of Louis of Bavaria. Charles, to gratify the pope, sent Nicolo in custody to him. Some time after this Francesco Baroncegli, following as it were the example of Nicolo, seized the office of tribune at Rome, and once more the senators were driven out, whereupon the pope, the more promptly to crush Francesco, released Nicolo and sent him with the prerogatives of tribune to Rome, where he recovered the reins of power and put Francesco to death; but Nicolo himself, incurring the enmity of the Colonnesi, was by them shortly afterwards slain and the senators were restored to their dignities. Meantime the King of Hungary, having driven out Queen Giovanna, returned to his own kingdom, but the pope, who preferred the queen to the king as a neighbour to Rome, contrived that she should be restored to her kingdom, so long as her husband Lodovico should be content with the title of Taranto and not be called king. The year 1350 was now come, and it occurred to the pope that the jubilee, which had been ordained by Pope Boniface IV. to be held every one hundred years, might be re-ordained for every fifty years, and this was decreed by him. The Romans pleased with this change suffered him to depute four cardinals to reform the administration of the city and to mould the senate to his will. The pope also proclaimed Lodovico of Taranto King of Naples, for which act of grace Queen Giovanna gave Avignon, which was her patrimony, to the Church. At this time Luchino Visconti died, and Giovanni, the archbishop, became the sole lord of Milan. He engaged in many wars, both in Tuscany and the neighbouring provinces, and in this way acquired great power. On his death Bernabo and Galeazzo his nephews succeeded; but shortly after Galeazzo died, leaving his son Giovanni Galeazzo, who shared the government with Bernabo. Charles, King of Bohemia, was now emperor, and Innocent VI, pope. The latter had despatched into Italy Cardinal Egidio, a Spaniard, who by his energy had revived the fame of the Church not only in Rome and Romagna but throughout Italy. He recovered Bologna, which had been seized by the Archbishop of Milan; forced the Romans to accept a foreign senator, to be annually nominated by the pope; made an honourable convention with the Visconti; defeated and took prisoner the Englishman Sir John Hawkwood, who with 4000 Englishmen had fought in Tuscany on the side of the Ghibellines. Urban V. succeeding now to the pontificate, and hearing of so many victories, decided to visit Italy and Rome, whither also came the Emperor Charles; but after a few months Charles returned to Germany and the pope went back to Avignon. After Urban's decease, Gregory XI. succeeded, and Cardinal Egidio being now dead, Italy fell back into the old dissensions, caused by the people combining against the Visconti, insomuch that the pope first despatched a legate with 6000 Breton soldiers, and afterwards came in person, and brought back the court to Rome in 1376, after it had been seventy-one years in France. On the death of Gregory, Urban VI. was chosen in his place, but shortly after, at a synod of ten cardinals in Fondi, his election was declared invalid, and Clement VII. was created pope. At this time the Genoese, who for many years had lived under the rule of the Visconti, revolted, and between them and the Venetians there arose a quarrel concerning the island of Tenedos, sufficient to set the whole of Italy in flames. Artillery, a new engine of war introduced by the Germans, was first employed in this struggle. Although the Genoese had the upper hand for a time, and kept Venice in a state of siege for many months, yet at the end of the war the Venetians were victors, and with the aid of the pope peace was made in the year 1381.

In this year there had arisen, as we have said, a schism in the Church, in which disunion the Queen Giovanna declared for the schismatical pope. For this reason the pope caused Charles di Durazzo, a descendant of the royal house of Naples, to make an attempt upon her kingdom; which he did, wresting the crown from her and making himself master of the kingdom. Giovanna fled to France; and the French king, furious at these events, despatched Louis of Anjou to Italy to recover the kingdom for her, expel Urban from Rome, and install the anti-pope. Louis, however, died in the midst of this great undertaking, and his army having suffered some reverses returned to France. The pope himself now went to Naples, where he imprisoned nine of the cardinals for having taken the part of France and the anti-pope. Afterwards he took offence at the king, who refused to make one of his nephews Prince of Capua, but, dissembling his vexation, he begged Charles to give him Nocera for a residence, which he fortified, making ready to take the kingdom by force from Charles. Whereupon the king took the field against him and the pope fled to Genoa, where he put to death those cardinals whom he had imprisoned. Thence he went to Rome, and to increase his dignity he created twenty-nine cardinals. At this time Charles, King of Naples, went into Hungary, where he was crowned king, and shortly after was murdered, leaving at Naples his wife and his two children, Ladislao and Giovanna. Giovanni Galeazzo Visconti at this time murdered his uncle Bernabo and seized the government of Milan, and not content with becoming the Duke of the whole of Lombardy wished to seize Tuscany also. But while he was thinking to assume this dominion, and ultimately the crown of Italy itself, he died. Meantime Urban VI. was followed by Boniface IX., and the anti-Pope Clement VIII. also dying was succeeded by Benedict XIII. During these times there were many English, German, and French soldiers in Italy, some brought there by princes who at various times had come into Italy, and some sent thither by the pontiffs when they were at Avignon. With these the princes had mostly conducted their fighting, until Lodovico da Cento, a Romagnaian, chanced to enrol a body of Italian soldiers entitled San Giorgio, the bravery and discipline of which soon deprived the foreign troops of their prestige and restored it to the Italians, whereupon the Italian princes made use of the latter in the wars which they waged between themselves. Owing to the disputes which he was constantly having with the Roman people, the pope had gone to Scesi, where he was residing when the 1400 jubilee was celebrated; at which time the Romans, to induce him to return to Rome for the good of the city, submitted once more to accept a foreign senator at his hands and allowed him to fortify the castle of San Angelo, under which conditions he returned. To enrich the Church he decreed that on the vacancy of any benefice a year's revenues should be paid to the papal treasury. After the death of Giovanni Galeazzo, Duke of Milan, who left two sons, Giovanmariangelo and Filippo, the state was split up into many parties. In the trouble which followed, Giovanmaria died, and Filippo was held for a time shut up in the fortress of Pavia, whence he was only liberated by the devotion and bravery of the castellan. Among others who seized cities which had belonged to the fathers of the Visconti was Gugliemo della Scala, who having been banished had placed himself under the protection of Francesco da Carrara, lord of Padua, with whose help he recovered the lordship of Verona. Here, however, he kept his position but for a short time, for at Francesco's bidding he was poisoned. In consequence of this the Vicentines, who had lived in peace under the ægis of the Visconti, alarmed at the power of the lord of Padua, joined themselves to the Venetians; whereupon the Venetians declared war upon Francesco, and took from him first Verona and afterwards Padua.

Meantime Pope Boniface died and Innocent VII. was elected his successor. To him the people of Rome made supplication that he should hand them over the fortresses and restore their liberties, but the pope would not consent, and the people thereupon called to their aid Ladislao, King of Naples. Ultimately they came to terms, and the pope returned to Rome from Viterbo, whither he had fled for fear of the people, and where he had made his nephew Lodovico, Count della Marca. After a time Innocent died, and Gregory XII. was made pope on his undertaking to renounce the papacy whenever the anti-pope should also renounce it. At the instigation of the cardinals, and in order to see if the Church could not be reunited, Benedict the anti-pope was induced to come to Porto Venere and Gregory to Lucca, where they discussed many things but decided nothing, the cardinals finally throwing them both over, and the pontiffs themselves departed, Benedict going into Spain and Gregory to Rimini. The cardinals on either side by the help of Baldassare Cossa, cardinal and legate of Bologna, called a council at Pisa, where they elected as pope Alexander V., who at once excommunicated King Ladislao and invested Louis of Anjou with the crown. With the Florentines, the Genoese, and the Venetians, also with Baldassare Cossa the legate, he attacked Ladislao and took Rome from him. But in the height of the war Alexander died, and Baldassare Cossa was made pope and assumed the title of John XXIII. Leaving Bologna, where he had been elected, John XXIII. went to Rome, where he found Louis of Anjou had arrived with his army from Provence. Louis came to an engagement with Ladislao and defeated him, but owing to the defection of the Condottieri he could not follow up his victory, thus enabling Ladislao presently to recover his strength and retake Rome, whereupon the pope fled to Bologna and Louis back to Provence. The pope, plotting how he might best lower the power of Ladislao, contrived that Sigismund, King of Hungary, should be elected emperor and encouraged to come into Italy. With Sigismund the pope had an interview at Mantua, and it was agreed to call a general council, at which the Church should be united, and should thus be enabled the more readily to withstand its enemies.

There were at this time three popes, Gregory, Benedict, and John, a circumstance which enfeebled the Church and robbed it of all authority. Constance, a city in Germany, was chosen for the place of meeting of the council, against the wish of John. And although the death of Ladislao had removed the pope's motive for calling the council, nevertheless he was so committed that he could not refuse to attend. He was conducted to Constance, but after some months he recognised his mistake and attempted to escape; whereupon he was made prisoner and forced to renounce the papacy. One of the anti-popes also, Gregory, voluntarily renounced it, and Benedict, the other anti-pope, on refusing to give it up was condemned as a heretic. Finally, being abandoned by his cardinals, he also was compelled to renounce it, and the council appointed Odo, of the house of Colonna, afterwards called Pope Martin V. Thus was the Church reunited after forty years of schism under many pontiffs.

At this juncture Filippo Visconti found himself, as we have already seen, in the stronghold of Pavia. Now, Fazino Cane — a man who during the recent troubles in Lombardy had made himself master of Vercelli, Allesandria, Novara, and Tortona, and accumulated vast wealth — having died without issue, had left Beatrice his wife heiress to his estates, and had enjoined his friends to bring about a marriage between his widow and Filippo. By the accomplishment of this alliance Filippo became a most powerful prince, regained Milan, and the entire dominion of Lombardy. Later on, to show his gratitude, in the way that princes often do show it, for these great benefits he accused Beatrice of adultery and caused her to be murdered. Having now become very powerful, he began to prepare for war upon Tuscany, in order that he might fulfil the intentions of Giovanni Galeazzo his father. Ladislao, King of Naples, at his death had left to his sister Giovanna, besides the kingdom, a great army captained by the foremost condottieri in Italy, among the first of whom was Sforza of Cotignola, most highly esteemed among that class of soldier. The queen to avoid the scandal of keeping one Pandolfello, whom she had brought up, took in marriage Jacques de la Marche, a Frenchman of the royal blood, on the condition that he should be content with the title of Prince of Taranto and leave to her the regal title and prerogatives. But on his arrival at Naples the soldiers proclaimed him king, and a great struggle arose between husband and wife, first one and then the other obtaining the upper hand; but in the end the queen maintained her position as head of the state, which afterwards became very hostile to the papacy. Hence it came about that Sforza, to reduce her to such straits that she would be compelled to throw herself into the arms of the pope, surprised her by resigning his command. Thus she found herself powerless at one stroke, and having no other remedy she had recourse for aid to Alfonso, King of Aragon and Sicily, whom she adopted as her son; she also enlisted Braccio da Montone, who was reputed the equal of Sforza in arms, and who was himself an enemy of the pope, since he had seized Perugia and certain other cities belonging to the Church. Peace was presently concluded between the queen and the pope; but King; Alfonso, fearing that she might treat him as she had done her husband, sought to make himself privily master of the fortresses. The queen, who was astute enough, forestalled him, and fortified herself within the stronghold of Naples. Suspicion still growing between them, they had recourse to arms, and the queen with the aid of Sforza, who had returned to her service, overthrew Alfonso, drove him out of Naples, and deprived him of his heirship, adopting Louis of Anjou in his stead; whereupon war again broke out between Braccio, who espoused the cause of Alfonso, and Sforza who favoured the queen. Sforza, however, while directing operations was drowned in fording the river at Pescara, and thus the queen was again in peril, and would have been driven from her kingdom but for the aid of Filippo Visconti, Duke of Milan, who compelled Alfonso to take refuge in Aragon. But Braccio, undeterred by the desertion of Alfonso, pursued his operations against the queen and laid siege to Aquila. Whereupon the pope, who regarded Braccio's success as against the interests of the Church, took into his pay Francesco, the son of Sforza, who met Braccio at Aquila, where he defeated and slew him. Of Braccio's party there now remained only his son Odo, whom the pope deprived of Perugia, leaving him Montone. But Odo dying soon after while fighting in Romagna for the Florentines, Nicolo Piccinino alone remained of any reputation of all those who had served under Braccio.

Now that we have arrived in the course of our history near to those times which I have particularly to trace, for there remains nothing of much importance to relate beyond the wars that the Florentines and Venetians waged with the Duke of Milan—which will be narrated when I treat of Florence in detail—I will not proceed further, but will only briefly remind my readers in what condition Italy, with its princes and armaments, stood at the time of which we are writing. Of the chief states, Queen Giovanna II. held the kingdom of Naples, the Marca, the Patrimony, and Romagna. Part of these lands were under the rule of the Church, part of them were held by their several deputies or tyrants, as Ferrara, Modena, and Reggio by the da Este; Faenza by the Manfredi; Imola by the Alidosi; Furli by the Odolaffi; Rimini and Pesaro by the Malatesti; and Camerino by the family of da Varano. Of Lombardy, part was under the sway of the Duke Filippo, part under that of the Venetians; because all those who had hitherto held individual states there had been exterminated, except the house of Gonzaga, who were lords of Mantua. Of Tuscany, the Florentines were master for most part; Lucca alone and Siena lived under their own laws, Lucca under the Guinigi, Siena free. The Genoese were at one time autonomous and at another under the rule of either the kings of France or of the Visconti; they were of little importance, and were reckoned among the smaller powers. Of the powers of first class importance not one possessed an armed force of their own. The Duke Filippo, shut up in his chamber and never permitting himself to be seen, carried on his wars by means of commissioners. The Venetians, in their desire for conquest on land, turned their back on those arms that at sea had rendered them so glorious, and following the customs of other Italian states placed their armies under the command of foreigners. The pope being a churchman was unused to arms, and the Queen Giovanna of Naples, being a woman, did of necessity what the others did from an evil choice. The Florentines, their nobility being extinct by reason of incessant feuds, and the government in the hands of men bred up to mercantile pursuits, followed in this respect the customs and fortunes of the rest. The armaments of Italy were therefore in the control either of the lesser princes or of men without territory; because the lesser princes, not for love of fame, but either for the sake of wealth or of security, followed the profession of arms; whilst the men without possessions, and ignorant of trades, were trained to arms from their childhood, and looked to them to gain either wealth or power. Among the soldiers of fortune most spoken of in those days were Carmignuola, Francesco Sforza, Nicolo Piccinino, pupil of Braccio, Agnolo della Pergola, Lorenzo and Micheletto Attendolo, Tartaglia, Giacopaccio, Ceccolino da Perugia, Nicolo da Tolentino, Guido Torello, Antonio dal Ponto ad Era, and many others like them. With these were the lords of whom I have spoken above, and to whom may be added the barons of Rome, the Orsini and Colonnesi, with other lords and gentlemen of the kingdom and of Lombardy, who taking a delight in war had made, so to speak, a league and understanding among themselves, and reduced it to an art, to which they accommodated themselves in such a way that the parties who engaged in war found themselves almost always the losers. In a word, fighting was reduced to a trade so vile that any peddling captain, in whom the mere ghost of ancient valour had reappeared, would have laughed them to scorn — to the amazement of all Italy who in her folly paid them respect. Therefore my history will be full of these slothful princes and of these most degraded fighters. Before I come to them, however, it is necessary for me, as I promised at the outset, to revert to the history of Florence from her first beginnings, and to set forth at large for all my readers what the condition of the city was at this early time, and by what steps — among all the troubles which have fallen upon Italy in a thousand years — it has arrived at this condition.

SECOND BOOK

1 2 1 5 - 1 3 4 3

AMONG other great and admirable customs of the ancient republics and principalities which in our times have perished, was that of founding and restoring towns and cities at every opportunity, nothing being more worthy of an excellent prince, or of a well-ordered republic, or more advantageous to a country, than the building of towns, where men are able to gather together for means of defence or industry. In former days this policy was easily pursued, because the state was accustomed to send what were termed colonies to such lands as it had conquered or as needed inhabitants; and of all institutions this of founding new towns secured the conquered territory more permanently to the conquerors, filled waste places with inhabitants, and kept the population properly distributed over the land. For when men are settled in a country in comfort they multiply more rapidly, and are more ready in attack and more secure in defence. But this institution, through the improvidence of princes and republics, has in our day become quite extinct, and by reason of its extinction realms have come to impotence and ruin; for through this policy alone can governments be rendered secure and countries be kept abundantly populated. Safety results from colonisation, because a colony founded by a prince in a territory which he has recently conquered serves as a stronghold and a garrison to keep the natives in subjection. Further, a country cannot be kept well populated, nor its people properly distributed, without this expedient; for all places are not alike productive or healthful, and thus in some places the population is abundant and in others scanty, and unless the expedient is adopted of shifting men from those regions where they abound, and settling them where they are wanting, the country soon deteriorates, because some parts of it become desert for lack of occupants, while others through their surplus population become impoverished. And inasmuch as nature cannot correct this anomaly it must be corrected by man's ingenuity, for unhealthy places become healthy through the concentration therein of a large body of men who quickly render the soil salubrious by cultivation, and with their fires purify the air— results which nature could never have achieved. The city of Venice furnishes a proof of this; for situate though she was in a marshy and insanitary spot, she became salubrious by reason of the crowds that flocked thither in a body. Pisa, again, owing to the insalubrity of the air, never became fully populated until Genoa and the surrounding country had been ravaged by the Saracens, when the refugees flocked into Pisa in such numbers that she soon became populous and powerful. But if for any reason there has been a failure to despatch colonies, then greater difficulty has been found in holding the conquered territory, while the uninhabited lands remain unsettled, and those that are overcrowded get no relief. Hence many parts of the world, and of Italy more particularly, are now, in comparison with what they were of old, mere deserts; and this has all come and will still come to pass from the lack, in princes, of all desire for true glory, and in commonwealths of such praiseworthy institutions. In ancient times, then, by virtue of these colonies, cities either sprang into existence, or being already in existence grew and prospered. Such was the city of Florence, which derived its origin from Fiesole, and was increased by colonies.

It is perfectly true, as Dante and Giovanni Villani show, that, because Fiesole was situate on the summit of a hill, the site for the new city was fixed not on the hill but in the plain, between the foot of the hill and the river Arno, in order that its markets might be more easy of access, and that such as desired to bring their merchandise thither might do so more conveniently. These markets, which were the occasion of the first buildings being raised in that place, made the merchants desire to have their commodities received there, and their storehouses became in time substantial buildings. Afterwards, when the Romans had driven back the Carthaginians and rendered Italy secure from foreign invasions, these buildings multiplied in great numbers; because men never remain in inconvenient quarters unless compelled to do so by necessity, as when the fear of invasion forces them to live in strong and rough places; but, so soon as their fears are past, their desire for comfort appeals to them, and they prefer to live in homely and accessible places. The security, therefore, which the renown of the Roman Republic conferred on Italy would serve to multiply the habitations already commenced in the above-mentioned way in such numbers as ultimately took the shape of a town, to which was first given the name of Villa Arnina. Later on there arose in Rome the civil wars, at first between Marius and Sylla, then between Cæsar and Pompey, and next between the murderers of Cæsar and those who desired to avenge his death. By Sylla, therefore, at first, and afterwards by those three Roman citizens who, after having revenged Cæsar, divided the empire, settlers were sent to Fiesole, of which all or some succeeded in establishing themselves in the plain adjacent to the town already begun. Thus by this process of increase the place grew so full of buildings, and of men, and of civil institutions of every kind, that it came to be counted among the cities of Italy, but regarding the origin of the name Florence there are various opinions. Some will have it that the city was so called after Florino, one of the heads of the colony. Others insist that its name was originally "Fluentia," not "Florentia," from its propinquity to the flowing Arno; and they call to witness Pliny, who says that the Fluentini dwell beside the flowing Arno. This reasoing is fallacious, for Pliny in his History is showing the position of the Florentines, not their name. And that term "Fluentini" may possibly be a textual corruption, because Frontinus and

Cornelius Tacitus, who wrote about the time of Pliny, speak of Florence and the Florentines; and already in the time of Tiberius they were governed according to the customs of other cities in Italy. Cornelius Tacitus relates that the Florentines sent deputies to the emperor to beg that the waters from the marshes should not be allowed to overflow their lands; and it is not reasonable to believe that the city had at one and the same time two names. On these grounds I hold that the city was at all times called Florentia, for whatever reason it was so named; and whatever may have been the circumstances of its birth, it sprang into being under the Roman rule, and in the time of the earliest emperor it began to be mentioned by historians. When the empire was overrun by the barbarians, Florence was destroyed by Totila, the king of the Ostrogoths, and was rebuilt by Charlemagne 250 years after; from which time until 1215 A.D. it shared the fortunes of other sovereign states of Italy. In those days the dominant power in Italy was first the House of Charlemagne, next the Berengarii, and finally the German emperors, as in our general statement we have shown, and in those times the Florentines were unable to increase, or to do anything memorable, owing to the power of those to whose domination they submitted. Nevertheless in 1010 A.D. on the festival of San Romolo, which the people of Fiesole kept as a holiday, the Florentines attacked and destroyed Fiesole. This was done either with the consent of the emperor, or in the interregnum between the death of one emperor and the election of another, when every one claims more liberty. But when the pontiffs acquired more authority in Italy, and the German emperors' power declined there, all the towns in the country guided their affairs with less deference to the ruling princes, in such wise that in the year 1080, in the reign of Henry III., all Italy became split, in open division, between the emperor and the Church. Nevertheless the Florentines maintained unity among themselves until 1215 by submitting to the conqueror of the moment and seeking the protection of no other power. Yet, as our bodily infirmities are the more dangerous and fatal the later they appear, even so

Florence, the more backward she was in imitating Italian intrigues, the more severely was she punished through them. The causes which led to the first and most noted division, since they have been recounted by Dante and many other celebrated writers, must only be briefly retold by me.

There were in Florence, among other very powerful families, the Buondelmonti and the Uberti, of whom the Amidei and the Donati were neighbours. In the family of the Donati there was a rich widow, who had one daughter of surpassing beauty. This lady had in her own mind intended to marry the girl to Messer Buondelmonte, a young cavalier, chief of the house of Buondelmonti, but whether through negligence or procrastination she had never made her intention known. His family, meanwhile, had arranged a marriage between Messer Buondelmonte and a daughter of the Amidei, whereat the lady was much displeased, and resolved with the aid of her daughter's beauty to upset the marriage before it should be celebrated. On seeing Messer Buondelmonte one day approaching her house alone, she came down from her chamber, bringing her daughter with her, and as the young man was passing advanced to meet him, saying, "I am rejoiced truly that you have chosen a wife, although I had reserved this, my daughter, for you," and she pushed open the door that he might see her. The cavalier saw the exquisite beauty of the girl and, knowing that her birth and dowry were not inferior to that of her to whom he was affianced, became so inflamed with passion to possess her that, recking nothing of his plighted word, or of the wrong he would do in breaking it, or of the troubles that would gather round him through his breach of faith, exclaimed, "Since you have kept her for me I should be ungrateful to refuse, there being yet time." Without delay the marriage was celebrated. This affair, once it was known, enraged the houses of the Amidei and of the Uberti, who were akin to them; and at a family council attended by many others related to them they decided that this injury could not be submitted to without disgrace nor be expiated by any other penalty than the death of Messer Buondelmonte. Whilst some discoursed of the evils that

might ensue, Moscha Lamberti said, "He who considers everything will never do anything," quoting that old and well known
line, "Cosa fatta, capo ha." Upon this they placed the killing of
Messer Buondelmonte in the hands of Moscha, Stiatta Uberti,
Lambertuccio Amidei, and Oderigo Fifanti, who meeting on the
morning of Easter Day, 1215, at the house of the Amidei, posted
themselves between the Ponte Vecchio and San Stefano, where
presently Messer Buondelmonte as he was crossing the bridge on
a white horse, and possibly thinking that it was just as easy to forget an injury as to break a promise, was attacked by them at the
foot of the bridge and killed beneath a statue of Mars. This murder threw the whole city into turmoil, part joining the Buondelmonti and part the Uberti. Being strong in houses, fortresses, and
men, the two families contended for many years without either
prevailing against the other, and from time to time their feuds,
albeit never extinguished by peace, were suspended by truce, and
thus, according to circumstances, they subsided for a time and
then flared out afresh.

Florence submitted to these troubles until the time of Frederic
II., who persuading himself that because he was King of Naples
he could increase his strength against the Church, and so consol-
idate his power in Tuscany, favoured the Uberti and their following, until with his help they drove out the Buondelmonti; and
thus, even as all Italy has been divided before, so now our city also
came to be divided into Guelf and Ghibelline. I do not consider it
beside the mark to commemorate the names of those families
which followed either faction. Those who followed the Guelph
party were Buondelmonti, Nerli, Rossi, Frescobaldi, Mozzi, Bardi,
Pulci, Gheradini, Foraboschi, Bagnesi, Guidalotti, Sacchetti,
Manieri, Lucardesi, Chiarimontesi, Compiobbesi, Cavalcanti,
Giandonati, Gianfigliazzi, Scali, Gualterotti, Importuni, Bostichi,
Tornaquinci, Vecchietti, Tosinghi, Arrigucci, Agli, Sizi, Adimari,
Visdomini, Donati, Pazzi, della Bella, Ardinghi, Teldaldi, Cerchi.
For the Ghibellines were the Uberti, Mannelli, Ubriachi, Fifanti,
Amidei, Infangati, Malespini, Scolari, Guidi, Galli, Cappiardi,

Lamberti, Soldanieri, Cipriani, Toschi, Amieri, Palermini, Miglio-
relli, Pigli, Barucci, Cattani, Agolanti, Brunelleschi, Caponsacchi,
Elisei, Abati, Tedaldini, Giuochi, Galigai. Besides this many of the
commoners joined the party of one or other of these noble families, so that the whole city was infected by their quarrels. When the
Guelfs were driven out they settled in the Valdarno, where they
built many fortresses, and in this way were enabled to protect themselves against the eruptions of their enemies. When Frederic came
to die, those Florentines who favoured a compromise, and were in
credit with the people, thought that it would be better to reunite
the city than to continue these ruinous dissensions, and they
worked in such a manner that the Guelfs, discarding the memory
of their wrongs, returned, and the Ghibellines, laying aside their
distrust, made them welcome. Being united, it appeared to them
time to adopt an independent way of living and to take measures
for self-defence before the new emperor should become powerful.

They therefore divided the city into six quarters, and elected
twelve citizens, two, entitled "Anziani," to rule each quarter, and to
be replaced annually. To remove all grounds of enmity such as
may arise out of judicial decisions, they made provision for two
foreign judges, to be called the one Captain of the People and the
other Podesta, who should judge in the suits, whether civil or
criminal, which arose among the citizens. As no institutions are
permanent without provision for their defence, they set up twenty
banners in the city and seventy-six in the surrounding districts,
under which they enrolled all the youth, and they decreed that
each one should be ready and armed under his banner whenever
he should be called up by the captain or the anziani. The device
on the banner varied accordingly as the arms under it varied; thus
the archers bore one device, and the soldiers with shields another;
and every year on the day of Pentecost they gave the ensigns over
to new men with great ceremony, and assigned new leaders to
their army. And to give dignity to their battalions, and a rallying
point for all such as might become scattered in the course of
battle, where they could re-assemble and make headway afresh

54

against the enemy, they furnished a large car drawn by two oxen with red trappings, with red and white colours flying overhead. Besides its use in the army, whenever they desired to assemble the citizens they brought the car into the Mercato Nuovo, and with solemn rites handed it over to the leaders of the people. To further enhance the dignity of their enterprises they had a bell, called Martinello, which was rung continuously for a month before they drew their army out of the city, so that the enemy would have time to prepare himself. Such valour was there in the men of those times, and with such generosity were their souls animated, that whereas to-day it is counted valorous and prudent to take an enemy unawares, it was then held dishonourable and treacherous. This bell they also carried with the army, and by it sentinels were posted and other functions of the army carried out.

Such were the institutions, civil and military, by means of which the Florentines laid the foundations of their independence, and it is impossible to conceive the degree of authority and power which in a short period she attained, for not only had she become the head of Tuscany, but she was counted among the first cities of Italy, and could have risen to any height of greatness if fresh and frequent dissensions had not afflicted her. The Florentines lived under this government for ten years, and within this time they had forced Pistoia, Arezzo, and Siena into a league with them. On their way back from the siege of Siena they took Volterra, and also destroyed some castles, and carried away the inhabitants to Florence. All these enterprises were carried out at the instigation of the Guelfs, who were much more influential than the Ghibellines, either because the latter were hated by the people for their haughty carriage during their predominance in the time of Frederic, or because the ecclesiastical party was more popular than the imperial; because with the aid of the Church the Florentines hoped to preserve their liberties, whilst under the empire they feared to lose them. Wherefore the Ghibellines, perceiving that their influence was declining, could not rest, and only awaited an opportunity to seize again the reins of government, and this seemed to have come to them when they found that Manfred, the son of Frederic, had established himself in the kingdom of Naples, and already humbled the power of the Church. Secretly, therefore, they conspired with him to regain their influence, but they were unable so to manage this as to prevent the authorities discovering the plot. Whereupon the anziani summoned before them the Uberti, who not only refused to obey, but took up arms, fortifying themselves in their houses. Upon this the enraged citizens flew to arms, and with the aid of the Guelfs drove out of Florence the Uberti who with the rest of the Ghibellines went to Siena. From here they sent to seek the assistance of Manfred, King of Naples, and by the exertions of Messer Farinata degli Uberti the Guelfs were shortly afterwards defeated by the royal forces near the river Arbia with so heavy a loss of life that the survivors of the rout fled not to Florence, which they deemed lost, but to Lucca.

Manfred had sent to the Ghibellines, as commander of his forces, Count Giordano, a man of great reputation in arms in those times. After the victory he accompanied the Ghibellines to Florence, brought the city into subjection to the King Manfred, abolishing the magistrates, and every other institution in which any semblance of liberty could be traced. These wrongs, inflicted without consideration, were received on all sides with intense anger, and from being merely ill-affected towards the Ghibellines the citizens came to hold them in the utmost detestation. And hence ensued ultimately the ruin of the Ghibellines. The Count Giordano having, through the urgent needs of the kingdom, to return to Naples, left in Florence as the viceroy the Count Guido Novello, Lord of Casentino. This man called a council of the Ghibellines, where it was unanimously decided that, if the Ghibelline party was to be maintained in power in Tuscany, it would be necessary to destroy Florence, inasmuch as that city having a Guelf population was of all places the best adapted for restoring the influence of the Church party. Against this cruel sentence, passed upon so noble a city, there was not found one citizen or friend to protest, save only Messer Farinata degli Uberti; he defended the city openly and without hesitation, saying that he would not have encountered so many difficulties and dangers if it had not been for the hope of once more residing in his native city; and that he had no desire now to seek another, or to refuse the home which fortune had bestowed on him; and that he would be no less an enemy to those who now spoke of destroying the city than he had been to the Guelfs; and if any of them, despairing now of his country, would seek to ruin it, he would defend it with all the valour which he had employed to drive the Guelfs out. Messer Farinata being a man of great courage and skill in war, and highly esteemed by Manfred, his authority put an end to the suggestion, and other plans had to be contrived for enabling the Ghibellines to keep their hold on the government.

In consequence of the threats of Count Novello, the Lucchese had dismissed the Guelfs who had taken refuge in Lucca, and they had gone to Bologna. Whilst there they were summoned by the Guelfs of Parma to assist them against the Ghibellines in that city. These Guelfs conducted themselves with such bravery that they conquered the enemy, and were rewarded by receiving their lands and possessions. Thus restored in wealth and reputation, and hearing that Pope Clement had called upon Charles, of Anjou to deprive Manfred of the kingdom, they hastened to offer help to the pope. The pope not only received them as allies, but conferred upon them his standard, which was afterwards always carried by the Guelfs in battle and is still in use in Florence. Manfred was despoiled of his kingdom and killed by Charles, upon which the Guelf party in Florence became more aggressive, whilst the Ghibellines declined in influence. Seeing which Count Guido Novello and those who held the government of Florence came to the conclusion that it would be wise for them to conciliate the people whom they had so short a time before outraged with injuries. These concessions, had they come earlier, might have been of use, but coming now by stress of circumstances they did no good and earned no gratitude, but only hastened the ruin of the Ghibellines. The count and his friends decided to restore to the people certain powers and dignities of which they had previously been deprived, and thirty-six middle class citizens were elected, together with two gentlemen from Bologna, to reform the government of the city. These deputies at their first meeting divided the city into guilds, and over each guild they placed a master, who was to be responsible for the members of the guild. Besides this they entrusted to each guild a banner, around which every man was to gather, ready armed, whenever the city had need of his services. There were in the beginning twelve guilds, seven greater and five lesser ones. Afterwards the lesser were increased to fourteen, so that finally there were twenty-one in all, as there are now. The thirty-six reformers also put into practice other suggestions for the benefit of the community.

In order to raise pay for his soldiers Count Guido levied upon the citizens a tax, which was so much resented that he dared not use force to collect it. Concluding from this that he had lost his authority, he decided in consultation with the Ghibelline leaders to deprive the people by force of those liberties which with so little prudence had lately been conceded to them. When it became known that this was to be carried out by the army, the thirty-six commissioners met and raised a tumult, whereupon the Ghibellines became alarmed and shut themselves up in their houses, whilst the banners of the guilds were brought out and many armed men flocked to them. Learning that Count Guido was at San Giovanni with his men, the people mustered at Santa Trinita, and placed themselves under the command of Messer Giovanni Soldanieri. The count, finding the people drawn up against him, moved out to meet them. Nor did the people avoid the fight but advanced against their enemy, and encountering him where stands to-day the Loggia of the Tornaquinci drove him back with the loss of many men; this utterly dismayed him, for he feared that the people would attack again during the night and that, his men being beaten and cowed, he would be killed. This idea so grew upon him that, thinking no other course possible, he sought safety in flight rather than in combat, and without consulting the leaders of his party he fled with all his men to Prato. But when he found himself in a safe place he forgot his fears, recognised his mistake, and wishing in the morning to correct it, set out again for Florence and arrived there at daybreak with the intention of re-entering by force the city which he had abandoned through cowardice. His design, however, did not succeed, for the people, who could only have driven him out with difficulty, could now keep him outside with ease, and in sorrow and chagrin he therefore retreated to Casentino, and the Ghibellines fled to their villages. Thus the people were the victors, and by the advice of those men who were desirous for the good of the republic, it was decided to restore the city to unity and peace by recalling all exiled citizens, whether Ghibelline or Guelf, with whom they could meet. So the Guelfs returned, and settled again in the city, six years after their expulsion, and the recent affronts of the Ghibellines were passed over. Notwithstanding the restoration of the Ghibellines they were still hated by the populace and the Guelfs, because the people remembered bitterly the tyranny of the Ghibelline rule, and the Guelfs could not erase from their memories the sorrows of their exile, consequently the mind of neither party was at rest. Whilst affairs stood in this position in Florence, the report was spread that Conradine, the nephew of Manfred, was marching that way with an army out of Germany to take possession of Naples; this inspired the Ghibellines with hopes of regaining their power, but the Guelfs, anxious for protection against their foes, sent to King Charles for assistance against Conradine when he should pass through their territory. When the army of Charles approached Florence, the Guelfs threatened the Ghibellines to such an extent that two days before the army arrived they all fled from the city, without any pressure being exercised upon them.

The Ghibellines having fled, the Florentines reorganised the government of the city, and elected twelve men, who were to hold the magistracy for two months and to be called buonomini. In place of the anziani, a council of eighty citizens was appointed with the buonomini, and was called the credenza. Also a further council of one hundred and eighty of the middle class citizens, thirty from each quarter of the city was appointed, which with the credenza and the twelve buonomini was called the general council. Another council was also ordained which was to consist of one hundred and twenty citizens from the middle class and the nobles, to whom was given the duty of revising the decisions of the general council, and the distribution of the republic's appointments. When this constitution was formulated the citizens proceeded to strengthen the Guelf party by the appointment of magistrates from among them, and by other regulations, in order to be able to defend themselves with the utmost effect against the Ghibellines. They also divided up into three parts the property of the Ghibellines, one part was given to the public; one to the magistrates, called the captains of the party; and the third part was assigned to the Guelfs as compensation for the losses they had incurred. The pope appointed King Charles the imperial Viceroy of Tuscany, in order to preserve that province more effectually for the Guelphs. The Florentines were now in a position, owing to the excellency of this new government, to maintain their credit within their own borders by their laws and without by their arms. At this time Pope Clement died, and after a dispute which extended over two years Pope Gregory X. was elected. This ecclesiastic having spent many years in Syria—even being there at the time of his election, far distant from the passions of parties—did not understand them in the manner that his predecessors had done, and having reached Florence on his way to France, he persuaded himself that it was his duty as a good pastor to endeavour to reunite the people of Florence. He, therefore, induced the Florentines to receive the syndics of the Ghibellines, and to discuss with them the terms upon which they could return to the city. Although an agreement was reached, the Ghibellines were so nervous they did not avail themselves of it. The pope laid the blame of this failure upon the city, and in anger he excommunicated it; it remained under this ban as long as he lived, but after his death the interdiction was removed by Pope Innocent V. The pontiffs had always lived in apprehension of those who attained any degree of power in Italy, whether such power was owing to the favour of the Church or not, and it was in the efforts of the Church to humble it that many disturbances arose and many changes occurred, because in its fear of one power it would seek to strengthen another, and when such a one had increased in power so as to become dangerous, the popes, fearing it, would in turn seek to lower it. This impulse caused one pope to wrest the kingdom from the rule of Manfred and yield it to Charles, and afterwards in fear of him another pope sought Charles' ruin. Thus it was that at this time Nicholas III., a scion of the house of Orsini, who had been raised to the pontificate, influenced by these fears, induced the emperor to take away from Charles the government of Tuscany, and the pope sent his own legate, Messer Latino, to govern that province in the name of the emperor.

Florence was now placed in a very unfortunate position, owing to the outrages committed by the Guelfic nobility and their want of respect for the magistrates—murders and other acts of violence occurring every day, and their perpetrators escaping without punishment, owing to their being favourites of one or other of the nobility. Whereupon the leaders of the people thought to curb this insolence by recalling the exiles, and thus giving the legate an opportunity of reuniting the city. They therefore allowed the Ghibellines to return, and in place of twelve governors they created fourteen, seven from each party, who were to hold office for one year, and were to be selected by the pope. Florence remained under this government for two years, when Martin IV., a Frenchman, came to the pontificate, and restored to King Charles all the authority which Nicholas had taken away from him. Thus at one stroke all the factions were revived throughout Tuscany, the Florentines taking arms against the imperial governor, depriving the Ghibellines of office, and instituting a new form of government to keep the nobility in check. It was now the year 1282 and the guilds, since they had been allowed officials and banners, had become so important that by their own authority they were able to ordain that, in place of fourteen governors, three only should be appointed who should be called priors. They were to have charge of the republic for two months at a time, and could be chosen from either the traders or the nobles, provided they were merchants or belonged to the guilds. Later they altered these leading magistrates to six, one from each of the six divisions of the city, and in 1342 they reduced the city into four quarters and the priors to eight in number, but owing to an accident once during that time they created twelve. This magistracy was the cause, as will be seen in time, of the ruin of the nobility, because by it they were gradually excluded from office under a variety of pretexts, and in the end deprived of all power. The nobility had acquiesced in this at first, since owing to dissensions amongst themselves, in their efforts to exclude each other from the government, they had lost all power. A palace was handed over to the magistrates, and they resided there constantly instead of meeting as formerly in churches, and they were also provided with officers and servants as an addition to their dignity, and the title of signori was conferred upon them, whilst in the beginning they had only been called priors. The Florentines remained quiet internally for some time, but they made war upon the people of Arezzo for having driven out of their city the Guelfs, and at Campaldino successfully overcame them. The city having increased much in population and wealth, it seemed advisable to enlarge its boundaries, and this they did in the way which is now seen; it is well known that its area was at first only that space which runs from the Ponte Vecchio to San Lorenzo.

War without and peace within had almost laid at rest the Guelf and Ghibelline feud in Florence, those animosities only remaining which prevail naturally in every city between the nobles and the people, and which arise from the nobles wishing to rule according to their own ideas, whilst the people desire to live according to the laws, and it is impossible for these two opposites to assimilate. This dissension did not come to a head as long as both parties were kept in awe of the Ghibellines, but as soon as they were tamed it began to show itself, and everyday some commoner was injured, and the laws and the magistrates were not strong enough to assert themselves, because every noble, with the aid of his friends and relations, would defend himself against the forces of the priors and captain. So the masters of the guilds came to the decision that, in order to put an end to these disorders, the signoria upon taking up office should appoint, as gonfaloniere of justice, a middle class man, who should enrol under twenty banners 1000 men, and with his own standard and men should be ready to execute justice whenever he should be called upon by them or the captain. Ubaldo Ruffoli was the first man elected. He raised his standard and destroyed the houses of the Galletti, because one of that family had slain a merchant in France. It had been easy for the guilds to pass this ordinance because of the dissensions prevailing among the nobles, who took no heed of its provisions until they saw the severity of the Galletti proceedings. This filled them with alarm for a time, but they soon recovered their insolent demeanour, because having always one of their order among the signori, they found many expedients for hindering the gonfaloniere in the execution of his duties. Beyond this the outraged party had need of witnesses, and none could be found who would be willing to bear witness against a nobleman. Thus Florence soon fell back into her old troubles, and her people submitted to many wrongs from the nobility because justice was slow, and her decisions often failed in execution. The people were quite at a loss what to do, but Giano della Bella, a lover of liberty, descended from one of the noblest Florentine families, inspired the masters of the guilds with courage, and by his advice it was ordained that the gonfaloniere should reside with the signori and have 4000 men under his command; that the nobles should be deprived of their power to sit as signori; that the harbourers of criminals should incur the same punishment as the criminals themselves; and that the public report of a crime should be sufficient evidence to adjudicate upon. By these laws, which were called the Ordinances of Justice, the people acquired immense power, but Giano della Bella brought down upon himself the hatred of the nobles, who looked upon him as the destroyer of their influence, and also of the rich merchants who were envious of his great authority. This hatred showed itself when shortly after a merchant was killed in a street fight in which a great number of nobles interfered. Among the nobles implicated was Messer Corso Donati, and he being the most aggressive in the disturbance the murder was attributed to him, and he was therefore arrested by the captain of the people. Whether Corso was innocent or the captain feared to condemn him, or however the matter was managed, he was acquitted. This displeased the people so much that they took up arms and ran to the house of Giano della Bella, and called upon him to enforce the laws of which he was the author. Giano desired that Messer Donati should be punished, but did not do as many thought he should have done, insist upon the people first laying down their arms, but he advised them to take their complaints to the signori and pray them to give them satisfaction. This advice further incensed the people, for now considering themselves abandoned by Giano, and wronged by the captain, they would not go to the signori, but attacked the palace of the captain and sacked it. This act offended all the citizens, and those who desired the ruin of Giano della Bella attributed all the mischief to him; whereupon he was accused by the captain of the insurrection and brought before the signori, among whom were several of his enemies. Whilst his case was being considered, the populace ran to his house and offered to defend him with their lives against the signori, but Giano was unwilling either to put the favour of the populace to the proof or to leave his life at the mercy of the magistrates, among whom were his sworn enemies, for he feared the fickleness of the one and the malignity of the other. Therefore, to take away from his enemies the opportunity of injuring him, and from his friends that of injuring the country, he decided to leave the city of Florence, which at his own peril he had freed from servitude to the nobles, and chose a voluntary exile.

After Giano della Bella had left the city the nobles were inspired with the hope of recovering their power, which they believed they had lost owing to the quarrels amongst themselves. Therefore they came to an agreement, and deputed two of their number to meet those signori, whom they thought favoured them, and to implore them to mitigate in some degree the asperity of the laws against the nobles. When it became known that these negotiations were proceeding, the middle classes were much disturbed, for they feared the signori would give way; thus, owing to the schemes of the nobles and the fears of the people, both parties armed themselves. The nobles took up their positions in three places, at San Giovanni, in the New Market, and in the Piazza de' Mozzi, and under three commanders, Messer Forese Adimari, Messer Vanni de' Mozzi, and Messer Geri Spini. The people assembled in great numbers under their banners at the palace of the signori, which at that time was situate near to San Procolo. As the signori had come under the suspicions of the people six citizens were deputed to sit with them in the council. Whilst both parties were thus preparing for the combat, some gentlemen from both the people and the nobles, together with certain priests of good character, came between them in order to endeavour to make peace. The nobles were reminded that the loss of their honours and the laws which weighed so heavily upon them were the result of their own arrogance and mismanagement, and that for them to take up arms to recover by force what they had lost by disunion and bad government was only to ruin their country and aggravate their own position. It was also pointed out to them that in numbers, riches, and determination the people were much superior to them, and that nobility, which seemed to them to raise them above other men, would not be of much avail in the fight when it came to blows, but was a mere name which could not defend them against the multitude. The people were reminded that it is not always wise to expect the ultimate victory, nor was it prudent to drive an enemy to despair, because he who cannot hope for any good will not fear any evil. Besides the people ought to remember that it was the nobility who had brought so much honour to the city in war, and that it was neither right nor just to pursue them with hatred; the nobles might endure being deprived of any share in the supreme magistracy, but what they could not endure was to be in the power of any man who, by means of the present ordinances, could drive them from their country. Therefore it would be wiser to mitigate these laws and by this favour induce the nobles to lay down their arms; the people should not tempt fortune further by confiding over-much in numbers, because they had often seen the many overcome by the few. This gave rise to much conflict of opinion among the people. There were many who thought that the quarrel should be fought out now, because it must by the nature of things come to a fight one day, and it was better that it should come at once, rather than it should be put off until the enemy was better prepared. If they could be persuaded that the nobles would remain content with a mitigation of the laws, then it would be well to mitigate them, but every one knew that the arrogance of the nobles was such that they would never rest until they were compelled by force. But many other men, wiser and calmer, said that, after all, the relaxation of the laws was not of so much importance or so serious as fighting, and in the end these views prevailed, and it was ordained that in accusations against nobles witnesses should be necessary.

Although arms were laid down both parties retained their suspicions of each other, and strengthened themselves with towers and armaments. The government was reorganised by the people and the number of rulers reduced, because it was recognised that the signori invariably favoured the nobles, among whom the leaders were the Mancini, Megalotti, Altoviti, the Peruzzi, and Cerretani. The government being firmly settled it was thought expedient, for the greater magnificence and security of the signori, to build them a new palace, the foundations of which were laid in 1298, and a piazza was made on the spot formerly occupied by the houses of the Uberti. They commenced also at this time to build the public prisons. These buildings were finished in the course of a few years when the city was more prosperous and powerful than it was then, being full of men, riches, and renown. The citizens who were trained to arms numbered 30,000, whilst there were 70,000 men in the districts around the city; and all Tuscany obeyed the Florentines, either as subjects or allies. Although there lingered some degree of soreness and suspicion between the nobles and the people, nevertheless it did not exercise any bad effect, because both parties lived together in peace. That peace might never have been disturbed had not new sources of dissension arisen, for from external affairs there was nothing to fear either from the emperor or from the exiles, because Florence was now in such a condition that she could have resisted all the combined forces of Italy with her own army. That evil which could not be effected by any outside means was to be accomplished from within.

There were residing in Florence two families, the Cerchi and the Donati, equally powerful by their descent, wealth, and the number of their retainers. They were also neighbours both in the city and the country; hence there had arisen between them slight disputes, but these were not sufficient to bring them to blows, and perhaps the peace would never have been broken between them had not fresh causes increased this jealousy in the following way. Among the first families in Pistoia was that of the Cancellieri, and one day Lore, the son of Messer Guglielmo, and Geri, the son of Bertaccio, both of this family, were playing together when Geri was slightly hurt by Lore. This accident displeased Lore's father, Messer Guglielmo, who, thinking that a little humility would avert further trouble, ordered his son to go to the house of the wounded lad's father and ask his pardon. Lore obeyed his father. Nevertheless, this considerate act only increased the trouble, and in no degree softened the harsh temper of Messer Bertaccio, for he ordered his servants to lay hold of Lore and cut off his hand; and as if for greater spite he had it done upon a manger. He then said to the lad, "Go back to your father, and tell him that wounds can only be cured by wounds, not by words." The cruelty of this deed so enraged Messer Guglielmo that he took up arms for revenge, and Messer Bertaccio also armed in his own defence, and not only did these families fight but the whole city of Pistoia became embroiled in the quarrel. As it happened that the two Cancellieri were descended from a Messer Cancelliere who had married two wives, the name of one being Bianca, so the partisans of the man who was son of this lady were called Bianchi, whilst the others, in order that they might have an opposite name, were called Neri. Many fights occurred with much loss of life and destruction of property, and wearying of this, yet unable to bring it to an end, they determined to embroil others in it, and with this view they carried their discords to Florence. Here the Neri, owing to their intimacy with the Donati, were assisted by Messer Corso, the head of the family, whilst the Bianchi, to obtain support against the Donati, had recourse to Messer Veri de' Cerchi, a man in every way the equal of Messer Corso.

This Pistoian discord revived all the old hatreds between the Cerchi and Donati, and this was already so manifest that the signori and other good citizens feared that it might break out into open fight at any moment and the whole city become embroiled. They had therefore recourse to the pope, praying him to use his authority to compose these troubles, which it was not in their power to remedy. The pope sent for Messer Veri and entreated him to make peace with the Donati. Messer Veri expressed his astonishment at this request and answered that he had no enmity against the Donati, and that to make peace presupposes war, and as there was no war he could not see that it was necessary to make peace. Messer Veri therefore came back from Rome without anything being concluded, and the animosity between the parties increased to such a pitch that any little accident, as indeed happened, might precipitate a fight. It was in the month of May when all Florence makes holiday in the streets, that some young men on horseback, among whom were the Donati and their friends, stopped to watch some girls dancing near to Santa Trinita, when suddenly some of the Cerchi also accompanied by many nobles rode up, and not knowing that the Donati were in front of them, and desiring also to see the dancing, spurred their horses among the people, some of whom were injured. The Donati took affront at this and drew their swords, to which challenge the Cerchi boldly responded; after many wounds given and received on both sides, the combatants were parted. This affray was the first of many, because all the city joined in the quarrel, people as well as nobles, and the two parties took the names of Bianchi and Neri. The Cerchi were leaders of the Bianca party, and allied with them were the Adimari, the Abbati, a number of the Tosinghi, of the Bardi, Rossi, Frescobaldi, Ncrli, and of the Mannelli, all the Mozzi, the Scali, Gheradini, Cavalcanti, Malespini, Bostichi, Giandonati, Vecchietti, and Arrigucci. Many of the citizen families also joined them, together with all the Florentine Ghibellines. Among the large numbers adhering to the Cerchi party were nearly all the rulers of the city. On the other side the Donati were the leaders of the Neri, and with them were the rest of the noble families who would not ally themselves with the Bianchi. They had also all the Pazzi, Bisdomini, Manieri, Bagnesi, Tornaquinci, Spini, Buondelmonti, Gianfigliazzi, and Brunelleschi. Not only did this discord contaminate the whole city, but it also spread through the country. It was much feared by the captains of the wards, whether Guelfs or supporters of the republic, that this new discord would bring about the resuscitation of the Ghibelline rule and ruin to the city in its train, therefore they sent again to the pope urging him to devise some remedy if he did not wish to see the city, which had always been a shield to the Church, either destroyed or turned over to the Ghibellines. The pope sent to Florence his legate, Matteo d'Acquasparta, a Portuguese cardinal. He met with many difficulties in dealing with the Bianchi, for they being the stronger had the least to fear, and making no progress in his negotiations he hurriedly left Florence in anger, first having placed it under an interdict. Thus the city was left in greater confusion than it had been before his coming.

Whilst men's minds were in this troubled state a number of the Cerchi and Donati happened to meet at a funeral, and from words they came to blows, but nothing of a serious nature occurred on that occasion. All of them, however, having returned to their houses, the Cerchi decided to attack the Donati in force, and with a crowd of men besieged the house of the Donati, but were driven back by the courage of Messer Corso, with a large number of their men wounded. The city was all up in arms, the signori and the laws were put on one side by the fury of the fighters, and the wiser and better citizens were filled with anxiety. The Donati and their party were now seriously alarmed because of their inferiority in numbers to the Bianchi, therefore Messer Corso, with the captains of the Neri and the ward captains, met together to discuss this serious condition of affairs, and it was decided to send once more to the pope and beg him this time to depute a prince of the royal blood to come to Florence and mediate between the parties. By this means the Neri hoped to gain some advantage over the Bianchi. This meeting and its decision were duly notified to the pope, and it was at once magnified by the opposite party into a conspiracy against their liberties. Finding that both parties remained under arms, the signori, among whom was Dante, by whose prudence and counsel they were largely guided, decided to arm the people, and to reinforce them with men from the surrounding country, and by these forces they compelled the Bianchi and Neri to lay down their arms. Messer Corso Donati and other leaders of the Neri were thrown into prison, and to give this action the appearance of impartiality they imprisoned also some of the Bianchi, but shortly after liberated them, under the pretence that they had been found to be innocent.

Messer Corso and his followers believing that the pope favoured their party went to Rome, desiring to present in person to him what they had previously written. They found at the court of the pontiff Charles of Valois, brother of the King of France, who had been called into Italy by the King of Naples to assist him in the conquest of Sicily. Being influenced by the representations of the Florentine exiles, the pope considered that he ought to send Charles to Florence until such time as it would be agreeable to him to continue his voyage to Naples. Charles therefore went to Florence, and although the Bianchi who were then ruling the city looked upon him with some suspicion, yet, being sent by the pope, and being the head of the Guelfs, they dared not resist him, but in order to conciliate him they placed the city at his disposition. Charles having received this authority at once armed all his friends and partisans. The people immediately suspected that he intended to take away their liberties, and arming themselves and fortifying their houses were ready in case Charles made any move. The Cerchi and the heads of the Bianca party carried themselves so haughtily as rulers that they fell into universal hatred. This encouraged Messer Corso and the other Neri exiles to return to Florence, knowing that Charles and the ward captains were favourable to them. Whilst the city was under arms watching Charles, Messer Corso and the exiles, with many armed men following them, entered it without any opposition. Although Messer Veri de' Cerchi had been pressed to oppose the entry of Messer Donati, he would not do so, but said that the people of Florence, against whom he came, ought to chastise him. But when Donati came, the very opposite happened, for the people who should have chastised him welcomed him, whilst Messer Veri fled to save himself. Having forced the Pinti gate, Messer Corso drew up his men outside San Pietro Maggiore, near to his own house, where his friends had assembled, with a great concourse of people desirous of seeing any novelty. The first thing Messer Donati did was to liberate from prison all who had been confined either for public or private offences; he also compelled the signori to resign their offices, which he filled with men of the Neri party or other commoners; and he gave over the houses of the leaders of the Bianchi to the sack for five days. The Cerchi and other leaders of the Bianchi, finding that Charles and the mass of the people were hostile to them, fled to their strongholds in the country. These men who would never accept any advice from the pope, were now compelled to have recourse to him for aid, and they pleaded to him that the coming of Charles had proved a source of disunion to Florence rather than union. Upon this the pope again sent his legate, Messer Matteo d'Acquasparta, who patched up a peace between the Cerchi and Donati and cemented it with betrothals and marriages. When, however, the legate proposed that the Bianchi should have a share of the public offices, the Neri who then held power would not consent; upon which the legate took himself off with scarcely more satisfaction, and with no less anger, than he did on the previous occasion, and he left the disobedient city again under an interdict.

Thus both factions remained in Florence and both were discontented, the Neri at finding the hostile party so near that at any time they might wrest the government from them, the Bianchi at finding themselves deprived of all authority and honours for which they were eager. To this natural fear and envy fresh injuries were now to be added. Messer Nicolo de' Cerchi with some of his friends was going to his country house, when on arriving at the bridge over the Affrico they were attacked by Simone, a son of Messer Corso Donati. The fight was sharp and had a sad ending for both parties, Messer Nicolo being killed on the spot and Messer Simone dying of his wounds the following night. This occurrence again disturbed the whole city, and although the Neri were most to blame they were shielded by those in power. However, before judgment could be given a conspiracy was discovered between the Bianchi and Messer Piero Ferranti, one of Charles' barons, with the object of restoring the government of the Bianchi. The affair was brought to light by the discovery of letters from the Cerchi to Ferranti, but the opinion was held by many that the letters were forgeries, produced by the Donati with the view of covering up the infamy which the murder of Messer Nicolo had brought upon them. For this conspiracy the Cerchi family and their following among the Bianchi, one of whom was the poet Dante, had their goods confiscated and their houses destroyed. These men and the Ghibellines who were in league with them were scattered through many lands, seeking with fresh troubles fresh fortunes. Charles having achieved his object in Florence, set out for Rome in order to pursue his enterprise in Sicily. He succeeded in this no better than he had done in Florence, and having lost the greater number of his men returned to France in disgrace.

After the departure of Charles from Florence the city remained for some time quiet, Messer Corso alone being restless. He did not consider that he held the position to which his merits entitled him, and owing to the government being a popular one he saw many men whom he considered his inferiors preferred to him in the management of the affairs of the republic. Moved by these feelings and thinking to disguise the dishonesty of his intentions with an honest motive, he charged many citizens who administered public funds with having converted them to their own uses. These charges were adopted by many men who had the same intentions as he had, and also by many others who, through ignorance, believed that Messer Corso was actuated by love of the country. On the other hand, the calumniated citizens had the people behind them. Thus the dispute quickly spread, and civil methods having failed they came to blows. Messer Corso and Messer Lottieri, the Bishop of Florence, with many nobles and some commoners, were on one side, and on the other were the signori with the greater part of the people, and fighting broke out in many parts of the city. The signori, finding themselves in great danger, sent to Lucca for assistance, and at once a great number of Lucchese came to Florence, and by their influence the affair was quickly settled; the disorders ceased, the people secured their liberties and retained their government, and the authors of the mischief had no punishments awarded to them.

A knowledge of these disturbances in Florence had reached the ears of the pope, and he had sent his legate, Messer Nicolo di Prato, to settle them. This gentleman had a great reputation for learning and courtesy and was a man of high rank. He at once gained every one's confidence, to such a degree that he was given authority to reform the government entirely in accordance with his own ideas. As he was a born Ghibelline, he had it in his mind to repatriate the exiles, but he knew that he must first gain the people to his views. To do this he revived the old brotherhoods of the people, which was the means of vastly increasing their power, whilst it diminished that of the nobles. The legate, believing that he had now laid the multitude under an obligation to himself, set about bringing the exiles back to Florence. This he attempted in various ways, and not only had he no success, but he fell under such suspicion of those he ruled that he was compelled to leave. He therefore returned to the pontiff bitterly enraged, and left Florence a prey to every sort of confusion and once more under an interdict. Florence was victimised, not by one faction but by many. There was the hostility between the people and the nobles, between the Ghibellines and the Guelfs, and between the Bianchi and the Neri. Thus the city was constantly under arms and filled with brawls. And now arose a new party, dissatisfied with the departure of the legate, because it desired the return of the exiles; the first to stir up this trouble were the Medici and the Giugni, who had already declared themselves to the legate in favour of the rebels. Whereupon there was fighting in most parts of Florence. To these evils there was added at this time a fire which broke out near the gardens of San Michele, in a house of the Abbati, thence it spread to that of the Caponaschi, and having burnt that it passed on to those of the Amieri, Macci, Toschi, Cipriani, Lamberti, Cavalcanti, and thence to the Mercato Nuovo; from there it spread to the Santa Maria gate, which it burnt entirely, and veering round by the Ponte Vecchio it destroyed the houses of the Gheradini, Pulci, Amidei, and Lucardesi, with many others, which added together would number more than 1300 houses. It was the opinion of many persons that the fire originated on the occasion of some fight; whilst others believed that it was caused by Neri Abbati, the Prior of San Scaragsio. He was a dissolute fellow, fond of evil, and seeing the people engaged in fighting, thought he could commit a piece of wickedness which, owing to people being otherwise occupied, could not be easily stopped; and in order that he might have a better opportunity for this, he started the fire in the house of one of his relatives. It was in the month of July in 1304 when Florence was so harassed by fire and sword. Messer Corso Donati alone was not under arms during these troubles, because he believed that when the two parties were tired of fighting, and desired to come to terms, he would be in a better position to arbitrate between them; but in due course they laid down their arms, not from any desire to come to terms with each other, but merely because they were satiated with misery. The only result of all this trouble was that the exiles did not return, and the party who wished to restore them still remained the weaker.

The legate, Messer Nicolo di Prato, had returned to Rome where he heard of these fresh disturbances in Florence, and he persuaded the pope that if he really intended to pacify the city it would be necessary for him to summon twelve of the principal citizens to Rome, and having thus drawn off the source of the mischief it would be more easily cured. This advice was accepted by the pontiff, and the citizens who were sent for, among whom was Messer Corso Donati, obeyed the summons. As soon as these gentlemen had left Florence the legate sent word to the exiles that now was the time for them to return, whilst Florence was deprived of her leaders. The exiles at once followed his advice and marched on Florence, entering the city where the walls were yet unfinished, and quickly reached the Piazza di San Giovanni. Then it was that a most remarkable thing happened; for those men who so short a time before had fought for the restoration of exiles when unarmed, were pleading for permission to return to their country, now, when they saw these same exiles with arms in their hands attempting to seize the city by force, joined the other citizens in expelling them. The citizens of Florence thus showed by their conduct that they held the welfare of the republic far above private considerations. One of the reasons why the exiles failed was that they had left part of their forces at Lastra, and again they would not wait for Messer Tolosetto Uberti, who was coming from Pistoia with 300 horsemen, on the grounds that swiftness rather than force was necessary to their success. As often happens in such enterprises, delay will let the opportunity slip, whilst haste brings failure from lack of force. When the rebels had been driven off, the people of Florence returned to their old quarrels, and determined to lower the pride of the Cavalcanti. With this object they destroyed the Stinche, a castle belonging to that family in the Val di Greve, and because those people who defended the castle, and were captured with it, were the first prisoners to be thrown into the new prison which was just completed, it was named after the castle from which they came, and has ever since been called the Stinche. At this time the leaders of the republic revived the brotherhoods of the people, and conferred on them the banners under which the guilds had previously assembled. The head standard bearers of the brotherhoods were called colleagues of the signori, and were to assist the signoria with arms in time of war and with counsel in peace. To them were added two governors and an executioner, and these with the standard bearers were to take action against the nobles who committed any wrongs.

About this period the pope died, and Messer Corso with the other Florentine citizens returned from Rome, and all would have remained quiet in Florence had it not been for the restless soul of Messer Corso. In order that he might concentrate attention on himself he always espoused opinions contrary to the men in power, and he lent the whole of his authority to whatever he saw the people desired. He did this in order that he might curry favour with them and become their leader in all their discontents and reforms, and all those who desired anything out of the usual course went to him. Many citizens of repute disliked him, and this dislike increased to hatred until, finally, the Neri broke out into open hostility against him. Although Messer Corso could only rely on private help in this matter, whilst his adversaries had the full power of the state at their back, yet so great was the force of his personality that every one feared him. His opponents, however, adopted a course which ruined Messer Corso in the eyes of the multitude; they spread abroad a report that he was intending to establish a tyranny. There was much in his manner of living that supported such a charge, for in this he far exceeded any private standard, and as he had recently married a daughter of Uguccione della Faggiola, the leader of the Ghibellines and Bianchi, and the most powerful man in Tuscany, this report was readily believed.

When this marriage came to the knowledge of his enemies, it inspired them with fresh determination to proceed against him, and they at once took up arms, whilst the people, influenced by the reports spread against him, did not come to his assistance, but sided with his enemies. The chief men among his adversaries were Messer Rosso della Tosa, Messer Pazzino di' Pazzi, Messer Geri Spini, and Messer Berto Brunelleschi. These gentlemen with their retainers and many citizens met at the Palace of the Signori, and by their order Messer Corso was arraigned by Messer Piero Bianca, the captain of the people, for attempting to make himself tyrant with the aid of Uguccione. Messer Corso was then summoned to appear before them, after which he was declared a rebel for contumacy. Between the arraignment and the passing of judgment not more than two hours elapsed. Having pronounced judgment, the signori with the brotherhoods of the people under their banners sought out Messer Corso. Although he found himself abandoned by his friends, judgment given against him, a multitude of enemies and the whole authority of the signori arrayed against him, he was not in the least alarmed, but fortified himself in his house, hoping to defend it until such time as Uguccione, to whom he had sent, should come to his assistance. He had not only barricaded his house, but the approaches to it, and manned them with his retainers, and although his assailants were very numerous they could not capture his positions. The fight went on for a long time and much loss was sustained on both sides, until the attacking party, seeing they could make no headway against Messer Corso, occupied the houses which ran close up to his and forced an entry into it. Messer Corso finding himself surrounded on all sides by his enemies, and seeing no hope of help from Uguccione, decided that he must at once seek other means of safety. Therefore Gherado Bordoni and himself placed themselves at the head of some of their most trusty and boldest soldiers, and dashed out against their foes. These they scattered and by dint of hard fighting got out of the city by the Porta della Croce. They were, however, pursued by a great number of men and Gherado was killed upon the bridge over the Affrico by Boccaccio Cavicciulli, whilst Messer Corso was taken prisoner at Rovezzano by some Catalan cavalry in the pay of the signoria. In order to avoid appearing before his victorious enemies, Messer Corso allowed his horse to fall with him as he approached Florence, and one of his captors ran him through; his body was taken possession of by the monks of San Salvi, and buried by them without any ceremony. To such an end came Messer Corso, from whom his country and his party had received much good and much evil. If his spirit could have lived with more tranquillity, his memory would have been far more esteemed; yet he deserves to be enumerated among our choicest citizens, although his restless mind caused his country and his party to forget the obligations they owed him, and in the end his restlessness brought upon his country an infinity of evils and to himself death. Uguccione, hastening to the assistance of his son-in-law, learnt at Remoli how Messer Corso had been overcome by the people, and that he could effect no good; in order that he should not be the cause of any further evil without benefit to himself, he went home.

The death of Messer Corso in 1308 removed the disturbing elements in the affairs of Florence, until it was reported that the Emperor Henry VII. was coming into Italy accompanied by a great number of Florentine exiles, whom he had promised to restore to their country. The government of Florence considered it expedient to reduce somewhat the number of their enemies, therefore they decided to reinstate all rebels, excepting those who had been specially named in laws which prohibited their return. This proviso prevented from returning many Ghibellines and some of the Bianchi, amongst whom were Dante Alighieri, the sons of Messer Veri di' Cerchi, and of Giano della Bella. The government also sent to Robert, King of Naples, but as he would not enter into an alliance with them they induced him to accept the protection of the city for five years. The emperor entered Italy by way of Pisa, and passed thence across the marshes into Rome, where he was crowned in the year 1312. He now decided that he would tame the Florentines, and marching against them, passing by Perugia and Arezzo, and reaching Florence he posted his army about a mile from the city near to the Monastery of San Salvi, where he remained fifty days without achieving any results. Despairing of effecting anything against the city or its government, he retired to Pisa, and here he arranged with Frederic, King of Sicily, to invade the kingdom of Naples. But as he was moving forward with his army full of the hopes of victory, and Robert was threatened with ruin. Henry met his death at Buonconvento.

A short time after this Uguccione della Faggiuola became lord of Pisa, then, assisted by the Ghibelline party, he also took possession of Lucca, and thus became a menace to his neighbours. In the hope of freeing themselves from this danger, they begged King Robert to allow his brother Piero to take the command of their army. Uguccione in the meanwhile increased his own power to the utmost, and by force or fraud seized many castles in the Val d'Arno and the Val di Nievole, and laid siege to Monte Catini; but the Florentines determined to relieve it, not wishing that the flames of war should spread in their territories. They gathered together a great army and marched into the Val di Nievole, where they attacked Uguccione and were routed after a great fight. The Florentines lost about 2000 men, amongst whom was Piero, the brother of King Robert, whose body was never found. Nor was the victory a bloodless one to Uguccione as he lost his son and many of his best captains.

After this defeat the Florentines fortified their city on all sides, and King Robert sent Count d'Adria, better known as Count Novello, to command their army. But notwithstanding the war which was raging with Uguccione, the city split itself into two parties, one calling itself the king's friends and the other the king's enemies; this may have been caused by some action on the part of Count Novello, or it may rather have arisen from the ingrained disposition of the Florentines to grow tired of any government and to divide themselves into parties. At the head of the party against the king were Simone della Tosa, the Magalotti, and some of the merchants, far outnumbering the supporters of the government. They managed also to send into France and afterwards into Germany to raise men and officers with the view of driving out the count, who was ruling the city on behalf of King Robert. Fortunately for the city they were unable to get any. Nevertheless this disappointment did not induce them either to abandon their enterprise or their search for accomplices, and finally they obtained some men from Agobbio. With these they first expelled the count, and then brought in Lando d'Agobbio, and appointed him as deputy, or bargello, with supreme power over the citizens. He was a rapacious and cruel fellow, who ravaged the country with an armed following, taking away the lives of this man or that man at the will of those who had appointed him. Becoming bolder by immunity, he debased the coinage and stamped it with the Florentine stamp; to such a depth had the discords of the city sunk her that none dare oppose him. Truly a great and miserable city which neither the memory of former discords, nor the fear of Uguccione, nor the authority of the king, had any influence to restrain; thus she is brought down to this miserable position, Uguccione ravaging her lands outside, and inside her walls she is robbed by Lando d'Agobbio.

Noble families, wealthy commoners, and every Guelf were on the side of the king and against Lando and his followers, yet they could not declare themselves without great danger, because all the resources of the state were in the hands of their enemies. They plotted, however, to get rid of this dishonest tyranny, and secretly advised the king to appoint Count Guido da Battifolle as his viceroy in Florence. The king accepted this advice, and the count was appointed, in this the signori and the opposition to the king were compelled to acquiesce because of the renown of the count, but the favour which Lando received from the gonfaloniere and the party in power prevented the count from achieving any good result. Whilst these troubles were afflicting Florence, the daughter of Albert, King of Germany, passed through the city on her way to meet her husband, Charles, the son of King Robert. She received much honour from the friends of the king, with whom she condoled on the condition of the city, and the cruelty of Lando and his followers, and with her help, assisted by the king's party, the citizens were united before she left, and the authority was taken from Lando, and he himself sent back to Agobbio, blood-stained and laden with plunder. In the change of government which ensued the protection of King Robert was continued for a further three years, and as previously there had been seven signori who had supported Lando, there were now elected six additional members from the king's party, and to these thirteen members of the signoria there were added some magistrates. These numbers were afterwards reduced to seven in accordance with the former custom.

The lordship of Lucca and Pisa was taken from Uguccione at this time, and Castruccio Castracani, a citizen of Lucca, became master of those cities. Being young, bold, and ardent, besides very fortunate in all his enterprises, Castruccio rose in a very short time to be the leader of the Ghibellines in Tuscany. For the first time for many years the Florentines put on one side their civil discords with the intention of curbing the power of Castruccio before it should get too much for them, but it had now increased far beyond their expectations, and they had to consider how they should defend themselves against him. In order to assist the signori in their deliberations on this subject, and to strengthen them in carrying out their decisions, twelve citizens were appointed, called buonomini, whose consent and advice were necessary before any important steps could be taken by the signori. It was at this time that the over-lordship of King Robert came to an end and Florence was once more her own master. The governors and magistrates were again appointed, and were kept united by their fears of Castruccio. After inflicting many defeats upon the Lords of Lunigiana, he was now besieging Prato, and the Florentines determined to march at once to the defence of that city. Therefore, closing their shops, they took up arms and set out — 20,000 footmen and 1500 horsemen. In order that they might reduce the forces of Castruccio and add to their own, the signori issued a proclamation to the effect that all Guelf rebels, who should come to the assistance of Prato, should be restored to their country. In virtue of this promise more than 4000 rebels came in. This immense army, gathering to the relief of Prato, alarmed Castruccio to such an extent that, without putting his fortune to the test of battle, he retired towards Lucca. Upon this there arose great dissension in the Florentine camp between the people and the nobles. The people wished to follow Castruccio in order to completely annihilate him; the nobles wished to return to Florence. The nobles urged that it may have been quite right to imperil their city in order to relieve Prato — the necessities of the case compelling them to take that risk; but now that Prato was out of danger they should not again tempt fortune, and possibly, in attempting to gain a little more, lose all. Being unable to come to a decision in the camp, the question was remitted to the signori. Here, however, the same differences were to be found as had raged between the nobles and the people in the camp. When this deadlock came to be known throughout the city the people flocked to the Piazza, and with menaces compelled the signori to yield. This resolution to follow up Castruccio, however, came too late, and was carried out with much manifest ill-will that he had ample time to escape to Lucca.

This misadventure enraged the people against the nobles, and the signori were not permitted to redeem the pledge they had given to the exiles, although it had been given with the consent and approval of the people. The exiles appear to have had some presentiment that the word of the signori would be broken, and they decided to anticipate the refusal by presenting themselves at the city gates before the Florentine army should return from the camp. This also had been foreseen and did not succeed, because they were easily driven off by those who had remained in Florence. Failing to obtain restoration to their country by force, the exiles now sent eight envoys to recall to the signori the pledge they had given and the perils which the exiles had encountered in the hope of receiving the promised reward. The nobles, having personally promised to carry out what the signori had engaged to do, exerted all their interest on behalf of the exiles, as they were in duty bound; but the mob were so filled with rage that Castruccio had not been conquered in battle that the nobles were unable to obtain the fulfilment of the signori's promise. This brought reproach and dishonour to the city. Many of the nobles were so greatly incensed at this miscarriage that they determined to obtain by force what had been denied to them. They entered into a conspiracy with the exiles, and promised them that if they would attack the city from the outside, their friends inside should take up arms and assist them to gain an entrance. Before the day arrived to carry this plot into execution it was discovered, so that when the exiles reached the city they found it prepared for them in such a way that none within dare stir in their behalf, and they were compelled to retreat without achieving any results. After they had gone it was determined to punish those who were responsible for their coming; but although the delinquents were well known to every one, none dare name them or charge them with the crime. In order that these names should be obtained without any respect of persons, it was arranged that the names of the offenders should be written down in council and then given in secret to the captain. It was found that the accused were Messer Amerigo Donati, Messer Teghiaio Frescobaldi, and Messer Lotteringo Gheradini. These offenders, having judges more favourably inclined to them than their crimes deserved, were only fined.

The disturbances occasioned in Florence by the appearance of the rebels at the city gates, convinced the brotherhoods of the people that one captain was not sufficient. It was, therefore, decided that for the future each brotherhood should have three or four leaders, and that every gonfaloniere should be allowed two or three additional men, who should be called bannermen. Thus, in cases of future trouble, it would not be necessary for the whole of a brotherhood to be assembled in one place, but they could be employed under several leaders. As happens in all republics, every accident is made the occasion of an alteration in the laws, old ones are repealed and new ones passed; so in this case, whereas the signoria had hitherto been elected from time to time, it was now decreed that the signori and the colleges should have authority to appoint certain signori, who should for the future hold office for forty months; the names of these signori should be placed in a ballot box and drawn for every two months. But before the forty months had come to an end a new ballot was called for, because many citizens doubted if their names were in the box. From this arose the custom of electing by ballot all the magistrates required both for the city and for the country districts, in place of election by the council; these ballotings were afterward called Squittini. And as they were made every three or at most every four years, they took away from the city a frequent cause of turbulence, which had hitherto arisen at the election of magistrates owing to the large number of candidates. The Florentines had adopted this system of election to avoid the inconvenience of frequent elections, not foreseeing the evils that would arise in exchange for such a trifling advantage.

In the year 1325, Castruccio Castracani seized Pistoia, and again his power so greatly alarmed the Florentines, that they determined to snatch the city from his clutches before he could take over its governance, and with the aid of friends and their own citizens they raised 20,000 foot soldiers and 3000 horsemen. With this army they besieged and took Altopascio, thus closing the way to Pistoia, they then marched on Lucca, ravaging the country, but from want of prudence and loyalty on the part of their captain, did not make much progress. The captain was Messer Ramondo di Cardona. Ramondo had observed the readiness with which the Florentines had from time to time yielded their liberties to others; at one time to the king, at another to the pope's legate, and to men of even lower degree, and it occurred to him that if he could involve them in some urgent necessity he might easily become their prince. He had even suggested this to them, for he had demanded full authority over the city, such as he had in the field, stating that without it he could not command the obedience which it was essential for a captain to have. To this the Florentines would not consent. Ramondo had therefore lost opportunities and Castruccio had seized them. Castruccio had now received the aid promised him by the Visconti and other Lombardian tyrants, and was in a position to assume the offensive, but Ramondo, who had failed to make the most of his opportunities from want of loyalty, could not extricate himself from the difficulties by which he was now surrounded. Castruccio attacked him near to Altopascio, as he was marching leisurely along, and after a hard fight the Florentines were badly defeated. Many citizens were killed and many taken prisoners; among the killed was Messer Ramondo, and thus he was punished by fortune as he had deserved to be by the Florentines, for his evil counsel and disloyalty. The damage which Castruccio inflicted upon the Florentines in pillage, captivity, desolation, and fire cannot be estimated, for without having any one to oppose him after his victory he harassed the country in every direction, and the Florentines had enough to do to save their city.

The Florentines were not so seriously disheartened by all this calamity that they could not at once make attempts to raise money and soldiers and send to friends for help. Yet none of these expedients proved of much use in curbing so powerful an enemy as Castruccio, and they had to accept the over-lordship of Charles the Duke of Calabria, the son of King Robert, in exchange for his aid in their defence. These rulers were accustomed to holding the lordship over Florence, and preferred the obedience of her citizens to their friendship. Charles was at this time engaged in a war with Sicily and could not immediately come to the relief of Florence, but he sent a Frenchman, Walter, Duke of Athens. This nobleman took over the government of the city and appointed whom he pleased as magistrates, at the same time he appeared so fair in his dealings, and concealed his real nature so successfully, that everybody loved him.

When Charles had concluded his war in Sicily he came to Florence, and made his entry into the city with 1000 horsemen in July 1326. His arrival put some restraint upon the ravages which Castruccio had previously been committing upon the country round Florence. Nevertheless any reputation which Charles may have gained by his actions outside the city was entirely lost within, for Florence had now to endure injuries from her friends which previously she had only received from her enemies. The signori were quite powerless, and in the course of one year the duke extracted from the citizens no less than 400,000 florins, although the agreement was only for 200,000 florins. This was one of the troubles with which either Charles or his father harassed the city day by day.

Fresh anxieties and enemies were now to be added to the old ones, owing to the suspicions of the Ghibellines being aroused by the entry of Charles into Tuscany. Therefore to counterbalance Charles, Galeazzo Visconti and other Lombardian tyrants with money and promises brought into Italy Louis of Bavaria, who against the wishes of the pope had just been elected emperor. Louis reached Lombardy and passed thence into Tuscany, where with the assistance of Castruccio he became master of Pisa, and having extracted a large sum of money from that city he journeyed on to Rome. Charles became alarmed for the safety of the kingdom and left Florence, having appointed Messer Filippo de Saggineto his viceroy. After the emperor left Italy Castruccio made himself master of Pisa, and the Florentines having obtained Pistoia by capitulation, Castruccio took the field determined to regain it. He pursued the siege with such valour and obstinacy that the Florentines in spite of all their efforts were unable to relieve the town, although at one time they attacked the army of Castruccio and at another time his country. The Florentines being thus unable, either directly or indirectly, to compel Castruccio to raise the siege, the Pistolese had to receive him as their master. Although this achievement of Castruccio enabled him to chastise the Pistolese and get the better of the Florentines, as well as brought him great glory, yet it led to his undoing, for on his return to Lucca he died. Good or bad fortune rarely comes singly, and at the same time as Castruccio there died also at Naples Charles, Duke of Calabria, the lord of Florence. Thus at one stroke the Florentines were liberated, far beyond their hopes, from their fear of Castruccio and the dominion of Charles. Having recovered their freedom they reformed the government of the city and annulled all the ordinances of the old councils; they created two new councils, one consisting of 300 commoners and the other of 250 nobles and commoners; the first of these two councils was called the council of the people and the other the general council.

When the emperor arrived in Rome he created an anti-pope, and attempted many other things against the Church, which had no effect, and having brought himself into contempt, he went to Pisa. Here, either in disgust or for want of pay, about 800 German cavalry deserted him and fortified themselves in Montechiaro upon the Ceruglio. On the departure of the emperor from Pisa for Lombardy these men seized Lucca and expelled Francesco Castracani, who had been left in charge of the city by the emperor. The Germans thought to gain some advantage out of the city, and offered it to the Florentines for 20,000 florins. The Florentines, acting under the advice of Messer Simone della Tosa, refused the offer. If the Florentines could have adhered to this decision it would have been of the greatest advantage to their city, but shortly after they regretted having made it, and brought great trouble upon themselves. It is evident that at one time they had the opportunity of obtaining the possession of Lucca, peacefully and for a very small sum of money, but they had not then the inclination; afterwards when they wanted it, and would have paid a much higher price, they could not obtain it. It was from impulses such as this that Florence was so often changing her government to her constant injury. Lucca, being refused by the Florentines, was bought by Messer Gherardino Spinoli, a Genoese, for 30,000 florins. And as men are far readier to wish for that which is out of their reach than to take that which is within their grasp, so when the purchase by Messer Gherardino, and the small price he had paid, became known to the people of Florence they burnt with a fierce desire to have Lucca, and cursed themselves and those by whose advice it had been refused. And in order to take by force what they had refused to buy, they sent their army to rob and spoil the country round Lucca.

It was about this time that the emperor left Italy, and as soon as he had gone the anti-pope was sent a prisoner into France. After the death of Castruccio, which happened in 1328, the Florentines remained at rest within their city until 1340, only attending to foreign affairs. During this time they waged long wars in Lombardy with John, King of Bohemia, and in Tuscany with the Count of Lucca. They also during this period adorned their city with many new and beautiful buildings. They built at this time the Tower of San Reparata, according to the designs of Giotto, the most famous painter of those days. It was in the year 1333 that the waters of the Arno rose in flood to more than twelve fathoms in some parts of Florence, and many bridges and houses were swept away, but with great expense and industry the destruction was repaired.

When the year 1340 arrived, new causes for change arose. The ruling citizens had two expedients for perpetuating or enlarging their powers; they were able to control the balloting in such a way that either they or their friends were elected, and they could always manage to have the governors elected from amongst their own people, and thus were always assured of their goodwill. Of such importance was this second expedient deemed that it was sometimes not considered enough to have the ordinary number of governors, but a third was elected. Hence it happened that at this time they had elected one Messer Jacopo Gabbrielli of Gobbio out of the usual course, and had moreover made him captain of the guard with plenary powers over the lives of the citizens. This fellow, out of deference to those who had appointed him, contrived some injury or other to the citizens almost every day, and among those whom be had wronged were Messer Pietro de Bardi and Messer Bardo Frescobaldi. These noblemen, naturally of a haughty spirit, would not allow a foreigner wrongfully to abuse them, merely to please a few people in power; to revenge themselves they conspired against both Jacopo and the government. In this conspiracy were involved many noble families and many citizens who were displeased with the tyranny of their rulers. The plot was to assemble as many of their armed retainers as possible at their own houses, and on the morning of All Souls' Day, when everybody would be in church praying for their dead, sally forth and kill the captain of the guard with the leaders of the government; afterwards choose a new signoria, reform the government, and issue new ordinances.

But the more such dangerous courses are considered, the less willingly are they followed, and it will always happen that conspiracies which require a long time to mature will be discovered. Messer Andrea de' Bardi was among the conspirators, and, in thinking over the matter, he became more influenced by the fear of punishment than by the hope of revenge, and disclosed all to his brother-in-law, Jacopo Alberti. He conveyed the information to the signori, and they passed it on to the executive. As the peril was imminent, seeing that All Souls' Day was at hand, many citizens were convened at the palace, and believing that it would be dangerous to defer action, desired the signori to sound the bell and summon the people to arms. Taldo Valori, the gonfaloniere, and Francesco Salviato, one of the signori, were relatives of the Bardi, and unwilling to sound the bell. One of them stated that it was not prudent to call the people to arms upon every trifling occasion, for when once power was put into the hands of the multitude it was no longer exercised with restraint; that tumults are easy to start but difficult to stop; that the better course would be to learn the truth of the matter, and punish by the laws, rather than attempt tumultuously to chastise upon a mere unsupported story which might bring ruin to Florence. These words were not attended to in the slightest degree, but with threatening and abusive language the signori were compelled to ring the bell. On the sound of the bell the people swarmed fully armed into the Piazza, whilst the Bardi and Frescobaldi, knowing that they were discovered, flew to arms, determined to conquer with glory or to die without disgrace. They hoped to defend themselves in that part of the city on the far side of the river where their houses were, and having fortified the bridges they waited for assistance from the country nobles and other friends. This intention was frustrated by their neighbours rising in support of the signori, and thus caught between two fires the conspirators abandoned the bridge and retired to the street where the Bardi resided. This place was stronger than the other position, and they held it valiantly. Messer Jacopo was frightened almost to death, for he knew well that the conspiracy was directed against himself, and he remained utterly dismayed amid his soldiers near the palace; but among the other governors there was more courage and less blame, especially on the part of the podesta, Messer Maffeo da Marradi. This gentleman presented himself where the fighting was going on, and fearlessly passed the Rubaconte bridge, and getting among the swords of the Bardi made signs of wishing to speak. Whereupon, out of respect for his bravery and other qualities, they at once put up their swords and listened to him. Messer Maffeo in grave and restrained language condemned their conspiracy, pointing out to them their danger in refusing to yield to popular feeling; he gave them hope that they should be heard and judged with every consideration; and promised his assistance to them because he sympathised with them in their just complaints. Messer Maffeo then returned to the signori, and urged them not to desire a victory with the blood of their own citizens, or to condemn without first hearing. In deference to Messer Maffeo's pleading the signori agreed that the Bardi and Frescobaldi should retire to their castles in the country. When they had left the city, and the people had laid down their arms, the signori instituted proceedings against the families of the Bardi and Frescobaldi who had taken up arms, and to deprive the Bardi of some of their power the signori bought from them the castles of Mangono and Vernia; the signori also passed a law that no citizen should possess a castle within twenty miles of the city. A few months afterwards Stiatta Frescobaldi and several other members of his family were beheaded. As if it were not enough for the government to have conquered and chastised the Bardi and Frescobaldi, where there was at first only one captain of the guard to afflict Florence, the government now appointed one for the country districts also; for the more authority men acquire, the worse they use it and the more insolent they become. This captain possessed greater powers, so that men could neither reside inside nor outside of Florence in peace. Thus the nobles became so incensed with the government that they were ready to sell their city and themselves for revenge. And knowing how to wait for their opportunity, it came to them in due time, and right well they used it.

Owing to the many troubles which occurred in Tuscany and Lombardy the city of Lucca had come under the dominion of Mastino della Scala, the lord of Verona, who, although he had agreed to hand Lucca over to the Florentines, had failed to do so. He was also the lord of Parma, and therefore believed that he was strong enough to hold Lucca, and cared nothing for the pledge which he had given to the Florentines. To avenge this wrong the Florentines allied themselves with the Venetians and attacked Mastino so fiercely that he was near to losing all his estates. Nevertheless, there did not accrue to the Florentines any other advantage from this war than the small satisfaction to their feelings in having beaten Mastino, because the Venetians, like all who accept the alliance of those weaker than themselves, made terms with Mastino after the victories at Trevigi and Vicenza without any consideration for the Florentines. Shortly after this peace Mastino lost Parma, which was taken from him by the Visconti, the lords of Milan, whereupon it was evident to Mastino that he could no longer hold Lucca, and he determined to sell it. There were two competitors for the purchase of Lucca, the Florentines and the Pisans. In the negotiations for the purchase the Pisans quickly perceived that the Florentines, as the richer of the two, were likely to obtain the city, therefore they fell back upon force, and with the aid of the Visconti took the field against it. This did not cause the Florentines to withdraw from the negotiations, but rather induced them to close the bargain with Mastino, and they paid down part of the purchase money and gave security for the balance. They sent Nardo Rucellai, Giovanni the son of Bernardino de' Medici, and Rosso the son of Richiardo de' Ricci to take possession. These gentlemen entered Lucca by force, and the men of Mastino handed it over to them. Nevertheless the Pisans pursued their venture and attacked the city with the fiercest determination, whilst the Florentines did their utmost to compel the Pisans to raise the siege. In the end the Florentines were driven back with the loss of much treasure and reputation, and the Pisans became the lords of Lucca.

As might well be expected the loss of Lucca incensed the people of Florence to the utmost against their rulers, and in every street and piazza the government was openly reviled for its parsimony and incompetency. The administration of the war had at its commencement been placed in the hands of twenty citizens, and they had appointed Messer Malatesta da Rimini captain of the expedition. This man had conducted it with so little courage and foresight that the Twenty had sent for aid to Robert, King of Naples, and he commissioned Walter, Duke of Athens, to proceed to their assistance. As if it were the will of heaven that the Florentines should be prepared for future evils, this man appeared in Florence at the very point of time when the expedition to Lucca had so disastrously failed. When the indignation of the people found expression against the Twenty a new captain was appointed with the hope of at least putting some curb upon the people's anger, if not of removing the cause of it. As fear was uppermost in the minds of the Twenty they appointed the Duke of Athens. He was elected in the first instance protector, but shortly after, in order to shield them more effectually, he was made captain of their men at arms. In the meanwhile, for the reasons already named, the nobles were living very discontentedly, and many of them who knew Walter when he ruled Florence formerly in the name of Charles, Duke of Calabria, believed that the time had now arrived when they would be able to quench their anger in the ruin of the city; and they saw no other way of bringing down the pride of the people, who had over-ridden them, than by bringing them under the subjection of a prince whom they considered was well acquainted with the virtues of the one party and the insolencies of the other, and who was capable of rewarding the one and curbing the other. The nobles also hoped that, when Walter had attained the power he desired by their help, he would reward them according to their merits. They therefore held many clandestine meetings with him, and persuaded him to take over the government entirely, and offered him their aid. To the assistance and power of the nobles was added that of some of the merchant families, among whom were the Peruzzi, Acciajuoli, Antellesi, and Buonaccorsi, who encumbered with debts which they were unable to meet, and which they wished others to pay, hoped in the enslavement of their country to escape from the slavery of their debts. These persuasions sharpened the ambitions of the duke to a greater desire for power, and in order to gain a reputation for severity and justice, and curry favour with the people, he prosecuted those who had conducted the war against Lucca. He put to death Messer Giovan de' Medici, Naddo Rucellai, and Guglielmo Altoviti, and condemned many to exile and many others to be fined.

These executions terrified the middle class citizens, but pleased the nobles and the mob; the one because it is in their nature to take a delight in troubles, whilst the other party saw the wrongs which the people had suffered in the war revenged. When the duke passed through their streets the people shouted praise to him for his courage, and called upon him to search out the fraudulent citizens, and promised to aid him to chastise them. Thus the authority of the Twenty waned whilst that of the duke increased; but with it also grew a fear of him, so that many citizens wishing to demonstrate their goodwill to him displayed his coat of arms upon their houses. Thus he lacked nothing but the title to make him a prince. When it appeared to him that he might with safety assume the government, he informed the signori that he considered it would be for the good of the city that full powers should be conceded to him, and as the whole city had already consented, they also must consent. Among the signori were many who had foreseen the impending ruin of their liberties, and all were greatly distressed at this demand. Although they knew well the danger they were incurring, they did not fail their country, but courageously refused the request. At his first coming to the city the duke had chosen for his residence the Convent of the Minor Brothers of San Croce, as if to show his religion and friendliness to the people, and now that he desired to carry into effect his malignant intentions he issued a proclamation ordering all the people to assemble on the following morning in the Piazza di San Croce. This proclamation caused the signori more alarm than had his previous summons to them, and they associated themselves with other citizens whom they still might look upon as lovers of their country. They fully recognised the strength of the duke, and felt they had no other resource but in prayers to him, and now that force had quite failed them they would beseech him either to abandon his claim or to let his yoke lie less heavy upon them. Therefore the signori sought an audience with him, and one of their number spoke as follows: "My lord, we have come to you, impelled in the first instance by the demand which you have addressed to us, and secondly by the order you have issued to the people to assemble before you; because it appears to us that you intend to obtain by extraordinary means that which we have not been able to consent to your assuming by the usual methods. It is not our intention to oppose your designs by force, but only to point out to you the weight of the responsibilities which you are taking upon your own shoulders, and the perils of the course you are entering upon. We do this in order that you may afterwards recollect our advice, and compare it with that of others, who are not advising you for your advantage, but only that they may have the opportunity of giving vent to their own passions. Our city which you seek to enslave has always been a free city, because the over-lordship which we have conceded to the kingdom of Naples was given by us as an equal, not as a servant. Have you considered what this really means to a city like ours, to which the name of liberty is so dear? Force cannot tame it. Time cannot waste it. No merit of yours can compensate us for its loss. Think, my lord, how much force will be necessary to keep such a city in subjection. The foreigners who may help you to hold it will not suffice. You will not be able to trust the men of the city who are now your friends, and are coming forward to assist you, because when they have overcome their enemies with your assistance they will turn upon you and crush you and elevate themselves to the princedom. The mob in whom you now place your trust will rise in revolt against you at the first trifling accident. Thus in a short time you may expect to find the whole city hostile to you, and this will end in your ruin, and perhaps in the destruction of the city. Neither will you be able to secure yourself from disaster, for whilst tyrants maintain their power against a few enemies, whom they may wipe out by either death or exile, they find no security against a universal hatred, since they never know whence the trouble will come, for he who fears every one can trust no one. Should you attempt to trust any men you will but aggravate the evil, because those who are left out will burn with a greater hatred. That time never exhausts the love of liberty is most certain, for it has often happened that in a city where it has never even been tasted, but has only been known by the memory which their fathers have left of their love of it, when once it has been recovered it has been most obstinately defended against every danger. But even if the fathers have left no record of their freedom, it is recorded in their palaces, the seats of the magistrates, in the coats of arms of the free brotherhoods, and will constantly bring to the minds of the citizens the desire to regain it. What can you do that can possibly supersede the sweetness of liberty, or that will cause men to forget their chains? If you were to add to our state the whole of Tuscany, or were to return each day to the city in triumph over our enemies, it would not suffice; for all the glory would be yours, and our citizens would not gain subjects but fellow-slaves, in whose slavery they would see the reflection of their own. Even if your conduct should be proper, your behaviour kind, your judgments upright, it would not be sufficient to make us love you. If you think otherwise you deceive yourself, because to those who have been accustomed to live in freedom every bond frets and every thread binds. It is also impossible for a turbulent state to remain under a pacific prince, because of necessity either he soon becomes the same, or the state acquires his habits, or they quickly ruin each other. Therefore you will have either to trust this city or to hold it with the utmost severity, and to do this your citadels, fortresses, and foreign friends will not be sufficient for long; or you must be content with that authority which we have already given you. To encourage you in this we would remind you that that dominion alone is durable which is without compulsion. Do not wish, blinded by a little ambition, to get into a position where you can neither stand in safety nor mount higher, a position from which you must fall to your own and our ruin."

The obdurate heart of the duke was not influenced in the slightest degree by those words, but he said in reply that it was not his intention to take away the liberties of the city, but rather to restore them, because it was only faction-ridden cities which were in servitude, the united were free. If Florence by his means should put away factions, personal ambitions, and hatreds, then he would give her liberty, not take it away. It was not ambition which induced him to take this step, he took it in consequence of the prayers of many citizens. Therefore the signori should be content to accept that which other citizens desired. As to the dangers which he would have to face he did not consider them, for it was the act of a coward to avoid doing a good thing for fear of danger, and it would be mean-spirited in him not to pursue a glorious enterprise for fear of a doubtful ending. He believed that in a very short time they would recognise that they had feared him too much and trusted him too little. The signori now perceived they could effect no good, and therefore acquiesced in the people assembling in the Piazza the following morning and handing over on their own authority the government of the city to the duke, on the same conditions as those which had previously subsisted between the Florentines and Charles, Duke of Calabria. It was on September 8, 1342, that the Duke Walter, accompanied with Messer Giovanni della Tosa and many companions and citizens, rode into the Piazza, and with the signori mounted the Ringhiera, as those steps are called which are at the foot of the Palace of the Signori, and from whence the convention between the duke and the signori was read to the people. When it came to the reading of the clause in the convention which provides for the power being conferred only for one year, the people shouted, "For life." When Messer Francesco Rustichelli, one of the signori, rose to speak, and to calm the tumult, his words were drowned in the noise of the shouting. Thus the duke was elected with the concurrence of the people their signore, not for one year, but for life, and he was lifted high and carried among the shouting multitude through the piazza. The guard of the Palace is accustomed to close fast the gates of the palace during the absence of the signori, and at this time the office was held by Rinieri di Giotto. This fellow had allowed himself to be corrupted by the friends of the duke, and without waiting to be forced he admitted the duke and his companions. The signori deprived of all respect and terrified were refused admittance, and sought their own houses, whilst the palace was sacked by the associates of the duke, the city standard was torn to pieces, and the ducal standard raised in its place. These things were witnessed with great grief and regret by all honest men, and with delight by those who either from ignorance or malignity desired them.

The duke having got possession of the government, prohibited the signori from meeting in the palace and transferred their council to a private house; he also took away the banners from the brotherhoods of the people; suspended the ordinances of justice against the nobles; liberated the prisoners; recalled the Bardi and Frescobaldi from exile; forbade the carrying of arms; he did this so that he might deprive of all power those who might be disposed to fight for their liberties. In order that he might further strengthen his position against any opposition within the city he made friends with the people in the districts outside. With this view he conferred many benefits upon the people of Arezzo, and made peace with Pisa, although he had been elevated to the princedom in order to carry on the war against that city. He destroyed the securities which had been given to the merchants who lent the money with which to carry on the war against Lucca; he revived old taxes and created new ones. His governors were Messer Baglione from Perugia and Messer Guglielmo from Assisi, with whom, and with Messer Cerrettieri Bisdomini, he constantly consulted. The taxes he imposed were very heavy, and his judgments unjust, and the civility and honesty to which he pretended in the beginning were now changed to arrogance and avarice. Many of the great citizens and noble merchants were either condemned to death or tormented in some new way. His government of the country districts was not more lenient than that of the city, for he appointed six governors who harassed and robbed the country people in every direction. He also looked upon the nobles with a good deal of suspicion, although he had been raised to power by their means, and had restored many to their country, for he could not believe that the generous minds which one is accustomed to find among the nobility could rest contented under his rule. He therefore began to confer benefits on the mob, in the belief that by their help and that of his mercenaries he would be able to maintain his tyranny. When the month of May came, in which the people indulge in festivals, he caused many brotherhoods to be raised among the lower orders, and bestowed upon them banners and money and honoured them with splendid titles. Whereupon a number of these companies paraded the city, whilst the rest were drawn up to receive them with great rejoicings. When the fame of this new government of Florence spread through Europe many Frenchmen came to the duke for employment, and he gave positions to all of them as to men whom he could trust. Thus in a very short time Florence not only became subject to the rule of Frenchmen, but men and women copied the French in their behaviour and dress without any regard to shame or the decencies of life; but above all that displeased was the violence that the duke and his followers offered to women without any consideration of their position.

The citizens therefore lived in great indignation at seeing the majesty of their state lowered, their ordinances corrupted, their laws suppressed, every honest course of life depraved, and all ordinary modesty relaxed, whilst those who had never been accustomed to see any regal pomp could not view without deep vexation the armed satellites which confronted them on every side. But what brought their dishonour more home to them was their being compelled to pay respect to him whom they most hated. And to this dishonour had to be added deep fear arising from the frequent murders, and increasing taxation by which the city was being continually wasted and consumed. This rising anger and hatred was well known to the duke, and was a source of anxiety to him, nevertheless he desired to make it apparent to every one that he believed himself to be beloved by the people. Thus when Matteo di Morozzo, either to please the duke or to clear himself from suspicion, informed the duke that the family of the Medici with others were engaged in a conspiracy against him, the duke not only refused to inquire into it, but even put the informer to death. By this course he deprived those who would have warned him of danger of all spirit to do so, and at the same time gave encouragement to those who sought his destruction. On the other hand, he caused the tongue of Bertone Cini to be torn out with so much brutality that he died, for having complained of the heavy taxation with which the citizens were afflicted. All this increased the anger and hatred of the citizens against the duke, for they, having been accustomed to say and do what they liked, could not endure having their mouths shut and their hands tied.

This hatred and resentment increased to such a pitch that, not only the Florentines, who had never known how to keep their liberties or to endure servitude, but any other enslaved people would have burned to recover their freedom. Hence it was that citizens in every rank determined to sacrifice their lives or recover their liberties. Three separate conspiracies were formed among the three ranks of citizens, namely, the nobles, the merchants, and the artisans, all inspired, beyond other prevailing reasons, by these several facts; the nobles, that they had not recovered the government; the middle classes, that they had lost it; and the artisans, that their livelihood was endangered. Messer Agnolo Acciajuoli, the Archbishop of Florence, had formerly praised the actions of the duke in his sermons, and had been instrumental in bringing him into favour with the people, but now when he saw the duke elevated to the princedom, and recognised his tyranny, and realised that he had deceived the country, he came to the conclusion that no other course was open to him but that the hand which had caused so great a wound should heal it and wipe out the fault it had committed. Therefore the archbishop put himself at the head of the first and strongest conspiracy, in which there were the Bardi, Rossi, Frescobaldi, Scali, Altoviti, Megalotti, Strozzi, and Mancini. In the second conspiracy Messer Manno and Corso Donati were the heads of it, and with them were the Pazzi, Cavicciulli, Cerchi, and Albizzi. In the third plot Antonio Adimari was the head, and with him were the Medici, Bordoni, Rucellai, and the Aldobrandini. Some spoke of killing the duke in the house of the Albizzi, where it was thought he was going to see a horse race on San Giovanni's day, but this did not succeed because he did not attend. They thought to attack him when he took his walks in the city, but this was found difficult, because he always went well armed and accompanied by guards, and constantly changed his walks, making it impossible to lie in wait for him in a certain place. They discussed killing him in the council chamber, hut although this might be accomplished the conspirators would remain at the mercy of his guards.

Whilst these suggestions were being considered by the conspirators, Antonio Adimari, with the intention of obtaining some men from his friends in Siena, revealed the plot to them with the names of those who were taking part in it, and declared that the whole city was disposed to liberate itself. One of these Sienese communicated the plot to Messer Francesco Brunelleschi in the belief that he was one of the conspirators. Either from apprehensions of his own safety, or from hatred which he bore to some of the others, Messer Francesco revealed the entire matter to the duke. Whereupon Messer Pagolo del Mazecha and Simone da Monterappoli were seized, and their revelation of the numbers and ranks of the conspirators alarmed the duke. He was advised that it would be better to send for them to come to him rather than attempt to take them prisoners, because if they should seek safety in flight then he could secure himself without trouble by their exile. The duke, therefore, sent for Antonio Adimari, and he, placing reliance upon his companions, at once complied, and was placed under arrest. The duke was then advised by Messer Francesco Brunelleschi and Messer Uguccione Buondelmonti to march through the city and kill every one whom he should meet. This did not, however, recommend itself to the duke, for he did not believe that he had sufficient force for such a purpose, but he adopted a course which, had it succeeded, would have brought all his enemies into his power, and with which his forces could have coped. It had been the custom of the duke to summon all the citizens before him whenever he desired to consult with them upon any occurrence. He therefore sent into the country for men, and made a list of three hundred citizens, and caused them to be summoned by his sergeants, under the pretence of desiring to consult with them, and having collected them he intended either by death or imprisonment to wipe them all out. But the seizure of Antonio Adimari and the sending for the soldiers could not be kept secret, and had already alarmed the citizens, especially those concerned in the plot, and the boldest refused to obey the summons. As the conspirators had read the list they consulted with one another, and encouraged each other to take up arms and die like men with arms in their hands rather than be lead like calves to the slaughterhouses. In a very short time the conspirators had full knowledge of each other, and they decided that on the following day, July 26, 1343, they would go to the Mercato Vecchio well armed, and would raise a tumult and summon the people to liberty.

Next morning, at the stroke of nine, the conspirators as arranged took arms, and the people at the call to liberty armed themselves, and barricades sprang up in every street under banners bearing the escutcheon of the city, which had been secretly provided by the conspirators. The heads of the families, nobles as well as merchants, came together, and all swore to defend each other and to kill the duke. The families of the Buondelmonti and

Cavalcanti, and the four families of citizens who had assisted in making the duke master of Florence held aloof, and these people with the butchers and the lowest of the mob assembled in defence of the duke. As soon as the duke heard the tumult he secured himself in the palace, and his retainers who were lodging in various distant parts of the city mounted their horses and set out for the palace. They were attacked by the citizens in many places, and only about three hundred got through to the palace. In the meantime the duke was in doubt whether to sally out against the enemy or defend the palace. On the other hand the Medici, Cavicciulli, Rucellai, and other families who had been most oppressed by the duke, determined that he should not have the opportunity of leaving the palace, for fear that some of those who had now declared against him should turn their arms in his favour and thus increase his forces. Therefore they made head against the Piazza and attacked the enemy there. Upon the arrival of the Medici and their friends in the Piazza, many of those families who had previously been in favour of the duke now declared themselves against him, seeing with what impunity he could be attacked, and changed their sides as the duke's fortune changed and threw in their lot with the citizens. But Messer Uguccione Buondelmonte retired into the palace, and Messer Gianozzo Cavalcanti withdrew to the Mercato Nuovo with some of his followers. Here he mounted a bench and begged the people who were passing carrying arms to go to the Piazza and help the duke. To frighten them he magnified his forces, and threatened the people with death if they obstinately persisted in their revolt against the duke. But none listened to him, nor stopped to chastise his impudence, and finding that he laboured in vain he declared he would tempt fortune no longer and retired to his own house.

The fight in the Piazza between the citizens and the duke's men was very fierce, and although those within the palace lent what assistance they could, the partisans of the duke were worsted. A number of them remained prisoners in the hands of the citizens, whilst others, dismounting from their horses, took refuge in the palace. Whilst this fighting was going on in the Piazza, Messer Corso and Amerigo Donati broke open the Stinche and burnt the records of the podesta and those of the public offices; they sacked the houses of the governors, and killed every minister of the duke upon whom they could lay hands. The duke now saw that he had lost the Piazza, that the whole city was up against him, and that there was no prospect of assistance reaching him. He therefore tried if by some generous deed he could once more gain the people over, and causing his prisoners to be brought before him set them free with friendly and gracious words, and knighted Messer Antonio Adimari, although Adimari protested against it. He lowered his own standard from the palace and ran up that of the people. These concessions came too late, and being forced from him brought him no goodwill. He remained shut up in the palace, and now realised that by grasping too much he had lost everything, and that in a few days he must die by the sword or by hunger. The citizens assembled in San Reparata, and to reestablish the government appointed fourteen citizens, seven from the nobles and seven from the merchants, who with the archbishop were given authority to reform the government of Florence. Six citizens were also chosen to exercise the functions of the podesta until such time as one could be elected.

Among those who came to the assistance of the Florentines were men from Siena, and with them six envoys, all men of honour in their own city. These gentlemen endeavoured to bring about an agreement between the duke and the citizens, but the citizens refused to discuss an agreement unless Messer Guglielmo of Assisi and his son, with Messer Cerrettieri Bisdomini were first given up to them. To this the duke would not listen until he was threatened by the men who yet remained with him, when he consented. It would appear doubtless that wounds are far deeper and passions far higher when freedom has to be recovered than when it has to be defended. Messer Guglielmo and his son, not yet eighteen years of age, were delivered over to their enemies. The boy's youth and beauty and innocency could not save him from the fury of the mob, and those who could not reach to wound him when living gashed him when dead, and not content with outraging his body with their swords they tore him to pieces with their hands and teeth. And, as if they wished that all their senses should be satiated with vengeance upon their victims, after having heard their groans, seen their wounds, and torn their flesh, they gave their palates a taste, in order that internal as well as external senses should be satisfied and share alike. Whilst this savage fury worked itself out upon these two gentlemen it saved Messer Cerrettieri, because the mob, wearied with its cruelty to them, forgot him, and never being demanded by them he remained in the palace, and the next night was carried off in safety by his friends. The mob having worked off its fury on Messer Guglielmo and his son came to terms with the duke, by which he was to renounce all claims upon Florence and leave the city with his men and possessions, and to have these terms ratified at Casentino, outside the Florentine dominions. In accordance with the terms of the agreement, the duke, accompanied by many citizens, left Florence, August 6, and arrived at Casentino, where the renunciation was finally ratified. He did this very unwillingly, and would not have kept his word had not Count Simone threatened that he should be taken back to Florence. The duke was, as his rule showed, avaricious and cruel, difficult of access and haughty in speech. He only desired the servitude of men, not their goodwill, and for this reason he cultivated their fear rather than their love. In personal appearance he was no less hateful than he was in his character, for he was swarthy and insignificant, with a long ragged beard; thus in every way he incurred the hatred of the people, and in the space of ten months his bad behaviour had lost him all the position to which the bad counsel of others had raised him.

These occurrences in Florence encouraged the towns which were under her rule to recover their freedom, and Arezzo, Castiglione, Pistoia, Volterra, Colle, and San Gimignano rebelled. Thus Florence found herself at one stroke free of her tyrant and deprived of her dominion; in recovering her own liberty she had taught her subjects how to recover theirs. Therefore, the duke having gone, and the towns having rebelled, the fourteen commissioners and the archbishop determined to conciliate the rebellious subjects with peace rather than turn them into enemies by war. In order to prove to their subjects that they were as pleased for them to have their freedom as they themselves were to obtain theirs, the Florentines sent envoys to Arezzo to renounce all claims upon that city, and to close with them an agreement that, whilst they would not claim them as subjects, they would esteem them as allies. With other towns they also made such arrangements as would secure them as friends and bind them to assist each other to maintain their liberties. This course so wisely adopted had a most happy ending, because not many years after, Arezzo returned to the dominion of Florence, and the other towns followed after a few months. Thus one often obtains with less difficulty, and far sooner, the things one avoids than those which are pursued with obstinacy or force of arms.

Having settled these external affairs the citizens were able to turn their attention to city matters, and after some dispute between the nobles and merchants it was concluded that the nobles should have one-third of the appointments to the signoria and one-half of the other offices. The city, as before stated, was divided into six wards which returned six signori, one from each ward, unless they chose, as sometimes happened, twelve or thirteen, but shortly after it was decreed that only six should be returned. To carry such a reform as the above it was found that six wards was not a convenient division, because it now being desirable to give a share in the representation to the nobles, it was necessary to increase the number of seats. Therefore they divided the city into four quarters, and gave three seats in the signoria to each. They abolished the office of gonfaloniere of justice and the standard bearers of the brotherhoods of the people, and in the place of the twelve protectors they created eight councillors, four from the nobles and four from the merchants. Having re-established the government on this basis the city would have been at peace if the nobles had been content to live with that moderation which is necessary in civil society; but they did the very opposite. As private persons they would not brook any equals, and as magistrates they insisted upon being masters. Thus every day there occurred some instance of their insolence and pride. The people were highly displeased at this, for they saw that for the one tyrant they had got rid of a thousand had risen in his place. Thus wrongs were increasing on one side and anger was rising on the other. Whereupon the merchants complained of the lawlessness of the nobles and their bad citizenship to the archbishop, and persuaded him to attempt to induce the nobles to resign their seats in the signoria and content themselves with other offices. The archbishop was naturally a good man, but easily led away by others, first to one side and then to another. Thus, at the instance of his colleagues, he had at first espoused the cause of the Duke of Athens, afterwards on the advice of some citizens he had turned against him. Then he had favoured the nobles in the reorganisation of the state, and now, moved by the reasons the merchants had given him, he was ready to help the people. Expecting to find in others his own want of firmness of mind, he easily persuaded himself that he could induce the nobles to agree to the suggestion, therefore he convoked the fourteen commissioners who had not yet laid down their office. In such language as he thought most suitable, he exhorted them to yield up their seats in the signoria to the people, and promised them that it would completely pacify the city, otherwise he feared that it and they would be ruined. This speech greatly incensed the nobles, and Messer Ridolfo di Bardi with harsh words rebuked the archbishop, telling him he was an unreliable man, reproaching him for his false friendship to the duke, and describing his share in the expulsion of the duke as treachery, concluded by saying that, as the nobles had gained their honours by the sword, so they would keep them by the sword. He then left the council chamber with his friends, and at once informed the other nobles of what was demanded of them. The merchants also declared their intention to their friends. Whilst the nobles were preparing to maintain their position in the signoria, the people determined to be beforehand with them, and rushed armed to the palace, shouting the demand for the resignation of the nobles. The tumult and noise was immense. The signori were abandoned, because when the nobles found the people ready armed they dared not take up arms, but shut themselves up in their own houses. The merchants first calmed the people by affirming that their colleagues among the signori were good modest men; but unable to arrange terms for them the signori were sent away to their own houses, which they only reached with great trouble. The nobles having left the palace, the four noble councillors were deprived of their office and replaced by twelve merchants. To the eight signori who remained was added a gonfaloniere of justice and sixteen standard bearers of the brotherhoods of the people, and thus the council was reformed so that the entire government of the city was vested in the people.

Whilst these changes were taking place, a great famine occurred in the city which further intensified the feelings of the contending parties, the people being goaded by famine and the nobles by their loss of office. This state of affairs encouraged Messer Andrea Strozzi to make an attempt to capture the liberties of the city. This man sold his corn at a lower price than other merchants, and this occasioned a large concourse of people to assemble at his house. So one morning he was bold enough to mount his horse and with some of his retainers to ride through the city calling the people to arms, and in a very short time he had collected more than 4000 men. These he led to the Piazza of the signori, and demanded that the palace should be opened to him. But the signori with threats and force drove Strozzi and his men out of the Piazza, and afterwards so awed the people with proclamations that in a short time they had all retired to their houses. Strozzi being deserted by his followers fled, and with difficulty escaped falling into the hands of the magistrates.

This attempt, although it was rash and came to such a despicable end, inspired the nobles with the hopes of weakening the merchants, now that the lower classes were at strife with them. The nobles, therefore, availed themselves of this opportunity to arm themselves, in order to regain the rights which they considered had been unjustly taken away from them. They believed so confidently in victory that they openly fortified their houses, provided themselves with arms, and sent into Lombardy for assistance. The people and the signori also prepared for the struggle, arming and sending to Siena and Perugia for help. Already some of the adherents of either party had arrived, and all the city was up in arms. The nobles had taken up positions at three points on this side of the Arno, namely, at the houses of the Cavicciulli near to San Giovanni, at the houses of the Pazzi and Donati at San Piero Maggiore, and at those of the Cavalcanti in the Mercato Nuovo. Those nobles whose residences were on the Arno barricaded the bridges and streets leading to them. The Nerli defended the bridge of Carraja, the Frescobaldi and the Manelli that of Santa Trinita, and the Rossi and Bardi the Ponte Vecchio and the Rubaconte. The merchants on their side were assembled under the banners of the gonfaloniere of justice and of the brotherhoods of the people.

Matters having reached this point it no longer suited the people to delay the fight, and the first to move were the Medici and the Rondinelli who attacked the Cavicciulli at the point which leads to their house through San Giovanni. The fight was very fierce, the besiegers being struck with stones from the towers, whilst the garrison suffered from the cross-bow fire from below. The fight lasted three hours, during which the assailants increased so continually that the Cavicciulli found themselves overcome and no aid near. They surrendered to the people, and thus saved their houses and goods, only their arms were taken from them, whilst they themselves were distributed among their merchant friends and relations as prisoners. Having vanquished the Cavicciulli, the Donati and Pazzi were next attacked, and being less powerful than the others easily succumbed. There remained only the Cavalcanti on this side of the river, and they were strong in position and men, but nevertheless when they found all the companies arrayed against them, whilst the others had yielded to only three, they gave themselves up without attempting a strong defence. Thus were three parts of the city brought into the hands of the people, one only remained in the power of the nobles, but it was the strongest, owing to the number of its defenders and the strength of its position. It was protected on one side by the Arno, therefore it was necessary to capture the bridges, and these were, as before stated, heavily defended. The Ponte Vecchio was attacked first; it was gallantly defended, because its armed towers, barricaded ways, and parapets were held by the best men, and the people were driven back with severe loss. They recognised the difficulty they would meet with in this bridge, and consequently assailed the Rubaconte bridge. Here they were again repulsed, so leaving two companies to watch them they passed on against the bridge at Carraja. Although it was bravely held by the Nerli it could not withstand the fury of the people, partly because it did not possess any towers and partly because the Capponi and other merchant families in the neighbourhood also attacked it. Being struck at on every side, the barricades were abandoned and a way opened to the assailants, and thus the Rossi and Frescobaldi were overcome, the merchants on that side of the river joining in the attack. The Bardi only remained now unconquered, and neither the ruin of their friends, nor the union of all their foes, nor the despair of aid could quell them. They would rather see their houses sacked and ruined and themselves killed than yield. They defended themselves so bravely that many times the people were driven back, reduced by heavy losses, from the Ponte Vecchio and the Rubaconte. There had been a short time previously a street opened up which led by the Via Romana to the backs of the houses of the Pitti, and thence to the walls on the hill of San Giorgio. By this street the people sent six companies with orders to assault from there the backs of the Bardi houses. When the garrison heard of this attack they lost courage and enabled the people to overcome them, because those who were defending the bridge abandoned the struggle there in order to defend their houses. Thus the Ponte Vecchio was captured and the Bardi put to flight in every direction, and many found safety in the houses of the Quaratesi, Panzanesi, and Mozzi. The people in the meantime, those of the more ignoble sort, thirsting for booty, spoiled and sacked the palaces and towers with such rage that the most cruel enemy of Florence would have been ashamed to work such havoc.

As soon as the nobles were overcome the people set to work to reorganise the government, and as there were three grades of people, namely, the upper, middle, and lower class, it was ordained that the upper class should have two representatives in the signori and the middle and lower classes three representatives each; and that the gonfaloniere should be chosen first from one class and then from another. Beyond this, all the ordinances of justice were re-enacted against the nobles, and in order that they should be still further weakened, many of their families were merged into the ranks of the people. The destruction of the nobility was so complete, and the order so depressed, that never afterwards were the nobles bold enough to take up arms against the people, but gradually sank into a low and abject position. This was the cause of Florence losing, not only her fighting qualities, but every description of high-mindedness. After the nobles were wiped out, the city remained at rest until the year 1353. During that time there occurred the memorable pestilence, which has been narrated with so much eloquence by Messer Giovanni Boccaccio, when Florence lost no less than 96,000 souls. The Florentines also entered upon their first war against the Visconti, a war that was entirely brought about by the ambition of the Archbishop of Milan. This war had not ended when the factions again broke out in Florence. Although the nobility was destroyed, fate did not fail to find new dissensions through which to bring the city fresh trouble.

THIRD BOOK

1343-1414

THE ineradicable hostility which naturally exists between the people and the nobles is caused by the one wishing to rule and the other to resist, and from this follows all the evils which arise in cities; for this contradictory spirit fosters everything which tends to disturb a commonwealth. This kept Rome ever at strife within herself, and if it is permitted to compare small things with great ones, this has caused the disunion of Florence, although the effects produced in the two cities have been very different. The dissensions which arose between the people and the nobles in Rome were settled at their commencement by discussion, whilst those of Florence were terminated by fighting. Those of Rome ended in a constitution, those of Florence in the death and exile of many citizens. The dissensions in Rome tended to increase the warlike qualities of her citizens, but in Florence they were entirely wiped out. Whilst the dissensions in Rome transformed the equality of her citizenship to the utmost inequality, those of Florence have reduced her citizens from a condition of inequality to a wonderful equality. The different ends which these two people set before themselves undoubtedly were productive of these very different effects. For the people of Rome were desirous of sharing the supreme honours with the nobles, whilst the people of Florence fought in order that they alone should govern without the participation of the nobles. And as the desire of the Roman people was more reasonable, so the injuries which the nobles suffered were more endurable, and the nobles yielded without coming to blows; thus after any quarrel between the two orders a law was passed and both were pacified. Since the objects which the Florentine people had in view was unjust and injurious, the nobility were compelled to resort to force in its own defence, and thus came bloodshed and banishment to the citizens. And the laws which were afterwards passed by the victors were for their own advantage and not for the general good. The victories which the people of Rome thus obtained over the nobles assisted in the advancement of the city herself, because the people became eligible to assist the nobles in the administration of the empire, the army, and the laws, and all being animated with the same spirit the city grew in valour and increased in power. But in Florence, when the people overcame the nobles, these latter were deprived of power for ever; and in case they wished to regain power it was necessary for them, not only to assume the behaviour, spirit, and mode of living of merchants, but also to appear as such. Hence followed those changes in coats of arms and names of families to which the nobles submitted in order to give the appearance of belonging to the people. Thus disappeared all valour in arms and gallantry of spirit which are the distinguishing characteristics of the nobility, whilst in the people they could never be kindled, for they had never possessed the qualifications. Thus Florence ever grew more abject and mean-spirited. Whilst the valour of Rome raised her to such a pitch of pride that she could not exist without a prince, Florence reached such depths that any clever law-maker could turn the government into any shape he pleased. All of which can be clearly seen by reading the preceding book. Having traced the rise of Florence, the birth of her liberties, and the causes of her dissensions, and having shown how the factions of the nobles and the people ended in the tyranny of the Duke of Athens, and caused the total destruction of the nobility, it now remains to relate the enmities between the people and the plebeians, and the various events which these quarrels provoked.

After the nobles had lost their power and been defeated in the war against the Archbishop of Milan, no cause of further trouble apparently remained in Florence. But the evil fortune and the indifferent laws of our city caused animosities to arise between the families of the Albizzi and Ricci, which divided Florence as cruelly as the old quarrels of the Buondelmonti and Uberti, and later those of the Donati and Cerchi divided her. The pontiffs during their residence in France and the emperors from Germany had sent at various times great numbers of soldiers of various nationalities to maintain their authority in Italy; thus at this time numbers of Englishmen, Germans, and Frenchmen were to be met with there. When a war ended these men, finding themselves without either employment or pay, would then raise a flag of adventure and levy tribute first from one prince and then from another. Thus in the year 1353, one of these companies under Monsieur Reale, a Provençal, entered Tuscany and alarmed the cities throughout the country. The Florentines not only armed themselves as a community, but many citizens armed themselves for their personal safety, and among these were the families of the Albizzi and the Ricci. There was such hatred between the two that each one endeavoured to obtain the upper hand in the republic in order to oppress the other. They had not yet come to blows, but had only opposed each other in the magistracies and the councils. All the city being at this time under arms, a quarrel arose by chance in the Mercato Vecchio where crowds of men had assembled, as under the circumstances might be expected. A rumour spread and reached the ears of the Ricci that the Albizzi were intending to attack them, whilst the Albizzi were told that the Ricci were seeking them out. Upon this the whole city rose in arms, and it was only after much difficulty that the magistrates were able to restrain both families from proceeding to extremities, but both were blamed for the occurrence, although it arose by chance and no blame attached to either. This accident, although a slight one, caused the anger of both families to burn more fiercely, and each of them sought to draw more partisans to their side. The citizens, however, had already secured such complete equality by the destruction of the nobles that the magistrates were able to enforce the laws far more stringently than formerly; and therefore the Albizzi and Ricci determined to get the better of each other by ordinary courses and without resorting to private violence.

We have already related how the magistrates were selected from the Guelf party only, after the victory of Charles I., and were armed with supreme authority over the Ghibellines. These repressive measures had either by the effluxion of time, or by new feuds and other circumstances, passed into oblivion; thus many of the descendants of the Ghibellines now enjoyed the prime magistracy. Uguccione de' Ricci, the head of that family, now worked matters so that the old laws against the Ghibellines were revived, because among the many who had held Ghibelline views were the Albizzi, who many years ago had come to reside in Florence from Arezzo. By reviving these laws, especially the one which declared that if any descendant of a Ghibelline should take upon himself the office of a magistrate he should be punished, Uguccione hoped to deprive the Albizzi of their offices. This design of Uguccione was made known to Piero, the son of Filippo degli Albizzi, who decided to agree to it, lest by opposing it he should make it apparent that he was a Ghibelline. This law, which was revived to satisfy the ambition of one man, did not in any degree affect the position of Piero degli Albizzi, but rather increased his authority, yet it was the beginning of many evils. For no one can make a law which causes more trouble in a commonwealth than one which takes cognisance of matters long past. Owing to the support which he gave to the re-enactment of this law, which had been intended by his enemies to entangle him, Piero became more powerful than before, because he came to be considered the author of it, and having acquired more authority under it he was looked upon with great favour by the new faction of Guelfs.

As no magistrates could be found who were willing to search out the Ghibellines, the law became of little effect; therefore the authority was handed over to the captains, and on them devolved the duty of searching the Ghibellines out, warning them not to accept any office, and declaring to them that if they disobeyed such warning they would be punished. Thus it came to pass that all those who had been deprived of the power of exercising the functions of a magistrate by this admonition were afterwards known as "Ammoniti." In course of time the captains became more daring, and under the influence of ambition, or with a view to extort money, would admonish not only those who may have incurred the penalty with justice, but also those who appeared to them to deserve it. From 1357, when this ordinance was revived, to 1367 it was found that more than 200 citizens had been admonished. By these means the captains of the wards and the Guelf faction had become very powerful, especially in the case of the heads of that faction, Messer Piero degli Albizzi and Messer Lapo da Castiglionchio and Carlo Strozzi, because fearing to receive the admonition all the citizens bowed down to them. This insolent method of conducting the business of the city, however, was extremely displeasing to many, and the Ricci were the most discontented of all, because they were the authors of all the mischief which was now threatening the republic with ruin; and which, contrary to their intentions, had contributed entirely to the supremacy of their enemies the Albizzi. When Uguccione de' Ricci was elected to the signoria, he took steps at once to put an end to this evil, of which he and his supporters had been the origin, and a new ordinance provided that three additional captains of wards should be added to the six already appointed. Two of these new captains were to be selected from among the smaller artisans, and all declared Ghibellines were to have their sentences ratified by twenty-four citizens deputed for that purpose. This enactment at once reduced the power of the captains within reasonable bounds, and whilst some citizens were still admonished, the number of them became very few. Nevertheless the Albizzi and Ricci factions were animated by the utmost hatred, and watched and opposed each other in all discussions on law-making or undertakings. These troubles lasted from 1366 to 1371, by which time the Guelf party had entirely recovered its former position. In the Buondelmonti family there was living at this time a certain Messer Benchi, a cavalier who, for his merits in one of the Pisan wars, had received the freedom of the popolani or merchants, and had thus become eligible for the signoria. But when he expected to take his seat in the council he found a law had been passed which forbade any great person who had become a popolani to sit there. This gave much offence to Messer Benchi, and he at once joined Messer Piero degli Albizzi. They determined to use the power of declaring Ghibellines to the utmost, and by these means oppress the small traders and get the government back into their own hands. Thus the favour which Messer Benchi enjoyed among the old nobility, and the standing of Messer Piero with the wealthy traders, enabled the Guelf faction to accomplish this, and by change in the government they managed to increase the authority of the captains and diminish that of the twenty-four citizens. By these means they enforced the admonition with more audacity than before, and the house of Albizzi, as head of the faction, mounted still higher in authority. On the other hand, the Ricci were not idle, but threw every possible obstacle in the way of the execution of their rivals' plans. Thus all parties throughout the city lived in the greatest anxiety, with the fear of ruin ever present. This induced many citizens, moved by love of their country, to assemble in San Piero Scheraggio, and discuss among themselves the prevailing disturbances. They decided to appeal to the signori, and one with more authority than the rest was deputed to speak, which he did in the following words: —

"Many of us, my lords, feared to respond to a private summons and meet as we have done, although the matter is one of public interest, because we feared that we might be considered presumptuous, or that we might be censured as ambitious. But when we recollected that every day citizens assemble in their houses and in the streets, not out of consideration for the good of the commonwealth, but only for the advancement of their own purposes, we decided that if those men, who are conspiring together for the destruction of the republic, have no fear in meeting together, then we, who are uniting for the good of the public, should also have no fears. But, my lords, we do not care what others say of us, for they of whom we speak pay no regard to us. My lords, the love which we bear to our country first called us together, and now bids us come to you, and lay before you the evils under which she now suffers—evils which, though great, are yet constantly increasing. It bids us offer you our assistance in crushing these accumulating evils. Difficult as this will be for you, you need not despair of success; you have only to put on one side all personal considerations and use the official power with which you have been invested. The universal depravity of the cities of Italy, my lords, has infected and corrupted this city of ours; for since Italy shook off the dominion of the emperors, the cities within it have had no curb sufficiently powerful to restrain them. They have not organised themselves as free communities, but have divided themselves into factions. This has given birth to all the evils and disorders which are afflicting us. Neither union nor friendship can be found among their citizens, unless it is among those who consort together for the commital of some wickedness, either against the country or some private person. As for religion and the fear of God, it is quite extinct; and the taking of oaths and the pledging of faith is no longer of any value, for men will not plight their word with any intention of keeping it, but as a means for more easily betraying their victims. Accordingly, praise and glory are gained in proportion as the deceit succeeds with more or less ease and safety. Thus wicked men are praised as clever, whilst the good men are censured as foolish. And it is true that in every city in Italy there are gathered together those who corrupt and those who are ready to be corrupted. The young people are idle, and the old are dissolute, and every sex and every age is full of brutish customs, so that good laws supply no remedy when thus marred by wicked habits. Hence arises that rapacity which is found among the citizens, and that desire, not for true glory, but for shameful honours, followed by hatreds, hostilities, divisions, and factions, bringing again in their train murders and banishments, the persecution of good men, the promotion of bad ones. Good men, relying upon their innocence, do not defend themselves by means outside of the law, as the wicked men do, and they are consequently ruined without recourse or honour. From this state of affairs springs the love of factions and their power, because bad men will bind themselves together from greed and for ambitious reasons, whilst the good men will do so from the necessity of defence. But what is most pernicious in these schemes is, that the authors and principals in them cloak their evil intentions under specious names. Thus, although they are all enemies of freedom, they tyrannise over us under the pretence of a government by magnates or by the people. The reward which they seek in victory is not the glory of having freed the city, but the gratification of having overcome their opponents and of having wrested the government from them. Then, having succeeded in their schemes, what deed is too unjust, cruel, or rapacious for them to commit. Such laws and ordinances as they make are made only for their own advantage, not for that of the public. The wars which they enter upon, the alliances and treaties which they conclude, are not for the common glory, but for the satisfaction of the few. If other cities are full of these disorders, our city is more than others fouled by them, because our laws, statutes, and civil ordinances have been passed, not in accordance with a condition of freedom, but to meet the ambitions of the party which happens at the time to be uppermost. Thus it follows that, when a party has been driven from power and a faction has been extinguished, another always follows, because in a city which prefers to carry on its government by factions rather than by laws, no sooner is a faction deprived of opposition than it begins of necessity to divide amongst its own members, for no faction can defend itself by those peculiar methods which in the first instance it practised for its own safety. Both the bygone and recent dissensions in our city will prove this. It was universally believed that when the Ghibellines were destroyed the Guelfs would survive for long afterwards, happy and honoured. But in a short time they were divided into Bianchi and Neri. After the Bianchi were extirpated, the city did not remain long without parties, and there was soon fighting going on. At one time it was to restore the exiles, at another time it was owing to the hostility between the nobles and the people. Finally, unable or unwilling to enjoy our liberties in peace we surrendered them, first to King Robert, then to his brother, afterwards to his son, and finally to the Duke of Athens. Even under those conditions we were never at rest, for we are like those who will never be content to be free and who never will be slaves. For so prone is our nature to faction that we did not hesitate, although we were living under the sway of the king, to put that vile fellow from Aggobio into the place of his Majesty. For the honour of the city we ought to forbear mentioning the Duke of Athens, for his cruel and tyrannical temper should have made us wise and have taught us to keep ourselves free in the future. But no sooner was he driven out than, our swords once more in our hands, we were fighting with more animosity and rage than we had ever fought before, until our ancient nobility were entirely overcome and subdued to the will of the people. This result caused many citizens to believe that no further disturbance or faction could arise in Florence now that a curb had been put on those who, by their insupportable pride and ambition, had appeared the cause of all the discords. But experience shows how delusive men's reasoning is, and how often their judgment is at fault; for the arrogance and ambition of our nobility has not passed away, it has only reverted to the wealthy classes of our citizens, who, after the manner of all ambitious men, strive to obtain the first positions in the republic. These men, failing any other method of seizing power, have again plunged the city into strife by resuscitating the names of Ghibelline and Guelf. These names were utterly forgotten, and it would have been well for the republic if they had never been known. It has been ordained from above that human affairs should neither endure for ever nor be at rest for ever, therefore there are fatal families in every republic who are born for its ruin. Our republic more than any other has been overburdened by such families, who first like the Buondelmonti and the Uberti, then the Donati and the Cerchi, and now, to our shame and ridicule, the Ricci and Albizzi, have arisen to disturb and divide her. My lords, we have not recalled our corruptions and our ancient and perpetual feuds to alarm you, but to trace out their causes, and demonstrate to you that we bear them in our minds as well as you do, and to assure you from what has happened before that you need have no fear of being unable to curb these present families. The immense power behind the old families brought many of them into great favour with princes, and no ordinary and civil proceeding was sufficient to curb them. But now that the empire has no authority, and the pope commands no respect, and this city with others throughout Italy enjoys perfect equality under its own government, the difficulty cannot be so great as formerly. Our republic especially is able, notwithstanding what has passed before, not only to assert her unity, but to reform herself, if only your lordships are disposed to wish it carried out. As for ourselves, we are only moved by compassion for our country, not by personal motives, and we give you the utmost encouragement to attempt it. Although the corruption of the city may be appalling, now is the time to destroy the evils which infect us, the passions which consume us, the poison which saps our life. Think not that the old feuds are to be imputed to man's nature, they are due to the times. These being now changed, you may hope to place your city under better laws and better fortune, you may overcome the malignity of the trouble, by placing a curb on the ambitions of men, and repealing those laws which have fomented the factions, and keep those ordinances which tend to civility and freedom. Let it be your endeavour to carry out these reforms at once under the mild influence of the law, rather than by deferring them compel men to insist upon them at the point of the sword."

The signori were moved by what they heard, although they did not hear it for the first time; but encouraged by the promised assistance of these gentlemen, they now authorised the appointment of fifty-six citizens to take steps for the preservation of the republic. It is only too true that many men are more capable of observing a good law than they are of originating one. Thus these citizens thought more of putting an end to the present feuds than of removing the causes of future ones, and consequently they succeeded in accomplishing neither the one nor the other of their objects. They left untouched the source from which factions would spring in the future, and they made one of the present factions so powerful as to endanger the republic. To carry out their reforms they deprived of office for three years three members from each of the Albizzi and Ricci families, among whom were Piero degli Albizzi and Uguccione de' Ricci, from these families they excepted members of the Guelf party. They prohibited all citizens from entering the palace except when the magistrates were sitting. They provided also that any person who should be assaulted or deprived of his goods should be able to proceed in his complaint by petition to the council, and compel the council to declare the assailant to be a noble, and being so declared he should then be punished according to the law. This order greatly depressed the Ricci faction, but encouraged that of the Albizzi; for although both were equally proscribed the Ricci were the more heavily hit, because, although the Palace of the Signori was closed to Piero, that of the Guelfs was open to him, and there he had paramount authority. If he and his following had been previously hot for admonishing the Ghibellines, they became hotter still after these injuries had been inflicted on them. To these bad feelings fresh causes of trouble were shortly to be added.

Gregory XI. was at this time pope, and was residing at Avignon. He ruled Italy, as his predecessors had done, through legates — grasping and arrogant men who afflicted many cities. One of these legates, who resided at Bologna, availed himself of the famine in Florence to make an attempt upon Tuscany. He not only refused all assistance to the Florentines, but even destroyed their hopes of a future harvest by attacking them with a great army in the springtime. He might possibly have succeeded in overcoming them, as he hoped to find them famished and unprepared, if his armies had been less venal and disloyal, because there was nothing left for the Florentines to do in their defence but to give the legate's army 130,000 florins as an inducement to it to abandon the enterprise. Whilst men can commence wars at their own time they cannot stop them just when they wish. This war, which was commenced to satisfy the ambition of the legate, was continued at the pleasure of the Florentines. They concluded a treaty with Messer Bernabo and all the cities hostile to the Church, and appointed eight citizens to conduct the war with all its necessary operations, and incur the necessary expenses without having to render any account of same. Notwithstanding that Uguccione de' Ricci was dead, this war against the pontiff brought the Ricci faction again to the front, because it was they who had always supported Messer Bernabo in his opposition to the Albizzi, and who had been always hostile to the Church. Furthermore, the Eight were bitterly hostile to the Church. All this caused Messer Piero degli Albizzi, Messer Lapo da Castiglionchio, Carlo Strozzi, and others to combine still further for the injury of their opponents. Thus whilst the Eight carried on the war these men continued to issue admonitions to all Ghibellines. The war lasted three years, and terminated only with the death of Gregory XI. The Eight had carried on this war with so much satisfaction to the citizens that they were continued in their office year after year. They were called the Saints, although they took but little notice of the censures of the pope, despoiled the churches, and compelled the clergy to celebrate the services. Thus these citizens esteemed more highly the good of their country than their own souls, and they demonstrated to the Church that although at first they had defended it as friends, they were now able to afflict it as enemies, and they influenced all Romagna, the Marca, and Perugia to rebel against it.

Nevertheless, whilst the Florentines were able to wage war so successfully against the pope, they could not defend themselves against the captains of the wards and their factions. The hatred which now filled the minds of the Guelfs against the Eight increased and emboldened them to such an extent that they even assaulted some members of the council, together with other noble citizens. The arrogance of these captains of the wards reached such a pitch that they were feared more than were the signori, and more respect was paid to them. The palace of the captains was more resorted to than that of the signori; and no ambassadors ever came to Florence without a mission to the captains. Although Florence had no war on her hands now that Pope Gregory was dead, confusion reigned within her walls, where the audacity of the Guelfs was unendurable, and no means were to be found by which it could be curbed. Many believed it to be necessary for the two factions to come to blows in order to prove once and for all which was the stronger. On the side of the Guelfs all the ancient nobility were ranged, and a considerable number of the merchant traders, among whom were Piero, Lapo, and Carlo as leaders. On the other side were the smaller traders, including the eight directors of the war, Messer Giorgio Scali, Tommaso Strozzi, with the Ricci, Alberti, and Medici. The remnant of the multitude took, as usual, the side of the malcontents.

It now became apparent to the leaders of the Guelf faction that their opponents were too strong for them, and that they stood in great danger whenever a hostile signoria should wish to lower them, and they decided to meet together and consult upon the affairs of the city and their own position. It also appeared to the Guelfs that the ammoniti had increased in such vast numbers and had brought so much reproach to them that the city was now entirely hostile to them. For this condition of affairs the Guelfs saw no remedy but, having lost their own honour, to take away that of the city. In imitation of the Guelfs of an earlier day, who could never live in security in the city without first driving out of it all their adversaries, they determined to seize the Palace of the Signori and bring the government under the sway of their faction. All the Guelfs agreed to this plan, but could not agree as to when it should be carried out. Their meeting was held in April 1378. To Messer Lapo da Castiglionchio it did not appear wise to postpone action, for nothing injures opportunity so much as waiting for it, especially as in their case Messer de' Medici could be made gonfaloniere in the next signoria, and everybody knew that he was against their faction. Piero degli Albizzi, on the other hand, thought it best to wait, because their faction was weak in numbers, and their intentions would be at once betrayed if they were to assemble any considerable number of men together. Let them await, therefore, the approaching festival of San Giovanni, when great crowds would assemble, amongst whom it would be possible to conceal as many men as they could desire. To remove any fears they might entertain of Salvestro, let him be admonished, and if this should fail, then let one of the members of the college in his ward be admonished; and when drawing lots it would be easy to make the choice fall upon him or one of his colleagues, owing to the ballot box being now empty, and so take away from Salvestro the right to sit as gonfaloniere. With this decision they closed the discussion, although Messer Lapo consented unwillingly to this course, for he considered it dangerous to delay, since a time absolutely suitable for everything is never found, and he who waits until it is so either never accomplishes anything or he attempts it at a time greatly to his disadvantage. The Guelfs therefore admonished one of the college, but this did not prevent Messer Salvestro being elected gonfaloniere, because the plot was discovered by the Eight, and they managed so that the substitute was not chosen.

Thus Salvestro, the son of Messer Alammano de' Medici, was made gonfaloniere. He was descended from one of the noblest of the merchant families and was not inclined to permit the people to be oppressed by a few powerful persons. Having found the people and many noble merchant companies disposed to assist him in putting an end to the tyranny, he communicated his intentions to Benedetto Alberti, Tommaso Strozzi, and Messer Giorgio Scali, who promised him their assistance. They secretly formed a league among themselves to re-enact the ordinances of justice, which would lessen the authority of the captains of the wards and give the ammoniti an opportunity to recover their positions. In order to carry this proposal Salvestro had to submit it first to the college, and afterwards to the council, in both of which bodies Salvestro was provost, a position which made the holder for the time being equal to a prince in the city. Salvestro, therefore, issued summonses for both the college and the council to meet on the same morning. He brought his proposition first before the college, where, although the number of members present was very small, it met with great opposition, and he could not obtain their consent to it. Whereupon Salvestro, seeing that they thus closed to him the first methods of obtaining the law, pretended that his necessities compelled him to leave the college, and went to the council without being seen to do so, and mounting upon a high bench, where everybody could see and hear him, said that he believed he had been made gonfaloniere, not to adjudicate in private causes, for which they already had their judges, but to correct the wrongs inflicted by the powerful, and to moderate those laws which had been found to threaten the republic with ruin, to both of these subjects he had given the utmost attention, and as far as possible had provided for them. But the malignity of men so opposed the justice of his attempts that the opportunity of his working for the good of the citizens was taken away from him, and from the council the opportunity of discussing those plans, or even hearing what they were. Seeing, therefore, that he could do no good work for the republic, nor assist them, there was no longer any reason why he should hold his office, which, either he did not deserve, or others believed that he did not, therefore he would retire into private life as soon as the people were able to appoint his successor, whom he hoped might have greater virtues or happier fortunes. With these words he left the council for his own house.

Those members of the council who were aware of this procedure, and who favoured the new law, raised a great tumult, and the signori and colleges met in the council chamber, and seeing their gonfaloniere going away, led him back with prayers and force to the chamber, which was now in a state of great tumult. Noble citizens were threatened with angry words, and Carlo Strozzi was taken by the throat by an artisan and would have been killed if those around him had not rescued him at great hazard.

But Benedetto degli Alberti raised the most tumult by calling the people to arms in a high voice from the windows of the palace, and the Piazza quickly became filled with armed men. Seeing this, those members of the college who had refused to pass the law when they were asked to do so now yielded when they found themselves threatened. The captains of the wards and many citizens met in their palace to discuss how they could oppose this law of Salvestro, but when they heard of the tumult, and learnt what the council had decided to do, they all retired to their own houses.

Let no one who starts a change in a city expect either to stop it at will or guide it as he thinks fit. It was the intention of Salvestro to revive the ordinances of justice and to pacify the city, but the matter proceeded otherwise, because the feelings let loose inflamed the minds of the citizens, who fortified themselves in their houses, would not open their shops, but concealed their goods in monasteries and churches, and every one acted as if some great danger were at hand. The members of the guilds met together, and each of them appointed a syndic. Then the signori called their colleges together and consulted with the syndics the whole of one day, as to the best way to compose these disturbances, but owing to differences of opinion could not decide upon any course. Another day followed and nothing was done. Then the guilds drew out their bands, and the signori, fearing a collision between the factions, called the council together to discuss the steps that should be taken. At once the guilds under their banners, with great numbers of armed men, marched into the Piazza. Whereupon the council, in the hopes of pacifying the people and the guilds and removing the causes of the discontent, gave a general power, which is called in Florence a balia, to the signori, the colleges, the Eight, to the captains of the wards, and to the syndics of the guilds, so that the government of the city should be reformed for the general welfare. Whilst this balia was being passed in the council, some companies of the guilds and the mobs, prompted thereto by persons who desired to revenge themselves for the recent injuries they had received at the hands of the Guelfs, rose and sacked the house of Messer Lapo da Castiglionchio. When Messer Lapo heard that the people were in arms, and that the signori had entered into engagements against the Guelfic decrees, he saw no other recourse but flight. He first hid himself in Santa Croce, and afterwards disguised in the dress of a priest he fled to Casentino. He was heard frequently to blame Piero degli Albizzi for having deferred seizing the government until the festival of San Giovanni and himself for having agreed to it. When Piero degli Albizzi and Carlo Strozzi heard the tumult they also hid themselves, but remained in Florence, where they had many relatives and friends, and believed they would be quite safe until the disturbances were over. Although it may sometimes be difficult to start these troubles, yet they are easily increased, and thus the house of Messer Lapo being burnt, many others were burnt and sacked, either by public hatred or private malice. In order that the mob might have company in their depredations upon other peoples' property, who possibly would have a greater appetite for such work than they themselves, the prisons were broken open. Afterwards the Monastery of the Agnoli and the Convent of San Spirito, where so many citizens had stored their possessions, were sacked. The public offices would not have been saved from the hands of these robbers had it not been defended by one of the signori, who, mounted on horseback with many armed men behind him, opposed the fury of the multitude.

The firm stand which the signori took against the mob, as well as the approach of night, somewhat calmed the rage, and the next day the balia made some concessions to the ammoniti, with the proviso that they should only exercise the functions of magistrates after three years had passed. The balia also repealed the several laws which the Guelfs had carried to the prejudice of the citizens. It declared Messer Lapo da Castiglionchio a rebel, together with several others of his companions who were held in general hatred. After these things had taken place, the names of the new signori were published, and Luigi Guicciardini was made gonfaloniere to them. Great hopes were entertained that these men would put an end to the present disorders, because they appeared to the citizens to be men of peace and desirous of peace for the community. Nevertheless, the citizens did not lay down their arms, neither were the shops opened, and strong guards kept watch throughout the city. Consequently the signori were not installed in office with the usual ceremonies outside the palace, but within it, and without the observation of any pomp. The signori, who considered the pacification of the city to be the most important of their duties, compelled the citizens to lay down their arms, to open their shops, and to send away from Florence the host of countrymen whom they had brought in to assist them. The signori also appointed guards in many parts of the city, and matters would have remained quiet if the ammoniti had been content to rest. But they were not willing to wait for three years before recovering their privileges, therefore, in order that these might be granted at once, the guilds once more assembled. They demanded of the signori that, for the good and peace of the city, an ordinance should be at once passed to the effect that no citizen whatever who had ever been a signore of a college, a captain of a ward, or a consul of any of the guilds should be admonished as a Ghibelline; and further that a new balloting should be made for the Guelf party and the present ones burnt. These demands were at once conceded by the signori, as well as by the council, and it appeared as if all pretexts for the tumults, which had again commenced, were now completely removed.

As men are never satisfied with simply recovering their own possessions, but must needs out of revenge desire to seize those of others, it followed that those who had profited by the recent disorders now pointed out to the artisans that they would never be safe unless many of their enemies were driven out of the city or destroyed. The report of this reached the signori, and they at once summoned the magistrates of the guilds and the syndics before them, and Luigi Guicciardini, the gonfaloniere, spoke the following words to them: "If the signori and myself had not had a long experience of the fortunes of this city, which makes the closing of a war outside the city a signal for the commencement of one within, we should have been much surprised at these subsequent feuds, and they would have been the more displeasing to us; but those things which are anticipated annoy the least, and thus we have endured these tumults with patience. They were commenced through no fault of ours, and we had expected them to come to an end so soon as we had given you the satisfaction which we have done in so many and important matters. But it is represented to us that you will not rest in peace, but desire to inflict fresh injuries upon your fellow citizens by their banishment. Thus our displeasure rises at your injustice, and if we could have believed that during the time of our magistracy our city could have been ruined, either by opposing your wishes or by complying with them, truly would we have avoided these honours either by flight or exile. But we accepted those honours, believing that we should have to deal with men who have in them some humanity and some love for their country, and hoping by our generosity to overcome your ambitions. We now find by bitter experience that, the more deferentially we carry ourselves towards you, and yield to you, the more aggressive you become, and the more unjust you are in your demands. If we speak thus plainly to you, it is not to offend you, but to assist you in turning over a new leaf. Let others tell you what may be pleasing, we only speak what is for your advantage. Tell us on your honour what else we can do for you beyond what we have already done? You desired us to reduce the authority of the captains of the wards. We have done so. You wished the ballotings of the Guelfs to be burnt and reformed ones substituted. We consented. You wished that the ammoniti should be restored to their privileges. It is permitted. At your prayers we have pardoned those who burnt houses and robbed churches, and to satisfy you we have sent many powerful and honourable citizens into exile. Out of consideration for you the nobles have been further restrained by new regulations. Where will your demands end, and for how long will you abuse our liberality? Do you not recognise that we endure our defeats with more patience than you do your victory? Do you not see to what an end your dissensions will bring your city? Do you not recollect how Castruccio, a vile Lucchese, overthrew it when your government was disunited? How a Duke of Athens, a mere condottiere, brought it under his sway? But when your state was united, then a pope and an Archbishop of Milan could not overcome it, but after many years of war had to draw off in disgrace. Why should you, therefore, during this time of peace, seek to bring your city into servitude when so many powerful enemies have left her free after many years of war? What can your dissensions bring you but slavery? And what can the possessions which you have taken or will take from us bring you but poverty, since with our industry we support the city out of those possessions; and being robbed of them by you we should no longer be able to do so, and those who seize them, as things wrongly acquired, will not know how to keep them, and hunger and poverty will assuredly follow. I and these signori command you, and if honour would permit we would pray you, to set your minds at rest at once, and be satisfied with what we have already done for you. Should you wish for anything later on demand it quietly, not with tumults and arms, for when your demands are just they will be complied with. But above all things do not give wicked men the opportunity of ruining your country under your patronage and to your reproach and damage."

These words, because of their manifest truth, deeply affected the minds of the citizens; they unanimously thanked the gonfaloniere for his good offices towards them, and also for having discharged his duties to the city as a good citizen, and they proffered their prompt obedience to his injunctions. The signori appointed two citizens from among the higher magistrates to assist them, and these, with the syndics of the guilds, were to consult together as to what measures could be adopted for quieting down the community and report thereon to the signori.

Whilst the above matter was being discussed, there arose a disturbance which wrought more harm to the republic than anything that had gone before. The greater part of the plundering and burning which had happened on the previous days was the handiwork of the lowest classes of the city, and the men who had been the boldest in the destruction feared that they would be punished now that the graver dissensions were about to be settled. They were also alarmed lest, as always happens, they should be deserted by those who had instigated them to commit the depredations. To these troubles ought to be added the hatred with which the lower classes always regarded the rich citizens and the heads of the guilds, because the workmen were always dissatisfied with the wages they received, never considering them what they were justly entitled to. When in the time of Carlo I. the city was divided into guilds, and a master and a constitution were given to each of them, it was provided that the members of each guild should be judged in all civil matters by the masters of these guilds. These guilds in the beginning, as we have said, numbered twelve, but afterwards they were increased to twenty-one, and had risen to such power that in a few years they absorbed the entire government of the city. Some being found to be of more or less importance than others, they were divided into greater and lesser guilds, of which seven were called the greater and fourteen the lesser. Out of this division and the causes related above, the arrogance of the captains of the wards took its rise, because those citizens who had formerly been Guelfs, and under whose government the magistracy was always sworn, had favoured the rich merchants of the greater guilds and had oppressed the members of the lesser ones. This caused the innumerable tumults of which we have spoken. In addition to this, many industries in which only small traders or the lower classes laboured had no guild of their own, but submission was yielded to one of the guilds which happened to assimilate in some degree to their own industry. Hence it followed that when these people became dissatisfied with their wages, or oppressed by their masters, they had no other course open to them but to appeal to the syndics of the guild to which they had submitted themselves, and from them they rarely received that justice to which they believed themselves entitled. And of all the guilds that had, and still have, most of that description of labour affiliated to them, the Guild of Wool is the most powerful and of the greatest authority, and it supports with its trade the greater number of the small traders and the labouring classes.

Thus it came about that the lower orders, not only those who were in submission to the Guild of Wool, but also those under other guilds, were full of resentment for the above reasons, and feared punishment for the burnings and robberies committed by them. Therefore they assembled at night to consider what could be done to meet the dangerous position in which they stood. One of the boldest and most experienced among them addressed them in the following words: "If we had now to decide whether we should take up arms, burn and pillage the houses of the citizens, and rob the churches, I should be the first among you to suggest caution, and perhaps to approve of your preference for humble poverty rather than risking all on the chance of a gain. But as you have already had recourse to arms, and have committed much havoc, it appears to me that the point you have now to consider is, not how shall we desist from this destruction, but how shall we commit more in order to secure ourselves. I believe beyond all question that, when nothing else can teach us, necessity will. On every side the city is full of complaints and hatred against us. The citizens are united on this point, and the magistrates are always consulting with the signori. Believe me, they are setting snares for us, and preparing fresh measures for coercing us. Therefore in our deliberations we ought to keep two things in view: firstly, to escape chastisement for what we have already done, and, secondly, to secure for ourselves in the future more liberty and more comfort. Let us begin, therefore, by insisting upon a pardon for the old offences, and to secure this pardon it is necessary to commit new offences by multiplying the plunderings and burnings and redoubling the disturbances, and above all let us increase the number of our comrades, because, where small faults are chastised, great crimes are rewarded, and where many men are involved no one is punished. When many suffer, few seek revenge, because where the injury is universal it is borne with more patience than when it is particular. The multiplication of offences, therefore, will enable us to obtain pardon more easily and put us in the way of obtaining those things which we need for our liberty. It seems to me that we shall most certainly get them, because those men who would stand in our way are both rich and disunited, and their disunion will give us the victory, and their riches, when we possess them, will enable us to keep it. Do not let us fear that antiquity of blood of which they boast. Men have all the same beginning, nature casts them all in the same mould, and their blood is equally good. Strip us all naked, and you will find all are alike. Dress us in their clothes, and we shall be nobles beyond question; put them in ours, and they will appear commoners. It is only riches and poverty which make the difference between us. It grieves me to hear that some of you repent for conscience sake of what you have already done and wish to go no further with us. If this be true you are not the sort of men I thought you were, for neither conscience nor shame ought to have any influence upon you. Remember that those men who conquer never incur any reproach, and where there is, as with us, a dread of hunger and prisons, we should lightly esteem conscience with its apprehensions of hell. If you watch the ways of men you will see that those who obtain great wealth and power do so either by force or fraud, and having got them they conceal under some honest name the foulness of their deeds. Whilst those who through lack of wisdom, or from simplicity, do not employ these methods are always stifled in slavery or poverty. Faithful slaves always remain slaves, and good men are always poor men. Men will never escape from slavery unless they are unfaithful and bold, nor from poverty unless they are rapacious and fraudulent, because both God and Nature have placed the fortunes of men in such a position that they are reached rather by robbery than industry, and by evil rather than by honest skill. Hence it follows that men destroy each other, and he who can do the least injury always comes off worst. Therefore, you should always use your strength when you have the opportunity, and fortune never threw anything in your way better than your present chance, whilst the citizens are disunited, the signori hesitating, and the magistrates alarmed. Now is the time to conquer them, before they become united and find their courage. If we take this action we shall either become masters of the city, or we shall gain so much that not only will our past misdeeds be forgiven, but we shall be in a position to threaten fresh injuries. I confess this course is bold and dangerous, but when necessity drives audacity is the highest wisdom, and no courageous man takes any account of danger in great enterprises. For all undertakings that are commenced in danger are concluded in safety, and we can never avoid one danger without running into another. When we know that prisons, torments, and even death are being prepared for us, I believe there is more danger in remaining as we are than in seeking to make ourselves safe, because in the first case the perils are certain, and in the second case they are doubtful. How often have I heard you complaining of the cruelty of your masters and the injustice of your magistrates? Now is the time, not only to liberate yourselves from them, but to become so much their masters that they will have more to suffer and fear from you than you have ever had to endure from them. The opportunity flies that these chances have brought, and in vain will you seek to recall it when once it has passed. You see the preparations of our adversaries. Let us anticipate their plans, for doubtless those will be the victors who first draw the sword — they will succeed, and their enemies will be ruined. This course will bring honour to many of us and security to all."

These persuasive words set on fire the already inflamed minds of the people for mischief, and they decided to have recourse to arms as soon as they should have gathered together more of their fellows, and they bound themselves with oaths to support each other should any of them be hauled before the magistrate.

Whilst these fellows were maturing their plans to seize the republic, the plot was brought to the knowledge of the signori, owing to one Simone della Piazza falling into their hands and revealing to them the whole of the conspiracy. The danger was realised when it was learnt that the revolt was to take place on the following day, and the signori at once summoned the colleges and those citizens who, with the syndics of the guilds, were taking measures for the pacification of the city. It was evening before they could all assemble, and it was then advised that the consuls of the guilds should be sent for, and that every man-at-arms then in Florence should be ordered to assemble in the Piazza the first thing in the morning, and with them should come the gonfaloniere of the people. By chance, however, a person named Nicolo da San Friano was regulating the clock of the palace at the time when Simone was under torture and the citizens were assembling. Nicolo perceived at once what it all meant, and ran home, filling the whole neighbourhood with his cries, so that immediately more than a thousand men gathered in the Piazza of San Spirito. This uproar also reached the conspirators, and San Pietro and San Lorenzo, the places appointed by them, were quickly filled with armed men.

By this time the morning of July 21 had come, and there were not more than eighty men-at-arms assembled in the Piazza in reply to the summons of the signori, and none of the standard-bearers had arrived because, on learning that all the city was up in arms, they feared to leave their homes. The mob which first reached the Piazza came from San Piero Maggiore, and the men-at-arms made no movement on their arrival. Upon the heels of this mob followed another crowd who, finding no obstacle in their way, demanded with terrible shouts the release of the prisoners from the signori. Having failed to obtain the prisoners by threats they proceeded to force; they burnt down the house of Luigi Guiccardini, and compelled the signori to give their prisoners up for fear of worse happening. Having obtained them, the mob then wrested the standard of justice from the executioner, and marching under it proceeded to burn down the houses of those who were hated either on public or private grounds, for many citizens, merely to gratify their hate, led the mob against the houses of their enemies. So readily was this done that it was only necessary for a voice in the crowd to shout against such and such a house, or even for the man who carried the banner to point it in a certain direction. All the muniments of the Guild of Wool were also burnt. Having committed much destruction, the mob attempted to accompany it with the distribution of honours, and created Salvestro de' Medici and other citizens cavaliers, the number of which reached sixty-four. Among these cavaliers were Benedetto and Antonio degli Alberti, Tommaso Strozzi, and others who were in the confidence of the mob, but others were knighted against their will. It was to be remarked in these occurrences, and many did note it, that the mob burnt the houses of some of those whom shortly after they made knights, even on the same day, so quickly did honour follow the injury. This happened to Luigi Guicciardini, the gonfaloniere of justice. Amid this great riot the signori were completely disheartened at finding themselves deserted by their men-at-arms, the syndics of the guilds, and by the standard-bearers, none of whom had come, according to orders, to their assistance. Only two of the sixteen standard-bearers put in an appearance, namely those of the Lion d'Oro and Del Vajo under Giovenco della Stufa and Giovanni Cambi, and these left the Piazza very quickly when they found that none of the others followed them. On the other hand, many citizens, when they witnessed the fury of this roving multitude, and saw the palace abandoned, would not leave their homes. Some, however, followed the crowds of armed men in order to be in a better position to defend their own or the houses of their friends; and thus the power of the mob increased whilst that of the signori diminished. This tumult lasted the whole day, and when night came the mob stopped before the palace of Messer Stefano, which is situated behind the Church of San Barnaba. Their numbers exceeded 6000 men, and before daybreak they had compelled the guilds by threats to send them their banners. When morning came they marched to the Palace of the Podesta with the standard of justice and the banners of the guilds before them, and upon the podesta refusing to give up possession of the palace, they seized it.

Now that the signori discovered that they could not control the mob by force, they determined to make an attempt to come to terms with it. They therefore summoned four men from each of the colleges, and sent them to the people assembled at the Palace of the Podesta to learn from them what they wanted. These envoys found that the leaders of the people, with the syndics of the guilds and some other citizens, had already formulated what they intended to demand from the signoria. Therefore, accompanied by four representatives of the people, the envoys returned to the signoria with these demands: — that the Guild of Wool should no longer maintain a foreign judge; that three new trade guilds should be established, one for the wool carders and dyers, one for the barbers, doublet makers, tailors, and such like mechanical trades, and one for the lower classes; that these three new guilds should always have two signori and the fourteen lesser guilds should have three signori; that the signoria should provide halls for these new guilds; that no members of the guilds should be called upon to pay debts under fifty ducats for the period of two years; that the pawn shops should cease charging interest and should only be repaid the principal; that all banished or imprisoned citizens should be pardoned; that all ammoniti should have their dignities restored to them. They demanded for their special favourites many other privileges besides these, and at the same time they called for banishment and imprisonment for those who had opposed them. Dishonourable and unjust as these demands were the signori agreed to them, fearing that worse might follow their refusal. As it was desirable that the demands should be ratified, the consent of the general council had to be obtained. But as both councils could not sit on one and the same day, it was agreed to wait until the following day. The mob now appeared satisfied, and the guilds content, and a promise was given that as soon as the laws should be passed all rioting should cease.

Whilst the general council was deliberating next morning, the multitude, all impatient and noisy, marched under their banners into the Piazza, and with terrifying shouts alarmed the council and the signori so much that one of their members named Guerrante Marignolli was so terrified that, on the pretence of making the doors safe below, he fled away to his own house. He was not, however, able to steal away so secretly that the mob could not recognise him; but they did him no injury, only shouting out when they saw him that all the signori must leave the palace, and that if they would not do so then their children should be massacred and their houses burnt. In the meantime the laws had been confirmed and the signori had returned to their rooms; the council had descended the stairs and stood discussing matters in the portico and court-yard, in despair of their city. For never was there seen such foul play in a multitude, or such craven fears in those who ought to have curbed and kept them in order. The signori also were sorely perplexed and in despair for the safety of the country, also at finding themselves abandoned by one of their own number, and at receiving no assistance, either of strength or counsel, from a single citizen. Whilst they remained in this state of uncertainty as to what they could or ought to do, Messer Tommaso Strozzi and Messer Benedetto Alberti, moved either by their ambition to become masters of the palace or possibly because they believed it to be the wisest course, advised the signori to yield to the turbulent populace and retire to their own houses. This advice, preferred as it was by those who had been largely leaders in the disorders, was rejected with scorn by Alamanno Acciajuoli and Nicolo del Bene, two of the signori. These gentlemen with some show of vigour said that others might yield if they wished, and it could not be helped, but as for themselves, they did not intend to yield up their authority until the time came for them to do so, unless they did it with their lives. This resolution only redoubled the anxieties of the signori and increased the rage of the people, until finally the gonfaloniere, wishing rather to get rid of his office than imperil his life, entrusted himself to the care of Messer Tommaso Strozzi, who safely conducted him to his own house. The other signori, in much the same manner, one after the other, deserted the palace, even Alamanno and Nicolo, when they found themselves alone, also fled, preferring to be considered prudent rather than brave. Whereupon the palace fell into the hands of the populace and of the Eight commissioners of war who had not yet laid down their office.

When the mob entered the palace a man named Michele di Lando, a wool carder, bore in his hands the standard of the gonfaloniere of justice. This fellow, bare-footed and with but little clothing, mounted the stairs with the mob following him, and when he reached the audience chamber of the signori turned to the multitude and said: "You see the palace is yours, and the city is in your power. What do you wish to do now?" With a great shout they answered that he should be their signore and gonfaloniere, and that he might govern the gity as he pleased. Michele accepted the government, and as he was a shrewd and intelligent fellow, made up his mind to pacify the city and put down the rioting. In order to keep the people occupied, and give himself time to turn round, he ordered that Ser Nuto, who had been intended for the post of bargello by Messer Lapo da Castiglionchio, should be sought for and brought before him. Those who stood around him at once set out on this commission. Desiring to commence his government with justice, as he had acquired it by favour, he caused it to be published that it was his command that all burning and pillaging should at once cease, and as a warning to the mob he set a gallows up in the Piazza. To make a beginning with the reform of the government he discharged the syndics of the guilds and elected fresh ones; he deprived the signori and the colleges of their offices and burnt the ballot boxes. As for Ser Nuto, he was carried by the mob into the Piazza, and hanged by one foot from the gallows; when this was done those near to him began to cut him in pieces, and in a moment there was nothing left of him but the hanging foot. The Eight commissioners for war, on their part, believing that they were the leading people in the city since the signori had been driven out of the palace, had designated a new signoria. When, however, this came to the knowledge of Michele he informed them that they must at once leave the palace, as he intended to show every one that he could govern Florence without their assistance. Afterwards Michele assembled the new syndics of the guilds and appointed a signoria, choosing for this purpose four members from the lower classes and two each from the greater and minor guilds. Besides this he made a new scrutiny and divided the government into three parts, one of which was to be concerned with the greater guilds, one with the minor, and one with the new guilds. He gave to Messer Salvestro de' Medici the revenue arising from the shops on the Ponte Vecchio, and reserved to himself the podestaship of Empoli. To the citizens who had assisted the plebeians he gave many favours, not so much as recompense for what they had done, but to secure their assistance for his defence in time to come.

It appeared to the mob that Michele in his scheme of government had been too partial to the great merchants, and had not given to the plebeians that share of power which was necessary to enable them to keep their hold of it, or even to defend themselves. Whereupon, with their usual audacity, they at once took up arms and rushed tumultuously into the Piazza with their banners flying, and called for the signori to descend into the Ringhiera and discuss with them the plans which they were proposing to make for their own security. Michele saw clearly their insolence, but had no wish to incur their anger. Therefore, while not agreeing with their demand, he strongly condemned the way in which they put it forward, and advised them to lay down their arms, and they would then obtain what the dignity of the signori would not permit them to yield under compulsion. At this the mob became enraged with the palace, and went off to assemble at Sante Maria Novella, where they elected eight leaders from among themselves, with ministers and other appointments that would bring them both dignity and consideration. Thus the city had two factions and was governed by two different sets of rulers. The leaders of the mob decided among themselves that the Eight should always be chosen from out of their guilds, and should reside in the palace with the signori, and that everything which the government of the city wished to do should be confirmed by themselves. They deprived Messer Salvestro de' Medici and Michele di Lando of all that had previously been bestowed upon them. They assigned to many of their followers offices and appointments, and salaries with which to maintain their dignities. Having closed their deliberations the mob sent two of their leaders to the signori with the demand that their decisions should be confirmed, with the hint that if consent were not freely given force would be used. These fellows discharged their commission to the signori with great boldness and insolence. They reproached the gonfaloniere for his ingratitude and want of respect in exchange for all the honours and dignities they had conferred upon him. Towards the end of their discourse, when they proceeded to threaten him, Michele could no longer endure their insolence, and mindful rather of the rank which he then filled than that from which he had sprung, he determined to curb their extraordinary insolence with extraordinary means, and drawing the sword which he wore at his side he severely wounded one, and then had both bound and thrown into prison.

When this occurrence came to the knowledge of the mob, it was beside itself with rage, and, believing that it would easily gain by arms what it could not gain otherwise, set out at once amid great tumult to attack the signori. Michele, on the other hand, knew well what would happen and decided to anticipate the mob, thinking that it was more glorious to attack his enemy outside than to await him within the walls of the palace and have to fly in shame and dishonour as had his predecessors. He therefore gathered together a great number of the citizens who were beginning to recover their senses and, mounted on horseback with many armed men at his back, sallied forth to Santa Maria Novella in order to fight the mob. The populace had, as we have seen, come to the same determination; and at the very time Michele was moving against them, they had left Santa Maria for the Piazza, and by accident each of the parties took different ways and did not encounter each other. When Michele returned to the Piazza he found that it had been occupied by the mob and the palace heavily attacked.

He at once joined battle with the mob and overcame it, driving part of the enemy out of the city, and forcing the rest to lay down their arms or hide themselves. This advantage was gained and the tumults quieted entirely by the personal valour of the gonfaloniere, who in courage, prudence, and rectitude excelled all other citizens of that time, and deserves to be enrolled among those exceptional men who have conferred benefits on their fatherland. Had he been animated by either ambition or malignity, the republic would have completely lost its liberty, and would have fallen under a tyranny worse even than that of the Duke of Athens. But his conscience would never allow him to think of doing anything that was not for the general good, and his prudence enabled him to conduct the affairs of the republic in such a way that most of his party yielded to him, whilst he was able to overawe the rest by force of arms. This caused the populace to dread him, but the better class of artisans settled down to their business, thinking that it was very foolish of them, after lowering the pride of the nobles, to endure the foulness of the mob.

At the time when Michele obtained his victory over the mob a new signoria had already been elected, but among its members were two of such vile and low condition that the citizens determined not to endure such a disgrace. When the new signori entered upon their office on September 1, the Piazza happened to be full of soldiers, and a tumult arose as the late signori appeared outside the palace, and a great shout was raised that they would not have signori chosen from the lower class. Therefore the signori to satisfy them deprived the two men of whom we have spoken, Tira and Baroccio, of their seats, and chose in their places Messer Giorgio Scali and Francesco di Michele. The guilds of the lower classes were also abolished and their members were deprived of their offices, only Michele di Lando, Lodovico di Puccio, with some others of better quality being retained. The honours were divided, half going to the greater guilds and half to the lesser guilds. They decided that the signoria should consist of four members chosen from the greater guilds and five from the lesser ones, and that the gonfaloniere should be chosen first from one set of guilds and then from the other. This government secured some quietude for the city. But whilst the republic had been thus wrested from the hands of the lower classes, the artisan class had become far more powerful than the great traders. To this the latter yielded of necessity, in order that they might win over the lower classes from the lesser guilds by complying with their wishes. This was also the view of those who desired to keep under those men who as Guelfs had inflicted so many injuries upon the citizens. Among those who favoured this form of government was Messer Giorgio Scali, Messer Benedetto Alberti, Messer Salvestro de' Medici, and Messer Tommaso Strozzi, all of whom carried themselves like rulers in the city. The affairs of the city thus managed and ruled soon began to give rise to dissensions between the wealthy traders and the artisans, and these troubles were fostered by the rivalries of the Ricci and Albizzi. As from these dissensions there followed at sundry times the very gravest results, and as they will occur very often in our story, we shall call one the popular and the other the plebeian party. This form of government lasted three years and teemed with murders and banishments. For those who ruled lived in constant dread of the immense numbers of discontented people, both within and without the city. The malcontents within the walls were always attempting, or it was believed that they were, something against the rulers; whilst those who were outside, with no fears to restrain them, constantly raised trouble, first in one direction then in another, at one time through some neighbouring prince, at another through some republic.

There was residing at this time at Bologna Gianozzo da Salerno, one of the captains of Carlo di Durazzo, who belonged to the royal family of Naples and was at that time planning an attempt on the kingdom of Naples then under the rule of Queen Giovanna. This man had been admitted into Bologna with the assistance of Pope Urban, who was the Queen of Naples' enemy. There were also at Bologna many exiled Florentines who carried on secret designs with Gianozzo and Carlo. This caused great anxiety to those who ruled in Florence, and they lent a ready ear to all calumnies directed against those citizens whom they suspected. Whilst affairs stood thus, a conspiracy was revealed to the government of Florence by which Gianozzo di Salerno intended to appear with the exiles at the gates of Florence, and many citizens were to be ready to take up arms and deliver the city to him. As soon as this came to the knowledge of the government many citizens were arrested. The first to be seized were Piero degli Albizzi and Carlo Strozzi; then Cipriano Mangioni, Messer Jacopo Sachetti, Messer Donato Barbadori, Filippo Strozzi, and Giovanni Anselmi. All of whom, with the exception of Carlo Strozzi who fled, were thrown into prison. In order that none of the citizens should be tempted to take up arms on behalf of the prisoners, the signori deputed Messer Tommaso Strozzi and Messer Benedetto Alberti with armed forces to mount guard over the city. The prisoners were examined, but according to the evidence produced they did not appear to be guilty of the charges brought against them, so the captain would not condemn them. But their enemies so stirred up and provoked the people to rage against them that by their violence the death sentence was procured. Neither the nobility of his family, nor his great reputation, was able to save Piero degli Albizzi, although in his time he had been more feared and honoured than any other citizen. Once when Piero was giving a great banquet to a number of citizens, some one, perhaps a friend to suggest modesty to him in the midst of his greatness, perchance an enemy to threaten him with the mutability of fortune, sent him a silver cup filled with sweetmeats in which was hidden a nail. When this was discovered and shown to the guests, it was interpreted by them as a warning to Piero that he should fasten the wheel of fortune with a nail; for she had brought him to the very summit of her wheel, and if it were allowed to pursue its circle it must bring him to the bottom. This interpretation was verified, first in his ruin, then in his death.

After this execution the city remained in a very disturbed state, both conquered and conquerors being in dread of each other. But it was the apprehensions of the government which caused the most trouble, for upon the least accident happening they inflicted fresh injuries, by putting to death, admonishing, or driving into exile many citizens. To these penalites have to be added new laws and ordinances for consolidating the government, which inflicted fresh injustice upon all who in any way came under the suspicion of the ruling faction. To do this more completely, they appointed forty-nine commissioners, who, with the signori, were to purge the republic of all suspected persons. These men admonished thirty-nine citizens, and deprived many nobles of their rank, and raised many citizens to the rank of nobles. In order to deal better with their enemies outside the city, they took into their pay Sir John Hawkwood, an Englishman of great reputation as a soldier, who had done much fighting for the pope and others in Italy. The Florentines' dread of these outside enemies arose at this time from the fact that large companies of armed men had been engaged by Carlo di Durazzo for his enterprise against the kingdom of Naples, and among these forces were large numbers of Florentine exiles. The signori not only gathered their army together against these troubles but also provided themselves with large sums of money. When, therefore, Carlo reached Arezzo, the Florentines handed over to him 40,000 ducats and received from him his promise that he would not molest them. In his enterprise against the kingdom of Naples he was completely successful, and sent Queen Giovanna a prisoner into Hungary. This victory caused the greatest anxiety to the rulers of Florence, for they could not believe that their money would exercise the same influence over the mind of the king as would the ancient friendships which he held with the families connected with the Guelfs, upon whom they had recently inflicted so many injuries.

As these anxieties increased, so did the injuries, and these in their turn did not lessen the fears of the rulers, but added to them, until the greater number of the citizens were living in a state of terror. To such a pass had the insolence of Messer Giorgio Scali and Messer Tommaso Strozzi reached, their importance far exceeded that of the magistrates, and every one feared them owing to the support they received from the mob; the government appeared to be violent and tyrannical not only to the seditious, but also to the innocent citizen. But the insolence of Messer Giorgio had to be brought to an end at some time, and this happened when Giovanni di Cambio was charged by one of Giorgio's familiars with treason against the state, and was declared innocent by the captain. Then the judge determined to visit the accuser with the punishment which Giovanni would have suffered had he been found guilty, and Messer Giorgio was unable to save his associate either by his authority or his prayers. Therefore Messer Giorgio and Messer Tomassa Strozzi went with an armed mob and liberated the prisoner, and sacked the palace of the captain, who was compelled to hide in order to save himself. This act inspired the citizens with the greatest indignation against Messer Giorgio, so that his enemies hoped the time had now come when they might destroy him and deliver the city, not only out of his hands, but also out of the power of the plebeians, who had held it under their arrogant yoke for three years. This also gave the captain a great opportunity, for as soon as the tumult had subsided he went to the signori and said that he had willingly taken upon himself the office to which their lordships had elected him because he had believed that he would have to serve just men, who would take up arms to assist justice and not to hinder it. But having now proved by experience the spirit of the city, and its ways of government, he was ready to give back to them the dignity which, to acquire advantage and honour, he had accepted, but which had brought him danger and loss. The signori bade the captain take courage, and promised to recoup him for his recent losses, and to assure his safety in future. Some of the signori joined those citizens whom they considered lovers of their country and less suspected than others by the government, and came to the decision that the present was a good opportunity to get the city out of the power of Messer Giorgio and the plebeians, since this last act of violence had alienated the generality of the people from him. Therefore it appeared

wise for them to take advantage of these angry feelings before
they subsided, knowing that the favour of the multitude is lost and
gained by any little accident. They also knew that if they wished to
bring the affair to a successful issue they must draw Messer Benedetto Alberti into their schemes, because without his consent the
undertaking would be a very hazardous one.

Messer Benedetto was a very rich and courteous gentleman,
but an inflexible lover of his country, and as he had been greatly
saddened by the tyranny which prevailed it was easy to gain his
approval and consent to the destruction of Messer Giorgio. The
reasons which had aroused Messer Benedetto's hostility to the
wealthy merchants and the Guelf faction were their tyranny and
injustice, and now when he found that the plebeians were as bad
as the other party he ceased to act with them, and the injuries
which were inflicted by their leaders upon so many citizens were
entirely without his consent. Thus the reasons which made him
espouse the cause of the plebeians made him also abandon it. The
approval of Messer Benedetto being gained, as well as that of the
masters of the guilds, and arms being provided, Messer Giorgio
Scali was seized, but Messer Tommaso Strozzi fled. The next day
Messer Giorgio was beheaded, to the great dismay of his party,
none of whom dared to stir on his behalf, but on the contrary
strove with one another to witness his execution. When he learnt
that he had to die in the presence of the people who a short time
before had worshipped him, he complained bitterly of his cruel
fate and of the ingratitude of those citizens for whom he had committed so many unjust deeds, to do which he had courted the
favour of the multitude on whom no reliance could be placed.
Recognising Messer Benedetto Alberti among the armed men, he
said; "And thou, Messer Benedetto, art willing that this injustice
should be done to me, when I would not at any cost have allowed
it be done to thee? But I tell thee, this day which is the end of my
misery is the beginning of thine." He then reproached himself
with having trusted too much in the people, whom any voice, any

act, any suspicion will turn and corrupt. Thus grieving he died in the midst of his armed enemies who rejoiced at his death. Afterwards some of his intimate friends were killed and their bodies dragged through the streets by the mob.

The execution of this man threw the whole city into a turmoil, because to effect it many people had taken up arms to assist the signoria and the captain of the people, whilst others had armed themselves either to further their own ambitions or because of their fears. Thus the city was full of warring passions, each with its different aim, which each faction intended to realise before it laid down its arms. The ancient nobility, called grandees, could not rest under the deprivation of their privileges, and strove with every art to regain them, and for this reason were in favour of the restoration of authority to the captains of wards. The wealthy merchants and the greater guilds were discontented with having to share their authority with the lesser guilds and the lower classes. On the other hand the lesser guilds were striving to increase their power rather than permit it in any way to be decreased. And the lower classes dreaded to lose the colleges of their trades. These dissensions caused many disturbances in Florence during the following year. At one time it was the grandees who took up arms; at another it was the greater guilds; then the lesser ones, and with them the lower classes; thus fighting often took place in different parts of Florence simultaneously. Besides this fighting there was constant strife between the factions and the palace guards, because the government, at one time negotiating and at another fighting, were always using their best endeavours to put an end to the disturbances. In the end, after two conventions had met and several balia had been created to reform the city, and after the gravest injuries, troubles and dangers had been endured, a government was successfully formed by which all those who had been banished from their country were to be restored, and Messer Salvestro de' Medici was again made gonfaloniere. All the privileges and salaries which had been granted by the balia of 1378 were taken away. Honours were restored to the Guelf party. Two new guilds were dissolved and their members distributed among affiliated guilds. The lesser guilds were deprived of their rights in the election of the gonfaloniere of justice and their share in honours reduced from one-half to one-third, those honours taken from them being of the higher grade. Thus the wealthy merchants and the Guelf party resumed once more the government of Florence, and the plebeians, who had ruled the city from 1378 to 1381, lost it when these changes took place.

The government of the wealthy merchants did not weigh less heavily on the citizens, or afflict less injuries upon them at its commencement, than had the government of the plebeians. Many traders of high position who were known to be supporters of the plebeians were banished, and with them considerable numbers of plebeians. Among them was Michele di Lando, who was not to be saved even by the memory of the benefits which he had conferred on the city when the frenzied multitude would have destroyed it— proving how little grateful his country was for his good deeds. It is due to princes and republics falling into such errors that, fearing to experience ingratitude from their masters, men will scheme in self-defence to injure them before they themselves can be injured. These murders and banishments were as displeasing to Messer Benedetto Alberti as they had previously been in former years, and he condemned them both in private and public. Hence the chiefs of the government looked upon him with suspicion, believing him to be one of the prime supporters of the plebeians and a consenting party to the death of Messer Giorgio Scali, not because of a dislike to his methods, but because he wished to secure the government to himself. Messer Benedetto's words and actions rather gave colour to these fears, and the party in power watched him narrowly in order to find an opportunity to overthrow him.

Whilst the Florentines lived under these circumstances, no events of importance to them occurred outside their city, although there were some few incidents which caused them more anxiety than harm. About this time Louis of Anjou came into Italy in order to restore Queen Giovanna to the throne of Naples and drive out Carlo di Durazzo. His approach gave some anxiety to the Florentines because Carlo, after the manner of old friends, sought their assistance, whilst Louis, after the manner of those who seek new allies, demanded they should stand neutral. So the Florentines, to make a parade of pleasing Louis and satisfying Carlo, dismissed Sir John Hawkwood from their service, and were privy to his entering that of Pope Urban, who was a friend of Carlo. This deceit was easily seen through by Louis and brought much trouble to the Florentines. When the war between Louis and Durazzo was at its height in Apulia, a body of troops went to the assistance of Louis from France, and as they passed through Tuscany the Florentine exiles in Arezzo seized that town and drove out the party who held it for Carlo. But whilst these exiles were plotting against the government of Florence with the object of upsetting it as they had done that of Arezzo, Louis died, and the position of affairs in Tuscany and Apulia was at once changed. By this event Carlo secured his hold upon the kingdom of Naples, which he had nearly lost, and the Florentines, who had been in fear of losing their city, secured Arezzo by purchase from the men who were holding it for Louis. Carlo having thus settled his affairs in Apulia left there to take possession of the kingdom of Hungary, to which he had lately succeeded by inheritance. He left his wife behind him in Apulia, together with his children, Ladislao and Giovanna, both of them still young, as we have shown in another place. Carlo took possession of Hungary, but was shortly afterwards murdered.

The acquisition of Arezzo caused great rejoicings in Florence, such in fact as many cities would have indulged in after a victory, and the rejoicings by the republic and the private houses prevailed to such an extent that many private persons entertained in rivalry with the state banquets. But the family of Alberti surpassed all others in the pomp and magnificence of their feasts and tournaments, which were more worthy of the estate of a prince than that of a private citizen. This display increased the fear and suspicion with which the government already regarded Messer Benedetto, and was the cause of his ruin. Those who now ruled

Florence could not rest, for it seemed to them that Messer Benedetto could at any time resume his old authority and drive them from the city. Whilst the government was entertaining these anxieties it happened that Benedetto's son-in-law, Messer Filippo Megalotti, was drawn for gonfaloniere of justice, whilst Benedetto himself was gonfaloniere of the companies. This occurrence redoubled the fears of the government, for they perceived that it would greatly increase the power of Messer Benedetto, whilst it would bring fresh danger to themselves. They desired, however, to free themselves from this embarrassment without disturbance, and encouraged his relative and enemy, Bese Megalotti, to intimate to the signori that Messer Filippo, not being of an age when he could take upon himself the position of gonfaloniere, was therefore not in a position to hold it and ought not to be allowed to do so.

This indictment was examined by the signori, some of whom actuated by hatred, others merely to raise trouble, pronounced Messer Filippo ineligible for the position. In his place Bardo Mancini was drawn — a man entirely opposed to the plebeians and most hostile to Messer Benedetto. As soon as Bardo had taken up his office he appointed a balia, which in taking over and reorganising the government banished Messer Benedetto, and, with the exception of Messer Antonio, admonished the rest of the family. Before Messer Benedetto left the city he called his friends together and, finding them greatly moved with grief, he said to them: "You see, my fathers and elders, how fortune has ruined me, and how she threatens you. I do not marvel at this, neither should you, for it always happens thus to men who amidst bad men wish to do good, or who wish to uphold that which the many seek to destroy. Love for my country made me agree with Messer Salvestro de' Medici and afterwards disagree with Messer Giorgio Scali. This same sentiment causes me to loathe the conduct of those men who now rule us — men who, as they have met with none to chastise them, now wish to have none to reproach them. And I am content that my exile should free them from the fear which they have, not only of me, but of all who have a knowledge of their wicked and tyrannical measures. Thus in striking me down they are threatening many others. But this banishment will not trouble me, because those honours which a free country conferred on me cannot be taken away when she is in slavery; and the memory of my past life will always bring me more pleasure than my exile will bring me pain. It grieves me beyond measure to see my country in the hands of a few men, and a victim to their pride and rapacity. I am grieved also for you, because I have no doubt that those troubles which are ended for me to-day will commence for you in a far greater degree; having me no longer to persecute they will fall on you. Let me therefore encourage you to steel your hearts against every misfortune, and carry yourselves in such a way that if any adversity should overtake you, as it certainly will, all the world will recognise that you are innocent and that you do not suffer from your own faults." Afterwards he visited the Holy Sepulchre of Christ, thus making his reputation abroad in no degree less than in Florence. On his return he died at Rhodes, and his bones were carried to Florence, and were buried there with great honour by those men who had persecuted him with every outrage and calumny whilst he lived.

It was not alone the family of the Alberti who suffered during these troubles, but many other citizens were admonished and banished, among whom were Piero Benini, Matteo Aldarotti, Giovanni and Francesco del Bene, Giovanni Benci, Andrea Adimari, and a great number of small traders. Among those families who were warned were the Covoni, Benini, Rinucci, Formiconi, Corbizzi, Manelli, and Aldarotti. It was the custom to create the balia for a certain period, but some citizens had from honest motives been in the habit of retiring when they had carried out the objects for which they were elected, although the period for which the balia was created had not expired. It appearing to the members of the balia then sitting that they had accomplished what they were elected for, they wished to retire according to the custom. But when this became known crowds ran armed to the palace and demanded that more citizens should be warned and banished.

This greatly displeased the signori, but until they had strengthened themselves they entertained the mob with promises; when, however, their forces had arrived they threatened the mob, and compelled them to lay down the arms which they had taken up with such fury. Nevertheless, in some degree to satisfy this rabid humour, and still further reduce the power of the lower class of artisans, it was provided that, whereas the plebeians had formerly had one-third share in the offices, they should now only have one-fourth. In order that the signori should always have among them two men whom the government could trust, the gonfaloniere of justice, with four other citizens, was authorised to make a ballot from which two members for every signoria should be drawn.

Thus was the government of the city finally settled after its first institution in 1381, and remained fairly tranquil until 1393, During this time Giovanni Galeazzo Visconti, called the Count of Virtu, threw his uncle Bernabo into prison and claimed the whole of Lombardy. This nobleman believed that he was strong enough to become King of Italy as easily as by treachery he had become Duke of Milan. So in 1390 he commenced war vigorously against the Florentines, the course of which varied to such an extent that at one time the duke was in great peril and at another time the Florentines were near total defeat. Nevertheless the defence of the Florentines was wonderfully courageous for a republic, and they were more fortunate in its conclusion than they had been in its progress, because after the duke had captured Bologna, Pisa, Perugia, and Siena, and had even prepared the crown with which he was to be crowned in Florence, he died. Thus death did not permit him to taste the fruits of victory, nor the Florentines to endure the stings of defeat.

During this war against the duke, Messer Maso degli Albizzi, whom the death of Piero had made an enemy to the Alberti, was created gonfaloniere of justice. And as party spirit still ran very high, Messer Maso determined to be revenged upon the Alberti family before he went out of office, in spite of the fact that Messer Benedetto degli Alberti had died in exile. The opportunity for this arose when a man, who was being examined concerning certain communications which had been made to the rebels, implicated Alberto and Andrea degli Alberti. These gentlemen were at once seized and thrown into prison. Whereupon the city became greatly excited; the signori took up arms and called the people to a conference. A balia was created, and by its means many citizens were banished and a new ballot for offices was made. All the Alberti were exiled and many citizens were put to death and others were admonished. The guilds of the lower classes, afflicted by these many injuries, immediately took up arms, fearing to be robbed not only of honours but also of life. One part of the men assembled in the Piazza, whilst the other ran to the house of Messer Veri de' Medici, who after the death of Messer Salvestro had become the head of the family. In order to pacify those who reached the Piazza, the signori sent Messer Rinaldo Gianfigliazzi and Messer Donato Acciajuoli to them as leaders, and as men who possessed the confidence of the plebeians. With them went the banners of the Guelf party. Those who went to the house of Messer Veri begged him to seize the government and liberate the people from the oppression of those citizens who were destroying the commonwealth and all good men.

According to the writers who have left us memorials of those times, it appears that if Messer Veri had been as ambitious as he was virtuous, he would have become the chief man in the city without any difficulty, because the heavy wrongs which, rightly or wrongly, the artisans and their friends had suffered had so inflamed their minds with revenge that if they could have found a leader they would not have failed to satisfy their craving. Nor did Messer Veri fail to have suggested to him what he could accomplish, for Antonio de' Medici, who had long borne Messer Veri a bitter hatred, would have persuaded him to assume the leadership of the republic. To him Messer Veri replied: "As your menaces gave me no anxiety when you were my enemy, so your counsels shall do me no harm now that you are my friend." He turned to the multitude and bade them be of good courage, and he would defend them if they would permit him to give them some advice. Passing through the midst of them he led the way to the Piazza, and from thence ascended into the presence of the signori sitting in the palace. To them he said that he could not in any way regret having so lived among the people of Florence that they should love him as they did, but it grieved him much that they should entertain an opinion of him which nothing in his past life had shown him to deserve. He had never set an example of restlessness or ambition, and he could not conceive where the idea had originated that he was the author of this trouble or ambitious to seize the government. He would therefore pray their lordships not to impute the ignorance of the multitude to him as a sin, because from the first, and to his utmost, he had always submitted himself to their authority. He warned them to use their good fortune in moderation, because it was better to enjoy the fruits of a moderate victory, with safety to the city, than to bring about its entire ruin. The signori commended Messer Veri, and begged him to persuade the mob to lay down its arms, after which they would not fail to do what he and other citizens counselled. With these words Messer Veri returned to the Piazza, and his following having been joined by that of Messer Rinaldo and Messer Donato, he addressed them, saying that he had found the signori very favourably disposed towards them, that many things had been suggested, but nothing was concluded owing to the lateness of the hour and the necessity of obtaining the consent of the magistrates. He therefore begged them to lay down their arms and render obedience to the signori, and pledged his word that gentleness rather than arrogance, prayers rather than threats, would influence the signori, that neither their interests nor safety should be overlooked if they would allow themselves to be guided by him. Under this assurance the multitude dispersed, and every one went to his own house.

The signori having secured the laying down of arms at once proceeded to fortify the Piazza, after which they enlisted 2000 trusty citizens and enrolled them under banners to which they were ordered to rally whenever they might be called upon to assist the signori. All other citizens were prohibited from carrying arms. Having completed these precautions they banished or put to death many of those artisans who had been prominent in the recent disturbances. With a view to securing more dignity and reverence for the position of gonfaloniere of justice, it was ordained that all who should be elected to the office should not be less than forty-five years of age. In their endeavours to strengthen the government they made many provisions which were not only extremely burdensome to their opponents, but even obnoxious to many good citizens of their own party. No one should consider a government either good or secure which requires violence to support it. Not only did this violence aggrieve those members of the Alberti who remained in the city, and the Medici who reproached themselves for the deception practised on the people, but many other citizens. The first man who made any attempt to overthrow it was Messer Donato, son of Jacopo Acciajuoli. This nobleman held a great position in the city, and was considered the superior rather than the equal of Messer Maso degli Albizzi, and because of his fine conduct when gonfaloniere of justice he was looked up to as the head of the republic. He could not rest contentedly in the midst of so much misery, nor would he turn, as so many would have done, public troubles to his own private advantage. He therefore made a resolution to restore the exiles to their country, or at least to restore the ammoniti to their rightful honours. To accomplish this, Donato went about the city pouring into men's ears his opinions, and saying that it was impossible to dissipate party spirit or pacify the citizens by any other method. Neither would he wait until his election to the signoria to carry his plans into effect. And as in our own affairs procrastination breeds indifference, whilst haste brings danger, so Donato determined to face the danger rather than incur the indifference. Among the signori was his relative, Messer Michele Acciajuoli, and his friend, Nicolo Ricoveri, and this appeared to Messer Donato to afford an opportunity which ought not to be lost. He therefore begged these gentlemen to introduce an ordinance into the council permitting the restoration of the exiles. Persuaded by Messer Donato these gentlemen spoke to then colleagues, who replied that it was not their duty to propose new measures of which the benefits were doubtful and the dangers certain. Whereupon Messer Donato, having failed in this attempt, angrily let his friends understand that, having rejected his plan for setting the city at rest, it should be accomplished by force of arms. This speech so much displeased his friends that the matter was communicated to the heads of the government, and Messer Donato was cited to appear before them. This he did and, being convicted upon the testimony of those to whom he had stated his intention, was banished to Barletta. Messer Alamanno and Antonio de' Medici were also banished with all the family of Messer Alamanno, together with many small traders who had sympathy with the plebeians. These events occurred two years after Messer Maso had taken over the government.

Whilst affairs in Florence remained in this position, with malcontents within and exiles without, there were among the exiles at Bologna Picchio Cavicciuli, Tomasso de' Ricci, Antonio de' Medici, Benedetto degli Spini, Antonio Girolami, Christofano di Carlone, and two others of humbler class, but all young and bold and ready to risk their lives in the hope of regaining their country. These men were secretly urged on by Piggiello and Baroccio Cavicciulli, who were living in Florence under an admonition, and encouraged that if they would come into the city they would be secreted there. This would give them the opportunity of killing Messer Maso degli Albizzi and calling the people to arms. The citizens, who were very discontented, were sure to rise, especially when they learnt that the Ricci, Adimari, Medici, Manelli, and many others would assist them. Moved by these hopes the conspirators entered Florence secretly on August 4, 1397, as had been arranged, and were sent out to watch for Messer Maso, with the intention of starting the tumult with his death. Messer Maso had, however, left his house and gone to an apothecary's near to San Pietro Maggiore. The man who had been told off to watch for him ran at once to inform the conspirators, who, seizing their arms, went in search of him, but they found that he had left. Whereupon, fearing nothing, they turned towards the Mercato Vecchio, where they killed one of the opposite party. Raising a great cry of "People! to arms, liberty, death to the tyrant!" they moved towards the Mercato Nuovo, where they slew another man at the end of the Via Calimala. Pursuing their way with the same cry, and no one joining them with arms, they turned back to the Loggia della Nighittosa. Here they took up an elevated position with a great multitude around them, and shouted to the men to join them and put an end to the slavery for which they had such a hatred. They told the crowd that it was the complaints of the malcontents in the city, rather than their own injuries, which had inspired them with the desire to liberate them, and that they knew that many citizens had prayed God for the opportunity of revenge which would come whenever they had leaders. Now the chance had come, and here were leaders ready to lead them and protect them, yet they stood like fools until those who wished to liberate them would be killed and their slavery aggravated. Was it not marvellous that, whilst they were ready enough to take up arms for trifling injuries, they would not stir to remedy greater wrongs; and were they able to endure that so many of their citizens should be driven into exile and so many deprived of their rights by the admonitions. All this was very true, but it did not move the multitude in the least, either because of fear or because the death of the two men had rendered their murderers hateful. The authors of the tumult found that neither deeds nor words had power to stir any one to revolt, and slowly it dawned upon them that it is a dangerous enterprise to attempt to offer liberty to a people who prefer to remain in bondage. The conspirators now despaired of their enterprise and retreated to the Church of San Reparata, where they shut themselves up, not to save their lives, but to defer their deaths. The signori were much disturbed at the first reports and armed and fortified the palace, but when afterwards they learnt how matters stood, who were the authors of the trouble, and where they were shut up, they were reassured. They ordered the captain to proceed against them with a body of armed men and make them prisoners. Without much trouble the doors of the church were burst open, and those who defended themselves were killed, whilst those who surrendered were taken prisoners. Upon being examined it was found that they alone, with Baroccio and Piggiello Cavicciulli, were guilty, and all were executed.

After this incident there followed another of graver significance. It will be remembered that during these times the city had been at war with the Duke of Milan, and that he having failed to conquer by force of arms had now recourse to conspiracy. With the assistance of the exiled Florentines, of whom Lombardy was full, the duke devised a project, to which many citizens were privy, that on a certain day a large party of exiles, properly armed, should be gathered from places round Florence, and should enter the city by means of the river Arno. These men, with their friends inside, were to meet at the various houses of the members of the government, and having killed them to reform the government according to their wishes. Among the conspirators within the city was one of the Ricci family, named Samminiato, who, seeking to enlist a confederate, found a traitor, for it often happens that conspiracies which cannot be carried through by a few men are divulged when the conspirators are many. This Ricci spoke of the plan to Salvestro Cavicciulli, whose fidelity should have been ensured by the wrongs suffered by his family and himself; but he, thinking more of present dangers than of future hopes, revealed the affair to the signori, who at once seized Samminiato, and forced him to disclose the whole conspiracy. None of the participators in it were taken excepting Tommaso Davizi, who entered Florence from Bologna without learning what had happened, and was seized as soon as he arrived; all the others fled—alarmed by the seizure of Samminiato. He and Davizi having been punished according to their misdeeds, a balia was created, and under its authority all delinquents were searched for and the government safe-guarded. The signori outlawed six of the Alberti and six of the Ricci, two of the Medici, three of the Scali, two of the Strozzi,

Bindo Altoviti, Bernardo Adimari, with many of the lower classes. They also admonished all except a few members of the families of the Alberti, Ricci, and Medici for ten years. Messer Antonio Alberti was not warned, he being considered an inoffensive and peaceful man, but it happened that, before the anxieties of this conspiracy were forgotten, a monk was seized who had been frequently seen passing between Bologna and Florence whilst the plot was being hatched. He confessed that he had often taken letters to Messer Antonio Alberti. Messer Antonio was at once thrown into prison, and although he stedfastly denied the charge, he was convicted on the evidence of the monk and fined a large sum of money, as well as banished to a distance of more than three hundred miles from the city. Inasmuch as the Alberti family were seen to be a constant source of danger to the government, all over the age of fifteen years were banished.

These events happened in 1400, and two years later the death of Giovanni Galeazzo, the Duke of Milan, brought to a close the war which, as we have seen, had lasted twelve years. At this time the government of the city was extremely powerful, and having no enemies either inside or outside, undertook operations against Pisa, in which it was gloriously successful. Florence remained at peace from this time until 1433, excepting in the year 1412 when, the Alberti disregarding their sentences of banishment, a new balia was created, which reinforced the government and prosecuted them with fines. During this time the Florentines also made war against Ladislao, the King of Naples, who, being proved the weaker, was compelled to yield the city of Cortona, of which he was lord, to the Florentines. Shortly afterwards, however, he gathered fresh forces together and renewed the war. The Florentines were often in the greatest danger, and had not the war been stopped by the death of the King of Naples, as the previous one had been stopped by the death of the Duke of Milan, Florence would have incurred the peril of losing her liberties, as she had done in the case of the duke. Neither was this war with the king finished at a less fortunate time than the previous one, because it came to an end just as the king had captured Rome, Siena, and all the Marca and Romagna. It only needed the possession of Florence to enable him to concentrate his whole power against Lombardy when he died. Thus death once more was more gracious to Florence than any friend, and more powerful to save her than even her own valour. After the death of the King of Naples, Florence remained at rest both within and without its walls for about eight years, at the end of which time the party spirit was renewed over the question of war against Filippo, Duke of Milan. These dissensions did not end until the destruction of the government, which had ruled the city from the year 1371 until 1434, and which had carried on so many wars, conquered Arezzo, Pisa, Cortona, Livorno, and Monte Pulciano. Still greater renown would Florence have achieved if she had remained united and had not allowed those ancient strifes to be rekindled, as in the following book will particularly be shown.

FOURTH BOOK

1414-1434

CITIES which are administered under a republican form of government, especially those in which the constitution has not been wisely framed, frequently change their government and their rulers, not on the score of liberty and slavery, as so many believe, but on the score of slavery and unbridled licence. For it is only the name of liberty which is honoured, because when rulers are of the trader class the government inclines to anarchy, and when they are of the nobility it inclines to severity; and neither of these classes will submit itself readily to either authority or law. It is true that, when by rare good fortune, a wise, honest, and powerful man does come to the front in a city, and institutes laws to keep in subjection the party spirit which prevails between nobles and traders, or restrains it so that but little evil results, that city may then be considered free and its government well-founded and strong; because being founded on good laws and ordinances it does not require the abilities of one man to sustain it, as other cities need. With such laws and ordinances many ancient republics were endowed, especially those which were long-lived. But where such laws and ordinances are entirely wanting, states have frequently changed from one government to another, from the tyrannical to the licentious. In such states all parties have very powerful enemies, and consequently there neither is, nor can be, any stability. For the one form of government will not please good men, and the other will not please the wise ones. Under one form evil can be done with ease, whilst under the other only good with difficulty. Under one the insolent will have too much authority, and under the other the foolish. And either forms may have to be sustained by the ability and good fortune of one man, who may become ineffective by misfortune or carried off by death.

I have already stated that the government which took its rise on the death of Messer Giorgio Scali in 1381 was founded by the valour of Messer Maso degli Albizzi, and was continued afterwards by that of Nicolo da Uzzano, and the city existed very tranquilly from 1414 to 1422. King Ladislao was dead, and Lombardy was much divided, so that neither within the city nor without was there any cause for anxiety. Following Nicolo da Uzzano, the citizens of most authority were Bartolommeo Valori, Nerone di Nigi, Messer Rinaldo degli Albizzi, Neri di Gino and Lapo Nicolini. The feuds which existed between the Albizzi and the Ricci had never been quite extinguished, and were afterwards revived by Messer Salvestro de' Medici to the great disturbance of the city. Although the Ricci faction only ruled for three years until 1381, when it was overthrown, yet it was popular with the mob, and the greater part of the citizens, understanding its aims, would not allow it to be entirely exterminated. It is true that the frequent conventions and the continual persecutions carried on against the heads of the faction between the years 1381 and 1400 had reduced it almost to impotency. The principal families of those persecuted were the Ricci, Alberti, and Medici, who suffered great loss of life and property, whilst those members who did remain in the city were deprived of their rights. Thus continual punishments brought the party to a very low ebb, indeed almost destroyed it. Nevertheless the memory of these wrongs, and the desire for revenge, lay hidden in the breasts of many men, waiting for an opportunity to show themselves. The wealthy traders who governed the city peacefully during these years made two mistakes which brought their government to ruin. One was that they became arrogant with their long continued power; and the other was the jealousy with which they regarded each other. Besides this, with their long possession of power, they ceased to watch with the care which ought to have been exercised those men who could injure them. The result of this was that the hatred of the people revived against them and their sinister methods of governing, and the rulers no longer fearing any trouble ceased to be watchful for it, whilst the jealousy that reigned among them enabled the Medici family to regain its old authority. The first member of this family to come to the front was Giovanni, the son of Bicci de' Medici. This gentleman had grown very rich, and being of a pleasant and kindly disposition had been admitted to the supreme magistracy, owing entirely to the complacency of the ruling party. The multitude believed that in Giovanni it had found a protector, and its elation caused some natural misgivings among the more far-seeing of the rulers, for it seemed to them likely to arouse the old strifes. Among these men was Nicolo da Uzzano, who missed no opportunity of impressing his views upon his colleagues. He pointed out to them the danger of tolerating one who was in such great repute with the majority of the citizens, and that it was easy to deal with such a trouble at its commencement, but difficult after it had been allowed to grow. He also said that he knew that Giovanni was of greater ability than ever Messer Salvestro had been. Nicolo was not listened to because of the jealousy in which some of his colleagues held his reputation, and they watched for a confederate to assist in pulling him down.

Whilst the people of Florence were occupied with these reviving feuds, Filippo Visconti, the second son of Gian Galeazzo, had succeeded to the lordship of the whole of Lombardy on the death of his brother. Believing himself to be strong enough for the enterprise, he entertained an idea of making himself master of Genoa, which at that time was living in freedom under its doge, Messer Tommaso da Campo Fregoso. But Filippo was somewhat doubtful if he could carry that, or indeed any other enterprise, to a successful issue unless he could announce a new agreement with the Florentines, the prestige of which would enable him to attain his wishes. He therefore sent his envoys to Florence to negotiate a treaty. Many citizens were of opinion that it should not be entered into, as they were persuaded that the peace which they had enjoyed for so many years could only be maintained by avoiding it. They recognised that whilst the treaty would be of the utmost advantage to Filippo, it would be of little assistance to their city. To other citizens it appeared the wiser course to enter into an agreement with Filippo, because if he should break it all the world would be convinced of his evil intentions, and then a war against him would be justifiable. Thus the affair was hotly disputed, but in the end a treaty was entered into, by which Filippo undertook not to interfere with anything on this side of the rivers Magra and Panaro.

Having made this treaty, Filippo seized Brescia, and shortly afterwards Genoa. All this was very contrary to the expectations of those people in Florence who had advocated the treaty, for they expected that the Venetians would have defended Brescia and that Genoa would have been able to defend herself. Inasmuch as in the compact between Filippo and the Doge of Genoa it was agreed that Serezana and other towns on this bank of the Magra should be surrendered to the Genoese if at any time Filippo desired to part with them, it followed that he had broken his treaty with Florence. In addition to this, Filippo had entered into an agreement with the legate of Bologna. All this caused our citizens to alter their minds, and to cast about for new expedients to meet impending troubles. When the knowledge of these anxieties reached the ears of Filippo he sent ambassadors to Florence to justify his proceedings, and to sound the minds of the Florentines, as well as to soothe them. The ambassadors expressed Filippo's surprise at their suspicions of him, and offered to forego anything that had caused them anxiety; but these declarations had no other effect on the citizens than to divide them into parties. One party, and that the most respectable one in the government, considered that they had better arm themselves and be prepared for hostile action, because if these preparations were made, Filippo would hesitate to declare war and peace would be preserved. Other citizens, either out of dislike to the government or from fear of war, urged that they should not lightly throw suspicions upon a friend, and that Filippo had done nothing to occasion alarm, but every one knew that to summon a council of ten, and enlist soldiers, would lead to war, and that such a war, against so great a prince, would not alone bring no advantage, but would involve the city in certain ruin. Besides which Florence could not keep possession of any territory she might conquer, seeing that Romagna intervened, and they dare not look at Romagna because of its close neighbourhood to the Church. Nevertheless the city listened more to those who advocated preparation for war than to those who spoke for peace. Therefore the council of ten was appointed, soldiers were enlisted, and new taxes imposed, and as this taxation fell more heavily upon the poor than upon the rich, the city was filled with complaints. The rulers were cursed for their ambition and rapacity, and were charged with oppressing the people in order that they might indulge their appetite for dominion and provoke a war which was not necessary.

Although the Florentines had not come to an open rupture with the duke he was greatly distrusted, owing to his having acceded to the request of the legate of Bologna to send troops to protect him against Messer Antonio Bentivogli. Messer Antonio had been driven out of Bologna, and had established himself in one of the Bolognese castles; and this castle, being adjacent to Florentine territory, had caused considerable uneasiness to the state. But what caused the greatest anxiety, and was largely the cause of the war, was the enterprise of the duke against Furli, Giorgio Ordelaffi, the lord of Furli, was dead and had left his son, Tibaldo, in the care of duke Filippo. But as the mother suspected the guardian, she sent the boy to Lodovico Alidossi, her father, who was lord of Imola. Nevertheless the people of Furli compelled her to observe the will of the father of the boy, and to hand him over to the care of the duke. Whereupon Filippo, to divert suspicion from himself, and thus conceal his intentions the better, ordered the Marquis of Ferrara to send Guido Torello, as his procurator, with

troops to take over the government of Furli. The town of Furli
thus fell into the hands of the duke. When this news, coupled with
that of the despatch of troops to Bologna, became known in
Florence, the urgent need for war was more apparent. Notwithstanding, there was still considerable opposition to it, and Messer
Giovanni Medici publicly discouraged it. He pointed out that,
although the evil intentions of the duke were now clear, it would
be wiser to await his attack rather than first attack him; because in
the latter case war would appear far more justifiable in the sight of
the princes of Italy on the part of the duke than on theirs. Whilst,
should the duke attack them, he could not then seek allies with
the same confidence which he would otherwise be able to show,
for his ambition would be unmasked. Neither would the Florentines defend the possessions of others with the same courage and
determination they would their own. By others it was urged that
victory was not to be won by awaiting their enemies at home, but by
going out to meet them, and that fortune is more friendly to him
who attacks than to him who defends. And that although the cost
may be heavier when war is waged in the territories of others, there
is less destruction than when it is made in one's own. This opinion
finally prevailed, and the Ten were authorised to use all the means
in their power to rescue Furli from the hands of the duke.

When Filippo saw the Florentines were determined to capture
those places which he had undertaken to defend, he put on one
side all considerations and sent Agnolo della Pergola with large
forces to Imola to prevent the lord of Imola from assisting his grandson at Furli by forcing him to devote himself to his own defence.
Whilst the Florentine army lay at Modigliana, Agnolo approached
Imola, where he found the moat frozen over owing to the intense
cold, and by stealth he seized the town and sent Lodovico a prisoner to Milan. The Florentines sent their army against Furli and
closely besieged it as soon as they heard that war had commenced
and that Imola was taken. With a view to prevent the forces of the
duke from concentrating for the relief of Furli, the Florentines
took the Count Alberigo into their pay, in order that from his town

of Zaganora he should harass the country even up to the gates of Imola, and this he did. Agnolo della Pergola, finding that he could not operate effectively against our men at Furli owing to the strong positions which they occupied, decided therefore to attack Zaganora. He was convinced that the Florentines would not permit the loss of this place, but would endeavour to succour it, and to do this would abandon the the siege of Furli, and be brought to battle in some situation of disadvantage to themselves. The army of the duke forced Alberigo to come to terms, which were granted, with the stipulation that the town should be surrendered within fifteen days unless it was relieved by the Florentines. When the news of this untoward event reached the city and the camp, the Florentines declared that the enemy should not have the town. This decision, however, resulted in Agnolo gaining a far greater victory, for the Florentines at once broke up their camp and marched to the relief of Zaganora. They were encountered on the way by the enemy and utterly routed, not so much by the valour of their adversaries as by the inclemency of the weather, because our men had marched several hours in soaking rain through deep mud, and had to fight against an unwearied enemy, who easily gained the victory. Nevertheless in this great defeat, which was famous through all Italy, none were killed excepting Lodovico degli Obizi, and he with two of his men was thrown from his horse and suffocated in the mud.

When the news of this defeat was brought to Florence the citizens were greatly depressed, especially those who had advocated the war, for they saw their enemy triumphant, their army defeated, and their country without allies. Moreover their people were against them, and followed them through the streets with insults and cursings against the oppressive taxes, saying that the war was declared without any just cause. The burden of their cry was: "Was it to strike terror into the enemy that the Ten were appointed? Have they relieved Furli or recovered it from the hands of the duke? No! Their intentions are now laid bare, and the end for which they worked is known. It was not to defend our liberty, for they regard that as their enemy. It was to swell their own power, and in this God has justly brought them to nought. This is not the only enterprise with which they have afflicted the city, there were many others, the war against King Ladislao being as bad. To whom could they go for help? To Pope Martin, whom they outraged out of consideration for Braccio? To Queen Giovanna, whom they abandoned, and forced into the arms of the King of Aragon?" Many other things were said such as might be expected from an angry people. Therefore it occurred to the signori to call together some of the citizens, who with reasonable words might attempt to soothe the feelings of the multitude. Whereupon Messer Rinaldo degli Albizzi, the eldest son of Messer Maso, who, encouraged by the memory of his father and his own abilities, aspired to a leading position in the city, addressed the people at length. He pointed out to them that it was not always wise to judge by results, because it may happen that well considered plans fail, whilst bad ones succeed. And if badly laid plans are to be praised because of their successful issue, men will inevitably be encouraged to act carelessly. This would result in grave injury to the commonwealth, because ill considered plans are not often successful. For the same reason it would be wrong to condemn a wise decision because it was not crowned with success. If this were done citizens would no longer have the courage to advise the city or to speak freely. He then passed on to the war, and proved that it was necessary to conduct it as they had done, for it would assuredly have come into Tuscany had it not been waged in Romagna. Although God had willed that their army should be defeated, yet the loss would become far heavier if they were now to abandon the war. Let them show a bold front to fortune, and put into force those remedies which still remained in their hands, then they would neither think so seriously of their defeat nor would the duke esteem his victory so highly. They ought to have no anxiety as to future charges and taxes, for they might expect these to change and to be far lighter in the future, because less provision is needed for defence than for attack. Finally he encouraged them to imitate their fathers, who had never lost their courage in spite of any adverse circumstances they may have encountered or the princes by whom they may have been attacked. Influenced by the courage of Messer Rinaldo, the citizens enlisted Count Oddo, the son of Braccio, and appointed Nicolo Piccinino his lieutenant. Nicolo had been a pupil of Braccio, and was one of the most distinguished men who had ever fought under his flag. To them the citizens added other condottieri, and remounted such of their cavalry as had lost their horses. Twenty citizens were appointed to levy new taxes, and when it was seen that the ruling citizens were depressed by the recent defeat, the Twenty taxed them heavily without any respect to their position.

This taxation gave great offence to the rich citizens, and although they did not complain at once lest their patriotism should be called in question, they condemned the principle of it, and debated among themselves how they could obtain relief. This came to the knowledge of the citizens and was defeated by them in the council. Thereupon the council instructed the tax-gatherers to insist upon payment with severity, in order that the burden of it should be felt and that it should become odious, and authority was given to the tax-gatherers to kill all who should oppose their officers. Many grievous events followed this order, owing to the wounding and death of several citizens. It appeared as if the factions must come to bloodshed, and everybody expected that great trouble would result, for the great citizens who had been accustomed to be revered could not endure being ill-used, whilst the other party desired that all citizens should be equally taxed. Therefore many of the foremost citizens assembled together and resolved that it was necessary to recover their authority, acknowledging that their own indifference had encouraged men to question official decisions, and had emboldened those who were always ready to head the mob. Having discussed the position of affairs many times, they decided to meet once more and come to some resolution, therefore more than seventy of them met in the Church of San Stefano with the consent of Messer Lorenzo Ridolfi and Francesco Gianfigliazzi, who were sitting at that time as signori. Giovanni de' Medici did not attend the meeting, either because the others were suspicious of him and did not ask him, or because, not being in sympathy with the objects of the meeting, he refused to attend.

Messer Rinaldo degli Albizzi addressed the meeting. He described the condition of affairs, how by their own negligence the city had drifted into the hands of the plebeians, and how it had before been recovered by their fathers in 1381. He recalled to their memory that iniquitous government which had ruled from 1377 to 1381; all those who were present had fathers or grandfathers who had suffered death under it, and the same perils would recur if such a government were to return to power. Already the mob had imposed such taxes as best suited it, and soon would be creating magistrates in its own interests, if it were not stopped by force or law. When this should happen the mob would take their place, and the government which for forty-two years had ruled the city with so much glory would be destroyed. Then Florence would either be governed by the will of a licentious mob or another danger would arise — a government under the dominion of one man, who would be made a prince over them. Therefore he declared that every man who loved his country and his own honour was bound to rise; he recalled to their memory the valour of Bardo Mancini, who rescued the city from its dangers by the destruction of the Alberti. The perils which were now imminent were caused by the wide franchises, which emboldened the multitude to fill the palace with contemptible and unknown persons, and this again was caused by their own negligence. He concluded by saying that the only plan he could see to remedy this was to restore the government to the grandees, take away all power from the smaller guilds, and reduce their number from fourteen to seven. This would give the plebeians less power in the council by the decrease in their number, and at the same time increase the authority of the grandees, who owing to their ancient hostility to the plebeians might be relied upon to thwart them. He declared that it was true wisdom to use men according to the circumstances of the time; and seeing that their fathers knew well how to use the plebeians to destroy the grandees, now that the grandees were humbled and the plebeians had grown insolent, it would be wise to curb the insolence of the plebeians by the aid of the grandees. As to the means by which to effect this, force or stratagem was needed, and either could be used, seeing that some among them were members of the Ten and able to bring men secretly into the city. Everybody present approved the advice of Messer Rinaldo, and he was much praised for it. Nicolo da Uzzano, among others, said that everything which Messer Rinaldo had said was true, and his remedies good and sure, if they could be carried into effect without dividing the city, but this could only be done by bringing Messer Giovanni de' Medici into their plans. When they had secured him, the populace, deprived of its leader, would lose much of its power to do harm. But should this not be accomplished, then they would be unable to effect their desires without arms, and recourse to arms he believed to be dangerous, either by failure to win or ability to enjoy the fruits of victory. He modestly brought to their recollection his past warnings, and their failure to deal with these troubles when it would have been easy to do so. But now that time had passed, and it could only be done at great hazard; there remained indeed no other recourse but to gain over Messer Giovanni. Accordingly Messer Rinaldo was commissioned to see Giovanni and induce him to join them.

The knight carried out his commission, and in the best possible terms pressed Messer Giovanni to join them in their undertaking, and not assist the populace in becoming more grasping, and thus destroy both the government and the city. To this Giovanni replied that he considered it to be the duty of a good and prudent citizen not to change the accustomed ordinances of his city; that nothing injures so much as frequent changes, because such changes must offend many, and where many are discontented some evil occurrence may be expected any day. Their resolution appeared to him to entail most disastrous results, inasmuch as it conferred privileges upon persons who, never having enjoyed them, would value them but lightly, whilst it would deprive many of honours which they had been accustomed to enjoy, and who would never rest until they had regained them. Thus the injury done to one party would be far greater than any benefit conferred on the other, and the authors of the change would gain but few friends, yet many enemies. Moreover, whilst the enemies would be bold to attack, the friends would be slow to defend, because men are by nature more ready to revenge wrongs that to recognise benefits, seeing that the loss will prove greater to those who lose than the advantages to those who gain. Messer Giovanni then addressed himself specially to Messer Rinaldo and said: "Had you well considered what will follow this action of yours, and amid what snares one walks in this city, you would not be so eager for this proposal. The party who advocates it has destroyed the power of the people with your assistance, and it will now use the people to destroy you; you whose former deeds have made them your enemy. And it will happen to you as it did to Messer Benedetto Alberti, who was persuaded by those who had no reason to love him to consent to the ruin of Messer Giorgio Scali and Tommaso Strozzi, and was himself sent into exile by those very men to whose persuasions he had listened." Giovanni therefore urged Messer Rinaldo to reconsider his decision and rather imitate his father, who, in order to earn the goodwill of the people, reduced the price of salt, proposed that all whose taxes amounted to less than half a florin should be allowed to pay them or not as they wished, and that on such days as the council met all persons should be secure from their creditors. Giovanni finally said that, as far as he was concerned, he advocated leaving the city to enjoy its present ordinances.

When this discussion became known outside it increased the reputation of Giovanni, but brought much odium to the other party. Giovanni separated himself entirely from them in order to discourage them from attempting any schemes under his patronage. He let every one with whom he spoke know that he was not one to encourage faction, but to discourage it, and that nothing need be expected from him but what would tend to the union of the city. Many of his followers were much discontented with this declaration, as they would have preferred his taking a more active part in affairs. Among these was Alamanno de' Medici, who, being by nature bold, never ceased urging Giovanni to favour friends and persecute enemies, condemning his indifference and slow methods of proceeding, which Alamanno said were the reasons why Giovanni's enemies did not hesitate to plot against him. His son, Cosimo, was also animated with the same feelings. Nevertheless Giovanni was not to be moved from his resolution by anything that had either happened or been threatened. There were at this time in the palace two secretaries to the signori, named Ser Martino and Ser Pagolo, one of whom favoured the party of Uzzano and the other that of the Medici. When Messer Rinaldo became convinced that Giovanni did not intend to join him, he determined to turn Ser Martino out of office, with the object of putting someone into his place more favourable to himself. This intention of Messer Rinaldo came in due course to the ears of his opponents, and not only was Ser Martino secured in his office but Ser Pagolo was deprived of his, to the great displeasure of his friends. This action would have been followed by dire effects had not the city been occupied by the war and thoroughly alarmed by the recent defeat at Zaganora. Whilst these affairs were occurring in Florence, Agnolo della Pergola, with the army of Duke Filippo, had captured all the towns of Romagna possessed by the Florentines except Castrocaro and Modigliana. The capture of the towns was partly due to their defenceless condition and partly to the treachery of their garrisons. In these sieges there occurred two instances which prove that bravery is much appreciated by men, although it may be displayed by an enemy, and cowardice and treachery are despised.

Biagio del Melano was the governor of the fortress of Monte Petroso. When almost stifled by the flames, and hopeless of escape, he threw beds and mattresses from the part of the fortress not yet burnt, and on to them he dropped his two little children, saying to his foemen: "Take for yourselves those possessions which fortune has given me, and of which you are able to deprive me, but those attributes of the soul—my honour and glory—I will not give you, neither shall you take them from me." The enemy ran to save the children and to offer ropes and ladders with which to save himself; but these he would not accept, choosing rather to perish in the flames than owe his life to the adversaries of his country. All that was saved from the flames was restored to the children, who were handed over to their relatives with the greatest care, and the republic regarded them with the greatest affection, and maintained them at the public expense as long as they lived. This is truly an example worthy of antiquity, and is the more to be admired inasmuch as in our days such deeds are rare. The opposite to this occurred at Galeata, where Zanobi dal Pino, the podesta, surrendered the fortress to the enemy without any attempt at defence. Moreover he strongly advised Agnolo to leave the mountains of Romagna, and carry the war into the hills of Tuscany, where it could be conducted with far more ease and advantage. Agnolo could not endure such cowardice and treachery, but abandoned Zanobi to his servants, who gave him only cards to eat upon which were painted serpents, and told him that by such food they would turn him from a Guelf to a Ghibelline, and thus he died in a few days of starvation.

Meanwhile Count Oddo, accompanied by Nicolo Piccinino, entered the Val di Lamona with the intention of inducing the lord of Faenza to join the Florentines, or at least to prevent Agnolo della Pergola from so freely harassing the Romagna. But the valley was strongly fortified and the natives accustomed to war, and Count Oddo was killed whilst Nicolo was taken prisoner and sent to Faenza. But fortune willed that the Florentines should gain by their defeat what they possibly would not have gained by a victory, because Nicolo worked matters so well with the lord of Faenza and his mother that they became friendly to the Florentines. Nicolo Piccinino was then sent at liberty, but he did not follow the course which he had recommended to others, because when discussing afterwards his agreement for hire as condottiere to the Florentines, either the terms did not appear high enough or he was offered better elsewhere, at any rate he abruptly left Arezzo, where he was then residing, and went into Lombardy, and entered the service of the Duke Filippo.

The Florentines, much alarmed by this desertion, and by the increasing burdens of war which they were no longer able to bear alone, sent envoys to the Venetians, and prayed them, while there was yet time, to take the field against the duke, lest he should increase so much in power as to become as dangerous to Venice as he was to Florence. The Venetians were encouraged to take this view by Francesco Carmignuola, who was considered one of the first soldiers of the day, and who had formerly been in the service of Duke Filippo, but had recently deserted him. The Venetians were doubtful how far they could trust Carmignuola, as they feared the enmity between him and the duke was only feigned. But whilst opinions were thus wavering, the duke attempted to poison Carmignuola by the hand of one of his servants, and although it was not sufficiently strong to kill him, it brought him to the brink of death. When this wickedness was discovered the scruples of the Venetians vanished, and the Florentines persisting in their solicitations, a league was formed, both parties undertook to prosecute the war at their joint charge, and agreed that any captures made in Lombardy should be for account of the Venetians, whilst those made in Tuscany and Romagna should be for the Florentines, and that Carmignuola should be the captain-general of the league. Thus by the means of this treaty the war was diverted into Lombardy, which came virtually under the control of Carmignuola, because in a few months he had captured many of the duke's towns, among which was the city of Brescia, a capture which, according to the system of warfare of those days, was considered marvellous.

This war lasted from 1422 to 1427, and the citizens of Florence were greatly displeased with the manner in which the taxes had been imposed up to that time and determined to have them levied in some new way. In order to proportion the taxes to a man's property it was decreed that every man should pay at the rate of half a florin on every one hundred florins worth of property. The public authorities were to levy this tax, and not individuals, and thus it fell heavily upon the richer citizens. It was, however, fiercely contested before it passed into law. The only gentleman who recommended it was Giovanni de' Medici, and by his voice it was carried. And as in levying this tax it fell upon the possessions of every citizen it was called the "Catasto." This system of taxation in some degree checked the tyranny of the upper classes, because they were not able to browbeat the plebeians and with threats make them be silent at the council, as they formerly did. Thus it followed that whilst this taxation was approved by the generality of men, it was regarded with great displeasure by the rich. Moreover, as often happens, men will not rest content with what they have obtained, but will desire something further; so the people in this case, not content with the equality of this system of taxation, demanded that the law should have a retrospective effect, in order that the affairs of the rich should be investigated with a view to discover who among them had paid less than his catasto, and that they should now be made to pay up, so that their contributions should equal the payments of those citizens who in past times had been compelled to sell their possessions to enable them to pay taxes which they ought not to have been called upon to pay. This demand angered the rich classes more than the catasto had done, and they condemned it on every opportunity. They contended it was most unjust to tax movable goods, because they might be possessed one day and lost the next; besides which many men had money hidden away which the catasto could not touch. Then again, those who left their business in order to assist in governing the republic ought to be less burthened, for it was surely enough for them to give their services to it, and it was not just that the republic should claim their property as well as enjoy their labours, whilst it only claimed the money of others. Those citizens who were advocates of the catasto rejoined that when the movable property varied then the tax would vary also, and if there were many variations means would be found to remedy any injustice. It was not worth while to take account of hidden money, because if money was not fructifying it was not reasonable to tax it, and if it came into circulation it would at once be discovered. If it did not please men to work for the republic, then let them leave it to others; this would make no difference, because there were plenty of patriotic citizens to be found who were ready enough to assist the republic, not only with their counsel, but also with their money. Besides which there were many advantages and honours attaching to the office of rulers which ought to be sufficient without men desiring to shirk the burdens. The opponents to the tax, however, had not disclosed the real reason of their opposition, which was that the rich could no longer wage war without paying for it, or having to share its burdens with other citizens. If this system of taxation had been in effect before, Florence would have had no war with King Ladislao, nor would there have been the present one with the Duke Filippo, neither of which were necessary, but were undertaken in order to fill the pockets of the rich. These controversies were checked by Giovanni de' Medici, who pointed out that it was not wise to go back on past events, for wisdom consists in learning how to provide for the future. If taxes had formerly been levied unjustly, let them now thank God that a way had been found by which they could be levied with justice. Let every one aim at making this a means of reuniting the city, and not of dividing it, as would be the case if the back taxes were enforced on a basis equal to the present. The man who is moderate in victory always chooses the better part, for it often happens that those who insist upon having all will end the losers.

By the good offices of one of the pope's legates this war between the Florentines and the Duke of Milan was brought to a close, and peace was signed at Ferrara. The conditions of this peace, however, were not observed by the duke, so the league once more took up arms and inflicted a severe defeat upon him at Maclovio. After this defeat the duke proposed fresh terms for peace, which were finally accepted by the Venetians and the Florentines. The Florentines had themselves grown somewhat suspicious, fearing their sacrifices were only likely to contribute to the aggrandisement of their allies, whilst the Venetians felt they could no longer trust Carmignuola, finding him very dilatory in his movements after the defeat of the duke. Therefore, all parties accepted this peace, which was concluded in 1428. By it the Florentines regained their lost towns in the Romagna, and the Venetians retained Brescia, and were presented by the duke with Bergamo and the surrounding country. The Florentines had expended in this war 3,500,000 ducats, and had brought upon themselves poverty and disunion, whilst they had contributed very largely to the increase in territory and importance of the Venetians. No sooner had the Florentines secured external peace than strife broke out within the city, because the great citizens would no longer endure the imposition of the catasto; and being unable to secure its repeal, they contrived to raise up fresh enemies against it. These gentlemen pointed out to the officials deputed to collect the tax that the law compelled them to levy it upon the possessions of all Florentines who resided in the districts round Florence, and that all neighbouring towns should be searched for this purpose. All Florentine subjects were, therefore, cited to appear with written proof of their possessions at a certain time. Whereupon the Volterrans sent a deputation, to the signori to complain of these acts. This incensed the officials so much that they threw eighteen of the deputation into prison; but although the Volterrans were deeply offended, they dare not rebel, out of consideration for the prisoners.

About this time Giovanni de' Medici was taken very ill, and feeling that his malady was mortal sent for his sons, Cosimo and Lorenzo, to come to his side, and spoke to them as follows: "I believe I have now lived the time which was allotted to me at my birth by God and nature. I am ready to pass away with contentment, because I am leaving you in the possession of riches, good health, and esteem. And, following in my footsteps, you will continue to live in Florence honoured and loved by all. Nothing brings me so much satisfaction, now that I am dying, as to remember that

I have never injured any one, but rather that I have assisted every-body according to my opportunities. Thus I encourage you to act. If you desire to live securely you must only accept those offices which are conferred on you by the citizens and the laws, and which will bring you neither danger nor envy. For it is what a man seizes, not what is given to him, which brings him hatred. It is always those who possess more than others, and yet wish to obtain the possessions of others, who lose their own, and who before they have lost it will live in continual anxiety. Acting upon these princi-ples I have not only maintained but improved my position in this city, where there has been so much that was hostile, and where opinions have been so divergent. Thus, if you follow in my foot-steps, you will maintain and increase your reputation, but if you act otherwise you must not expect to be more fortunate than others, who in our time have ruined themselves and their families." Giovanni died shortly after, much regretted by the great majority of the citizens, who justly admired his great qualities. He was very gen-erous, not only giving aid to those who asked it, but to all in poverty who did not ask it. He loved all men; he praised the good and pitied the bad. He never sought honours, although he possessed them all. He never went to the palace unless he was sent for. He loved peace and avoided war. He remembered men in their adversity, and was ready to assist them in their prosperity. He was opposed to public rapacity, yet willing to increase the public wealth. In his magistracy he was gracious, not eloquent, but profoundly wise. Personally be appeared melancholy, but his conversation was pleasing and witty. He died very rich in treasure, but far richer in fame and goodwill. These great inheritances of wealth as well as of mind were not only maintained but increased by his son Cosimo.

The Volterrans, having become weary of remaining in prison, promised all that was required of them in order to regain their lib-erty. Upon being liberated they returned to Volterra, and arrived there at the time of the election of new priors, among whom was a plebeian named Giusto, who was one of the deputation who had been imprisoned in Florence. This man, who was in great favour with the plebeians, was consumed with hatred because of public and private injuries received at the hands of the Florentines; being further encouraged by a nobleman named Giovanni di (surname missing), with whom Giusto sat in council, and aided by the authority of the priors, he incited the mob to wrest the town out of the hands of the Florentines and make him their governor. A great tumult was raised, the captain who acted for the Florentines was made prisoner, and Giusto was declared master of the town. The Florentines were much incensed at this outbreak in Volterra, but having come to terms with the Duke of Milan had not much doubt about soon regaining it. They, however, did not delay action, but commissioned Messer Rinaldo degli Albizzi and Messer Palla Strozzi to undertake the enterprise. As soon as Giusto realised that the Florentines intended to attack him, he sent for aid to the Sienese and Lucchese. The Lucchese promptly refused on the plea that they were in alliance with the Florentines, whilst Pagolo Guinigi, who was then lord of Lucca, not only refused all assistance, but sent Giusto's envoy as a prisoner to Florence. Pagolo's object in doing this was to attempt to regain the good graces of the Florentines, which be appeared to have forfeited in the late war by having exhibited some partisanship for the duke. In the meanwhile the Florentine commissioners advanced against Volterra, hoping to find it unprepared. They assembled their men-at-arms, and levied men from the lower Valdarno, and brought infantry from the country round Pisa. Although Giusto was abandoned by his neighbours, and heard of the preparations against him by the Florentines, he did not despair; but relying upon the position of the fortress and the strength of the town, prepared himself for defence.

There was at this time in Volterra a man of much repute with the nobility named Arcolano, a brother of that Giovanni who had per-suaded Giusto to seize the government. Messer Arcolano assembled a number of confederates and pointed out to them that God had come to the aid of their city by this event, since if they would con-sent to take arms and deliver the city up to the Florentines they would get rid of Giusto and become themselves the leading men in Volterra, and regain all the ancient privileges for the city. Having come to this determination, they armed themselves and went to the palace where the signore resided. Messer Arcolano left most of his men below, and himself with three others went upstairs into the hall above, and here he found Giusto and some other citizens. They drew him on one side as if they would speak with him on affairs of importance, upon which Giusto led them into another room, where they at once attacked him with their swords. They were not, however, sufficiently quick to prevent Giusto drawing and severely wounding two of the confederates before they could despatch him. Having killed him, they threw him from the windows of the palace. Messer Arcolano and his party then surrendered the city to the Florentine commissioners, who being close at hand with their army at once entered the city without any terms being arranged. It followed, however, that Volterra only changed her condition from bad to worse, for among other things the Florentines deprived her of her territory and placed her under the jurisdiction of a deputy.

Volterra having been lost almost at a single stroke, and as quickly regained, there appeared nothing more to fight about, had not the ambitions of men stirred up fresh trouble. When peace was declared by the Florentines after the recent war, Nicolo Fortebraccio, a son of the sister of Braccio of Perugia, who had fought for a length of time for the city of Florence, was allowed to leave its service, and at the time of the trouble with Volterra was in quarters at Fucecchio. The Florentine commissioners, in their expedition against Volterra, took advantage of the services of Fortebraccio and his men. It was the opinion of many at the time that Messer Rinaldo instigated Fortebraccio under some pretended insult to attack the Lucchese whilst accompanying him; Messer Rinaldo promised to work matters in such a way that the Florentines should espouse his quarrel with Lucca, and that Fortebraccio should be appointed captain-general. The war, however, against Volterra collapsed, and Fortebraccio had to return to his quarters at Fucecchio, whence, either by the persuasions of Messer Rinaldo or on his own initiative, he entered the territory of the Lucchese with 300 cavalry and 300 infantry and seized the castles of Ruoti and Compito. Afterwards, he over-ran the surrounding districts and carried off great booty. When the news of this raid reached Florence it gave rise to great excitement and was discussed by groups of men all over the city, the greater number of whom demanded that Lucca should be at once attacked. Among the leading citizens who favoured this course were the Medici party, and with it Messer Rinaldo, influenced either by his judgment that it was for the advantage of the republic, or by his ambition that a victory would redound to his credit. Those who did not look with favour upon the enterprise were Nicolo da Uzzano and his party. It seems scarcely credible that such a diversity of opinion could have arisen in this very city on the question of entering upon this war, and that those citizens and people who had condemned the recent war against the Duke Filippo, although it was entered into after ten years of peace and to preserve their own liberties, were now, after such vast expense and so many privations, insisting upon war against Lucca in order to destroy her liberty. Whilst, on the other hand, those who had advocated the war against Filippo now condemned this against Lucca. Thus will opinions change with time, and men be much more ready to seize the possessions of others than to guard their own, and be far more influenced by the hope of gain than by the fear of loss, because loss is never expected until it is very apparent, whilst gain, although it may be far distant, is always hoped for. The people of Florence were stimulated in their hopes of gain by what Fortebraccio had already accomplished, and by what he was promising in the future, also by the letters received from the governors of Pescia and Vico, asking for permission to receive the submission of the castles in their neighbourhood, thus it appeared as if almost all the country round Lucca could be captured. The ambassador sent by the lord of Lucca to Florence to complain of the attack upon him by Fortebraccio, and to beseech the signoria of Florence not to make war upon a neighbour, and upon a city that had always been friendly, contributed his share to the trouble. This ambassador was Giacopo Viviani, who a short time previously had conspired against Pagolo Guinigi and been thrown into prison. Although he had been found guilty, Pagolo had pardoned and liberated him. Believing that Giacopo had forgotten his injuries, Messer Pagolo had entrusted him with this mission to Florence. But Messer Giacopo was more impressed by the perils he had passed through than the pardon he had received, and when he reached Florence he secretly encouraged the citizens to persist in their intentions, it was this encouragement which had inflamed their hopes. The signoria caused a general council to be convened in order that the leading men in the city might debate the question before it. Four hundred and ninety-eight citizens were present at this council.

Among the leading men who advocated this enterprise, as we have already seen, was Messer Rinaldo. This gentleman pointed out all the advantages which would follow the acquisition of Lucca, and he proved the opportuneness of the time for the undertaking by showing that the Venetians and the Duke Filippo had left the city as it were a prey for them; and since the pope was fast entangled in the affairs of the kingdom of Naples, he could not interfere with them. To this could be added the facility with which the city could be seized, seeing that it had come under the yoke of one of its own citizens, and had thus lost much of its ancient vigour and of its desire to preserve its liberty. It might, therefore, be expected to be yielded up at the first summons, either by the people in their desire to get rid of their tyrant, or by the tyrant out of fear of the people. Rinaldo spoke also of the injuries which the lord of Lucca had done the Florentines, and of his sinister intentions, and how dangerous he would become if the pope or the duke were to declare war against their republic. And he concluded by saying there would never be another war undertaken by the Florentine people which would be more feasible, advantageous, or just. Against this view Nicolo da Uzzano urged that Florence could not possibly undertake an enterprise more unjust, more dangerous, or one from which might arise greater peril to herself. In the first place they ought not to injure a Guelf city which had always been friendly to the Florentine people, and which had often sheltered the Guelfs in her bosom at her own peril when they had been driven from their homes. Never could they find in their memories a time when Florence had been injured by Lucca; but if Lucca had wrought her harm when in servitude, as happened when Castruccio formerly held her, and as now under the present lord, the blame should not be imputed to the city but to the tyrant. And if war could be made against the tyrant, and not against the city, he would dislike it the less. But because this could not be done, he would never consent to a city, previously friendly, being despoiled of its possessions. But as things went nowadays, justice and injustice did not weigh much, and he would leave this part of the subject and turn to the question of advantages to this city. He believed that such affairs can only be considered advantageous when the risk of loss is not considerable. Now, he could not understand that any one could call this enterprise one of advantage, when the risks were so sure and the utility so doubtful. The certain loss was the cost of the undertaking, of which they had already had such a bitter taste, and which was enough to stagger a city which had been long at rest, and still more one like their own exhausted by a long and weary war. The advantage which might accrue was the acquisition of Lucca, which he confessed would be a great one. But let them consider the difficulties of accomplishing such a feat, which to him appeared so great as to be impossible, for he could not believe that the Venetians or Filippo would allow them to acquire the city of Lucca. It might be that the Venetians would consent, in order not to appear ungrateful for the vast territories which they had so recently gained with the money of the Florentines. Filippo would be delighted to see the Florentines involved in a new war and fresh expenditure, in order that when broken and weary on every side he could again fall upon them. Even in the progress of the enterprise, and to assist in the defeat of Florence, Filippo would not fail to aid the Lucchese both secretly with money or by dismissing his soldiers, who as soldiers of fortune would go to the assistance of Lucca. For these reasons he begged them to abandon the enterprise and manage affairs in such a manner that the tyrant would create enemies within his own city, because there is no surer way of bringing a city under subjection than by allowing it to live under a tyrant, by whom it will be weakened and afflicted. Thus, if they conducted this affair prudently, Lucca would be brought to such a pass that the tyrant could no longer hold it, and not knowing how to govern itself, it would of necessity fall into their hands. But when Nicolo saw that the council were not listening to him, he prophesied that they would enter into a war in which they would spend immense treasure and incur many losses. By chance they might emerge from the struggle the conquerors of Lucca, but it would only result in liberating it from a tyrant; and Lucca, from being a city friendly, enslaved, and weak, would arise a city free but hostile to Florence, and in the time to come a bar to the greatness of their own republic.

This finished the speaking, and on a vote being taken of those present for or against the war, it was found that out of the entire number only ninety-eight voted against it. Having come to this decision and created the Ten to manage the war, horse and foot soldiers were enlisted. Astorre Gianni and Messer Rinaldo degli Albizzi were appointed commissioners, and it was agreed that Nicolo Fortebraccio should keep the towns which he had captured on the understanding that he continued the war on account of the Florentines. The commissioners with their army arrived in the territories of the Lucchese and then divided: Astorre spread himself over the plain towards Camaggiore and Pietrasanta, whilst Messer Rinaldo drew off towards the mountains; for it was believed that the surrounding country being wasted, the city would be more ready to surrender. This course proved most unfortunate, not because few towns were captured, but because of the incompetency which both of the commissioners displayed. Astorre, in fact, brought all his troubles upon himself. There is a valley near to Pietrasanta named Seravezza, rich and populous, the inhabitants of which went out to meet Astorre when they heard of his approach and begged him to accept their submission to the Florentine people. He pretended to accept their offer, but afterwards ordered his men to seize the passes and strong places in the valley. He then assembled the men of the valley in a large church and made them all prisoners. After which he sacked and ravaged the valley with the utmost cruelty and violence, sparing no holy place, nor woman, whether married or virgin. When these outrages became known in Florence they caused the gravest displeasure, not only among the magistrates, but throughout the city.

Some of the Seravezzians escaped from the hands of the commissioner and made their way to Florence, where through every street, and to every person they met, they told the story of their wrongs in such a manner that they were taken before the Ten by those people who desired to see the commissioner punished, either as a wicked man or as one of the opposite faction. One of the Seravezzians addressed the Ten as follows: "We are sure, noble sirs, that our words will find belief and compassion among your lordships when you hear that our country has been seized by your commissioner, and the manner in which we have been treated by him. Our valley, as your memory will confirm, has always been a sure refuge from the earliest times for your citizens who have come to us when persecuted by the Ghibellines. Our fathers and ourselves have always revered the name of this illustrious republic, as the head and chief of the Guelfs, and as long as the Lucchese were Guelf we willingly yielded fealty to them. But since they have submitted to a tyrant, and have deserted their old friends and followed the Ghibelline party, we have obeyed under compulsion, rather than willingly. God knows how many times we have prayed that a chance should be given us of showing our love for the old party. But how often men are blinded by their desires! What we had looked forward to as our salvation has become our destruction. As soon as we heard that your banners were advancing towards us we went out to meet them, not as enemies, but as if to our ancient lords, and we placed our valley, our fortunes, and ourselves in the hands of your commissioner, relying on his words, and believing that if he had not the feelings of a Florentine he had at least those of a man. Your lordships must pardon us if we are unable to endure in silence the wrongs we have suffered, and of which from our souls we speak, but this man, your commissioner, had nothing human about him but his appearance, and was nothing of a Florentine but in name. A deadly pest, a cruel wild beast, a horrid monster, such as no writer has ever described. He summoned us to our church, under the pretence of wishing to speak with us, and there imprisoned us. He then burnt and destroyed the whole valley, and the inhabitants, robbed and stripped of their possessions, he beat and murdered; the women were wronged, and virgins were torn from the arms of their mothers and thrown to the soldiery as prey. If we, for any injuries done to the people of Florence or to him, had deserved such evil treatment, or if armed and opposing him we had been captured, we should grieve the less, indeed we should have blamed ourselves for what our arrogance or offences had brought down upon our heads, but seeing that we surrendered our arms willingly, and were then robbed with such cruelty and shame, we bring our complaints to you. Although we could have filled all Lombardy with our lamentations, and spread the story of our wrongs throughout Italy, thus bringing universal hatred on this city, yet we have not done so, lest a noble republic should be stained with the injustice and cruelty of a wicked citizen. Had we been aware of his cruel nature before our destruction we would have done our best, had it been possible, to satiate him, for although we might have lost all we possessed, yet we should have saved our honour. Although it is all too late, we come to you for shelter and beg you to relieve the miseries of your subjects, so that others may not fear to suffer our fate by coming under your rule. If our infinite sorrows do not move you, let the fear of the anger of God do so who has seen his temples sacked and burnt and our people betrayed on his altars." Having spoken thus they threw themselves to the ground, crying and begging that their country and possessions should be restored to them, and that wives should be restored to husbands, and children to parents, although it was no longer possible to give them back their honour. These atrocities, which had only previously been reported, were now confirmed by the evidence of those who had suffered, and disturbed the magistrates to such a degree that without delay they recalled Astorre, and afterwards condemned him to the loss of all civil rights. The property of the Seravezzians was sought for and restored as far as possible, and other claims were in time settled by the city of Florence in various ways.

Messer Rinaldo degli Albizzi, on the other hand, who was generally considered to have been the author of the war, was reported to be conducting it, not for the advantage of the people of Florence, but for his own. It appeared that as soon as he had gained the appointment of commissioner his interest in the capture of Lucca evaporated, and he was content to waste the country, to stock his lands with cattle and his house with booty. As if the plunder which he and his satellites accumulated was not enough for his advantage, he bought that of the soldiers, and thus from a commissioner he became a merchant. When these calumnies reached his ears they stirred his bold and haughty spirit more than they should have done a more serious man, and so enraged was he against the magistrates and citizens that without waiting for permission he returned to Florence, and at once presented himself before the Ten. He said he knew well how difficult and dangerous it was to attempt to serve a free or factious city, because the one is always filled with rumours and the other persecutes those who fail and never rewards success. Accusations are made where there is any doubt; those who conquer receive no praise; those who err are blamed by all; those who lose condemned by all. Friends persecute out of spite, and enemies out of hatred. Nevertheless the fear of idle accusations had never caused him to neglect any duty which he considered would be for the advantage of his city. True it was that, having lost his patience over the present unjust calumny, he had departed from his usual custom in such matters. Therefore he begged the magistrates in the future to be more ready to defend their citizens, and thus enable them to throw all their energies into the defence of the country. And as to the people, although they might not concede a triumph to their captains, let them, at least, defend them from false charges, recollecting all citizens were of the same city, and any day might bring them into similar trouble, when they would understand what pain such calumnies cause to a proud spirit. The Ten endeavoured to appease him under the circumtances, but committed the further care of the enterprise against Lucca to Neri di Gino and Alamanno Salviati. These gentlemen desisted from harassing the country and drew their forces nearer to the city of Lucca; but as winter was now approaching and the weather severe, the army would go no further than Capannola, although it seemed to the commissioners, who were desirous of closely investing the city, that the men were only wasting time. The Ten would not listen to any excuses and ordered the camp to be struck, but the soldiers refused to obey owing to the inclemency of the season.

There was in Florence at this time a most excellent architect by name Filippo, the son of Ser Brunellesco, of whose work the city is full. So great was his genius that after his death a statue in marble was placed to his memory in one of the principal churches in Florence with an inscription testifying to bis merits. He pointed out to the Ten that, taking into consideration the situation of the city of Lucca and the course of the river Serchio, he would undertake to flood that city, and persuaded the authorities to allow him to make the attempt. But this resulted in disaster to the Florentines, without any harm whatever being done to their enemies, because the Lucchese raised a high bank in the direction towards which the Florentines were turning the Serchio, and in the night time pierced the bank of the dyke by which the water was being conducted. Thus when the bank of the canal broke, the water rushed out, and meeting with a bar to its progress towards Lucca, spread itself over the plain, flooding the Florentine camp, which had to be removed to a considerable distance from the city.

For these reasons the war against Lucca did not prosper, and the newly appointed Ten sent as commissioner Messer Giovanni Guicciardini, who once more moved the camp into the neighbourhood of the city. When the lord of Lucca found his enemy closing around him, he accepted the advice of Messer Antonio del Rosso, a Sienese gentleman who was stationed in Lucca on behalf of Siena, and sent Salvestro Trenta and Lionardo Buonvisi to the Duke of Milan. These gentlemen besought the duke to lend his aid to the lord of Lucca; but not finding him inclined to assist, they begged him to give them secretly the help they needed, and they, in the name of the people, promised to surrender their lord to him as a prisoner, together with the possession of the city. They warned him that if he did not accept this proposal quickly their lord would surrender the city to the Florentines, who were soliciting him with many promises. The prospect of this contingency caused the duke to put on one side all other considerations, and he at once ordered his general, Count Francesco Sforza, to publicly ask of him permission to go into the kingdom of Naples. Having obtained this, the count marched off with his troops to Lucca. The Florentines, notwithstanding the device which had been employed, were apprehensive of his intentions, and sent his friend. Count Boccaccino Alamanni, to turn him aside. The count, however, having entered Lucca, and the Florentines withdrawing their forces to Librafatta, he passed on to attack Pescia, of which town Pagolo da Diacceto was governor. This man, influenced more by fear than any other motive, fled to Pistoia, and Pescio would have been lost had it not been for Giovanni Malavolti who preserved it. Giovanni defended it so successfully that Sforza failed to carry it, but captured the suburb of Buggiano, and burnt the castle of Stigliano hard by. When the Florentines witnessed this destruction they had recourse to the remedy which has so often saved them, knowing that corruption will prevail with mercenary soldiers where force is powerless. Therefore they proffered money to the count, in return for which he was not only to leave the city but give it up to them. As it appeared to the count that there was no more money to be obtained from Lucca, he turned to those who had it, and came to terms with the Florentines. He would not agree to give Lucca up to them, for his conscience would not allow that, but to abandon it to them as soon as he should have received the 50,000 ducats. In order that he should be excused for this act to his master, it was arranged that the people of Lucca, who were his accomplices, should drive out their lord.

There was in Lucca, as we have already seen, Messer Antonio del Rosso, the Sienese ambassador. This man, on the authority of Sforza, plotted with the citizens the ruin of Pagolo. The leaders of the plot were Piero Cennami and Giovanni de Chivizzano. Count Sforza lay with his forces outside the city on the banks of the Serchio, and he had with him Lanzilao, son of Pagolo. Everything having been arranged, armed conspirators, to the number of forty, sought out Pagolo at night, who much astonished demanded the cause of the tumult. Piero Cennami replied that his government had brought down upon them such a number of enemies as were likely to destroy them all either by the sword or by hunger, and they had, therefore, decided to govern themselves, and demanded from him the keys of the city and its treasure. To this demand Pagolo replied that as for the treasure it was spent, but the keys of the city and himself were at their disposal. He begged only that they should be content to end his reign as he had commenced and carried it on, namely, without bloodshed. Pagolo and his son were taken by Count Francesco to the duke and shortly afterwards died in prison.

The departure of the Count Francesco having relieved Lucca of her tyrant, and the Florentines of their fear of his army, the Lucchese prepared for their defence, whilst the Florentines returned to their attack. The Count of Urbino accepted the command of the Florentines force, and pressed the Lucchese so closely that they were once more compelled to send for aid to the duke, who despatched Nicolo Piccinino to their assistance, under the same pretext as he had sent the Count Sforza. Piccinino drew near to Lucca and encountered our army on the banks of the

Serchio, attacked and defeated it whilst crossing the river. Our commissioner with a few of his men found refuge in Pisa. This defeat threw the whole city of Florence into mourning, and as the war had been undertaken at the wish of the people themselves they did not know on whom to turn; therefore, as they would admit no blame themselves, they blamed the administrators; they, however, revived the charges against Messer Rinaldo. But Messer Giovanni Guicciardini was more defamed by a slanderous report which alleged that it was in his power to have closed the war after Count Francesco had left the scene of operations, but that he was bribed by money, of which he had transmitted large sums; it was alleged that the men who brought it and those who received it could be produced. So persistently were these accusations repeated that the captain of the people, in deference to the demands of the public, and the incitements of the opponents of Guicciardini, was compelled to summon him before him. Messer Giovanni was greatly angered at this, and appeared before the captain, but his relatives, for the sake of the family honour, brought so much influence to bear upon the captain that the charges were abandoned.

After their victory on the banks of the Serchio the Lucchese not only regained possession of their own towns, but captured many round Pisa, except Bientina, Calcinaia, Livorno, and Librafatta, and Pisa itself would have been lost if a conspiracy in that city had not been discovered. The Florentines reorganised their army, and appointed Michelotto, a pupil of Sforza, to be their leader. At the same time the duke continued to press the Florentines, and inflicted heavy losses upon them. He also brought about a league between Genoa, Siena, and the lord of Piombino in defence of Lucca, and engaged Nicolo Piccinino for its captain; thus the intentions of the duke now became perfectly apparent. Thereupon the Venetians and Florentines renewed their convention, and the war was openly prosecuted in both Lombardy and Tuscany. It was carried on with varying success in these two provinces, until all parties were so thoroughly worn out that peace was declared between them in May 1433, whereby the Florentines,

Lucchese, and Sienese returned to each other the many castles that had been captured during the war, and all parties were reinstated to their possessions.

During the progress of this war the malignant passions of all parties held full sway in the city of Florence, amid which Cosimo de' Medici after the death of his father, Giovanni, played his part in public affairs with the greatest spirit, and with far more zeal and liberality on behalf of his friends than his father had ever shown. So that those who had exulted over the removal of Giovanni were in far worse plight now that they had to deal with Cosimo. He was a very far-seeing man, generous in his disposition, liberal in his opinions, of a dignified and pleasant appearance; he never attempted anything against the state, or the two great factions in it; but he was ready to assist all men, and by his generosity made many citizens his partisans. By carrying himself in this manner he appeared a standing reproach to the men who were ruling the state; yet Cosimo believed that by so doing he might continue to live secure in Florence, and powerful enough to be able to overcome his enemies if their ambitions should lead them to attempt anything against him. The chief instruments in establishing the power of Cosimo were Averado de' Medici and Puccio Pucci—Averado with his bold spirit and Puccio with his prudence and sagacity. So greatly was the counsel and judgment of Puccio esteemed, and so well was it recognised, that Medici adherents were called after the name of Puccio rather than after Cosimo. The enterprise against Lucca had been undertaken by a city steeped in faction, and although friends of Cosimo had advocated the war, its administration was carried on by persons opposed to him—being men of higher reputation in the state. But Averado de' Medici and others, not being able to condemn the war, endeavoured with every art and at every opportunity to calumniate its management. If losses occurred, as they did pretty frequently, it was not ascribed to the good fortune or skill of the enemy, but it was all attributed to the blundering of the commissioners. It was this policy which caused them to magnify the sins of Astorre Gianni, and which drove Messer Rinaldo degli Albizzi in anger to throw up his commission without leave. It also brought the pressure to bear on the captain of the people which induced him to summon Messer Giovanni Guicciardini before him. Hence arose all the troubles which the magistrates and the commissioners had to meet, since if the complaints were justifiable they were magnified, and if they were not just they were made to appear so. But whether true or false they were invariably believed by the populace who hated their rulers.

These methods and the extraordinary state of affairs produced by them were perfectly well understood by Nicolo da Uzzano and other leaders of their party, and although they had often discussed them amongst themselves they had never been able to devise a remedy. For whilst it appeared dangerous to allow this condition of affairs to continue, it was difficult to oppose it successfully. Nicolo da Uzzano was the principal man who would not consent to violent measures being taken against Cosimo, but when the war with Lucca and the troubles in Florence were at their height, Nicolo Barbardori took the opportunity of urging Nicolo da Uzzano to agree to the removal of Cosimo; and finding him pensive in his study, pressed him by all the reasons which it was possible to adduce to agree with Messer Rinaldo to drive Cosimo out of Florence. To this proposal Nicolo da Uzzano replied in the following words: "It would be better for thee, for thy house, and for our republic that thou and others who follow thee should have beards of silver rather than of gold, as thy name would have it, because their counsel coming from grey beards and long experience would then be wiser and of greater advantage to the commonwealth. It seems to me that those who think of driving Cosimo out of Florence should first measure their strength with his. You have baptised our party the party of the nobles, and opposed it to that of the plebeians, and if these names represent the truth of the case the victory would in any event be doubtful, but reasoning from the fate of the ancient nobility of this city, who were entirely destroyed by the plebeians, we should have far more to fear than to hope in such a contest. But we are really standing in much more peril, seeing that our party is divided, whilst that of the adversary is united. In the first place, Neri di Gino and Nerone di Nigi, two of our foremost citizens, have never proved themselves more friendly to us than to our adversaries. And there are many families, as well as houses, divided, and out of envy to brothers or relatives unfavourable to us and favourable to our enemies. I will only recall to you some of the most important, others will suggest themselves to you. Think of the son of Messer Maso degli Albizzi, Luca, who out of jealousy to Messer Rinaldo, has thrown himself into the arms of the opposite party. In the Guicciardini house, of the sons of Messer Luigi, Piero is hostile to Messer Giovanni and favours our adversary. Tomaso and Nicolo Soderini, out of the hatred which they bear to their uncle Francesco, openly take sides against him. So that if we are to weigh properly those who belong to our party, and those who are of theirs, I know not why our party should be called noble more than theirs. And if they are followed by all the plebeians, then we are in a much worse position; and if it should come to blows or to votes, we should not have a chance. If we should take a stand upon the dignity of our position and the reputation of our government, which has stood for fifty years, when it should be put to the proof our weakness would be discovered and we should lose all. If thou shouldst urge that the justice of our cause would bring us strength, whilst for the same reason they will lose theirs, I reply that justice must be recognised and appreciated by others as well as by ourselves to have any force. But in this case it is exactly the opposite, for the reasons upon which we should take action are entirely founded upon our fears lest Cosimo should be made a prince, and the suspicions which we entertain of him are those which others have of us; and what is worse, they accuse us of the same design of which we accuse him. The acts of Cosimo that have given rise to this fear are that he places his money at the service of any man, not only of private persons, but also of public men, and not only of Florentines, but of strangers; that he favours any citizen who needs an appointment; and that his friends are promoted by the influence which he exercises with the crowd. Therefore the reasons why he should be hunted from the city are that he is charitable, obliging, generous, and friendly with every one. Tell me briefly what law is there which prohibits or condemns and fines a man for his charity, liberality, or friendship? And while there are all sorts of ways by which a man may attain sovereignty, these are not believed to be among them; nor should we be able to persuade the people that they are, because our own methods have destroyed their confidence in us; and being naturally factious, through having lived so long under factions, they are corrupt and unwilling to pay attention to such suggestions. But let us suppose that you have succeeded in exiling Cosimo, which could easily be done, seeing that the signoria is disposed to do it, how would you prevent him from returning when there would remain behind so many of his friends, burning with desire to have him back? It would be impossible, and you could never be secure from it, seeing that he has the goodwill of so many. And the more of his friends whom you banish the greater number of enemies you raise against yourselves, so that after a short time he and they would return. What will you have gained then? For you will have banished a good man, and a bad one will have returned. His naturally good disposition will have been changed by those who have recalled him, to whom he would owe everything, and whom he would not be able to restrain. If you attempt to put him to death by the ordinary means of the law you will not succeed, because his money and the corruptibility of your minds will always save him. But supposing that he is dead or driven out never to return, I do not see what our republic will have gained; because if we have liberated her from Cosimo, she will fall into the arms of Messer Rinaldo; and I, speaking for myself, am one of those who desire that no citizen should become superior to another in power and authority. But if it be necessary that one or other of these two men has to prevail, I do not know why I should love Messer Rinaldo more than Cosimo. I wish to say no more to thee, unless it is, may God preserve this city from one of its own citizens becoming its prince, but when for our sins we deserve one, let it not be Messer Rinaldo whom we shall have to serve. Do not, therefore, persuade me to take a course which is full of danger, or make me believe that with the few men who follow you, you could successfully withstand the will of the multitude; because all of these citizens you name, partly through ignorance, partly through malice, are ready to sell our republic. In this fortune is their friend, for they have already found a buyer. Be therefore governed by my advice. Take care to live modestly, and to have, as regards liberty, as much suspicion of some of our party as of those of the opposite faction. And when any trouble does arise you will be in favour with all parties if you keep neutral; thus will you do good to yourself and no harm to your country."

These words somewhat chilled the ardour of Barbadori, and the matter lay at rest during the war with Lucca; but when peace was declared, and the death of Nicolo da Uzzano happened at the same time, the city had neither war nor curb to restrain it. Whereupon the most malignant party passion broke out without any restraint, and Messer Rinaldo, who had now become the sole chief of his party, did not cease to prompt and importune any citizen whom he thought might become gonfalonier to take arms and free the country of Cosimo, who otherwise, by the malignity of a few men, and the ignorance of the many, would lead the country into slavery. These proceedings of Messer Rinaldo, as well as those of the opposite party, kept the city in a constant uproar; and whenever the election of a magistrate occurred, it was publicly discussed how many of one party and how many of another would support him. And at an election for the signori the whole city was disturbed. Every case that came before the magistrate, even the most insignificant, was made an opportunity for a contest; secrets were published; both right and wrong was conferred by favour, and the good men as well as bad were equally hurt; no magistrate did his duty.

Whilst affairs were in this confused condition in Florence, with Messer Rinaldo determined to lower the power of Cosimo, it came to the knowledge of Rinaldo that Bernardo Guadagni might possibly become the gonfalonier; therefore, in order that Bernardo should not be ineligible for the position owing to his debts to the public, Rinaldo paid his taxes for him. When the drawing for the signori took place, it was found that, fortune favouring our discords, Bernardo was drawn for gonfalonier, and would act in September and October. Messer Rinaldo went at once to visit him, and to assure him that the nobles' party, and all who wished to live quietly, congratulated themselves on his having attained the dignity, and that it rested with him to show that their hopes were not in vain. Rinaldo pointed out to Bernardo the dangers which they ran from disunion, and that the only way to secure union was to destroy Cosimo, who alone, by the popularity which his riches brought him, kept their party weak; and that Cosimo had reached such a height he would be made a prince unless care was taken to prevent it. Rinaldo also said that it was the duty of Bernardo, as a good citizen, to remedy this. He ought to summon the people to the Piazza, declare a reform in the government, and restore to the country its liberty. He recalled to his memory how Messer Salvestro de' Medici had unjustly limited the power of the Guelfs, to whom, by the blood of their fathers, the government belonged, and why should he, Bernardo, with justice on his side, hesitate to do against one what Salvestro did not hesitate wrongfully to carry out against many. He bade him not fear, for many friends would flock with arms in their hands to his aid; nor should he fear what the plebeians would do, for Cosimo would get no more assistance from them than did Giorgio Scali in his hour of need, because although they adored him now they would betray him then; nor need the wealth of Cosimo cause Bernardo to hesitate, for when once the signori had him in their power they would deprive him of it. Rinaldo concluded by saying that this deed would make the republic united and secure, and cover Bernardo himself with glory. To all of this Bernardo briefly replied that he believed what Rinaldo had said to be necessary, and that the time had arrived when it should be carried out. He should therefore prepare his forces in order that he might be ready when his friends were.

As soon as Bernardo was installed in his office he, in collusion with Messer Rinaldo, influenced his colleagues, and cited Cosimo to appear before them. Although Cosimo was advised by many friends not to comply with the summons, he obeyed and went, relying more on his own innocency than on the mercy of the signori. When he reached the palace he was at once arrested; whilst Messer Rinaldo with many armed men sallied forth from his house and took possession of the Piazza, whither the signori had summoned the people, and two hundred men were chosen for the balia, in order to reform the government of the city. The reform of the government, and the question of the life or death of Cosimo, were considered by this balia as soon as possible. Many desired that he should be sent into exile, many that he should be killed, many others were silent, either out of compassion to him or out of fear for their colleagues. These differences prevented them coming to a decision. In the tower of the palace was a place as large as the space would allow called the Alberghettino, into which Cosimo was shut, and committed to the custody of Federigo Malavolti. From this place Cosimo could hear the turmoil and noise of arms in the Piazzo, as well as the frequent ringing of the balia bell. All this caused him deep anxiety for his life, but his chief fear was that his personal enemies would make away with him by some secret means. For this reason he abstained from food, and in four days only tasted a small morsel of bread. When Federigo perceived this he said to him: "Let not the fear of being poisoned, Cosimo, cause you to kill yourself with hunger. It is small honour to me, if you think I would take a hand in such wickedness. For myself, I do not believe that you will lose your life. You have too many friends, both inside and out of the palace. But should you lose it, you may rest content they will use some other means than me as a medium to take it. I will not stain my hands with any man's blood, least of all with thine, who hast never wronged me. Therefore be of good cheer, take your food, and live long for your friends and country. In order to give you confidence, I will eat of the same food as you do." These words greatly cheered

Cosimo, and with tears in his eyes he embraced and kissed Federigo, and with earnest words thanked him for his kind and compassionate feelings, and he promised that if ever fortune should give him the chance of rewarding him he would not be forgetful.

Cosimo was reassured by this, and whilst the citizens were still undetermined what to do with him, Federigo, in order to provide some amusement, took with him to supper with Cosimo a witty and facetious fellow named Farganaccio, a familiar friend of the gonfaloniere. Supper being almost finished, it occurred to Cosimo that he might avail himself of the visit of this man, whom fortunately he knew, and he made a sign to Federigo that he should leave them alone. Federigo understood this, and left them under the pretence of going outside for something for the meal. Cosimo, after some ingratiating words, entrusted Farganaccio with a countersign, and instructed him to go to the master of the hospital of Santa Maria Nuova for 1100 ducats. He was to keep 100 for himself and 1000 he was to carry to the gonfaloniere, and beg him to find some plausible reason for coming to see him. Farganaccio fulfilled this mission, the money was handed over to Bernardo, who became more amenable, and obtained the banishment of Cosimo to Padua in opposition to the wishes of Messer Rinaldo, who desired that he should be killed. Averardo was also banished with many other members of the Medici family, and with them Puccio and Giovanni Pucci. In order to overawe those who might be averse to the banishment of Cosimo, a balia was conferred upon eight of the guard and the captain of the people. When the above decision had been made Cosimo was brought before the signori, and on October 3, 1433, received his sentence of banishment. He was warned to obey it, otherwise they would proceed to extremities both against his life and possessions. Cosimo accepted his exile cheerfully, saying that he was willing to go wherever the signoria desired to send him. He begged them, however, now that his life had been spared by them, to defend him, for he had been informed that many who desired his blood were waiting for him in the Piazza. He offered his possessions, wherever he should be, to the city, the people, and the signoria. The gonfalonier bade him be of good courage, and kept him at the palace until after nightfall, when he led him to his own house and supped with him. Afterwards he gave him an escort through the Florentine territories. Wherever Cosimo passed he was received with the greatest honour — the Venetians visited him officially, not as an exile, but as a man occupying the most exalted position.

Thus Florence was left, robbed of one of her best citizens, and one universally beloved. Every one was despondent, those who had emerged successful from the recent struggle equally with those who had been defeated. Messer Rinaldo began to be apprehensive of the future, and, determined not to allow either himself or his party to fail, assembled a number of friendly citizens and blamed them for the ruin which he foresaw approaching in having allowed themselves to be influenced by the prayers, the tears, and the money of their enemies; he asked them if they did not already recognise that they themselves would soon have to pray and to weep, that none would listen to their prayers, and none would pity their tears. And as to the money which they had accepted, they would soon have to refund the capital, and the interest they would be called upon to pay would be in torture, exile, and death. It would have been better for them to have died than to have allowed Cosimo to get off with his life, or to have allowed friends of his to be left behind in Florence. Great men should not be struck at, or, if they are, it should be to utterly destroy them. He saw no other remedy but to strengthen their party in the city, in order that they should expel their enemies, whom he foresaw would soon awake, with arms in their hands, since the civil methods were unavailing. And the remedy which he had so often suggested was to restore the great families to their positions and honours in the city, and thus strengthen their own party, as their opponents had strengthened theirs by the addition of the plebeians. By doing this their party would become once more vigorous in action, with more tenacity, courage, and spirit. In conclusion he threatened that, if this last and true course were not adopted — and

he could see none other by which to save the government among
so many enemies—the ruin of their party and the city was at hand.
To this harangue Mariotto Baldovinetti, one of those present,
replied that the nature and unendurable pride of the nobles was
such that it would be folly to incur a certain tyranny under them in
order to avoid an uncertain one under the plebeians. When
Messer Rinaldo found that his advice was not listened to, he
cursed his evil fortune and that of his party, attributing everything
to the will of heaven rather than to the ignorance and blindness of
men. Whilst affairs were in this position, without any course being
decided upon, a letter was discovered which had been written by
Messer Agnolo Acciajuoli to Cosimo, in which the writer pointed
out the goodwill of the city to Cosimo, and urged that he should
provoke a war, and make a friend of Neri di Gino, because it was
believed that when the city came to be in want of money, and
could find no one to supply it, the need of it would bring back to
the citizens the memory of Cosimo, and they would demand his
recall; and that if Neri di Gino could be detached from the party
of Messer Rinaldo, it would be so weakened there would be no further occasion for fear. Upon this letter reaching the hands of the
magistrates, Messer Agnolo was thrown into prison, tortured, and
then sent into exile. But even this example did not in any degree
stem the tide which was rising in favour of Cosimo.

A year had almost elapsed since Cosimo had been banished,
and the end of August 1434 had arrived, when Niccolo di Cocco
was elected gonfalonier for the ensuing two months, and with him
eight signori, all of whom were friends of Cosimo. Such a signoria
filled Rinaldo and his party with alarm, and in the interval of three
days, during which the signori remained in complete privacy,
Rinaldo again called together the heads of his party, and pointed
out to them the impending and certain danger, saying that they
should at once take arms whilst Donato Velluti still retained the
office of gonfalonier as the only recourse left; they should also
summon the people to the Piazza, obtain a new balia, deprive the
new signoria of office and create another more favourable to the

government, bum the ballot lists and make new ones, which should be filled with the names of friends. These proposals were considered by many of the persons present to be prudent and necessary, by others far too violent and likely to bring too much danger. Among those who dissented from Messer Rinaldo was Messer Palla Strozzi, a man of peace and very courteous, far more fitted for the study of letters than the control of party. He said that all policies appear to be equally good at the beginning, whether they are for a bold course or for a cautious one, but as they develop the difficulties arise, and in the end they prove disastrous. He believed that the fear of external war, arising out of the duke's army having mustered on the frontier, would be considered by the signori of far more importance than any internal discord. But if it should become apparent that the signori were bent on changes, which could not be carried out without their knowledge, then would be the time for fighting, and for taking such steps as might be necessary for their common safety. The necessity for arming would then be so evident that it could be done without alarming the people and without danger to themselves. The party, therefore, agreed to allow the signori to take office, but their proceedings should be very narrowly watched, and should any act against the party be observed every one should at once take arms and assemble in the Piazza San Palinari, near to the palace, whence they could take action in whatever direction it should be needed.

With this decison the new signori were allowed to take office, and the gonfalonier, to obtain some reputation and inspire respect for his position among those who might oppose him, threw his predecessor, Donato Velluti, into prison on a charge of misappropriating public funds. He next sounded his colleagues upon the subject of the recall of Cosimo, and finding them disposed to it he spoke to those whom he considered the head of the Medici party, and upon their advice he summoned Messer Rinaldo before him, together with the two other chiefs of the party opposed to the Medici, Ridolfo Peruzzi and Nicolo Barbadori. When Messer Rinaldo received this summons he determined no longer to put off an insurrection; therefore he issued from his house with a large armed following, and was at once joined by Ridolfo Peruzzi and Nicolo Barbadori. With them were many citizens and some soldiers who happened to be in Florence without occupation, and all met as arranged in the Piazza San Pallinari. Messer Palla Strozzi, although he had collected a number of men, did not leave his house, neither did Messer Giovanni Guicciardini. Messer Rinaldo sent to them, reproaching them for their delay in coming. Messer Giovanni replied that he had enough to do in preventing his brother from going to the assistance of the palace. Messer Palla, after many urgent messages, went unarmed to San Palinari on horseback, attended by only two footmen. Upon this Messer Rinaldo rode up to him and warmly upbraided him for his negligence in not coming out with the others, telling him that such conduct arose either from lack of loyalty or courage, and that any man who considered his reputation ought to avoid such an accusation. And if Messer Palla believed that because he failed in his duty to his party the victorious enemy would either spare his life or fail to send him into exile, he was deceived. As for himself, he said, if anything unfortunate did happen he had the satisfaction of knowing that he had not failed his party in counsel before the danger did come, and had not failed in courage now that it had come. But to Messer Palla and others there would be the ever-to-be-remembered regret that three times had they betrayed their country; once when they saved the life of Cosimo, the second when they refused to follow his, Rinaldo's, advice, and a third time when they refused to join him in arms. To these words Messer Palla answered nothing that could be heard under the circumstances, but murmuring to himself he turned his horse and rode back to his house.

When the signori heard that Messer Rinaldo and his party had taken up arms, and found themselves deserted by the citizens, they knew not what to do, so shut themselves up in the palace. But Messer Rinaldo delayed going to the Piazza until the arrival of the forces which never came, and thus lost the opportunity of victory, and inspired the signori with courage to resist. Many citizens now obtaining access to the signori encouraged them to offer such terms to the rebels as would induce them to lay down their arms. Therefore some of the signori, who were less obnoxious than others to Rinaldo, went to him and said the signori could not understand the reason of this tumult, because there had never been a suggestion of injuring any citizen, and if the reason for the disturbance was the fear that Cosimo might be recalled, there really was no cause for such a suspicion, and they would give Rinaldo an assurance to that affect; and if he and his friends wished to come to the palace they would be welcome, and all their demands should be satisfied. These words did not affect the intention of Messer Rinaldo, who said that he would only be satisfied with the resignation of the signori, in order that he might reorganise the government for the benefit of all the citizens. But as always happens in affairs in which personal authority is equal and opinions differ, anything of value is rarely effected. Ridolfo Peruzzi, influenced by the opinions of some of the citizens, said that, as far as he was concerned, he wished for nothing more than that Cosimo should not return, and having secured this it was to him a sufficient victory, and he had no desire for a greater one by causing the city to run with blood, therefore he would obey the signori, and entering the palace with his men was joyfully received. The failure of Messer Palla's courage and the action of Ridolfo having caused the complete failure of Rinaldo's enterprise, he remained at San Palinari, and soon the zeal of his followers began to evaporate. Added to this the pope intervened with his authority.

It happened that Pope Eugenius was in Florence at this time, having been driven out of Rome by the citizens, and hearing of these tumults he considered it to be part of his duties to appease them. Therefore he sent Messer Giovanni Vitelleschi, the patriarch, a great friend of Messer Rinaldo, to beg Rinaldo to come to him, saying that his influence with the signori, and their obedience to him, could not fail to obtain satisfaction and safety for Messer Rinaldo, without loss or bloodshed to the people. Persuaded by his friend, and accompanied by those who had taken up arms on his behalf, Messer Rinaldo went to Santa Maria Novella where the pope resided. Eugenius informed Messer Rinaldo that the signori had pledged their word and given him authority to settle all disputes to the malcontents' satisfaction as soon as they should have laid down their arms. Messer Rinaldo having already experienced the cowardice of Messer Palla, and the levity of Ridolfo Peruzzi, put himself into the pope's hands, for want of a better course, with the hope that the pope's authority would be able to save him. Whereupon the pope signified to Nicolo Barbadori, who with others was waiting outside, that they should lay down their arms, and that Messer Rinaldo would remain with him in order to negotiate the agreement with the signori. Nicolo and his followers with one voice agreed to disarm.

When the signori were informed that their adversary was disarmed, they at once gave their attention to the agreements promised by the pope in their name, and at the same time they sent secretly to the mountains round Pistoia for infantry. They caused these men with their own men-at-arms to enter Florence by night, and seize all the strong places in the city. Having done this, they summoned the people into the Piazsa and created a new balia, which at its first meeting recalled Cosimo and others who had been banished with him. The balia then sent into exile Messer Rinaldo degli Albizzi, Ridolfo Peruzzi, Nicolo Barbadori, and Messer Palla Strozzi, with many other citizens belonging to the hostile party. In such numbers were they exiled that few cities in Italy remained without them, and many cities outside Italy were filled with them. Thus did Florence, on this and similar occasions, lose not only men but wealth and industry. When the pope saw all this ruin fall on those who had laid down their arms at his instigation he was greatly disturbed at such wrongs. He condoled with Messer Rinaldo under these injuries, committed under his pledged word, bade him have patience, and look for a change of fortune. To this Messer Rinaldo replied: "The want of confidence shown by those who should have trusted me, and the reliance I placed on you, have ruined both me and my party. But I blame myself more than I do any one else for having believed that you, who had been hunted out of your own country, would have the ability to keep me in mine. Of fortune's tricks I have already had a plentiful experience, and as I never relied upon her in prosperity, so she injures me the less in adversity; I know that when it pleases her she will smile upon me again. Yet if she is ever pleased to do so I shall never think it an honour to live in a city where the laws are of less value than the individual. Because that country only is desirable where one's possessions and friends are to be enjoyed in security, and not one in which they can be readily taken away; and where friends, for fear of themselves, will not abandon you in the hour of your greatest need. To wise and good men it has always been less grievous to hear of the troubles of their country than to witness them. Thus it is more glorious to be an honourable rebel than an enslaved citizen." Messer Rinaldo then left the pope, full of anger, cursing himself, the indifference of his friends, his own bad judgment, and went into exile. On the other hand, Cosimo, having heard of his restoration, hastened back to Florence, and rarely has a citizen returning in triumph from victory been received by his country with such demonstrations of joy and by such a concourse of people as was Cosimo when he returned from exile. All saluted him as the benefactor of the people and the father of the country.

FIFTH BOOK

1434-1440

NATIONS, as a rule, when making a change in their system of government pass from order to disorder, and afterwards from disorder to order, because nature permits no stability in human affairs. When nations reach their final perfection and can mount no higher they commence to descend; and equally when they have descended and reached a depth where they can fall no lower, necessity compels them to rise again. Thus states will always be falling from prosperity to adversity, and from adversity they will ascend again to prosperity. Because valour brings peace, peace idleness, idleness disorder, and disorder ruin; once more from ruin arises good order, from order valour, and from valour success and glory. Hence it has been observed by wise men that arms take precedence of letters, and that captains are more needed in cities and countries than philosophers, because a state that has good and valiant armies achieves victories, and victories secure peace; and further, that the fortitude of brave armies cannot be corrupted by any surer means than by letters, nor can idleness find entrance into cities except by this great and dangerous deceit. This was perfectly well recognised by Cato, when the philosophers Diogenes and Carneades were sent as envoys from the Athenians to the Roman senate; for Cato, finding that the Roman youths followed admiringly the philosophers, and knowing the evil that would result to the country from this plausible idleness, passed a law that no philosophers should be allowed to enter Rome. By means such as these countries have been brought to ruin, but where men have learnt wisdom by suffering they have returned to good government, unless they have remained overwhelmed by some extraordinary disaster. These are the causes which have made Italy, first under the ancient Tuscans and then under the Romans, at one time happy and at another miserable. Although nothing has been rebuilt upon the ruins of Rome that could in any way renew her glory, as under some vigorous domination might have been effected, nevertheless there has arisen so much valour in some of the new cities and empires which have sprung from the Roman ruins that whilst no one of them has dominated the others, yet they have worked in harmony to free and defend themselves from the barbarians. Among these powers the Florentines, if they have been deficient in territory, have not been so either in energy or influence; for their situation in the midst of Italy, with their wealth and readiness to take the offensive, has placed them equally happy either to sustain a war brought against them or to secure a victory to those allied with them. But among these new principalities possessing high military qualities, peace could not be kept for any length of time; yet there was little of the harshness of war in their quarrels, because as there are none of the conditions of peace where principalities are constantly attacking each other, so there are none of the conditions of war where men are not killed, cities sacked, or territories laid waste. In those days war was carried on in such a desultory way that men entered upon it without any fear of its consequences, carried it on without danger, and concluded it without loss. So that whilst in other lands valour is enervated by long spells of peace, in Italy it was dissipated by the miserable way in which wars were waged, as can be clearly recognised in the events which will be related between 1434 and 1494, where it will again be seen that in the end a way was once more opened for the barbarians, and Italy was once more brought under their rule. If the deeds of our princes at home and abroad are not worth studying for their valour and dignity, as were those of their ancestors, yet they have other attributes which are not less worthy of consideration, which will show that even the noblest people can be held in check by a feeble and ill-regulated soldiery. If in the following description of the affairs of these corrupt communities one has nothing to relate of the fortitude of their soldiers, the valour of their captains, or the patriotism of their citizens, one will see with what deceit and with what craft and guile the princes, soldiers, and leaders of republics have achieved for themselves a reputation they have never deserved. It will be no less useful to study these actions than those of antiquity; for whilst the latter may inspire noble minds to follow them, the former will incite us to spurn and avoid them.

Italy had been brought into such a condition by those who dominated her, that when a peace was secured by common agreement between princes it would be almost immediately disturbed by the soldiers who remained under arms; thus war brought no glory and peace no rest. For example, when peace was made between the Duke of Milan and the league in 1433, the soldiers were unwilling to stand idle, and at once turned their arms against the Church. There were in Italy at that time two schools of arms, one the Braccescan and the other the Sforzescan. Count Francesco, the son of Sforza, was the head of one, whilst Nicolo Piccinino and Nicolo Fortebraccio were the leaders of the other. Almost all the soldiers of Italy deferred to one or other of these schools. The Sforzescan school was held in the higher estimation, because of the valour of the count and the prospect which the Duke of Milan held out to him that he should have in marriage his natural daughter. Madonna Bianca, the expectation of this connection bringing the count the highest consideration. For various reasons both of these two parties united in attacking Pope Eugenius after the conclusion of the peace of Lombardy. Nicolo Fortebraccio was moved to it by the ancient hatred between the Braccio and the Church; the count was only influenced by his ambition. Thus while Nicolo attacked Rome, the count made himself master of La Marca. The Romans, being unwilling to become involved in this war, drove Eugenius out of Rome, and he with difficulty and danger reached Florence. Eugenius, recognising the danger in which he stood, for he was abandoned by those princes who having only recently been anxious to lay down their arms were quite unwilling to take them up again for him, came to terms with Count Francesco, and yielded to him the lordship of La Marca, although the count had added presumption to the wrong of usurpation by signing his letters to his agents with Latin words, according to the Italian customs, meaning: Ex Girifalco nostro Firmiano, invito Petro et Paulo. Nor was the count content with the concession of territory, but desired to be created gonfaloniere of the Church, and this office also was conferred on him. So much more terror had war for Eugenius than a dishonourable peace. By this the count came into alliance with the pope and hostile to Fortebraccio, and the war which ensued between them was waged for many months in the territories of the Church, and did far more damage to the pope and his subjects than to those who waged it. Finally a truce was negotiated by the Duke of Milan, and an agreement was concluded by which both contestants were established as princes in the territories of the Church.

No sooner was this matter settled at Rome than war broke out again in Romagna, instigated by Batista da Canneto. This man had put to death some members of the Grifoni family at Bologna and driven out the papal governor and others of his enemies. In order to maintain his position he had recourse to Filippo, whilst the pope looked to the Venetians and Florentines to redress his wrongs; so that at once two great armies were set on foot in the Romagna. Filippo's army was led by Nicolo Piccinino, and that of Florence and Venice by Gattamelata and Nicolo da Tolentino. A battle was fought near to Isola in which the Florentines and Venetians were defeated and Nicolo da Tolentino taken prisoner and sent to the duke at Milan, where he died in a few days, either by treachery or from grief at his defeat. The duke did not follow up his victory, either because it had weakened him too much or because he expected the league would back out of the war after their defeat, and thus time was given to the pope and his allies to rally. This they did by appointing Count Francesco Sforza their captain and attempting to drive Nicolo Fortebraccio out of the territories of the Church, and thus bringing the war to a conclusion favourable to the pope. When the Romans saw that the pope had courageously taken the field they sought to come to terms with him, and these being arranged they received one of his commissioners. Nicolo Fortebraccio held among other towns Tiboli, Montefiasconi, Citta di Castello, and Ascessi, and being unable to keep the field had taken refuge in the latter town, where he was besieged by the count. Owing to the vigorous defence which Nicolo made, the siege was unduly prolonged, and it became necessary for the duke to take decisive steps to prevent the league obtaining a victory there, or in case the town were taken, then to be in a position to compensate himself elsewhere. Therefore, with a view to compelling the count to raise the siege, the duke ordered Nicolo Piccinino to invade Tuscany through Romagna. Whereupon the league, considering it of more importance to defend Tuscany than to capture Ascessi, ordered Count Francesco to contest the passage into Tuscany with Nicolo, whose army had already reached Furli. The count therefore moved his army to Cesena, and left his brother Lione in charge of his estate and affairs in La Marca. Whilst Nicolo Piccinino was endeavouring to invade Tuscany and the count to prevent him, Nicolo Fortebraccio attacked Lione, defeated him, took him prisoner, and dispersed his army. He followed up his victory by seizing many towns in La Marca. This event disturbed the count exceedingly, and leaving part of his army to oppose Piccinino he set off with the rest against Fortebraccio, and meeting him, defeated and took him prisoner. In this battle Fortebraccio was so severely wounded that he died a few days afterwards. This victory restored to the pontiff all the towns which Fortebraccio had taken, and brought the Duke of Milan to terms, which by the good offices of Nicolo da Esti, Marquis of Ferrara, were accepted. By this peace all the towns which had been occupied by the duke were returned to the Church, and the army of the duke sent back to Lombardy. Batista da Canneto, following the invariable destiny of those who owe everything to the position and abilities of others, fled when the men of the duke left Romagna, having neither power nor ability of his own to hold Bologna, to which city Messer Antonio Bentivoglio, the head of the hostile party, returned.

All these events occurred during the exile of Cosimo, and after his return, those who had brought him back, with many citizens who had suffered injuries, only thought of securing their position with the government. The signoria who succeeded to the magistracy in November and December were not content with what their predecessors had effected in favour of the Medici party, but prolonged and changed the place of exile of many of their opponents, and also banished many others. These oppressive measures fell not only on the men opposed to them, but was extended to their possessions, their relatives, and private friends, and if the proscription had been accompanied with bloodshed it would have equalled those of Octavius and Sylla; yet it was just tinged with blood inasmuch as Antonio, the son of Barnardo Guadigni, was beheaded, together with four other citizens, among whom were Zanobi Belfratelli and Cosimo Barbadori, who, leaving their place of exile, had gone to Venice. The Venetians, valuing the friendship of Cosimo higher than their own honour, sent these gentlemen prisoners to Florence, where they were shamefully put to death. These executions secured respect for the ruling party and dismayed its enemies, when they saw that so powerful a republic as Venice was ready to barter its honour with the Florentines for the lives of these men. At the same time it was believed by some to have been done not so much to please Cosimo, as to inflame the parties against each other in Florence, and by this bloodshed to make the divisions more acute, for the Venetians could see no barrier to their own greatness but Florentine unity.

The city being cleared of enemies and suspected persons, honours were conferred on new men with a view to encouraging the Medicean party; the Alberti family among others who had been guilty of rebellion against their country were restored; with few exceptions the nobility were absorbed into the ranks of the people; and the possessions of the rebels were divided at trifling prices among the citizens. Beyond these measures the party strengthened themselves with new laws and ordinances, and drew up fresh voting lists, taking their enemies out of the ballots and filling them up with the names of their own friends; and as if it were not sufficient for them to have selected the names for the ballot in order to keep their hold on the government—warned by the fate of their opponents—they determined that the magistrates, with whom rested the death penalty, should always be taken from among the heads of their party. It was therefore agreed that the accopiatori—the men who took charge of the balloting for the new voting—together with the old signoria, should have authority to appoint the new signori. They gave to the Eight of the guard the power of life and death. They provided also that all exiles who had completed their terms of banishment should not return unless the lords of the colleges, who numbered thirty-seven, should first record thirty-four votes in favour of restoration. The writing and receiving of letters was prohibited, and every word, sign, or familiarity that offered any affront to the government was to be heavily punished. If there remained in Florence any disaffected person whom these provisions did not reach, then he was to be afflicted by new penalties. Thus in a short time all of the hostile party were driven out or reduced to poverty and the government established firmly in the hands of the ruling party. In order to further secure assistance to themselves from outside, and to hinder those who might be inclined to avail themselves of such and to injure them, a league was formed with the pope, the Venetians, and the Duke of Milan for the defence of the state.

Whilst affairs in Florence were shaping themselves in this way, Giovanna, the Queen of Naples, died, and by her will left the kingdom to René d'Anjou. Alfonso, the King of Aragon, who was at that time in Sicily, was also preparing with the assistance of many barons to seize the kingdom. The Neapolitans and the remainder of the barons favoured the claims of René, but the pope, for his part, had no desire that either René or Alfonso should possess it, and desired that its affairs should be administered by one of his deputies. Alfonso, however, invaded the kingdom, and was received by the Duke of Sessa, whom he took with many other noblemen into his pay; and having Capua in his possession, which was held for him by the Prince of Taranto, it was his intention to force the Neapolitans to accept his terms; he also sent his fleet to attack Gaeta, which was held by the Neapolitans. Upon this the Neapolitans had recourse for aid to the Duke Filippo, who persuaded the Genoese to go to their assistance. This they were quite willing to do, not only for the satisfaction of the duke, who was their prince, but for the security of their commerce with Naples and Gaeta, and they at once fitted out a powerful fleet. When this came to the knowledge of Alfonso he strengthened his navy, set out in person to meet the Genoese, and brought them to an engagement off the island of Ponzio. His fleet, however, was defeated, and he with many princes was captured and sent as prisoners to Filippo by the Genoese.

This victory caused much anxiety to those princes who feared the power of Filippo in Italy, for they considered it would give him the opportunity of making himself master. But he, so contradictory are the actions of men, took a course entirely opposite to that which was expected of him. Alfonso was a clever man, and as soon as he was able to speak with Filippo, he pointed out to him that he was deceiving himself by favouring the cause of René and not his; because if René should become King of Naples he would use all his influence to bring Milan under the sway of the King of France, in order to have French aid close at hand, and not be obliged to open a way for it whenever he was pressed; for René could never be secure in Naples without the destruction of the Duke of Milan and the absorption of his state into that of France. Exactly the opposite would result if he, Alfonso of Aragon, became the King of Naples, for he would then have no enemies but the French, and it would be necessary for him to keep on terms with and support the duke and not the French, because he would always be compelled to obey the man who was in a position to open the door to his enemies. For this reason the real power and authority of the position would rest with Filippo, although the title of king would belong to Alfonso. Therefore it was of vital interest to Filippo to weigh well the danger of the one course and the advantages of the other, unless he should be more desirous of satisfying his revenge than of securing the safety of his state. In the one case he would remain a prince and free, in the other case he would be wedged in between two powerful princes, and would either lose his kingdom or live in continual fear, and as a slave he would have to yield obedience to his neighbours. These words so impressed the duke that he changed his intentions and liberated Alfonso, and sent him with all honour back to Genoa, and from thence to the kingdom. Alfonso then entered Gaeta, which had been seized by some of his partisans, as soon as his liberation was known.

The Genoese were most indignant with the duke for liberating the king without any consideration for them; for whilst they had encountered all the expenses and dangers, he had reaped the honours; on them had fallen all the abuse for the king's capture, whilst the duke had usurped the position of his liberator. During those times in which the city of Genoa had enjoyed its freedom, it had appointed by free votes a head of affairs, whom it called a doge. This officer did not thereby become an absolute ruler, nor even had he the control of affairs, but rather as one who should propose to the magistrates and council what had to be discussed. Genoa has many noble families so powerful that they render a very grudging obedience to the magistrates. Of these families the Fregosi and the Adorni are the most considerable. From this fact arises all those dissensions which completely upset public order, for these families not only fight among themselves, but often against the state, and thus it follows that first one party and then the other is trodden down or, in turn, overcomes it opponents. Sometimes it happens that those who have lost their positions appeal to foreigners. From this it followed, and it does so still, that he who rules in Lombardy will also rule in Genoa, as indeed it did when Alfonso was taken prisoner. Among the leading Genoese who had been instrumental in bringing Genoa under the rule of the Duke of Milan was Francesco Spinola, who, not long after he had brought his country into subjection, fell, as often happens in such cases, under the suspicion of the duke. Whereupon Spinola, indignant at the charge, went into a sort of voluntary exile at Gaeta, where he was residing at the time of the naval battle with Alfonso. Having carried himself in that engagement with great gallantry he appeared to have regained the approbation of the duke, and was able to claim as his reward permission to reside at Genoa in security. But finding that the duke still regarded him with suspicion, for the duke never believed that the man who loved the freedom of his country could ever love him, Spinola decided once more to tempt fortune, and to strike a blow for the restoration of his country to liberty and himself to fame and safety. He believed there was no other way by which to regain the good opinion of his countrymen than by making the hand which inflicted the wound carry the medicine for the cure. He judged that now, when the indignation against the duke was universal, was the time to carry his plan into execution. He communicated it to several men whom he knew to be like-minded to himself and persuaded them to join him.

The Feast of San Giovanni Batista had arrived, and was to be made the occasion of the entry into Genoa of Arismino, the new governor sent by the duke. He had already nearly reached the city accompanied by Opicino, the late governor, and many Genoese. Spinola would no longer delay carrying his plans into execution, so sallying forth from his house fully armed, accompanied by those who had shared his counsels, he went into the Piazza opposite to his house and shouted the name of liberty. It was a marvellous sight to see the incredible swiftness with which the people ran together at the sound of that name, giving those who for some reason or other were supporting the duke no time to sieze their arms, or even to find safety in flight. Arismino, with some citizens, sought refuge in the fortress which was held for the duke, while Opicino tried to find shelter in the palace where he had 2000 men under his command, hoping there to defend himself and inspire his followers with confidence. He therefore turned in that direction, but before he could reach the Piazza he was killed, torn to pieces, and his limbs scattered through the streets of Genoa. The Genoese then placed their city under the control of free magistrates; in a few days the castle and other strong places held for the duke were captured, and then the whole city was free from its bondage to the Milanese.

When affairs took this turn the princes of Italy, who had been so desperately alarmed lest the duke should become too powerful for them, hoped now to curb him. Seeing what had happened to him, and notwithstanding their recent league with Milan, the Florentines and Venetians made peace with the Genoese. Whereupon Messer Rinaldo degli Albizzi with other leaders among the Florentine exiles, finding affairs disturbed in this way and the world as it were turned upside down, were inspired with the hope of inducing the duke to declare war against Florence, and in an audience which they had with him in Milan, Messer Rinaldo spoke as follows: "If we who were formerly your enemies now come with confidence to enlist your aid in restoring us to our country, neither you nor any one else ought to be surprised, when political affairs are considered and the changes which fortune is making. Notwithstanding our past and present conduct, and what we have already done to you, and what we propose to do to our country, we shall always be able to show good and sufficient reason for our actions. No just man blames those who seek to defend their country by all the means in their power, and it was never our object to injure you, but to defend our country. You can bear witness that in the course of the great victories of the league, as soon as we found you inclined to peace we encouraged its conclusion as much as you yourself did. Therefore we are not conscious of having done anything to forfeit your goodwill. Nor should our country complain that we now ask you to employ those arms against her from which we formerly so obstinately defended her, because that country only deserves to be loved by its citizens which loves all its citizens equally, not that one which honours a few and neglects the rest. Besides this, the using of arms is not entirely reprehensible, because although cities are very composite bodies, yet they resemble simple ones, and as in the latter case there often arise infirmities which cannot be cured without fire and steel, so in the former there are many troubles which a good citizen would err greatly in leaving to rankle rather than in curing them, even though the sword should be necessary. What greater evil can there be in the body politic than slavery? What medicine is more necessary than that which has so often been employed before to cure it? Those wars only are just which are necessary, and those arms are hallowed when recourse to them is the only hope. I know of no necessity greater than ours, and no more pious action than to rescue one's country from slavery. Most surely, therefore, our cause being so holy and just, it ought to be so considered by us both. Nor is justification wanting on your side, because the Florentines have disgraced themselves by coming to terms with your rebellious lieges, the Genoese, after concluding a peace with you and consummating it with all solemnity. Thus if our cause fails to move you, your resentment at that indignity will do so. This enterprise would be especially easy now, for you need not expect to repeat your past experiences when you encountered the bravery of the Florentines in attack and their obstinacy in defence. These two virtues might reasonably cause you anxiety if that people were animated by the same spirit as before, but that has now been changed, for you cannot expect the same virtues to reside in a city which has so recently expelled the greater part of its wealth and industry. What steadfastness in defence can be looked for in a people torn by so many warring feuds? These terrible dissensions are also reasons why such wealth as remains will no longer be available, because men willingly offer their patrimony when they know it is to be spent for the honour and glory of the state, for they hope to recover in peace what they have lost in war; but they will not do so when they find themselves oppressed in peace by the same taxation as in war —having to endure in war the depredations of their enemies and in peace the injustice of their rulers. Citizens are injured far more by the rapacity of their fellows than by that of their enemies, for in one case it is unlimited whilst in the other it can be limited. In the late war you attacked a united city, now you will be against a disunited one; then it was to seize the state belonging to good citizens, now it is to take it from bad ones; then it was to destroy the liberty of a city, now it will be to restore it. It is not reasonable to expect that where so many different circumstances prevail a result similar to the last will follow; rather you should be inspired with a confident hope of victory. You can easily judge what aggrandisement to your state will follow. You will have Tuscany for your friend, bound to you by so many and great obligations, that she will be of more service to you in your enterprises than even Milan herself. And whereas at another time such an acquisition would be termed ambitious and violent, in the present circumstances it will be deemed just and righteous. Therefore let not this opportunity pass, and remember that if your other enterprises against Florence have only brought forth waste, disgrace, and disaster, this will be carried through with ease, and will bring you the greatest advantages and the most enduring fame."

Few words were really needed to persuade the duke to declare war upon Florence, impelled as he was by hereditary hatred and blind ambition, and spurred on by the recent injury he had received at the hands of the Florentines by their league with the Genoese. Nevertheless he recalled the treasure he had expended and the defeats he had experienced, and the illusory hopes of the exiles only added to the anxiety which such a perilous undertaking naturally brought him. But as soon as he heard of the rebellion in Genoa he sent Nicolo Piccinino with all the cavalry and infantry he could get together against it, in order that he might recover it before the citizens could arrange its defence, and he relied much upon the castle which still held out for him. Although Piccinino drove the Genoese from the hills round Genoa, and captured the valley of Pozeveri which they had fortified, and beat them back into the city, he could advance no further owing to the defence which the obstinate courage of the Genoese made, and finally was compelled to retire. Whereupon the duke, at the instigation of the Florentine exiles, ordered his army to cross the Levante and approach the borders of Pisa, where he could carry out operations on a larger scale than in the country of the Genoese, whence he would be able to develop his attack at leisure in such directions as might, be necessary. Nicolo therefore set his army in motion, attacked Serezana and captured it; then passed on towards Lucca, committed much havoc, and by this aroused the suspicions of the Florentines to the utmost; but he announced that he only wished to enter the kingdom of Naples, whither he was going to assist the King of Aragon. When these troubles broke out. Pope Eugenio retired from Florence to Bologna, where he endeavoured to compose matters between the duke and the league; but as the duke would not listen, he was informed that unless he consented to a treaty the pope would have to transfer the services of Count Francesco, who was in his pay, to the league. Although the pope took much trouble over the affair it was labour in vain, because the duke would not give way unless Genoa was yielded to him, and to this the league, who wished Genoa to retain her freedom, would not consent, therefore both parties despairing of peace prepared for war.

When Nicolo Piccinino reached Lucca the object of the new movement became apparent to the Florentines, and they despatched their army into the neighbourhood of Pisa, under the command of Neri di Gino, and having obtained the consent of the pope to Count Francesco joining them, they made their head-quarters at Santa Gonda. Piccinino from Lucca demanded entry to the pass in order that he might cross into the kingdom, and when this was refused he threatened to take it by force. The strength of the armies and the abilities of the captains were equal, and they remained for many days without moving, as neither of them were willing to tempt fortune, and both were delayed by the severity of the weather, it being now December. The first to move was Piccinino, who was informed that he could easily take Vico Pisano.

This he attempted, but did not succeed; he, however, laid waste the country round Vico, and burnt the suburb of San Giovanni alla Vena. Although this enterprise was in a great measure a failure, the inactivity of Count Francesco and Neri tempted Nicolo to undertake further operations, and he attacked Castello and Filetto and captured both towns. Even this did not cause the Florentine army to move, not because the count feared his enemy, but because the magistrates in Florence, out of respect for the pope, who was still labouring in the cause of peace, had not yet decided upon war. What the Florentines did from prudence their enemies believed they did from fear, and were encouraged by it to undertake fresh forays, and having decided to attack Barga appeared before it in great force. This caused the Florentines to put all considerations on one side, and not only determine to relieve Barga but to carry the war into the Lucca country. Count Francesco therefore marched against Piccinino, and having brought him to battle before Barga, inflicted a severe defeat upon him and forced him to raise the siege. The Venetians now decided that by these acts the duke had broken the treaty of peace, and therefore sent Giovanni Francesco da Gonzaga, their captain, to Ghiaradadda to lay waste the country of the duke and compel him to recall Nicolo from Tuscany. The recall of Piccinino and the victory they had obtained over him determined the Florentines to prosecute the war against Lucca, in the hope of capturing the city, and of this they had not much doubt seeing that the duke, the only man they had to fear, was deeply engaged with the Venetians. It was felt that the Lucchese had no just cause to complain of this attack, for they had sheltered the enemies of the Florentines and enabled them to attack their dominions.

In April, 1437, the count again set his army in motion, but the Florentines desired first to recover their own towns before attacking those of others, so they re-took Castello and all the towns which had been seized by Piccinino. They then turned in the direction of Lucca and attacked Camajore, which was at once surrendered; for although the citizens of that town were quite loyal to their lords, the present danger was more powerful than loyalty to distant friends. For these reasons Massa and Serezana fell before them. Having effected these captures they turned their faces towards Lucca about the end of May; they destroyed the standing corn and grain, cut down trees and vines, drove off the cattle, and stopped at nothing which would harass the enemy. The Lucchese, when they found themselves deserted by the duke, withdrew from the country districts which they despaired of defending, and with bastions and other fortifications strengthened the defences of their city. Having a strong garrison, and plenty of time to prepare themselves, they had great hopes of being able to hold their own, and in this hope they were encouraged by the memory of what had happened in their previous encounters with the Florentines. They only feared that the hardships of the siege might cause the mob, whose courage is unstable, to regard their own safety of more importance than the freedom of the city, and force it into some disadvantageous and shameful compact. Whereupon the people were called into the Piazza and inspired to the defence of their country by an address from one of their wisest and most respected countrymen.

"You ought to understand," said he, "that deeds which are determined by necessity deserve neither praise nor blame. Therefore if you are charged with the responsibility of this war which the Florentines have declared against you, under the belief that you rightly deserve it for having admitted into your city the soldiers of the Duke of Milan and permitted them to attack the Florentines, you err greatly in accepting that charge. Remember the persistent hostility of the people of Florence to you, caused neither by your injuries to them nor by their fear of you, but only by your weakness and their ambition; for the first gives them hopes of conquering you and the second provokes them to attempt it. Do not imagine that any merits of yours will remove that desire of theirs, or that any offences of yours will inflame it more to your injury. It is part of their nature to attempt to take away your freedom; it is yours to defend it. Whatever they do, or we do, to attain that end, let no one complain and let no one be surprised. Why, therefore, should we complain that they attack us, lay siege to our towns, bum our houses, and waste our country? Which of us is so foolish as to be surprised at it? Because, if we were able, should we not do the same or worse? Although the admission of Nicolo Piccinino into our city has afforded the Florentines a pretext for declaring war against us, yet if hc had not come they would have found some other excuse, and should the war have been deferred it might have been the worse for us. Thus it is not the admission of Nicolo into your city which you can blame, but rather your bad fortune and the ambitious nature of the Florentines. Then again you were not in a position to refuse the duke an entrance for his men, or when they were here to prevent their prosecution of the war. You know very well that without the assistance of some other power you are not safe, nor is there any power upon whom you can place so much reliance as upon the duke. He gave us our freedom, and it is only reasonable to expect that he will defend it. He has always considered our enemies as his. If, therefore, in order not to injure the Florentines, we had offended the duke, we should have lost a friend and increased the power of an enemy, and enabled him the more readily to injure us. Therefore it is far better to enter upon this struggle with the duke for our friend than to have peace with him for an enemy. Since he has been instrumental in drawing us into this trouble it is not reasonable to expect that he will abandon us. Let me recall to your memories the fury with which the Florentines have so often attacked us, and with what glory we have repulsed them, and how often we have been preserved with no other allies but God and time. And shall they not assist us again if we are only willing to exert ourselves? Formerly all Italy left us a prey to Florence; now we have the duke on our side, besides which we have every reason to think that the Venetians will not consent to our destruction, because they will look askance upon any increase in the power of the Florentines. On former occasions the Florentines were less hampered and had more expectations of assistance than now, and were, therefore, more powerful whilst we were weaker in every respect. At that time we defended a tyrant;

now we defend ourselves. Then the glory of our defence belonged to others; now it will be ours alone. In those days our enemies were united; now they are so no longer, for Italy is filled with sedition. But if we had none of these incitements to hope, a binding necessity should make us stand firm in defence of our homes. All enemies should be equally feared by you, because all desire your ruin and their own glory; but above all others the Florentines must be dreaded, because they would never be satisfied with our tribute and obedience to their rule, but would seize our persons and possessions and satiate their cruelty with our blood and their rapacity with our property; thus every one in every station of life ought to dread them. Do not let yourself be moved by seeing your fields laid waste, your villages burnt, your towns seized; because if our city itself can only be saved the rest of necessity will be saved also; but if we lose the city, then the safety of the rest would be of no advantage. If we maintain our freedom, the enemy can then only hold our outside possessions with difficulty; but if we lose our freedom then the possession of them would be useless to us. Take, therefore, your arms, and when you fight remember that the reward of victory will be the safety, not only of your country, but of your homes and your children."

The last words of the speaker were received with the utmost enthusiasm by the people, all swore to die rather than yield or listen to terms which would touch their liberty, and everything that was necessary to the defence of a city was taken in hand.

The army of the Florentines meanwhile had lost no time, and after having captured Monte Carlo, and committed immense damage in the surrounding country, it went into camp before Uzzano, intending to force the Lucchese who had been beaten back in every direction, and had no hopes of assistance, to surrender from hunger. The castle at Uzzano was too strong and well defended to be taken as easily as the others. The Lucchese, as was to be expected, finding themselves hard pressed, had recourse to the duke, and with words both rough and gentle sought his assistance.

At one time they enlarged upon their own merits, at another upon the offences of the Florentines, and they urged on him that his defence of them would encourage his other friends, whilst his desertion would dishearten them. If they were to lose life and liberty, he would lose his honour with his allies and credit with all those who for love of him had ever encountered any peril. To words they added tears, hoping that if his obligations did not influence him compassion might. Finally the duke, recalling his old hatred of the Florentines, also recognising his obligations to the Lucchese, and desiring above all things to prevent the Florentines from acquiring such possessions, decided to send a large army into Tuscany and attack the Venetians in such strength that the Florentines would be compelled to relinquish their enterprise against Lucca.

This conference and the decision of the duke to send an army into Tuscany were soon known in Florence, and damped the government's hopes of success in Lucca; the Venetians, however, were called upon to press the duke with all their forces and keep him occupied in Lombardy. But the Venetians themselves were in a bad position at this time, because the Marquis of Mantua had deserted them for the service of the duke, and consequently they were unable to take the field unless the Florentines at once sent Count Francesco to take over the command of their army, with the condition that he should bind himself to cross the Po in person, for they no longer wished him to abide by the long standing obligation whereby he was bound not to pass beyond that river. They stated that they could no longer maintain the war without a captain, and they would trust none other but the count, yet he would be of no use unless he could carry the war wherever it was necessary. It appeared of the utmost importance to the Florentines that the war should be prosecuted with vigour in Lombardy, but they also saw that without the count their attempt on Lucca would have to be abandoned, and they knew perfectly well that this demand of the Venetians was made rather to disturb them in that enterprise than because they needed the count. On the other hand, the count was willing to go into Lombardy to please the league, but he was unwilling to vary the conditions, fearing to endanger his prospects of the marriage promised him by the duke.

Thus the Florentines were distracted by two opposing passions — the wish to possess Lucca and the fear of war with the duke. As usually happens, fear predominated, and it was agreed that after the count had captured Uzzano he should go into Lombardy. There remained, however, another difficulty, the solution of which, although it did not rest with the Florentines, gave them more trouble and anxiety than the first, and this was the unwillingness of the count to cross the Po, for unless he did so the Venetians were unwilling to employ him. The only possible settlement was for one or other party to yield; under the assurance that no private promise was sufficient to break a public compact, and that he could thus avoid crossing the river, the Florentines induced the count to write a letter to the signoria of Florence promising to cross the river. It would follow from this arrangement that the Venetians having once begun the war would be obliged to continue it, and that the diversion of troops, upon which the Florentines were relying, would take place. On the other hand the Florentines assured the Venetians that this private letter would be quite sufficient to bind the count and that they ought to be content with it; that where it was possible to respect the engagements of the count to his father-in-law it should be done, and that there was no advantage to any of the parties in revealing the understanding without pressing necessity. By these means the transference of the count to Lombardy was secured, and, Uzzano being captured, the army was entrenched round Lucca to hold it securely, whilst the count handed over the command to the commissioners, crossed the mountains, and entered Reggio. In the meanwhile the Venetians had become somewhat suspicious of the count's real intentions, therefore, to put the matter to the test, they requested him before doing anything else to cross the Po and join the rest of their army. This was distinctly refused by the count; an angry scene ensued between him and Andrea Mauroceno, the Venetian envoy, in which they accused each other of arrogance and want of honesty; charges and counter charges were made, one party saying he was not engaged for that service, and the other that there should be no pay; finally the count returned to Tuscany and Mauroceno to Venice. The Florentines quartered the count in the country around Pisa, and hoped to induce him to rejoin them in the war against the Lucchese, to which he showed no inclination. When it came to the knowledge of the Duke of Milan that the count, out of consideration for him, had refused to cross the Po, he hoped to negotiate the safety of the Lucchese by the same means. He therefore begged the count to do his best to bring about a peace between the Lucchese and Florentines, and the duke let him understand that if he were able to include Milan in it, he should then have his daughter in marriage. The duke having no male child, this promise had great influence with the count, because in it he saw a way to become master of Milan. He therefore threw obstacles in the way of prosecuting the war, and, informed the Florentines that he would not move until the Venetians observed the terms of his agreement for pay, and that such payment was not sufficient in itself, for desiring to live securely in his estate he looked for other supporters than the Florentines. Therefore, if he were abandoned by the Venetians, it would be necessary for him to think of his own affairs, and he cleverly threatened to come to terms with the duke.

This quibbling and deceit highly displeased the Florentines, for they clearly saw that their enterprise against Lucca was lost, and that if the duke and the count were to join forces their own state would become threatened. Believing that the influence of Cosimo de' Medici with the Venetians would weigh with them, they sent him to Venice to persuade the senate to keep to the terms of their agreement with the count. The position of their affairs was discussed by him at length in the Venetian senate, and their relations with the rest of Italy, as well as the forces upon which the duke could rely; in conclusion he proved that if the duke and the count were to become allies, they would deprive the Florentines of their freedom and drive the Venetians into the sea. The Venetians replied that they knew well their own strength and also that of the rest of Italy, and believed themselves to be perfectly capable of holding their own; they were not accustomed to pay soldiers who fought for other people, therefore the Florentines ought to pay the count, since it was they whom he had served; but if the Florentines really wished to enjoy perfect freedom they must lower the pride of the count rather than pay him; there are no bounds to the ambition of men, and if they are to be paid for doing no service, they will soon demand something more dishonourable and dangerous; therefore it was necessary for the Florentines to take steps at once to curb the insolence of the count and not allow it to grow until it became incorrigible; if on the other hand, from fear or any other motive, they wish to keep on terms with him they must pay him. So Cosimo returned to Florence without having achieved anything.

Nevertheless the Florentines did their best to prevent the count breaking loose from the league, which indeed he was loth to do, but his desire for the marriage with the daughter of the duke kept him hesitating, and it only required a slight accident, as indeed happened, to dissolve his doubts. The count had left his estates in La Marca in charge of one of his most trusty leaders, a man named Furlano. This man, instigated thereto by the duke, threw up his position under the count and accepted the duke's pay. This caused the count anxiety for his own fate, and waiving all other consideration, he came to terms with the duke, and among the clauses of this agreement was one by which the duke was bound not to interfere in the affairs of either Romagna or Tuscany. Upon the conclusion of this treaty the count persuaded, and in a way compelled, the Florentines to make peace with the Lucchese, and seeing no other course open to them, they did so in the month of April 1438. By this treaty the Lucchese were confirmed in their freedom, whilst the Florentines kept Monte Carlo and a few other fortresses. After this the Florentines circulated throughout all Italy letters of complaint that as God and man were unwilling that the Lucchese should come under their rule, peace had been concluded with them; and seldom has there been such grief manifested over the loss of one's own possessions as the Florentines expressed at not having secured the possessions of Lucca.

Whilst the Florentines occupied themselves with these great enterprises they did not cease beautifying their city, or watching carefully the affairs of their neighbours. At the time of his death, Nicolo Fortebraccio, as we have shown, was married to a daughter of Count di Poppi. The count had held the town and fortress of Borgo a Santo Sepolcro in the name of his son-in-law, and had lived and ruled there until the death of Fortebraccio. After this he claimed to hold them as the dower of his daughter, and refused to surrender them to the pope, who claimed them as the property of the Church; whereupon the pope sent some forces under the patriarch to seize them. The count, finding that he was not in a position to repel the attack, offered the town to the Florentines, but they would not accept it; and the pope visiting Florence at this time the Florentines negotiated an arrangement between the count and the pope. Some hitch, however, occurred in the proceedings, and the patriarch invaded the Casentino and captured Prato Vecchio and Romena, and immediately offered them to the Florentines. These also were refused unless the pope would consent to their being given to the count. After much dispute the pope consented, on the understanding that the Florentines should use their best endeavours to induce the count to surrender the Borgo. Having settled this matter to the satisfaction of the pope, it occurred to the Florentines to ask the pope to personally consecrate the cathedral church of their city, Santa Reparata, the building of which had occupied many years, and which was now sufficiently finished for divine service to be celebrated there. To this the pope willingly consented, and in order to increase the honour due to him, as well as confer greater dignity on the city and Church, a scaffolding was erected from Santa Maria Novella, where the pope resided, to Santa Reparata of the width of four braccio and the height of two, covered entirely, both above and around, with the richest cloth. Upon this the pope, with his court, walked, together with such magistrates of the city and citizens as were deputed to accompany him; the rest of the citizens and people were assembled in the streets, houses, and in the church itself to witness the spectacle. When all the ceremonies which are customary on these occasions had been performed, the pope, desiring to show his appreciation to the people, conferred the honour of knighthood upon Giuliano Davanzati, a citizen of the highest repute and gonfalonier of justice at the time; the signoria not wishing to be outdone by the pope in honouring their own citizens, bestowed upon Davanzati the captaincy of Pisa for one year.

Differences arose about this time between the Roman and Greek Churches over the ritual of divine worship, and in the last council at Basle much had been said upon the subject by the prelates of the Western Church. It had been decided to bring pressure to bear upon the Greek emperor and prelates to induce them to attend another council, also to be held at Basle, when efforts were to be made to bring the Greek service into harmony with that of the Roman Church. Although the suggestion to yield in this matter to the Roman pontiff offended the dignity of the Greek empire and hurt the pride of the Greek prelacy, yet as they were experiencing at this time much trouble from the Turks, against whom they feared they would not be able to defend themselves without assistance, they decided to yield in order that they might ask for aid with more assurance. The emperor, the patriarchs, and the Greek prelates assembled at Venice, but the fear of the plague drove them to Florence. A council was held in the cathedral church of Florence, and after discussions carried on for many days the Greeks yielded and came into accord with the Roman Church and its pontiff.

It had been hoped that the treaties which had recently been agreed upon between the Florentines, the Lucchese, the Duke of Milan, and the Count Francesco Sforza, would put an end to strife in Italy, particularly in Lombardy and Tuscany. As to the struggle which was being waged in the kingdom of Naples, it was generally agreed that it could only be ended by the destruction of one or other of the combatants—René of Anjou or Alfonso of Aragon. Although the pope was very discontented at the loss of some of his territory, and the ambitions of the duke and the Venetians were well known, it was expected that the one from necessity, and the others from exhaustion, would rest awhile. But matters fell out otherwise, for neither the duke nor the Venetians could remain long at rest, and arms were soon again taken up, and Lombardy and Tuscany once more filled with strife. It was the possession of Bergamo and Brescia by the Venetians which stirred the haughty spirit of the duke, for he could not endure witnessing the marching and counter-marching threatening and disturbing his adjoining country, and he believed himself not only able to put an end to it, but even to retake his towns, if he could only detach the pope, the Florentines, and the count from their alliance with the Venetians. His plan was to seize Romagna, thinking that the possession of that province would put it out of the power of the pope to injure him, and that the Florentines finding the flames of war on their own borders would not stir, and if they did it would only be at a great disadvantage. The duke also bore in mind the grudge which the Florentines owed the Venetians for the Lucca affair, and believed that it would make them very loth to go to war for their sake. As to Count Francesco, the duke relied upon their recent alliance, and the prospect which was held out to him of becoming his son-in-law, to keep him neutral. To confine the trouble as far as possible, and to give less reason for others to interfere, at the same time to abide by the article of his agreement with Count Francesco that he should not attack the Romagna, the duke incited Nicolo Piccinino, as if moved by his own ambition, to invade that province.

When the agreement was fixed between the duke and Count Francesco, Nicolo Piccinino was in the Romagna, and in collusion with the duke spread abroad the report that he was extremely indignant at this arrangement being made with the count who was his mortal enemy, and in consequence of it he betook himself with

his army to Camurata, between Forli and Ravenna, and there fortified himself as if with the intention of staying until some new
enterprise should engage him. After the report of his indignation
against the duke had spread through Italy, Nicolo let the pope
know of all that he had done for the duke, and of the ingratitude
with which he had been treated, and that the duke had informed
him that, having now nearly the whole force of the armed men of
Italy under his two captains, he intended to seize Italy. But if his
Holiness desired it, one of these two captains whom the duke flat-
tered himself he controlled would be hostile, and the other not
available, to the duke; because if the pope would provide the
money, Nicolo would provide the men, and the states of the count,
which he had taken from the Church, should be attacked, and the
count then having to attend to his own affairs would be unable to
assist the ambitious designs of Filippo. These suggestions appearing feasible to the pope, he believed them and sent Nicolo 5000
ducats and many promises of promotion for him and his sons.
Although the pope was warned by friends to beware of deceit, he
would listen to no one who spoke of it. It appeared to Nicolo that
he ought no longer to delay action because his son Francesco had
already sacked Spoleto, to the great indignation of the pope,
therefore Nicolo decided to attack the city of Ravenna, at that
time held for the Church by Ostasio da Polenta. Either because
the undertaking was easy, or that he had a secret understanding
with Ostasio, the city capitulated in a few days upon terms. After
this Bologna, Imola, and Forli were occupied by him, and of the
twenty fortresses which were held in that state for the pope, wonderful to say, there was not one that did not fall into the hands of
Nicolo. As if it were not enough for Nicolo to have injured the
pope by robbing him of these fortresses, he insulted him by writing that it was only right his property should be taken from him,
for having deceitfully attempted to sever the friendship which had
existed so long between himself and the duke by sending broad-
cast throughout Italy letters stating that he, Nicolo, had deserted
the duke and joined the Venetians.

Having seized the Romagna, Nicolo left it in the care of his son, Francesco, and with the greater part of his army passed into Lombardy, where he joined the rest of the duke's army. He then occupied the country round Brescia, and laid siege to the city. The duke, who had only the one desire of being left alone to deal with the Venetians, now sent envoys to the pope, the Florentines, and the count with the view of clearing himself of the responsibility for Nicolo's actions in Romagna, stating that if what had been done was contrary to the articles of agreement, then it was contrary to his wishes, and letting them understand that, for this disobedience, Nicolo should suffer, as time and opportunity would show. To this the Florentines and the count gave no credence, but believed, as the truth was, that these declarations were only made to keep them quiet until he should have subdued the Venetians. These latter, full of confidence in their own power to overthrow the forces of the duke, did not intend to seek assistance from any one, but to carry on the war by themselves under their captain, Gattamelata. Count Francesco had fully intended, with the help of the Florentines, to go to the assistance of King René in the kingdom of Naples had not these disturbances in Romagna and Lombardy broken out. Although the Florentines were quite ready to assist René for the sake of the ancient friendship which bound them to the House of France, yet the duke would have replied by immediately offering his assistance to Alfonso, because of the friendship contracted with him during his detention at Milan. But both the Florentines and the duke, with their attention occupied by the war close at hand, were not in a position to meddle with one at a distance. The Florentines, however, seeing Romagna invaded and the Venetians driven back by the forces of the duke, and foreseeing in the ruin of others a presage of their own fate, sent urgently to the count to come into Tuscany and consult with them. They stated to him that some action must be immediately taken to counteract the ambitious projects of the duke, supported as they were by greater forces than ever before, otherwise every state in Italy would shortly have to suffer. The count knew perfectly well that the fears of the Florentines were well founded, yet he was held back by his desire to realise his hopes of marrying the duke's daughter. The duke was also aware of this wish of the count, and, in order to keep him quiet, encouraged him in his hopes. As the girl had already attained a marriageable age there was no reason for longer delaying, therefore all the customary arrangements for the wedding were made, and to induce the count to give more credence to his promises the duke added deeds, and sent the count 30,000 florins, which had to be given under the marriage settlement.

The war, however, continued to spread in Lombardy, and the troops of the Venetians were driven back in every direction, the vessels they had placed on the river were taken by the duke, the country around Verona and Brescia was occupied, and the cities themselves so closely besieged that, according to general opinion, they could not hold out for long. The Marquis of Mantua, who had been for many years in the pay of the Venetian Republic, had deserted its service and entered that of the duke. The republic was now thoroughly alarmed, and compelled to adopt the course which pride had forbidden in the beginning of the war. They recognised now their only hope of safety lay in an alliance with the Florentines and the count, and this they at once sought, although in fear and trembling, expecting a similar reply to that which the Florentines had received from them in the case of Lucca and the trouble with the count. They obtained, however, an answer more favourable than they expected or their previous conduct deserved, because the hatred of an old enemy prevailed with the Florentines over their anger with an old and well tried friend, and having foreseen the trouble which the Venetians would inevitably incur, they had pointed out to the count that his ruin would follow that of the Venetians, that he only deceived himself if he believed that he would be more highly valued in the time of the duke's good fortune than he had been when it was at its lowest ebb, and further that the only reason why the duke had promised him his daughter was because he was feared. Since promises which necessity compels us to make necessity alone compels us to keep, the duke must be kept to his by necessity, and this could not be done unless the Venetians were maintained in their position. Therefore it was for the count to remember that if the Venetians were driven to renounce their inland territories, he would then lose not only such advantages as might accrue to him from their holding such dominion, but also the advantages to be derived from the fear which such power would inspire in others; and if the count would but consider the affairs of Italy closely, he would recognise that there remained only those states who were hostile to him or were of no account. Nor, as he had often maintained, were the Florentines alone able to support him, therefore under all circumstances he ought to do his utmost to keep the Venetians in their position as an inland power. These considerations, and the resentment which the count felt against the duke for his trickery over the marriage question, now induced him to join the league, although even now he was not to be obliged to cross the Po, and a convention was signed between them in February 1438. The Venetians undertook to find two-thirds of the expenses and the Florentines one-third, whilst each party bound themselves to defend at their own cost the estates which the count possessed in La Marca. The league was not contented with its own forces, but increased them by enlisting those of the lord of Faenza, the sons of Messer Pandolfo Malatesti da Rimino and Pietrogiampagalo Orsino; although they tempted the Marquis of Mantua with the most lavish promises, they could not seduce him from his service with the duke. The lord of Faenza, although he had signed his agreement with the league, returned to the service of the duke with better terms. These circumstances reduced the hopes of the league of making a rapid settlement of their difficulties in Romagna.

Affairs in Lombardy were at this time also a source of great anxiety; Brescia was so hard pressed by the army of the duke that the news of her surrender might be expected any day, and Verona was in the same straits, and should one of these cities yield, all the preparations for war which had been made would be in vain and the treasure already expended would be lost. The only remedy which suggested itself to the Florentines was to send the Count Francesco into Lombardy, but there were three obstacles in the way. Firstly, the refusal of the count to pass the Po and carry the war beyond it; secondly, the dread of the Florentines lest they should stand at the mercy of the duke if the count were to leave them, for there was nothing easier than for the duke to retire behind his fortifications and hold the count at bay, whilst with a portion of his army he reinvaded Tuscany, and it was this probability which caused the gravest apprehensions among the party who now ruled in Florence; thirdly, the question of the route to be adopted by the count by which his army might unmolested reach Padua where the Venetian army then lay. It was the second of these difficulties which most concerned the Florentines, but recognising the situation, and wearied by the importunities of the Venetians who demanded the count, pleading that without him they were lost, the Florentines placed the necessities of the Venetians before their own perils. There then remained only the difficulty of the route, and this it was decided must be left to the Venetians to secure; and as Neri di Gino had already carried through the negotiations with the count, and had induced him to agree to cross the Po if ordered, the signoria instructed him to proceed to Venice to lay stress on what the Florentines had done, and to arrange the route and security of the count.

Neri set out at once by ship from Cesena for Venice, and no prince could have been received with more honour by the signoria than he was, for it was believed that the safety of the Venetian empire depended upon the results of his embassy. Neri being introduced to the senate spoke as follows: "Most serene prince, it has always been the opinion of my masters in Florence that the power of the Duke of Milan would be the ruin of their republic and your state, and that the safety of both was bound up in the strength of both. If this had always been acted upon by your signoria then we should have found ourselves in a better position, and your state would have been safe from the perils which now threaten it. But as you gave us neither assistance nor trust at the time when you should have done so, we have not been able to come swiftly to your aid; nor indeed have you been ready to ask it of us. You have known so little of us, either in your prosperity or adversity, that you have never realised that we always love those whom we have once loved, and always hate those whom we have once had cause to hate. The love which we bear to your city has been more than once proved by our readiness to send armies into Lombardy to assist you, even at our own peril; whilst the hatred we bear to Filippo, and always shall bear to his house, is well known to all the world. It is by no means easy to cancel an old friendship or an old enmity by a new injury or a new benefit. It is very evident to us that we could have remained neutral in this struggle with little hazard to ourselves and to the great satisfaction of the duke, because although by that he might destroy you and become lord over all Lombardy, yet we should not despair, for there would still remain enough energy in Italy to defend us. With every increase in power and dominion there comes fresh envy and hatred, from which wars and troubles are bound to arise. We know also that, in remaining neutral, we should avoid much expense as well as many dangers, for whilst the seat of war is now in Lombardy it will speedily spread to Tuscany if we move. Nevertheless all these anxieties have been thrown to the winds by us in our long-standing affection for you, and we have resolved that we will defend you with the same resolution as we should ourselves. To this end my masters have considered it necessary to relieve Verona and Brescia at all costs; and as this appeared impossible without the assistance of Count Francesco Sforza they deputed me, as his obligations compelled him not to cross the Po, to induce him to cross over into Lombardy and to carry the war into those districts. The count, recognising the force of those reasons which have influenced us, has signified his consent, and, unequalled in courtesy as he is invincible in war, he desires also to surpass that liberality which he sees we have extended to you, for he well knows in what danger Tuscany will stand after his departure, and recognising that we have preferred your safety to our own peril, he has determined also to sacrifice his own interests to the same object. Therefore I am here to offer you the services of the count and his 7000 horsemen and 2000 footmen, ready to meet your enemy wherever he can be found. I pray you, my lords, as do my masters and the count himself, that as the number of his men exceeds that which he was compelled to provide, you also will make him suitable recompense out of your liberality, in order that he may never repent having accepted service with you, nor we for having persuaded him to do so." This speech of Neri was listened to by the senate with the greatest attention, and if he had been an oracle he could not have influenced his audience more completely; for they did not wait for the doge to respond as was usual, but rising to their feet, with hands uplifted and their eyes filled with tears, they thanked the Florentines for their timely assistance, and Neri for being the man to bring it. They promised also that at no time should the memory of this help be banished from the hearts of themselves or their children, and that Venetia should always be as much a fatherland to the Florentines as to themselves.

When this enthusiasm had somewhat subsided, they began to discuss the route for the count to follow, in order that bridges should be built, roads made, and other matters arranged. There were four possible routes: one along the coast via Ravenna, but the greater part of this being along the shore and through marshes was not approved; the second was the more direct, but it was closed by a fortress called Uccellino which was held by the duke, and would have to be taken before it could be passed; this was a difficult task in the short time at their disposal, the utmost haste being necessary if they wished to succour the two cities; the third route was through the forest of Selvo, but the Po had flooded that part of the country and the way was difficult if not impossible; the fourth was through the Bologna district, across the bridge at Puledrano and thence to Cento and Pieve, skirting Bondeno and Finale, to Ferrara, whence by road and river the army could reach Padua, and join the forces of the Venetians. This route was finally chosen although it was difficult and enemies barred the way in places, but as soon as the count was notified of the decision he set off with the utmost despatch, and reached Padua on June 20, 1439. The arrival of this great captain in Lombardy filled the empire of the Venetians with the most sanguine hopes, and whereas they had despaired of their safety so recently, they now began to dream of new conquests. The first thing the count did was to march to the relief of Verona, and with a view to intercepting him, Nicolo moved his army to Soave, a castle situate between Vicenza and Verona, surrounded by a moat reaching from Soave to the marshes of the Adige. The count, finding himself stopped by the way of the plains, decided to carry his army through the mountains to Verona, assuming that either Nicolo would not expect him to make the attempt, the country being very rough and wild, or if expecting him to do so, would not have time to stop him. Providing himself, therefore, with provisions for eight days, he and his men crossed the mountains and descended into the plain close to Soave. Nicolo had erected some slight fortifications to bar the way, but they were quite insufficient to stop the count, and when Nicolo found that, contrary to all expectations, his enemy had successfully crossed the mountains, he at once retreated beyond the Adige, and the count entered Verona without opposition.

The first difficulty—the raising of the siege of Verona—having been easily overcome by the count, there remained the second— the relief of Brescia. This city is situate in such a manner near the lake of Garda that, although it may be closely invested by land, it can be provisioned by water. The duke had therefore put a fleet of galleys upon the lake, and in the very beginning of his victories had occupied all those towns which were able to provision Brescia from the lake side. The Venetians also had galleys there, but not in sufficient force to contest the supremacy of the lake with the duke. The count, therefore, decided to support the Venetian fleet by land, and by these means get into his possession those towns which withheld supplies from Brescia. To this end he planted his camp before Bardolino, a castle on the lake, and hoped that its capture would induce the others to surrender. But fortune was hostile to the count, and a fever breaking out among his men, he was compelled to retire to a pleasant and healthy place, the Veronese castle of Zevio. When Nicolo found that the count had retired, he determined to seize the opportunity of making himself master of the lake, therefore leaving his camp at Vegasio, with a party of chosen men, he attacked the Venetian fleet with the greatest energy and captured almost all the vessels. By this victory but few castles remained on the lake that did not at once surrender to him.

The Venetians were much alarmed by this disaster, and fearing that Brescia would surrender in consequence, they sent messengers and despatches to the count urging him at all costs to relieve the city. The count saw that all hope of succour to the besieged city by the way of the lake had failed, and that the trenches, barricades, and other impediments which Nicolo had raised in the open country made an attack on that side very hazardous, he therefore determined again to cross the mountains and in that manner come to the aid of Brescia as he had done to Verona. Having laid all his plans, the count left Zevio by the Val d'Acri and reached the lake of Sta Andrea, thence he marched to Torboli and Peneda on the lake of Garda. Hence to Tenna, which it was ncessary for him to capture before he could reach Brescia. Nicolo had in the meanwhile penetrated the designs of the count and conducted his army to Peschiera. He then, with the Marquis of Mantua and a picked body of men, went to meet the count, and coming to battle with him was severely defeated. Of his men a large number were taken prisoners, some found refuge on the galleys, and some found their way back to the main army. Nicolo himself turned back into Tenna, which he reached at nightfall, but fearing that if he remained there until the morning he would certainly fall into the hands of his enemies, he took a chance of much peril to avoid what was a very sure danger. He had with him only one servant, a German of great bodily strength, who had always served him with the utmost fidelity. Nicolo persuaded the man to put him into a sack and carry him over his shoulder, as if he were carrying baggage for his master, and thus get him out of the town to a place of safety. The army of the enemy lay all around Tenna, but in the hour of victory no guards were set, and but little order maintained, so that the German was easily able to save his master, whom he carried on his shoulder as a bag of booty; and thus passing through the whole encampment without any stoppage, brought Nicolo back in safety to his army.

Had this victory been taken advantage of with the same energy with which it had been achieved, it would have brought succour sooner to Brescia and greater success to the Venetians. But no advantage was taken of it, and the opportunity soon passing, Brescia remained in the same difficulties as before. Nicolo having returned to his men, pondered how to wipe out his recent defeat and prevent the Venetians from relieving Brescia. From some prisoners whom he had taken in the course of a skirmish, he learnt that the citadel of Verona was indifferently guarded and might be easily captured. Therefore it appeared to Nicolo that fortune had placed in his hands an opportunity to recover his own honour and turn the rejoicings of his enemy for his recent victory into lamentations over a great disaster. The city of Verona is situate in Lombardy at the foot of the mountains which divide Italy from Germany, and is built partly on the hills and partly in the plain. The river Adige rises in the valley of the Trento, but instead of spreading itself at once through the plains it turns to the left towards the mountains, whence it reaches the city and flows through its midst, not, however, dividing it equally, but leaving much more of it extended towards the plain than towards the hills. Upon these hills are two fortresses, one called San Piero and the other San Felice, which being well placed command the city, but are much stronger in position than in armaments. In the plain beyond the Adige and upon the walls of the city are two more fortresses, one thousand paces apart, one called the old and the other the new citadel. A wall stretches from one to the other of these strongholds, as it were a string to a bow formed by the usual city wall, and between the two walls there is a district of houses called the San Zeno suburb.

Nicolo Piccinino determined to seize these citadels and the suburb, believing that it would be easy to do so owing to the negligence of the guards, increased as it was since their recent victory; besides which there is no enterprise in war more likely to succeed than that which your enemy does not expect. Making, therefore, a selection of his men, Nicolo with the Marquis of Mantua went by night to Verona and, without being discovered, scaled the walls and captured the new citadel. From there the men descended into the town, broke open the San Antonio gate, and admitted their cavalry. Those of the Venetians who held the old citadel, and who had first heard of the attack when the guards of the new citadel were killed, and whom the bursting open of the gates had now told that their enemy was upon them, at once called the city to arms. The more courageous of the citizens when aroused flew to arms and gathered in the Piazza dei Rettori. Nicolo's men having in the meanwhile sacked the suburb of San Zeno had revealed to the citizens who had pressed forward that it was the duke's army which had regained possession of their city. Thereupon, despairing of protection, they implored the Venetian governors to seek refuge in the fortresses, and by surrendering the city preserve it and the citizens for a better fate. Therefore the governor and all others of Venetian nationality took refuge in the fortress of San Felice, whilst the chief citizens sought Nicolo and the Marquis of Mantua and begged them to spare the city rather than destroy it to their everlasting reproach, especially as in the service of their first masters they had earned no thanks, or any resentment from the invaders by defending themselves. Nicolo and the Marquis reassured them in some degree by telling them that, as far as military needs would permit, the city should be protected, but as they were convinced the count would hasten to retake the city, they must with the utmost speed get possession of all the strong places in it, and separate by ditches and barricades those which they could not capture from the rest of the town, in order that the enemy might experience the utmost difficulty in effecting an entrance.

The Count Francesco was at Trenta with his army when the news of the capture of Verona reached him. He at first believed it to be false, but when he learnt later from an indisputable source that it was true, he at once burned with a desire to retrieve his negligence. Although his captains counselled him to abandon the Verona and Brescia enterprises and march on Vicenza, to avoid being in turn besieged by the enemy, he would not consent, but determined once more to tempt fortune by attempting the recovery of Verona; and turning to the Venetian army contractors, and to Benedetto de' Medici, who had been sent by the Florentines as a commissioner, he assured them of the certain recovery of the city if but one fortress would hold out for him. He accordingly put his army in motion with the utmost despatch and set out for Verona. Upon hearing this Nicolo believed, as indeed he had been advised by this people, that the count was marching towards Vicenza, but soon learning that he had turned in the direction of San Felice, Nicolo at once ordered its defence. There was, however, no time for this now, as the fortification of the fortress was incomplete and the soldiers were scattered in all directions in their search for booty and ransom, and could not be assembled rapidly enough to oppose the count before he reached the fortress. From there the count descended into the city and speedily recovered it, to the confusion of Nicolo and his men. Nicolo and the Marquis of Mantua first took refuge in the citadel, but afterwards fled into the Mantuan country; here they collected the remnant of their men and rejoined the others who were besieging Brescia. Thus was Verona won and lost by the ducal army in four days. Having achieved this victory, and thrown supplies into Brescia, the count went into winter quarters at Verona. He also arranged for the building of galleys during the winter at Torboli, to enable him in the spring to attempt the relief of Brescia by water as effectively as by land.

The Duke of Milan now found himself with the fighting suspended for the present, and with but small hope of gaining possession of either Brescia or Verona. He attributed this to the money and counsel which the Venetians had received from the Florentines, who, in spite of all the injuries they had received from the Venetians, and all the promises the duke had made, were not to be alienated from their ancient friendship. The duke, therefore, decided to attack Tuscany in order that he might make Florence reap more effectually the fruits of the seed she had sown. He was encouraged in this determination by the Florentine exiles and Nicolo Piccinino. Both importuned the duke with reasons suitable to their motives; Nicolo was influenced by a desire to drive Count Francesco out of La Marca and to possess the estates of Braccio; the desire of the exiles was to return to their country. Nicolo demonstrated to the duke that he could invade Tuscany and yet maintain the siege of Brescia, being master of the lake and having the place closely invested by strong field works well defended and provisioned, and that should the count attempt any fresh enterprise there were plenty of captains and men left to oppose him, but it was not at all likely that he would attempt anything of the sort without first relieving Brescia, and this being impossible it was perfectly easy for the duke to invade Tuscany without abandoning his enterprise in Lombardy. Nicolo also proved to him that the Florentines would be compelled to recall the count, or be utterly undone, and that whichever course they adopted the victory would remain with the duke. The Florentine exiles, on their side, declared that as soon as Nicolo approached Florence with his army the people, wearied with the exactions and arrogance of their rulers, would throw down their arms; the exiles could promise an easy approach to Florence by the Casentino route, owing to the friendship between Messer Rinaldo and the lord of Casentino. All this confirmed the duke in his determination to invade Tuscany. During this time the Venetians did not cease to urge the count to push on the relief of Brescia, although the winter was extremely severe, but the count refused to do this, alleging that he ought to wait for the open season when his fleet would be ready, and then by both land and sea the attempt should be made. This reply caused the Venetians much displeasure, and they became dilatory in their supplies to the army, causing many men to desert.

These events gave much alarm to the rulers of Florence, for not only were they making no progress in Lombardy, but the war was approaching their own doors in Tuscany. At the same time the army of the Church was inspiring them with some anxiety, not that the pope was hostile to them, but it was the fact that the army gave more obedience to its commander, the patriarch, than to the pope himself. Cardinal Giovanni Vitelleschi Cornetano, now the Patriarch of Alexandria, was formerly the Apostolic Notary, then Bishop of Recanati, and ultimately received the hat and was created Cardinal of Florence. He was a bold and astute man, greatly beloved by the pope, who placed him at the head of the army of the Church, and made him captain of all the papal undertakings in Tuscany, Romagna, the kingdom, and in Rome. He knew well how to manage men, and had thus acquired so great an authority both with the pope and the army that the one feared to refuse him anything, whilst the other refused to obey any one but him. The patriarch was in Rome when the report spread that Nicolo was intending to invade Tuscany, and it was his presence there which had caused so much anxiety to the Florentines; the patriarch's hostility to Florence had been caused by the banishment of Messer Rinaldo, because the terms of the agreement which had been fixed by him as mediator between the parties had never been observed by the Florentines, but, on the contrary, as soon as Messer Rinaldo had laid down his arms the agreement was broken and Messer Rinaldo driven into exile. This caused the rulers in Florence to immediately suspect that if Messer Rinaldo should join Nicolo when he came into Tuscany then the time had arrived when Messer Rinaldo's restoration was to be attempted. At the same time it appeared to the Florentines that the intentions of Nicolo were exceedingly doubtful, for why should he abandon an enterprise half completed, to undertake one so uncertain as this one, and in absence of more information they believed that some deceit was intended. These suspicions they communicated to the pope, who had already repented of his error in parting with so much of his authority to the patriarch.

Whilst these suspicions were occupying the minds of the Florentines, fortune threw in their way a weapon against the patriarch. The republic was accustomed to keep in many places persons who carefully watched all who carried letters, in order to discover anything that might be plotted against their government. By chance some letters written by the patriarch to Nicolo, without the knowledge of the pontiff, were discovered at Montepulciano, and at once sent to the pope by the commissioners for war. Although the letters were written in cypher, and their meaning put in such a way that no one could draw any definite conclusions from them, yet their very obscurity, and the fact that they were addressed to an enemy, so alarmed the pontiff that he decided to make sure of the patriarch, and he entrusted the execution of his design to Antonio Rido of Padua, the castellan of San Angelo in Rome. This man was empowered to execute his commission swiftly and only waited for his opportunity. The patriarch had determined to march into Tuscany at once, and had arranged to leave Rome on the following morning. He wrote the castellan that he would be upon the bridge early and had some matters to discuss with him. This was Antonio's opportunity, and having given his men their orders he waited for the patriarch at the appointed time. To ensure the safety of the fortress this bridge could be lifted up or let down as required, and as soon as the partiarch had reached it Antonio gave the appointed signal to his men to close the bridge, and at one stroke the patriarch passed from the head of an army to a prison. His men at first were inclined to make some disturbance, but retired on learning that what had been done was at the instance of the pope. The castellan endeavoured to soothe the patriarch with gentle words, and gave him encouragement that all might yet be well, to which the patriarch replied: "Great men are not thrown into prison merely to be set free again, and men who deserve to be imprisoned do not deserve to be set free again." He died in prison very shortly afterwards, and the pope made Lodovico, the Patriarch of Aquileia, the leader of his army. The pontiff who had never had any wish to be backward in a war between the duke and the league was now glad to take a hand in it, and he promised to assist in the defence of Tuscany with 4000 cavalry and 2000 infantry.

The Florentines were thus freed from this danger, but there still remained the anxieties connected with Nicolo's actions, and the trouble in Lombardy arising from the difference between the count and the Venetians. In order to compose these latter they sent Neri di Gino Capponi and Messer Giuliano Davanzati to Venice, commissioning them to discuss the manner in which the war was to be conducted in the coming year, and they further instructed Neri that, having learnt the views of the Venetians, he should then proceed to the count and learn his, and he was also to impress upon the count the points which were essential to the well-being of the league. The ambassadors had scarcely reached Ferrara when they heard that Nicolo had crossed the Po with 6000 cavalry, whereupon they hurried on to Venice. Here they found the signoria fully determined to relieve Brescia in spite of the winter season, because the city could not hold out until the spring when the galleys would be ready, and any aid that was to be given must be given at once, otherwise the city would surrender; the loss of all their possessions on land would follow this, and the sphere of the duke's influence would be greatly enlarged. With this in his mind, Neri went on to Verona to hear what the count had to say against it. The count demonstrated very clearly that to march against Brescia at this time was folly and perilous to their success in the future, for nothing of any benefit to the city and nothing but discomfort and disgust to the army would result; that when the proper time did arrive for action, the army would be compelled to return to Verona to replenish its stores and arms which had been wasted in the winter months, and which would be then required; thus instead of employing their time in fighting it would be consumed in passing to and fro between Brescia and Verona. Messer Orsatto Justiniani and Messer Giovanni Pisani had been sent on the part of Venice also to discuss this matter with the count; after much consideration it was decided that the Venetians should pay the count 90,000 ducats and his men forty ducats per lance for the coming year, and that as soon as possible the entire army should take the field, attack the duke, and compel the return of Nicolo to Lombardy. Having concluded this the deputies returned to Venice. Owing to the enormous sums of money required, the Venetians met with much difficulty in collecting it.

In the meanwhile Nicolo Piccinino had followed up his intentions, reached the Romagna and induced the sons of Messer Pandolfo Malatesti to desert the Venetians and join the duke. Whilst this was displeasing to the Venetians it was much more so to the Florentines, because they had hoped to be able to hold their own in the Romagna, but this rebellion of the Malatesti alarmed them, for they feared that their captain, Giampagolo Orsino, who was then in the territory of the Malatesti, would be seized and disarmed. This news also caused great alarm to the count, and fearing for his estates in La Marca, which the arrival of Nicolo endangered, he left Verona for Venice in order to go to their defence. In his interview with the doge he pointed out to him that it would be to the interest of the league that he should be sent into Tuscany, for war must be carried on against the captains and armies of the enemy wherever they can be found, not against towns and their garrison, because if the armies are beaten the war is then ended, whereas if they be left unfought the war spreads far and wide. He declared that La Marca and Tuscany would be utterly lost unless a vigorous opposition was made to Nicolo, and their loss would bring no advantage to the cause in Lombardy. But whilst the remedy rested with him he did not intend to abandon his friends or his subjects, and since he went into Lombardy as a lord, he did not intend to leave it as a mere condottiere. To this the doge replied that it was very evident that if the count not only left Lombardy but repassed the Po, all the inland territories of the Venetians would be lost, and they need expend no more money in the attempt to defend them, for it was not wise to defend a thing that must be lost in the end; and it would be less reproach to them to lose the territory and save their money than lose both. When these territories were lost, it would soon be seen of what importance the reputation of Venice had been towards the maintenance of Romagna and Tuscany. Therefore, said the doge, they differed entirely from the count, because they believed that whoever was master in Lombardy would be master elsewhere, and the victory in Lombardy should be easy, because the policy which Nicolo had adopted exposed the duke to attack and ruin before he could recall Nicolo or provide any other defence. If the count would only examine carefully what had happened, he would see that the duke had sent Nicolo into Tuscany to draw the count out of Lombardy, and so remove the seat of war from his own territory. And if the count should follow Nicolo, when there was no need for it, the duke would see and enjoy the success of his plans. On the other hand, if the Venetians maintained their army in Lombardy, and made such provision as they could in Tuscany, the duke would see too late the false move he had made, and having lost in Lombardy and gained nothing in Tuscany he would stand in the utmost peril. Each party having stated his views, it was decided that nothing should be done until the result could be seen of the agreement between the Malatesti and Nicolo, whether the Florentines could rely upon Giampagolo, and whether the pope would support the Florentines in earnest, as he had promised. Soon after this conclusion was reached, it came to their knowledge that the Malatesti had been influenced more by fear in coming to terms with Nicolo than by any evil intentions, that Pietro Giampagolo had reached Tuscany with his troops, and that the pope was more determined than ever to assist the league. The count was satisfied with this information, and decided to remain in Lombardy, and also to allow Neri Capponi to take back with him to Florence 1000 cavalry and 500 men of other arms. And should affairs in Tuscany fall out in such a way that the assistance of the count was necessary, then Capponi must write to him and he would go at once. Neri Capponi reached Florence in April, and was joined by Giampagolo the same day.

Nicolo Piccinino in the meanwhile had settled affairs in the Romagna and arranged a descent into Tuscany. He decided to cross the mountains at San Benedetto, and thence pass through the valley of Montone; but having found this pass held in force by Nicolo da Pisa, he considered it vain to attempt it with his troops. When the Florentines found themselves suddenly threatened, without either leaders, soldiers, or munitions, they at once sent some citizens to defend these passes. Among these men there was one Messer Bartolommeo Orlandini, a knight, who was placed in charge of the castle of Marradi and of the pass which it commanded. Nicolo Piccinino, finding that he could not force the pass of San Benedetto owing to the energy of its defender, bethought himself of the castle of Marradi, which he might carry, relying on the pusillanimity of its guardian. Marradi is placed at the foot of the mountains which separate Tuscany from Romagna, and faces Romagna at the entrance to the Val de Lamona. Although it was not fortified, yet the river and the mountains gave it great strength, and its garrison was loyal and well armed. The river banks were steep and rugged, and it was impossible to approach the castle if the little bridge over the river were defended, and thus the position was very secure. Nevertheless the cowardice of Messer Bartololommeo so infected the garrison that all the advantages of position were lost, because on the first rumour of the enemy's approach everything was abandoned, and Bartolommeo fled with his men, not stopping until he reached the suburb of San Lorenzo. Nicolo having entered the abandoned castle, astonished at finding it undefended and marvelling at the ease with which it had been acquired, passed on to Mugello, where he seized several castles. At Pulicciano he rested his forces. From here he harried all the country to the hills around Fiesole, and even crossed the Arno and robbed and burned up to within three miles of Florence.

The Florentines were not in any way alarmed by this raid upon their territory, but they recognised the importance of keeping the city under firm government; and in this they met with no difficulty, for Cosimo was held in high esteem by the people, and the magistracy was in the hands of a few powerful men, who repressed with severity those who were inclined to be discontented with the government or who desired any change. The Florentines also knew of the forces with which Neri would return, according to the agreement made in Lombardy, and they also were expecting the pope's army. Neri arriving and finding the city in this posture, decided to move into the country and exercise some check upon Nicolo in his daily raids. Therefore with the cavalry he had brought with him and some infantry raised among the citizens, he recaptured Remoli which the enemy held, and encamping there effectually kept Nicolo in check. Nicolo having seen with what indifference the Florentines had endured his raiding of their country, and having observed the calmness with which the city had maintained itself, decided upon some enterprise which would induce the Florentines to follow him, when he would have a chance of bringing them to battle, in which his previous experience led him to hope that he would prove victorious.

Among the men whom Nicolo had in his army was Francesco, the Count of Poppi. He had formerly been in alliance with the Florentines, but when Nicolo reached Mugello he joined him. Although the Florentines had reason to doubt his loyalty, they had tried to ensure it by conferring many benefits upon him and entrusting some neighbouring towns to his command. Nevertheless the love of faction has such influence over men that neither the fear of danger nor receipt of favours could loosen the ties which bound the count to Messer Rinaldo degli Albizzi and other chiefs of his party who had ruled in Florence. As soon as Nicolo approached Mugello the count joined him, and provided him with supplies and transport to enable him to move on to Casentino; he also gave him advice as to the strength of the Florentines, and the best means of harassing them. Nicolo took his advice and marched to Casentino, seized Romena and Bibbiena, and afterwards encamped before Castel San Nicolo. This castle is situated at the foot of the mountains which divide Casentino from the Val d'Arno, and being well placed and defended was difficult of capture, although Nicolo continually battered it with catapults and other engines of war. This siege lasted for more than twenty days, during which the Florentines were enabled to get their forces together, consisting of 3000 cavalry under several condottieri, and assemble them at Fegghine. Pietro Giampagolo was the captain, and with him were Neri Capponi and Bernardo de' Medici. To them came four men from San Nicolo, begging for assistance. The commanders examined the position, but concluded that no help could be sent, because the only route into the Val d' Arno was over the mountains, the passes of which could be more readily seized by the enemy than by them, as the enemy were close to the passes and the advance of the Florentines could not be kept secret. Thus the Florentines would not attempt a relief which would probably be unsuccessful, and might be the ruin of their army. The commissioners bestowed great praise upon the garrison for its loyalty, and begged them to hold the castle as long as possible before surrendering, Nicolo got possession of the castle after thirty-two days' fighting, and the expenditure of so much time over so trifling a matter was largely the cause of the failure of his expedition. Had he kept his army round Florence the government would have experienced far more trouble with the enemy at the gates in assembling their forces, getting provisions, and raising money from the citizens; it would have also given encouragement to those within the city who, seeing the serious character of the war, would endeavour to bring about a peaceful arrangement with Nicolo. But the desire of the Count di Poppi for revenge on the garrison of the castle, who had long been his enemies, led him to give the counsel which Nicolo accepted to please him, and which finally ruined both men. The indulgence of private passions are generally injurious to affairs of state. Nicolo followed up his success at San Nicolo by capturing Rassina and Chiusi. Count Poppi endeavoured to persuade him to remain in these parts, pointing out to him with what advantage he could extend his operations round Chiusi, Caprese, and Pieve, make himself master of the mountains, descend thence upon Casentino, the Val d'Arno,

Chiana, and the Trevere, and be always ready for any movement which his enemy might develop. But Nicolo, looking at the rocks, said to the count, "My horses cannot eat stones," and proceeded to the suburb of San Sepolcro, where he was well received. From here he made overtures to the people of Castello, who, however, having friends in Florence, would not listen to him. He then went to Perugia with forty cavaliers, desiring the inhabitants to pay him homage. He was received with every mark of respect, being a citizen of that place, but in a few days he incurred their suspicions, and after attempting to come to terms with the legate and the Perugians, he received 8000 ducats and rejoined his forces. He also made an attempt to seize Cortona by treachery, but the plot was discovered and failed. This happened owing to a warning which Bartolommeo di Senso, one of the chief citizens, received from a countryman, a friend of his, as he was going one evening to mount guard at one of the gates. He was told that unless he wished to be killed he ought not to go, and upon Bartolommeo inquiring further he learnt all the particulars of the conspiracy. These he revealed to the captain, who secured the leaders in the plot and doubled the guards at the gates. He then waited for Nicolo, who came at night according to the time appointed, but finding the conspiracy discovered returned to his quarters.

Whilst these affairs were transpiring in Tuscany with but little gain to the forces of the duke, those in Lombardy were hastening towards his ruin. As soon as the season permitted the count to take the field with his army, he prepared to drive the duke from the lake by the fleet which the Venetians had fitted out during the winter, believing that if he could accomplish this the rest would follow. Thereupon he attacked the fleet of the duke and defeated it, and at the same time put his army in motion and captured several strongholds of the duke. Upon hearing of these disasters, and of the ruin which was impending, the remainder of the duke's army investing Brescia, at once raised the siege, and Brescia after three years' close investment was free. The count followed up the retreating foe to Soncino, a castle situate on the river Oglio, and drove him thence to Cremona, where the duke made a stand in order that he might strike a blow in defence of his state. Here the count pressed him day by day, until the stupidity of sending Nicolo into Tuscany was brought so forcibly home to the duke that he wrote Nicolo informing him of the position in which he found himself, and ordering him to leave Tuscany and return to Lombardy with the utmost despatch.

During these events the Florentines had joined their army with that of the pope and encamped at Anghiari, a castle at the foot of the mountains which divide the Val di Tevere from the Val di Chiana, four miles from the Borgo San Sepolcro, amid plains suitable for the manœuvres of cavalry and other movements of armies. When the Florentines heard of the count's victories and the recall of Nicolo, they fancied they had conquered without powder and shot or drawing a sword, and the commissioners gave orders that as Nicolo would only remain a few days longer in Tuscany no battle was to be fought. These instructions came to the knowledge of Nicolo, and although he was under the necessity of leaving Tuscany he would not go until he had struck a blow at the Florentines, therefore he decided to force a battle upon them, in the expectation of finding them unprepared and with no thoughts of fighting. In this he was encouraged by Messer Rinaldo and the Count di Poppi and also the Florentine exiles, who all saw their hopes destroyed if Nicolo should leave, but believed that if he could be induced to fight he might conquer, or at least be defeated with honour. Nicolo, having made his resolution, moved his army from its encampment between Castello and the Borgo, and reached the latter place without the knowledge of the enemy. Here he was joined by 2000 men, who came to his standard relying on his valour and the promise of plunder.

Nicolo formed up his forces in battle order and marched towards Anghiari, and had approached within about two miles of it when the dust he raised betrayed him to Micheletto Attendolo, who, perceiving that it was the enemy, gave the alarm. There was immediately great disorder in the Florentine camp, for all discipline had been neglected, owing to the belief that the enemy was at that time far distant and more disposed to flight than fight; many men had put away their arms, many were away from their quarters, many seeking shade from the prevailing heat, and many away on their own business; yet by the energy of the commissioners and captains the men were mounted and in battle array before the enemy arrived. And as Micheletto was the first to discover so he was the first who was ready to fight, and getting his company together he rode swiftly to the bridge over the river which crosses the highway not far from Anghiari. Pietro Giampagolo had upon his arrival levelled the ditches which bound the road running between the bridge and Anghiari, so that Micheletto was able to station himself upon the bridge, with Simoncino, a condottiere of the Church, and the legate flanking him on the right, and with Pietro Giampagolo and the infantry lined up on the left bank of the river. The bridge was therefore the only spot on which the enemy could get at the Florentines, whilst they had only the bridge to defend. The infantry of the latter had orders that, if the enemy's infantry should approach the road in order to give flank support to their cavalry, they were to fire upon them with their cross-bows and so prevent them from taking the Florentine horse who might cross the river in the flank. The first body of the enemy who appeared were received by Micheletto and driven back, but Astorre and Francesco Piccinino, coming up to their support with a chosen body of troops, smote Micheletto with such fury that they drove him off the bridge and pursued him to the foot of the road which leads to the suburb of Anghiari. But here the Piccinino men were taken in the flank, and they in their turn were driven back, and once more the bridge was in the possession of the Florentines. The fight lasted two hours, during which Nicolo and the Florentines were alternately masters of the bridge, although Nicolo was fighting at great disadvantage both on his own and also on the far side of the bridge, because when his men succeeded in getting across they found large bodies of men drawn up on the levelled plain ready to receive them, and fresh troops ready to take the place of those who were exhausted. On the other hand, when the Florentines were established on the far side of the bridge, where the ditches and banks had not been levelled, Nicolo could not bring up his reserve troops; and although Nicolo captured the bridge several times he was unable to hold it, because the enemy poured in fresh troops and drove him back. When, however, the bridge was finally taken and held by the Florentines, and they had their men established on the road, the fury of their attack, and the nature of the ground, as we have seen, prevented Nicolo from bringing up his reserves; the front ranks of his men becoming inextricably mingled with the rear, they broke; the entire army was soon in confused flight, and never stopped until it reached San Sepolcro. The Florentine soldiery at once fell to plunder, which in men, horses, and booty was immense, not more than a thousand horse escaping with Nicolo. The men of the Borgo who followed Nicolo for the sake of plunder were plundered themselves, for they were all captured and held for ransom, and their ensigns and equipments taken from them. This victory brought much more advantage to the Tuscans than loss to the duke, since had the Florentines lost the day all Tuscany would have fallen to the duke, but in losing the battle the duke had only lost arms and horses which money would soon replace. There never was a period in our history when war could be waged in the country of others with less peril to the invader than in those days, for in such a rout as at Anghiari, following a long battle lasting from the twentieth to the twenty-fourth hour, only one man was killed, and he died by neither wound nor gallant blow, but fell from his horse and was trampled to death. Men could fight in security in those days, because they were all on horseback covered with armour and safe from death. Whenever they surrendered there was no reason they should die; therefore, defended in combat by armour, when unable to fight any longer they surrendered.

This fight and its results are a signal example of the miserable character of the fighting of those days. The Florentines, having conquered Nicolo and driven him into Borgo, were for following the victory up, besieging him there, and thus ending the war; but the condottieri and their soldiers would not consent, alleging they had their wounded to attend and their booty to secure; and what was more, on the following day they left for Arezzo without the permission of the commissioners or the orders of the captains. Having deposited their plunder in that town they returned to Anghiari. Action so contrary to all recognised ideas of duty or military order ought to have been punished if the remnant of the army retained any conception of discipline, by depriving them of the fruits of a victory which had been gained by no merit of theirs. Besides this, the commissioners desired to retain as prisoners the men-at-arms who had been captured, but, contrary to their orders, they were liberated. It must be a wonder to all men that an army so constituted could possess sufficient valour to win a battle, or that an enemy could be found miserable enough to allow itself to be beaten by such fighters. However, in the passing and repassing of the Florentine army between Arezzo and Anghiari, Nicolo had ample time to get his men out of Borgo and start for Romagna. With him went the Florentine exiles, who had now lost all hopes of regaining their fatherland; they divided themselves into parties and settled in or away from Italy according to their opportunities. Among them Messer Rinaldo degli Albizzi chose Ancona for his home, and having lost his earthly country, to gain one in heaven; he went on a pilgrimage to the Holy Sepulchre; from there he returned, and whilst sitting at table, during the celebration of his daughter's marriage, he suddenly died, favoured in this by fate, since on the least unhappy day of his exile he passed away. It can truly be said that he was a man who bore honourably every change of fortune, or rather he would have done so more signally had he chanced to have lived in a united city, because those qualities which brought him to ruin in a divided city would have secured him many honours in a united one. After the departure of Nicolo and the return of their men from Arezzo, the commissioners presented themselves before Borgo, the people of which town were willing to give themselves up to the Florentines who were, however, unwilling to accept them. In the course of the negotiations the papal legate suspected that the Florentines were unwilling that the town should be taken possession of for the Church. Thereupon a dispute arose between them, which would have ended in a conflict between the Florentine and papal troops if the discussion had lasted much longer; but in the end the legate gained his point and the matter was settled without strife.

Whilst these events were happening at Borgo it was reported that Nicolo was marching on Rome, although some said it was toward La Marca. Under these circumstances it appeared right that the legate with the Sforzescan forces should march towards Perugia, in order that he could turn to Rome or La Marca, whichever place Nicolo should make for. With them went Bernardo de' Medici, whilst Neri and the Florentine forces invaded the Casentino. To fulfil this decision Neri proceeded against Rassina and captured it, and with equal despatch took Bibbiena, Pratovecchio, and Romena; from thence he attacked Poppi and closely invested it on two sides, one in the plain of Certomondo and on the other side from the hill near to Fronzole. The Count di Poppi, finding himself abandoned by both God and man, shut himself up in his town, not that he had any hopes of succour, but in order to obtain terms. Neri held him fast, and the count finally demanded terms, and obtained as good as he had reason to expect. The lives of himself and his family were to be spared, and he was allowed to depart with such possessions as he could carry, and he was to cede his town and estate to the Florentines. Before the capitulation was complete the count descended to the bridge over the Arno which flows at the foot of the town walls, and in his affliction thus spoke to Neri: "If I had correctly measured my strength with yours, I should have been rejoicing with you as a friend in your victories, instead of supplicating you as an enemy to make my ruin less heavy. As the present position of affairs is to you glorious and joyous, so to me it is grievous and sad. I had subjects, estates and riches, horses and arms, who wonders that I have no inclination to relinquish them? But if you have the power and desire to rule all Tuscany then of necessity the rest must obey; unless I had committed this error, my bad fortune would never have befallen me, and your liberality could never have been shown; because if you spare me you will give to the world for all time an example of clemency. Let, therefore, your mercy surpass my guilt, and allow this estate to descend to the children of those from whom your fathers received innumerable benefits." To this Neri replied that the count had relied too much on those who were able to perform so little, and had committed so many crimes against the republic of Florence that it was necessary in the present position of affairs to take from him those possessions which had become a source of peril to it, and which he had not been willing to hold as its friend. He had taught them the lesson that he was never to be trusted in any place, where he would be in a position to injure them, should any misfortune overtake them. It was not he but his state which was to be feared. If, however, he became a prince in Germany, Florence would give him its good wishes, and for the love of his ancestors, to which he had referred, he should have its favour. The count replied in anger that he wished the Florentines further, and the friendly parley ceased. When the count saw there was nothing more to be gained, he gave up the town and surrendered all his rights, and set off with his weeping wife and children, grieving at the loss of a state which his family had enjoyed for four hundred years. These victories having been reported to Florence were received with great rejoicings by both rulers and people, and as Bernardo de' Medici had found the rumour to be false that Nicolo had marched either on Rome or La Marca, he rejoined Neri and together they returned to Florence. The city decided to confer upon them the honours which are usually accorded to citizens returning with victory, and Bernardo and Neri were received in triumph by the signori, the leaders of the parties, and all the citizens.

1440-1459

It always was, and it is only reasonable that it always should be, the aim of those who go to war to enrich themselves and to impoverish their enemy; nor is victory sought for any other purpose but to take from others what you desire, in order that you may become powerful and your enemy weak. Hence it follows that whenever either victory impoverishes you, or an acquisition makes you no richer, then the war has either over-reached or stopped short of the object for which it was undertaken. The prince, or the republic, is benefited by victory when the enemy is wiped out and the victor remains master of the booty and ransom. But victory is only a mockery when the enemy, although conquered, is not utterly destroyed, or when the booty and ransom goes to the soldiers and not to the state. Princes and republics in that position are more unhappy in victory than in defeat, because they have to endure in defeat the injuries which their enemies inflict, whilst in victory they are defrauded by their allies, whose injuries inflicted without provocation are harder to endure, seeing that the state has of necessity to lay fresh burdens and taxes upon its subjects. If a prince has any humanity in him he cannot entirely rejoice in a victory which only brings fresh miseries to his people. In ancient and well ordered republics it was usual to fill the treasury with gold and silver after a victory, to distribute gifts among the people, to remit taxes, and with rejoicings and solemn festivals delight their subjects. But the victors in the days we are describing first emptied the treasury, then beggared the people, yet failed to effectively secure themselves against their enemies. This arose from the entirely wrong system upon which warfare was conducted, because a conquered enemy, who was deprived only of his horses and arms, and was neither held prisoner nor put to death, was given an opportunity to again attack his victor, and this he did as soon as he could refurnish himself with horses and arms. Seeing that all ransom was claimed by the soldiery, the prince who conquered received no payment whatever towards fresh expenses and the pay of his soldiers, but he had to extract it from the exhausted resources of his people, who themselves received no benefits from the victory, which indeed often caused princes to become more grasping and less considerate towards their subjects by harassing them with new taxes. To such a pass had this system of warfare reached that fresh supplies of money were equally necessary to the conqueror as to the conquered, if either desired to secure the services of this soldiery, because whilst one had to reward his men the other had to refit his, for the victors would not fight without their reward and the conquered could not fight without horses and arms. And whilst one prince would obtain but little satisfaction from his victory, little harm would be done to the other by defeat, because the victor would not be allowed to follow up his victory, and the defeated one would have time allowed him to recover.

This miserable and perverse method of warfare enabled Nicolo Piccinino to take the field again before Italy knew that he had been defeated, and also to make a harder fight of it than before. It enabled him to seize Verona after his rout at Tenna. It was the cause of his reappearance in Tuscany with a great army although his forces had been scattered at Verona. Although he was utterly routed at Anghiari, he was as active as ever in the field before he had reached Romagna. It was this also which encouraged the Duke of Milan to believe that Nicolo could retrieve the position in Lombardy, which had been almost lost in his absence; for whilst Nicolo was filling all Tuscany with the turmoil of battle the duke was brought to such a low ebb that he feared he would lose his state, and that nothing but the recall of Nicolo would save him. In order to gain time the duke had recourse to that subtlety which in similar situations had assisted him in past times, when he could no longer sustain an enterprise by force. He sent Nicolo da Este, the Prince of Ferrara, to Peschiera where the count lay with his army, and Nicolo on the part of the duke suggested a peace. He pointed out to the count that the continuance of war was not to the advantage of either, because if the duke should be driven from the field the count would be the first to suffer, because his services would no longer be required by the Venetians and Florentines; as a pledge of the sincerity of the duke in his desire for peace the daughter was again offered in marriage, and he promised to send the girl to Ferrara and place her in the count's hands as soon as peace was signed. The count replied that the duke could have peace at once if he really desired it, because the Venetians and Florentines were equally ready for it, but it was hard to believe that the duke was, for he well knew the duke never made peace unless necessity compelled him, and when that had passed away the desire for fighting returned; nor could the count put much reliance upon the promise of the marriage, because he had been deceived so frequently; nevertheless, when peace was concluded he would discuss the subject with his friends.

The Venetians, who are often suspicious of their soldiers without reasonable cause, looked upon this conference with disapproval, and the count desiring to efface this impression pushed the war vigorously. But between the ambitions of the count and the suspicions of the Venetians little progress was made during the remainder of the summer. By the time Nicolo Piccinino had reached Lombardy the winter had set in and all the armies retired into winter quarters, the count to Verona, the duke to Cremona, the Florentines into Tuscany, and the army of the pope into Romagna. This latter army after its victory at Anghiari had attacked Furli and Bologna, in order to wrest them from Francesco Piccinino who was holding them for his father, but he so bravely defended them that the pope did not succeed. The people of Ravenna, however, were so terrified at the prospect of coming under the dominion of the pope that, with the concurrence of their signore, Ostasio di Polenta, they placed themselves under the protection of the Venetians. The Venetians, as a recompense to Ostasio for having consented to the city being given up to them, and to put it out of his power to attempt to take back at any time what he had so incautiously surrendered, sent him and his son to die in Candia. Notwithstanding the victory at Anghiari, the pope was so pressed for money that he sold the castle of Borgo San Sepolcro to the Florentines for 25,000 ducats.

Whilst affairs were in this position every one felt safe from war in the security of winter, and no one thought any more of peace. The duke, to whom the winter season and the return of Nicolo had given fresh courage, broke off the negotiations with Count Francesco, and turned all his attention to getting fresh supplies of horses and other necessaries for the struggle in the spring. These preparations coming to the knowledge of the count, he went to Venice to discuss with the senate the operations in the coming campaign. Nicolo, on his side, brought affairs into order, and, seeing the enemy off his guard, would not wait until the arrival of spring, but crossed the Adda and invaded the Brescian country, seizing all that district excepting Oddula and Acri, and capturing more than 2000 Sforzescan cavalry. What caused most anxiety to the count and alarmed the Venetians was the disaffection of Ciarpellone, one of their chief captains. When the count received advice of this he at once left Venice, and upon reaching Brescia he found that Nicolo had returned to his quarters after doing much damage. Th& count, finding everything quiet, decided that it would be better not to stir matters up, but avail himself of the opportunity which time and the enemy gave him to reorganise his forces, in order that he might be in a better position to revenge himself in the future for his past injuries. Among other things he induced the Venetians to recall the men who were serving under the Florentines in Tuscany, and to put at their head Micheletto Attendulo in place of Gattamelata who was dead.

Nicolo Piccinino was the first to take the field in the spring. He laid siege to Cignano, a castle situate twelve miles from Brescia; Count Francesco went to its assistance, and the war was carried on between these two captains in the usual way. At the same time the count, feeling some anxiety for the safety of Bergamo, attacked Martinengo, a castle so placed that having taken it he could relieve Bergamo at his pleasure, although it was seriously threatened by Nicolo. Nicolo had foreseen that the relief of Bergamo could only be effected by way of Martinengo, and had therefore provided it with the strongest defence, so that the count was obliged to bring against it his whole force. Thereupon Nicolo posted troops in such a position that they could cut off the count's supplies, and with entrenchments so strengthened that of his own army that the count could not attack him except at a serious disadvantage; indeed the count was in such a situation that the besiegers were in greater peril than the besieged. Hence the count could no longer continue the siege as he was in danger of starvation, yet could not extricate himself from his perilous position; indeed he could see nothing in front of him but ruin to the cause of the Venetians and a decisive victory for the duke.

Fortune, who never fails to help her friends and hinder her foes, now raised up so much ambition in Nicolo Piccinino, and brought him to such a pitch of insolence, that, forgetful of the relative positions of himself and the duke, he wrote to him saying that he had fought under his standard for many years, and had not yet acquired any territory for himself, not even sufficient for a grave, and he wished to know what reward he was to obtain for all his labours, for it was now in his power to make the duke master of Lombardy and deliver all his enemies into his hands; and seeing that a certain victory should bring a certain reward, he desired to have the city of Piacenza conceded to him, in order that he might take some repose after his long-continued fighting. Nor did he hesitate to threaten the duke at the end of his letter that unless his request was granted he should retire from the field. This demand, put forward so unwisely and insolently, enraged the duke to such an extent that he determined to lose everything rather than submit to such dictation. He whom so many and dangerous enemies had never bent was now turned by the insolence of a subordinate, and he decided to come to terms with the count. He therefore sent Antonio Guido Buono of Tortona to the count offering his daughter in marriage, and suggesting conditions of peace, which were readily accepted by the count and his colleagues. These terms being secretly agreed between them, the duke sent Nicolo an order to sign a truce for one year with the count, explaining to him that the expenses of the war were so great that he could not refuse the offer of a certain peace for an uncertain victory. Nicolo was astonished at this decision, and could not understand what could have occurred to cause the duke to renounce the opportunity for such a glorious victory: he could not believe that it was to avoid rewarding his friends that he stepped forward to save his enemies. Nicolo opposed the decision with all the means in his power, until the duke had to threaten that if he did not do as ordered he would be abandoned to his own soldiers and enemies. Nicolo obeyed, but with the soul of one who is compelled by force to abandon friends and country—grieving over having the victory snatched from him, at one time by fortune and at another time by the duke. The truce being now signed, the marriage between the count and Madonna Bianca was celebrated, and the city of Cremona given as a dowry. The articles of peace were signed in November 1441, when Francesco Barbadico acted for the Venetians and Pagolo Trono and Messer Agnolo Acciaiuoli for the Florentines; by this treaty the Venetians gained Peschiera, Asola, and Lonato, all of them castles taken from the Marquis of Mantua.

Although war had ceased in Lombardy, there still remained strife in the kingdom of Naples, which could not be appeased, and finally became the cause of fresh trouble in Lombardy. Whilst the war was raging in Lombardy, King René had been worsted by

Alfonso of Aragon, and nothing of his kingdom remained to him but Naples. Alfonso, thinking that he had victory in his hand, decided whilst besieging Naples to take Benevento from Count Francesco Sforza, and also some other estates which belonged to him in that district; this he believed he could do without much risk, seeing that the count was fully occupied with the war in Lombardy. Alfonso succeeded with ease in his enterprise and captured all the towns; but when the news reached him that peace was signed, he feared that the count would come, not only for the recovery of his own estates, but also on behalf of René; and for the same reasons René also looked to the count, and sent to him for assistance, begging him to come to help a friend, and take his revenge upon an enemy. Alfonso, on his side, wrote to the duke, praying him for the friendship he had for him to keep the count so occupied with great undertakings that he would be unable to assist René. Filippo was ready enough to disturb the peace which had so recently been concluded to his disadvantage, and agreed to the suggestion. He therefore intimated to the Pope Eugenius that now was the time to recover those towns of which the count had deprived the Church, and offered to assist him with Nicolo Piccinino, whom he would pay as long as the war lasted, and who since the recent peace had remained in Romagna with his army. Owing to the hatred which Eugenius entertained for the count he eagerly swallowed this advice to recover his possessions, and although he had been deceived in former times by Nicolo over this same matter, he believed now that the duke intervened he need not fear any deceit, and he at once sent his men to join Nicolo in the attack on La Marca. The count, affronted at such an unexpected attack, put himself at the head of his army and took the field against his enemies. Alfonso, in the meantime, had captured Naples, and thus the whole of the kingdom was in his hands excepting Castelnuovo. René left this place safely guarded and set out for Florence, where he was honourably received. After remaining there a few days he left for Marseilles, seeing that he could effect nothing more toward the recovery of the kingdom of Naples.

Alfonso shortly after this had taken Castelnuovo, whilst the count, having realised that he was inferior in forces to the pope and Nicolo, had recourse to the Florentines and Venetians for men and money, pointing out to them that if they did not make up their minds to curb the king and the pope, whilst he himself was yet alive, they would have but little chance afterwards, for the king and the pope would join forces with the duke and divide Italy between them. The Florentines and Venetians remained for a time uncertain what course to pursue, for being occupied with some trouble with the Bolognese they did not consider it wise to enter into hostilities with the king and pope. The trouble in Bologna had been caused by Annibale Bentivogli driving Francesco Piccinino from the city; and Annibale, having done this, had sought the aid of the Florentines to defend him against the duke who espoused the cause of Francesco Piccinino, and this help they had not refused. Being, therefore, engaged in this affair they were not able to promise assistance to the Count Francesco. However, before deciding anything, they secured themselves with the duke by renewing their league with him. To this he was not averse, as he had only consented to hostilities against the count as long as King René was under arms, but now that he had been driven out of the kingdom, and Alfonso was in possession, he no longer desired the count to be deprived of his estates. Not only was he willing that assistance be given to the count, but he wrote to Alfonso that he would be obliged to him if he would retire to the kingdom and abandon the war. Although Alfonso was opposed to this his many obligations to the duke forced him to agree, and he re-crossed the Tronto with his army.

Whilst these events were happening in Romagna, the Florentines were not at rest among themselves. One of the first among the citizens of repute who ruled in Florence was Neri, the son of Gino Capponi, of whose great reputation with both citizens and soldiers Cosimo de' Medici was jealous. Gino had been at the head of the Florentine army many times, and had always distinguished himself by his ability and courage. Beyond this the memory of the victories that he and his father had gained endeared the army to him—his father having captured Pisa, whilst he himself had conquered Nicolo Piccinino at Anghiari. Thus Gino was admired by many, but disliked by those who did not wish him to share the government with them. Among the other captains in the Florentine army was Baldaccio d'Anghiari, one of the finest soldiers in Italy, unsurpassed in his mental and bodily qualifications. He had always commanded infantry, and had acquired in that service such reputation that men would follow him anywhere. Baldaccio was a great friend of Neri, whom he loved for those deeds of valour which he had often witnessed. This friendship aroused the suspicions of many citizens, and they determined to destroy Baldaccio, for they considered it was dangerous to retain him in their service and doubly dangerous to dismiss him; in this decision fortune favoured them. The gonfaloniere of justice at this time was Messer Bartolommeo Orlandini, the man who as we have seen was sent to defend Marradi when Nicolo crossed into Tuscany, and who fled leaving exposed the pass which nature more than half defended. Such cowardice was hateful to Baldaccio, and by letters and spoken words he had insultingly published Bartolommeo's want of courage. This had caused Bartolommeo to be shunned and despised, and he burned for that vengeance which would enable him to blot out the infamy of his own misdeeds with the blood of his accuser.

Messer Bartolommeo's thirst for vengeance was well known to certain citizens, and without much difficulty they persuaded him to satisfy it, and at one stroke avenge his own injuries and relieve the state of a man whom it was equally dangerous to keep or dismiss. Messer Bartolommeo, therefore, decided to murder Baldaccio; to accomplish this he had a party of armed men admitted into his offices, and Baldaccio having entered the Piazza as customary to discuss with the magistrates his affairs, the gonfaloniere sent for him; to this he complied without any suspicion of evil. The gonfaloniere received him, and walked up and down the corridor where the offices of the signori are located discussing business with him. Having spent some time in this manner, they approached the chamber in which the armed men were concealed. Bartolommeo gave a signal and they rushed forth; Baldaccio, alone and unarmed, was killed and his body thrown from the window of the palace that fronts the Custom House. From thence the body was carried into the Piazza, the head severed, and left as a spectacle for the people during the whole of the day. Baldaccio left only one son, whom Annalena, his wife, had borne to him a few years before, and who did not long survive him. Annalena thus deprived of son and husband, and unwilling to marry again, turned her house into a convent, and received there many noble ladies with whom she lived a saintly life until she died. The memory of this lady, through the convent which she instituted, and which was named after her, has lived until to-day, and will never fade. This murder somewhat undermined the position of Neri by depriving him of friends and authority, but it was not enough to satisfy the ruling faction, because ten years having passed since the establishment of their power the authority of the balia had expired, and many men presumed to speak and act with more liberty than was agreeable; the heads of the ruling party, therefore, came to the conclusion that, unless they wished to lose their position, it was necessary to renew the balia and thus invest their party with fresh authority and enable them to get rid of some of their enemies. Therefore in 1444 they created a new balia with the assistance of the councils, which reorganised the public offices, conferred power on a few leading men to elect a signoria, renewed the chancellory for improvements, deprived Ser Filippo Peruzzi of his office, and put in his place one who would act more in accordance with the views of those in power. They extended terms of banishment, threw Giovanni, the son of Simone Vespucci, into prison, deprived of their offices the accoppiatori, and with them the sons of Piero Baroncelli, all the Serragli, Bartolommeo Fortini, Messer Francesco Castellani, and many others. By these measures they re-established their power and cut down their enemies.

Having reorganised the government of the city, attention was directed to foreign affairs. Here, as we have seen, the aid of Alfonso had been withdrawn from Nicolo Piccinino, and the Count Francesco, reinforced by the Florentines, had become sufficiently powerful to attack him. This he did, utterly defeating him and capturing Fermo. Nicolo with the few men he saved threw himself into Montecchio, which he fortified and held so strongly that many of his soldiers rejoined him and enabled him to defend himself with ease against the count. Winter coming on, both captains sent their men into winter quarters. Nicolo spent the winter months in recruiting his forces, and in this the pope and King Alfonso assisted him. When the spring opened, both captains again took the field, and Nicolo having the stronger army reduced the count to great straits, and would have defeated him if the duke had not upset the plans of Nicolo. Filippo sent word to him that he desired to see him immediately as he had affairs of great importance to discuss with him. Nicolo, curious to hear what the duke had to say — abandoning a certain advantage for an uncertainty — left his son Francesco in command of the army, and went to Milan. Upon this news being communicated to the count he determined not to miss the chance of defeating his enemy in the absence of Nicolo; he therefore attacked the army near to the castle of Monte Loro, routed it, and took Francesco prisoner. When Nicolo reached Milan he soon discovered that he had been deceived by Filippo, and hearing also of the defeat and capture of his son he took it so deeply to heart that he died of grief. This was in 1445 and in the sixty-fourth year of his age. As a captain, Nicolo was more valiant than fortunate, and his two sons who survived him, Francesco and Jacopo, who with less abilities than their father, had even worse fortune. In them the Braccescan school of arms became almost extinct, whilst that of the Sforzescan, aided by fortune, became ever more glorious. The pope, finding the army of Nicolo dispersed and its leader dead, and with no expectations of succour from Aragon, sought peace with the count, and by the good offices of the Florentines obtained it. By the treaty which followed, Osimo, Fabriano, and Recanati, towns in La Marca, were restored to the pope, whilst the rest remained under the governorship of the count.

By the treaty of La Marca peace would have been secured to Italy had it not been for Bologna. In this city there were then two powerful families—the Bentivogli and the Canneschi, of which Annibale was the leader of one and Battista of the other. In order that their mutual interests might be consolidated, the two families had contracted many marriages between themsevles; but among men who are aspiring to the same honours it is far easier to make marriages than to ensure friendship. After Annibale Bentivogli had driven out Francesco Piccinino he had bound Bologna by treaty to the Florentines and Venetians, but the Duke of Milan desired to bring the city into alliance with him, and to this end he contrived with Battista Canneschi the death of Annibale. When the plans of the murderers were complete, Battista attacked Annibale and his family, and put all to death, after which he proclaimed the duke throughout the city—this happened on June 25, 1445. The commissioners of Florence and Venice were in Bologna when this occurred, and at the first sign of the disturbance retired to their houses, but afterwards, finding that the people were hostile to the murderers and had assembled in the Piazza lamenting the death of Annibale, they recovered their courage, and, picking up some soldiers, joined others and attacked the Canneschi. In a short time they overcame them, killed several, and hunted the rest out of the city. Battista escaped from the fight, but not having time to leave the city, hid himself in a pit for storing corn which was in his house. Although his murderers knew that he had not left the city, and had sought for him the whole day, they could not find him, but they so terrified his servants that one of the lads pointed out his place of concealment. Still armed, he was pulled from his hiding place and killed, and his body dragged through the streets and burnt. Thus the duke tempted Battista into this enterprise, but could give him no assistance in time to save him.

Bologna was greatly disturbed by this tumult, although the death of Battista and the flight of the Canneschi had in some degree composed it, but it was feared that dissensions would arise between the supporters of the Bentivogli, seeing that all the family were destroyed except one boy, named Giovanni, who being only six years old could not take upon himself the government, and the citizens were apprehensive that such dissensions might encourage the Canneschi to return. Whilst these matters were still in doubt, Francesco, — he who was Count of Poppi, and who was then in Bologna, — informed the leading men that, if they wished to be governed by a descendant of the house of Bentivogli, he knew where one was to be found. He related to them that about twenty years ago a cousin of Annibale Bentivogli, Ercole by name, came to Poppi and lived there with a girl by whom he had a son called Santi, and whom Ercole always treated as his son, indeed he would have had some difficulty in repudiating him, for all who had once seen Ercole would easily recognise the resemblance between the two. The citizens gave credence to this story of Count Poppi, and hastened to send a deputation to Florence to seek out the young Santi, and arrange with Cosimo and Neri that he should be allowed to return with them to Bologna. The reputed father of the young man was dead, and he resided with an uncle named Antonio da Cascese. Antonio was rich and childless and a friend of Neri. When Neri understood the purport of the deputation he said the request was one that should not be rashly refused or accepted, and desired that Santi be questioned by the men from Bologna in the presence of Cosimo. Having met together, Santi was not only approved but almost worshipped by the Bolognese, to such a pass will the necessities of faction bring some minds. Nothing, however, was concluded at this interview, for Cosimo taking the youth on one side said to him: "No one can give you better counsel than yourself in a case like this, because you ought to take that course to which your inclinations lead. If you be a son of Ercole Bentivogli you will turn yourself to those tasks which are worthy of your father and his family; but if you be the son of Agnolo da

Cascese you will remain in Florence and tamely spend the rest of your life in the wool trade." These words influenced the youth so much that, whereas he had been inclined at first to take the latter course, he now said that he submitted himself entirely to the opinion of Cosimo and Neri. An agreement was soon made with the envoys from Bologna, and Santi, being suitably provided with clothes, horses, and servants, set out with a great retinue for Bologna. Here he was entrusted with the governorship of the city and the care of Messer Annibale's son, and conducted himself with so much prudence that, whilst the greater number of his predecessors had been killed, he lived peacefully and died honoured by all.

After the peace of La Marca and the death of Nicolo Piccinino, the Duke Filippo, requiring a captain for the command of his armies, entered into a secret arrangement with Ciarpellone, one of Francesco's leading captains, and finally came to an agreement with him. Ciarpellone asked permission of the count to visit Milan in order to take possession of the castles yielded up by the duke after the recent war, but the count, fearing there was more in this request than appeared, arrested him, and on the plea of his complicity in frauds put him to death, and thus prevented the duke from having his services. This incident incensed the duke against Francesco and greatly pleased the Florentines and Venetians, for they always lived in dread that the ambitions of the duke and the abilities of the count would work together for a common end. This quarrel caused the war again to break out in La Marca. Gismondo Malatesti, the lord of Rimini, had, as son-in-law of the count, always looked forward to becoming master of Pesaro, but when the count seized it he conferred it upon his brother Alessandro. This displeased Gismondo, who was further enraged when he learnt that his enemy, Federigo di Montefeltro, had seized Urbino, also with the help of the count. Gismondo, therefore, joined the duke, and also begged the pope and King Alfonso to declare war on the count. Whereupon the count determined to anticipate Gismondo and give him an early taste of the fruits of the war which he was invoking, suddenly attacked him. The Romagna and La Marca were at once filled with strife, for the Duke Filippo, the king, and the pope poured in troops to the aid of Gismondo, whilst the Florentines and Venetians, unable to send men, sent money to the count. It was not enough for Filippo to carry the war into Romagna, but he attacked the dominions of the count and laid siege to Cremona and Pontremoli; but the latter was defended by the Florentines, and Cremona by the Venetians. Thus the war was in some measure rekindled in Lombardy, and after some skirmishing round Cremona, Francesco Piccinino, the duke's captain, was routed at Casala by Micheletto, the leader of the Venetians. This victory encouraged the Venetians to believe that they could conquer the duchy of Milan, and sending one of their commissioners to Cremona they invaded the Ghiaradadda, and occupied all that district except Cremona. After passing the Adda they swept up to the gates of Milan. The duke then had recourse to Alfonso, pointing out to him the danger to the kingdom should Lombardy fall, and begging him to come at once to his aid against the Venetians. Alfonso promised assistance, but this could only reach the duke after great delay unless it had the consent of the count.

Filippo, therefore, had recourse to the count, and begged him not to abandon him now that he was old and blind. The count justly considered himself much injured by the duke, inasmuch as it was he who brought the present war upon the count; on the other hand, any increase in the power of the Venetians did not please him. Besides this the league was at this time treating the count very parsimoniously in the matter of supplies; whilst the Florentines having now lost their dread of the duke had less need of the services of the count, and the Venetians were actually compassing his destruction as the only man who could keep them out of Lombardy. Nevertheless, at the time when the duke was seeking to draw the count into his service with the offer of the leadership of his armies, provided that the count deserted the Venetians and restored La Marca to the pope, the Venetians themselves were also ambassadors to him, promising him Milan when they had captured it, and the captaincy of their armies in perpetuity, provided that he followed up the war in La Marca and prevented Alfonso's forces from reaching Lombardy. Thus the promises of the Venetians were very tempting, besides which the Venetians themselves deserved every consideration at the hands of the count, for had they not entered into this war to preserve Cremona for the count? On the other hand the injuries which the duke had inflicted upon the count were very recent, and his promises hitherto had been utterly unreliable. Thus the count was troubled with doubts on each side. On the one there were his obligations to the league, his plighted word, his recent honours, and the promises for the future all weighing with him; whilst on the other side there were the prayers of his father-in-law, but, above all, there was the deceit which he feared lay hidden under the promises of the Venetians, because he could well see that whenever they should become masters of Milan he would stand at their mercy as far as their promises and the fulfilment of them were concerned; and he knew no prudent prince should allow himself to get into such a position. These doubts in the mind of the count were all dissipated by the ambition of the Venetians whose intentions of seizing Cremona were precipitated by a conspiracy which they were fostering within its walls. In collusion with the conspirators they drew their army near to the city, but the plot was discovered by those who watched the city for the count, and the hopes of the Venetians were in vain, for by this they lost both the count and Cremona, because the count, throwing on one side all considerations, joined the duke.

Pope Eugenio was dead and Nicolo V. had succeeded him, and the count was ready with his army at Cotignola to pass into Lombardy when he learnt that the Duke Filippo was dead. This event, which occurred on the last day of August 1447, brought much trouble to the count. His army was mutinous, not having received its full pay for some time; the Venetians were in arms against him for having deserted them and joined the duke; Alfonso, his implacable enemy, was also to be feared; the pope and the Florentines were not to be relied upon, because he held towns belonging to the Church, and the Florentines were in alliance with the Venetians. However, he determined to show a bold front to fortune and deal with events as they occurred, because it often happens that expedients declare themselves in action which remain hidden when nothing is done. What inspired him with the greatest confidence was the hope that the Milanese, having no army of their own, would turn to him for defence against the Venetians. In expectation of this he crossed over into Bolognese territory, and leaving Modena and Reggio behind him posted his army on the banks of the Lenza, and offered his services to the Milanese. When the death of the Duke of Milan took place a great number of the citizens desired a republic, whilst others wished to live under a prince. Of those who wished a prince, one half wanted to choose the count, whilst the rest preferred King Alfonso; but as those citizens who wished to live in freedom were more united in their desires than the others, they prevailed and a republic was established. Many cities, however, of the duchy would not recognise the republic, for they considered that if Milan could exercise the privilege of choice of government so also could they, and those who did not aspire to freedom did not wish for the over-lordship of Milan. Thus it came about that Lodi and Piacenza put themselves under the Venetians, and Pavia and Parma declared themselves free. When this came to the knowledge of the count, he went to Cremona where his envoys met those of the Milanese, and it was agreed that the count should be captain to the Milanese on the same terms as those which he had arranged with the late duke. To this was added the stipulation, that until such time as Verona should be recovered, Brescia should be ceded to the count when this city was to be returned.

Previous to the death of the duke the Pope Nicolo, on his elevation to the pontificate, had endeavoured to make peace among the princes of Italy, and had proposed to the Florentine envoys, who were present at his investment, that a diet should be convened at Ferrara to arrange the terms for a long truce or a permanent peace. Under these circumstances there had assembled in that city the pope's legate with envoys from Venice, Florence, and the Duchy of Milan, but King Alfonso sent none. The king had posted himself with a large body of horse and foot at Tivoli, from whence he could join the duke at any time, and as soon as the count had been drawn to their side he believed that he would be strong enough to openly attack the Florentines and Venetians, and it was with these intentions he had allowed the count to enter Lombardy with his army. The king gave as his reason for not taking part in the diet at Ferrara that he would confirm any agreement made by the duke. After many days spent in discussion it was decided to arrange a five years' truce or a permanent peace, whichever the duke should prefer. His envoys, however, found the duke dead on their return to Milan. Notwithstanding the death of the duke, the Milanese were quite willing to accept the agreement which had been arrived at, but to this the Venetians would not assent, because they now had great hopes of seizing the duchy, especially as Lodi and Piacenza placed themselves under their protection as soon as the duke was dead, and thus in a short time they would not only deprive Milan of her territory, but so oppress her that she would yield before any assistance could reach her. They were also encouraged in this view when they found the Florentines entangled in a war with King Alfonso.

The king at this time lay with his army at Tivoli, intending to attack Tuscany as he and the late duke had planned; and now that war had broken out in Lombardy the time and the opportunity had come. He first desired to obtain a footing in Florentine territory before declaring war, and with this view he intrigued with the garrison of Cennina and seized it. The Florentines were astonished at this attack, and saw at once that the king intended war; upon which the Ten commissioners of war were appointed, men enlisted, and the usual preparations for defence were made. After the capture of Cennina the king had led his men on to Siena, in hopes of inducing the Sienese to join him, but they held firm to their friendship with Florence, and would not admit him into

Siena or any of their other cities. They, however, gave him supplies, which action might be pardoned owing to the strength of the king and their own weakness. As it did not appear prudent to the king to pass through the Val d'Arno, as he had first intended, having again lost Cennina, and with the Florentines threatening his rear in force, he turned towards Volterra and seized some fortresses in that district. Thence he approached Pisa, and with the help of Arrigo and Fazio de' Conti of the Gheradesca family he captured some castles and laid siege to Campiglia. This place he was unable to carry, and winter coming on and the Florentines approaching, the king left garrisons in his captured strongholds to defend them and harass the country, and himself with the rest of his army retired into winter quarters round Siena. The season of the year having come to the aid of the Florentines they reorganised the army and placed at its head Federigo, lord of Urbino, and Gismondo Malatesti of Rimini. Although there were some disagreements between these two commanders, the prudence of Neri di Gino and Bernardetto de' Medici, the Florentine commissioners, kept them united. Whilst it was still the depth of winter the Florentines broke up their camp, retook the towns round Pisa and Pomerance in the Volterra, drove back the soldiers who were harassing the country along the sea coast, and made it difficult for them to hold the castles they were left to defend. As soon as spring came the Florentines assembled all their forces, consisting of 5000 horse and 2000 foot, at Spedaletto, whilst Alfonso with 15,000 men approached within three miles of Campiglia. The Florentines naturally thought he intended to lay siege to that place, but he turned his attention to Piombino. He expected to take this city with ease as it was ill provided for a siege, and desired to have it because it would assist him in harassing the Florentines. He considered that from it he could weary the Florentines of the war, and draw his supplies from the towns round Pisa. The Florentines realised at once the trouble this siege would cause them and called a council of war. It was finally decided to hold the woods of Campiglia, as this would oblige the king to retreat either disgraced or defeated. They also fitted out four galeasses which they had at Leghorn, threw 300 infantry into Piombino, and themselves took up a position at Caldane, where attack was not easy, and quitted the woods in the plain where defence was difficult.

The Florentine army was dependent upon the neighbouring towns for supplies, but as these had already been raided, and few inhabitants were left, there was little to be obtained from them. The army suffered many privations, especially in wine, for they could neither get it there nor elsewhere; whilst the king, although the Florentines kept him closely invested, was abundantly supplied with everything, excepting forage, being provisioned by sea. The Florentines, therefore, decided to try if the sea would not bring them supplies, so they loaded up their four galeasses and made the attempt; but the seven galleys of the king met them, captured two and put two to flight. The Florentine army now lost all hope of fresh supplies, and more than 200 soldiers deserted to the king, chiefly because they could get no wine, whilst the rest of the army complained bitterly at being in such a burning region where no wine was to be obtained and where the water was bad. The commissioners decided to abandon the place, and to attempt the recovery of some castles which still remained in the hands of the king. On the other side, the king, although he had not suffered from want of supplies, and was still superior in point of numbers, was losing many men from sickness, owing to the unhealthiness of the coast—many men died and the whole army was more or less infected. These conditions inclined both parties to a truce; the king demanded 50,000 florins and the surrender of Piombino. These terms being referred to Florence, many citizens desired to accept them, saying that they could see no possibility of Florence ever getting any advantage out of a war that required such a vast expenditure. However Neri Capponi, who had come to Florence, used such reasons against yielding that the people would not accept the offer, but took Piombino under their protection both in peace and war, as long as it should not surrender but defend itself as it hitherto had done. When the king learnt this decision, and found that his army was so reduced in numbers that it could not hope to capture Piombino, he raised the siege, leaving more than 2000 men dead; with the remnant of his plague stricken army retired as if routed into the country round Siena, and from thence into the kingdom of Naples, threatening fire and sword against the Florentines at some future time.

Whilst these events were transpiring in Tuscany, Count Francesco had been appointed captain of the Milan forces, and had made friends with Francesco Piccinino, who was fighting for the Milanese, in order that he should either assist him in attaining his ends or should hesitate before thwarting him. The count now took the field with his army, and the men of Pavia, fearing they had not sufficient strength to defend themselves against his forces, offered their city to him upon the condition that he did not hand them over to the Milanese, whom they had every reason to fear. The possession of this city, which the count desired, appeared to him a most favourable beginning to his schemes, and although he did not allow himself to be restrained by any feelings of shame at the deceit or the breaking of faith, for great men only consider it shameful to lose not to gain by deceit, he hesitated to accept the offer of the city. His fear was that, if he accepted the city, the rage of the Milanese would lead them to throw themselves into the arms of the Venetians, and on the other hand he feared that if he did not do so the Pavians would give themselves away to the Duke of Savoy. In either case his designs upon Lombardy were endangered. However, he finally agreed to accept it, believing there was less danger in this than leaving it to another. He persuaded himself that he would be able to make the Milanese understand the risks they would have run had he not accepted the city, because the citizens would have placed themselves under the Venetians or the Duke of Savoy, and in either case the Milanese would have lost their hold upon the city. The count easily assured himself that the Milanese would rather have him, their friend, as a neighbour than either of the others who were powerful and antagonistic to them. The people of Milan were greatly disturbed by this event, for it disclosed to them the ambitious motives which actuated the count and the end he had in view. Yet they dared not show any anxiety, because, if they quarrelled with him, they did not know where to turn for assistance, except to the Venetians and they feared their pride and heavy yoke. Therefore they decided not to break loose from the count, but to make use of him in warding off the perils which now threatened, and to hope that when they were free from those troubles they would free themselves from him. The Milanese were at this time not only attacked by the Venetians, but also by the Genoese and the Duke of Savoy acting on behalf of Charles of Orleans, the son of a sister of Filippo; the count, however, brought them to battle and easily defeated them. There remained only the Venetians to be dealt with, and they holding the cities of Lodi and Piacenza, threatened Milan; the count took the field against Piacenza and after a troublesome siege captured and sacked it. The winter approaching, both armies retired into winter quarters. The count went to Cremona, where he remained all winter with his wife.

When spring came the armies of Milan and Venice again took the field. The Milanese only desired to recover Lodi and then make peace with the Venetians, because the expense of the war was ruining them; they were doubtful also of the loyalty of their captain; therefore they were urgent for peace in order to reserve their strength and secure themselves in some way against the count. They determined, however, to move their army against Caravaggio, in the hope Lodi would surrender when it saw that fortress in the hands of the enemy. The count yielded to the orders of the Milanese, although he would have preferred to cross the Adda and attack the Brescians. However he commenced the siege of Caravaggio, and so fortified himself with field-works that the Venetians could only attack him at great disadvantage should they attempt to raise the siege. The Venetians brought their army under Micheletto up to within a couple of bow-shots of the count's position, where they remained for many days, and had much skirmishing with the enemy. Nevertheless the count pressed the castle hard, and brought it to the point of surrender; this caused the Venetians much anxiety, because the loss of the castle meant the failure of the whole enterprise. The captains gave the position the closest attention, yet they saw no other way of relieving the castle but to attack their enemy in his fortified camp, although such attack could only be made at great disadvantage. But so serious was the loss of the castle to the Venetians, although naturally hesitating and averse to doubtful or dangerous courses, they were ready to risk all rather than to lose the place.

Having determined to attack the count, they opened the assault upon his position at an early hour of the morning, and chose that part of his defence which appeared the weakest; but as often happens at a first rush when an attack is unexpected, the Sforzescan army was thrown into confusion. The count, however, soon restored order, and not only drove back the enemy but followed them up and completely routed them; so that out of an army of more than 12,000 horsemen not more than 1000 escaped; all the baggage and transport was captured, and never have the Venetians suffered a greater or more terrible defeat than on that day. Among the booty and prisoners was found a Venetian army contractor, who throughout the war and before this fight had spoken scornfully of the count, calling him a low-born fellow and a bastard; so that finding himself a prisoner, and recollecting all he had said, he had little doubt he would be punished as he deserved. He was brought before the count in fear and trembling, as is generally observed in men both proud and base, who in prosperity are arrogant and in adversity abject and contemptible; he threw himself on his knees and begged the count's pardon for all he had said and done. The count raised him up and, pressing his hand, bade him be of good courage and hope for the best. He then said to him that he wondered a man of his wisdom and serious disposition, as he had always wished to be considered, should have fallen into such an error as to speak disrespectfully of those who had not deserved it from him. And as to those charges which he had brought against him, the count was not in a position to say what passed between his father Sforza and his mother, Madonna Lucia, because he was not there and took no part in bringing them together; so that on that matter he deserved neither praise nor blame. He could only speak for affairs over which he had control, and could say that he had always conducted himself in such a way that none could reproach him, and of this Venice and its senate had recent experience. He bade him, therefore, in the future show more discretion in speaking of others, and more caution in attacking them.

The count with his victorious army then passed into the Brescian territory, occupied the whole of the country, and pitched his camp within two miles of Brescia. The Venetians anticipated that after their defeat the next blow would fall on Brescia, and had therefore provisioned and fortified it to the best of their ability, and garrisoned it with such troops as they could get together. By virtue also of their league with Florence they demanded assistance, and being at peace with King Alfonso the Florentines sent them 1000 foot and 2000 horse soldiers. With these forces the Venetians were now in a position to treat for peace. It seemed almost to be fated that, however severely the Venetians were defeated, they were bound to gain in the end by treaty, for what they lost by war was often restored to them doubled in value. They were at this time well aware of the doubts which the Milanese entertained of the loyalty of their captain, and of the hopes the count entertained of becoming the lord of Milan instead of its captain. They also knew that the choice of making peace with one or other of these two parties lay in their own hands—the one party desiring peace in the interests of his ambition, and the other desiring it because of its distrust. The Venetians in the end elected to come to terms with the count, because they were convinced that as soon as the Milanese discovered that the count had sold them, in their anger they would turn to any one rather than submit to him; and finding they could neither defend themselves nor trust the count, and unable to secure help elsewhere, they would throw themselves into the arms of the Venetians. Relying on these conclusions the

Venetians sounded the mind of the count and found him disposed for peace, for he desired that the victory at Caravaggio should be ascribed to him and not to the Milanese. An agreement was arrived at between them by which the Venetians bound themselves to pay the count 13,000 florins each month until he had acquired Milan, and that during the war they should furnish him with 4000 horsemen and 2000 infantry. The count on his side engaged to restore to the Venetians the towns, prisoners, or anything else of theirs which he had captured during the war, and to be himself content with those towns only of which the Duke Filippo had died possessed.

The grief caused in Milan at the news of this treaty was far greater than the rejoicing after the victory at Caravaggio: the princes grieved, the whole population lamented, the women and children wept, and all cursed the count for his disloyalty and treachery; and although they feared that neither prayers nor promises would turn him from his contemplated ingratitude, they sent ambassadors to him to see with what countenance and words he would supplement his wickedness. When the ambassadors appeared before the count one of them addressed to him the following words: "Those who desire to obtain something from another are accustomed to use either prayers, rewards, or menaces, in order that he may be moved either by pity, gain, or fear, and thus influenced he may grant their desires. But with cruel and avaricious men who trust in their own might, such means have no force, and in vain do men endeavour to move them with prayers, to gain them with rewards, or to terrify them with menaces. Although too late we learn your cruelty, ambition, and pride, we come with no desire to gain anything from you, nor do we believe that we could obtain any good thing from you if we were to demand it, but to put on record the benefits which you have received from the people of Milan, to show with what ingratitude you have repaid them; and that from amid our misery we may feel the satisfaction of having justly reproached you. You can easily remember your position at the death of the Duke Filippo. You were the enemy of the pope and the king; the Florentines and Venetians whom you had deserted were hostile to you, either through a just resentment or because they had no further need of your services; you were exhausted with the war which you were carrying on against the Church, for you had but few men, no friends, and no money; and were without hope of being able to retain either your estates or your reputation. This condition of affairs would have brought about your downfall if it had not been for the simplicity we showed in giving you shelter. We were moved to this because of the happy memory of our late duke, with whom you had just concluded a new alliance, confirmed by your marriage with his daughter, and because we believed your love to him would have passed to his heirs; and if you had added the benefits you received from the duke to those we conferred on you, you ought not only to have remained loyal to that alliance but inseparable from it. Therefore to the conditions of the former convention we added either Verona or Brescia. What more could we promise or give you? And as to yourself, what could you have obtained, I do not say from us, but from others at that time? However you received from us unhoped-for succour, and we as recompense have now received from you unexpected treachery. You did not conceal for long the iniquity of your intentions, because no sooner had you become the head of our army than against every sense of justice you accepted the city of Pavia. That act ought to have warned us what would be the end of your friendship to us. We however endured that injury, hoping that your ambition would have been satisfied with that prize. Alas! He who desires everything is never satisfied with a part. You promised that all your subsequent acquisitions should be enjoyed by us, well knowing that what is given by degrees can be taken away again at one stroke, as happened to us after the victory at Caravaggio, which, won by our blood and treasure, was used for our destruction. Unfortunate as those cities may be which have to defend their liberties against the ambitions of those who wish to oppress them, far more so are those who have to defend themselves against a disloyal mercenary such as you are. Let our fate go down to posterity, although the example of Thebes was lost upon us, when after the victory gained over her enemy Philip from a foe became her captain and afterwards her tyrant. We however can be accused of no other fault than of having trusted one who ought never to have been trusted. Your past life, your ambition, never content with any position or rank, ought to have warned us. We ought never to have placed any confidence in the man who betrayed the lord of Lucca, drained the Florentines and Venetians of their resources, despised the duke, and reviled the king, but who, above all, had ruthlessly persecuted God and His Church. Who could expect that such potentates would weigh less in the mind of Francesco Sforza than the Milanese, or that he who had violated his faith with so many others would keep it with us? Nevertheless want of prudence on our part is no excuse for perfidy on yours, nor does it purge your infamy which our just complaints shall spread through the world, nor will it prevent the stings of conscience pricking you, when that weapon which we forged to terrify and chastise others is turned against our own breast, because you will be justly considered to deserve that punishment which is the due of parricides. Although ambition may blind you, all the world bearing witness to your infamy will open your eyes. God Himself will open them, for perjurers, faith-breakers, and traitors offend Him still as they always have done, unless for some hidden reason He has now closed His eyes to the deeds of wicked men. Do not promise yourself therefore a certain victory, for the aroused anger of God may defeat you, and we will only part with our freedom in death. When we can no longer defend ourselves we will surrender to some other prince rather than to you. If, however, for our sins, and against every wish, we do fall into your hands, we have a firm belief that your rule, commenced in deceit and wrong, will end either with you or your sons in dishonour and disaster."

Although the count was deeply wounded by the language of the Milanese deputies, he did not show his feelings either in words or change of countenance, but he replied to them that he was content to attribute their unwise language to their angry feelings, but that he could answer their charges before any tribunal to whom it would be proper to submit their differences. It would then be seen that he had not injured the Milanese, but had only taken such steps as would prevent them from injuring him. All the world was perfectly acquainted with the intentions of the Milanese after the battle of Caravaggio, for instead of rewarding him with the gift of Verona or Brescia, they made an attempt to come to terms with the Venetians, in order that the odium of the war should rest upon his shoulders, whilst to them would belong the honour of making peace, the fruits of victory, and every other advantage. They really had no cause of complaint against him, for he had only succeeded in obtaining the terms of peace which they had tried to get; and if he had hesitated to take the course he had done, he would now be reproaching them for the ingratitude for which they were reproving him. Whether this were true or not, the result of the impending struggle would determine which of them was favoured by that God upon whom they called to avenge their injuries, and which of them had fought with the greater right on his side.

The ambassadors then left, and both parties prepared for war. The Milanese engaged Francesco and Jacopo Piccinino as their captains, who by reason of the ancient enmity between the Bracceschi and Sforzeschi arms remained faithful to Milan, and hoped to defend their liberties until such time as they could detach from the count the Venetians, whom they did not expect to remain either friendly or faithful to him for any length of time. The count had also the same fears of the Venetians, and believing that, when obligations are not strong enough to bind, it is wise to buy loyalty more effectually with rewards, he therefore, when arranging the campaign, agreed that the Venetians should besiege Crema and retain it after they had captured it. Their agreement bound the Venetians to maintain the alliance with the count until he had seized all the dominions of the Milanese, and he now held the city so closely invested that it could no longer obtain provisions. Despairing of any other help the Milanese sent envoys to Venice, praying the republic to have compassion on them, and imploring its aid against tyranny, which it had ever been its custom to give; because should Sforza become master of Milan no further limit would remain to his ambitions, for he would never rest content under any terms, nor would he recognise the ancient boundaries of the state. The Venetians were not yet masters of Crema, and wishing to capture it before they denounced the count, they replied officially that, having made an agreement with the count, they could not listen to the Milanese. But in private they spoke in such a way as would enable the envoys to give encouragement to the signori in Milan.

The count was now in possession of the suburbs of Milan, and the Venetians had captured Crema; therefore there was no longer reason to defer the agreement between the Milanese and the Venetians. Accordingly terms were agreed between them, by one of which the Venetians undertook to defend the liberties of the Milanese. Having made this agreement, the Venetian troops under the count were ordered to leave his camp and retire to their own. The conditions of the peace made with the Milanese were signified also to the count, and twenty days given him in which to accept them. The count was not surprised at this, because he had foreseen it and expected that it might happen any day; nevertheless, now that it had come, he could not help resenting it and experiencing the feelings of the Milanese when they had been abandoned by him. He at once decided to play with the Venetians, yet not abandon his designs on Milan. Accordingly he took advantage of the presence of the Venetian ambassadors, who had communicated the terms of peace to him, to announce that he was quite ready for peace, and would send his envoys to Venice to ratify it. But his secret instructions to these were that they were not to ratify, but to defer the signature under various pretexts. To induce the Venetians more readily to believe that he was in earnest, he entered into a truce with the Milanese, drew off his army from around Milan, and quartered his men in his own towns. This plan brought him the final victory and ruined the Milanese, because the Venetians, relying on peace, sent no further supplies of war to the Milanese who, being granted a truce and their enemy withdrawn, believed that the count would now abandon his proceedings against them, because of their alliance with the Venetians. This decision doubly proved their ruin; it caused them in the first place to relax their defence, and, secondly, the country being freed from the Venetians, and the seed time being at hand, much grain was sown; hence it followed that the count could starve the Milanese far easier than they could him. All these things were damaging to the enemy and advantageous to the count; in addition he gained time in which to rest and recruit his army.

During this war in Lombardy the Florentines had not declared themselves for either party, and had shown no favour to the count either when he was fighting for the Milanese or against them, for the reason that he had neither need of their help nor had he asked it; only after the rout at Caravaggio had they sent assistance to the Venetians by virtue of their league with them. But when the Count Francesco stood alone, and had nowhere else to turn, he was obliged to seek instant aid from Florence, both officially from the state and privately from his friends; especially from Cosimo de' Medici with whom he had always had friendly relations, and who had always assisted him with advice and money. Nor was the count abandoned in this necessity, but was freely assisted by Cosimo, and encouraged to persist in his enterprise. Cosimo also urged the city to assist the count, but in this he met with opposition. Neri di Gino was still very powerful, and it did not appear to this statesman at all advantageous for Florence to permit the count to take possession of Milan; he believed that it would be conducive to the welfare of Italy for war to cease, and for the count to ratify the terms of peace. In the first place, he doubted if the Milanese, in their resentment against the count, would not prefer to give themselves up to the Venetians, and in the next place he considered that it would be the ruin of all if the count were to acquire Milan. The count would become far too formidable if he were permitted to join his army to a great state like that of Milan; and if he had been found insupportable as a count, he would be still more unendurable as a duke. Therefore Neri maintained that it would be better for the republic of Florence, and all Italy, for the count to remain as he was, great in arms, whilst Lombardy might be divided into two republics; for Lombardy united under one leader would threaten all Italy, whilst divided it could injure no one. To attain this end he could see nothing but to refuse assistance to the count and maintain the league with the Venetians. The friends of Cosimo declined to accept these reasons, as they did not believe that Neri was influenced in his decision solely by love of the republic, but because it appeared to him that if the count, the friend of Cosimo, were to become duke, then Cosimo himself would become too powerful. Cosimo, on his side, insisted that to aid the count at this juncture would be of the utmost advantage to both Italy and the republic, for in his opinion it was not reasonable to expect that the Milanese would be able to maintain their freedom, since their standard of citizenship, their ways of living, and their ancient feuds were in every circumstance adverse to republican rule. Thus it must follow that either the Venetians would become masters in Milan or the count would become duke. No one could be so foolish as to doubt which was better for the republic, to have as a neighbour a powerful friend or a more powerful enemy. He was also doubtful if the Milanese would yield submission to the Venetians, although they were at strife with the count, because the count had plenty of adherents in Milan, whilst the Venetians had none; so that if unable to maintain their freedom they would be more likely to submit to the count than to the Venetians. This difference of opinion engaged the city for a long time, and finally it was decided to send ambassadors to the count in order to discover his chances of success; if they were good, then the ambassadors were to come to terms with him, if otherwise, then let them raise difficulties and temporise.

When, however, the ambassadors reached Reggio they learnt that the count was already master of Milan; for as soon as the truce expired the count had moved his army against the city and intended, in spite of the Venetians, to get possession of it. The Venetians could only send assistance by the Adda, and this route could easily be closed against them, and the count, relying on their not taking the field during the winter, believed that he would capture Milan before the spring, especially as Francesco Piccinino was dead, and there only remained his brother Jacopo as leader of the Milanese. The Venetians sent envoys to Milan to encourage the citizens to defend themselves to the utmost, and promised to come swiftly to their rescue. There was much skirmishing during the winter between the count and the Milanese, but until the weather became more favourable the Venetians, under the command of Pandolfo Malatesta, remained in their cantonments beyond the Adda. When information reached them that if they wished to succour Milan they must tempt the fortune of battle and attack the count, Pandolfo, knowing well the bravery of the count and his army, decided that he was not in a position to fight. But Pandolfo had hopes of winning without fighting, for the count was much pressed for want of grain and forage; he therefore advised that the army should be kept where it was, in order to give the Milanese hopes of succour and prevent them giving themselves up to the count in despair. This course was approved by the Venetians because it appeared a safe one, and because they still believed that if the Milanese were pressed by the privations of the siege they would be compelled to throw themselves upon their protection, persuaded as they were that the Milanese would never yield to the count, owing to the injuries they had received from him.

Whilst the Milanese were besieged, they suffered extreme misery, and poverty stricken by nature the people died of hunger in the streets; consequently there arose on every side cries and complaints, and the magistrates becoming alarmed took all possible care to prevent the citizens from assembling. Privation always disposes the crowd to evil and the slightest incident will cause it to break out. Thus it happened that two men of the lower order were speaking together near the Porta Nuova of their own and the city's miseries, and of what could be done to relieve them, when others began to gather round them until a large crowd had assembled, and a report spread through the city that the people near the Porta Nuova had risen in arms against the magistrates. Upon this the multitude, who were only waiting an opportunity, at once took up arms and made Gasparre de Vicomercato their leader. They then went to the palace where the magistrates were assembled and killed all who could not escape. Among those killed was Lionardo Veniero, the Venetian ambassador, whom they recognised as the cause of all their misery. The men who by these means had become the chief men in the city, then debated what should be done to escape from their troubles and regain peace. They all decided that, since they could no longer preserve their liberties by their own efforts, they must seek protection under some prince who was capable of defending them. Some named King Alfonso, some the Duke of Savoy, and others were for the King of France, but none named the count, so deep was their hatred of him. Nevertheless, Gasparre de Vicomercato, disagreeing with the others, was the first to name the count. Gasparre was only influenced by the desire to put an immediate end to the war, and he saw no way of accomplishing this but by calling in the count, because the people had need of immediate and certain relief rather than a deferred hope of future help. In so many words he explained away the action of the count, and blamed the ambitions and greed of the Venetians and princes of Italy, who had never really wished that the people of Milan should enjoy freedom. If after all they have to surrender their liberty, let it be to one who could defend them, and who would do it in such a way that their servitude would bring them immediate peace, and they would no longer have to endure the perils and hardships of war. Gasparre was most attentively listened to, and at the conclusion of his speech all demanded that the count should be sent for, and they appointed Gasparre as their ambassador. By command of the people he sought out the count and gave him the agreeable news, which the count was delighted to receive. The count therefore entered Milan as its prince on February 26, 1450, and was received with the greatest rejoicings by those who had so recently held him in the greatest hatred.

When the news reached Florence, the Florentines at once instructed their envoys, who were then on their way to the count, to congratulate the duke on his victory instead of negotiating with the count for a treaty. The envoys were very graciously received by the duke and honourably rewarded, because he well knew that in a struggle against the Venetians he could not find in all Italy a more loyal or gallant ally than Florence. The Florentines now saw that, having their fears of the house of the Visconti laid at rest, they would have to meet the forces, of the Aragonese and Venetians. The Aragonese King of Naples hated the Florentines owing to their ancient friendship with the house of France, and the Venetians because they saw that the suspicions with which the Florentines had always regarded the house of Visconti would now be transferred to them, and recollecting with what persistency the Florentines had always opposed the Visconti, and fearing the same treatment, they decided to ruin the Florentines. Such were the reasons which enabled the duke to conclude an alliance with the Florentines, and which caused the King Alfonso and the Venetians to regard him as their common enemy, and impelled them to determine to put their armies in motion at the same time — the king to attack the Florentines and the Venetians the duke. The Venetians believed that, the duke being new to his dominions, would be easily overcome by their own forces without the aid of others.

Owing, however, to the treaty which existed between the Venetians and the Florentines, and the peace which the king had made with the latter after the fighting at Piombino, it did not appear right to disturb the peace without some pretext to justify it. Therefore both the Venetians and the king sent ambassadors to Florence, who on behalf of their masters let the Florentines understand that the purport of the agreements between them was not for the injury of others, but for the defence of their mutual states. Then the Venetians complained that the Florentines had permitted the passage through Lunigiano of Alexandro, the duke's brother, who had used that route to reach Lombardy with his forces; and further, the Florentines had been the advisers and abettors of the treaty which had been concluded between the duke and the Marquis of Mantua, both of which acts they maintained were opposed to the interests of their states, and the friendship which existed between them; therefore they frankly informed the Florentines that those who injure others wrongfully give justification to others to injure them, and that those who act in contravention of treaties must expect war. Cosimo was requested by the signoria to reply, and this he did in a long and weighty oration, recounting all the benefits which Florence had conferred upon the Venetians, pointing out the wide dominions which the Venetians had acquired with the blood and treasure and counsel of the Florentines, and recalling the fact that as the friendship between them had always been at the instance of the Florentines, so now they would not be the cause of any hostility. Having always been lovers of peace they were able to appreciate the treaty recently concluded between the Venetians and King Alfonso, if it tended to peace and not to aggression. It was a cause of much surprise to them that complaint should be made of the small affairs pointed out, and that so great a republic should consider them for a moment; but even if they were worthy of consideration, the Florentines wished to let every one understand that their country was free to all, and that as for the duke, he was of such rank and position as would entitle him to enter into an alliance with Mantua without the aid or advice of any one. But as it was to be feared that these complaints concealed some hidden motives, the Florentines were ready to let it be known that, whilst their friendship would be of advantage, so their hostility would be dangerous.

Thus the trouble was lightly dismissed, and the envoys appeared to take their leave sufficiently satisfied, nevertheless the movements of the Venetians and the king, by virtue of their alliance, caused anxiety to the Florentines and the duke, and made them expect war rather than peace. This induced the Florentines and the duke to draw closer together, whilst the sinister intentions of the Venetians became more apparent; for at this time they formed a league with the Sienese, who, acting under its provisions, drove all Florentine subjects out of the city and state of Siena. This was followed shortly after by a similar act on the part of King Alfonso, without any justification or reason for it, and in spite of the treaty made with Florence the year before. The Venetians also attempted to capture Bologna by arming a number of exiles and sending them by night through the sewers into Bologna. The entrance of these men was not discovered until they raised their cries and awakened Santi Bentivoglio, who was told that the city was in the hands of the rebels. Many begged him to save his life by flight, since if he stayed he could not save them, but he preferred to show a bold front to fortune and encouragement to his friends by taking arms, and putting himself at the head of his adherents he attacked the rebels, routed them, killing many and driving the rest out of the city. After this deed of bravery everybody declared Santi to have proved himself a true scion of the house of Bentivoglio.

These acts indicated to the Florentines that war was impending, and therefore they followed their usual custom of creating the magistracy of Ten, enrolling men, and sending envoys to Rome, Naples, Venice, Siena, and elsewhere to seek the aid of friends, to allay fears, to guard against misunderstandings, and to learn the plans of enemies. From the pope nothing was received but expressions of general goodwill, from the king some empty excuses for having turned out the Florentines and the offer of safe conducts to any persons who should ask them. Although he endeavoured to conceal his plan of campaign, the ambassadors discovered it, as well as his preparations for attacking the republic. The Florentines also strengthened their league with the duke in several particulars, and through his good offices concluded an alliance with the Genoese, which settled their old quarrels over reprisals and other differences. The Venetians, on their side, took all possible steps to upset these arrangements, even going to the length of praying the Emperor of Constantinople to expel all Florentines from his dominion. Thus the Venetians were entering upon this war with the utmost determination, urged on by their lust of dominion, without any respect for those who had contributed so much to their grandeur in the past. However, they were not listened to by the emperor. The Florentine envoys were prohibited from entering the territories of the Venetian Republic, the senate alleging that in consequence of their understanding with King Alfonso they were not permitted to receive envoys without his participation. The Sienese received the envoys courteously, fearing they might be attacked by the Florentines before the league was in a position to defend them, therefore they thought it best to soothe with gentle words the enemy they were not yet capable of resisting. It is not believed that the Venetians and the king desired to send envoys to Florence to justify the declaration of war; but since the Venetian envoys would not be permitted to enter Florentine territory, it did not appear correct for those of the king to go alone, and the legation did not take place. The Venetians learnt by this that they were as little respected by the Florentines as the Florentines had been by them only a few months before.

In the midst of the anxieties caused by these events, the emperor, Federigo III., passed into Italy to be crowned, and on January 30, 1451, entered Florence with 1500 knights, and was most honourably received by the signoria. He remained in Florence until February 6, when he left for his coronation in Rome. Here he was most solemnly crowned, and afterwards celebrated his nuptials with the empress, who had come to Rome by sea. In May they passed through Florence, and were received with such honours as marked the first coming of the emperor. When the emperor was on his way home he received some honours from the Marquis of Ferrara, and in return for these conceded Modena and Reggio to him. The Florentines during this time lost no opportunity of preparing for the war which now appeared imminent, and to create an impression upon the enemy they and the duke entered into a treaty of offence and defence with the King of France, and published it with great ostentation throughout all Italy.

It being now May 1452, it no longer appeared prudent to the Venetians to defer their struggle with the duke, therefore, with 16,000 horse and 6000 infantry, they invaded his territory by the way of Lodi, and at the same time the Marquis of Monferrato, either through his own ambition or the incitements of the Venetians, attacked him on the other side near Alessandria. The duke assembled 18,000 cavalry and 3000 infantry, and having garrisoned Lodi and Alessandria, and fortified other places which the enemy were likely to attack, he invaded the Brescian territory, wasting the country in every direction, and sacking the weaker towns. Having defeated the Marquis of Monferrato at Alessandria, he was able to turn upon the Venetians and invade their country.

Whilst the war was carried on in Lombardy with varying and trifling successes, none of which are worthy of record, the fighting now occurring between King Alfonso and the Florentines was waged with no more energy and caused no more anxiety than the one in Lombardy. Ferrante, the illegitimate son of Alfonso, came into Tuscany with 12,000 soldiers under the command of Federigo, lord of Urbino. His first enterprise was against Fojano in the Val di Chiana, for owing to the treaty with the Sienese they had entered Florentine territory on that side. Fojano was a small castle with poor defences and a weak garrison, but according to those times considered brave and trusty; they numbered 200 men, and had been placed there by the Florentine signoria. Ferrante encamped before this place and laid siege to it, but whether it was that the prowess of his army was so insignificant, or the castle was so strong, or the valour of its defenders so great, it took thirty days to capture it. This delay gave ample time to the Florentines to put other places of greater importance in defensive order, and to get their men together for a proper and skilful resistance. The enemy having taken Fojano poured into Chianti, but were driven back from two small towns by the inhabitants. They then passed on to Castellina, a castle situated on the borders of Chianti, about twelve miles from Siena. This place occupied a very weak position, and was still more poorly defended; but the incompetency of the attack was such that, even with these drawbacks, it was able to withstand the assault, and after forty-four days' siege the army of Ferrante drew off in disgrace. So little were the armies of those days to be feared, and so little peril did the fighters experience, that towns which are now abandoned as incapable of defence were then considered impossible of capture. Whilst Ferrante lay with his army at Chianti he made several raids into the Florentine territory, and approached within six miles of Florence, causing great alarm and loss to the citizens. They had at this time stationed their army, numbering about 8000 men under Astorre da Faenza and Gismondo Malatesta, near Colle, in order to keep it out of reach of the enemy, lest it should be brought to battle, and losing it lose everything. For they knew very well that if the small castles were lost they would be returned after the peace, and that the larger towns were in a position to resist the enemy. King Alfonso had a fleet of about twenty galleys at sea near Pisa, which, whilst he attacked Castellina by land, took up a position off the fortress of Vada and captured it owing to the remissness of the castellan. By this capture the enemy were able to harass the country in its neighbourhood, but the Florentines soon checked this by sending men to Campiglia, who drove the raiders back to the coast.

The pontiff took no part in these struggles, except attempting to bring the parties to an agreement; yet although free from war himself, he encountered some perils at home. There resided in Rome at that time Messer Stefano Porcaro, a learned Roman citizen, of good family, but yet more distinguished for his lofty spirit. This gentleman, like many others whose minds hunger for glory, desired to accomplish something worthy of being handed down to posterity, and be believed there was nothing greater than to free his country from the dominion of the prelates and restore it to its ancient state; and when he had succeeded in this he hoped to be called a new founder, a second father of the city. What incited him to undertake this enterprise was the evil lives of the prelates and the discontent of the barons and people of Rome, and what inspired his hopes beyond all else were the verses of Petrarch in the *Cansone* which commences: "Spirto gentil che quelle membra reggi," where he says: —

> "Sopra il Monte Tarpejo, canzon vedrai,
> Un cavalier, ch' Italia tutto onora,
> Pensoso piu d'altrui, che di se stesso."

Messer Stefano knew that poets had often been inspired with a divine and prophetic spirit, and he believed that he had every reason to expect that what Petrarch had foretold in his verse would come to pass, and that he ought to be the fulfiller of such glorious hopes; for was he not far superior to any other Roman in eloquence, learning, accomplishments, and connections? He became, therefore, so possessed with these ideas that he could no longer regulate either his words or his actions sufficiently to conceal his intentions from others. Thereupon the authorities banished him to Bologna with a view to depriving him of the opportunity of doing any harm, and the governor of that city was commissioned to keep him under daily observation. Messer Stefano was in no way depressed by this first set back, but rather encouraged in his enterprise; at the same time, however, he began to show more discretion in his communications with his friends, and more than once he passed to and from Rome and Bologna with such swiftness that he was always in time to report himself to the governor, in accordance with the orders. When he had converted a sufficient number of men to his views he determined no longer to defer his attempt, therefore he communicated with his friends in Rome, and arranged to give a supper to which all the conspirators would be invited, and each one asked to bring a trusty friend. Messer Stefano promised to be with them before the supper was finished. All arrangements were carried out as he wished, and he had safely arrived in the house where the supper was held. As soon as the banquet was over, Messer Stefano appeared before the company dressed in cloth of gold, with chains and other ornaments upon him, all giving him a splendid and majestic appearance. Having saluted the company he delivered a long oration, encouraging them to be brave and resolute in their glorious enterprise. He then divided them into parties, and appointed one to seize the palace of the pontificate on the following morning, whilst the other should call the people of Rome to arms. News of the plot reached the pontiff that night, some say through the treachery of one of the conspirators, others that the presence of Messer Stefano was well known in Rome. However this may be, the pope, on the same night, after the supper, seized Messer Stefano with the greater number of his accomplices and put them to death, as their misdeeds deserved. Such was the end of the dreams of Messer Stefano Porcaro. His intentions may claim some merit, but his want of judgment in carrying them out deserves censure. Although some shadow of glory may appear to cling to such enterprises, the dangers which attend their execution are very real.

The fighting in Tuscany had now lasted nearly a year, and in the spring of 1453 the time had arrived when the armies were to resume the campaign. With their army increased by the Signore Alessandro Sforza, brother of the duke, who had come to the assistance of the Florentines, whilst the forces of the king had been weakened, it appeared possible to the Florentines to recover some of their lost towns with but slight effort. Therefore they took the field at Fogano, which owing to the remissness of the commissioners had been sacked, and found the inhabitants so scattered that it was only by offering them privileges and gifts that they were induced to return to the town; the fortress of Vada was also retaken, the enemy having fired it when they saw they could not hold it. Whilst the Florentines were carrying out these operations, the Aragonese army had retired on Siena, and although it dared not face the Florentine army it burnt and pillaged their territory, to the great loss of the inhabitants. Thus the king, failing to meet his enemies in the field, endeavoured to raise new foes against them and compel them to divide their forces.

Gherardo Gambacorti, the lord of Val di Bagno, either because of friendship or some other obligation, had always been, as had his ancestors, either in the pay or under the protection of the Florentines. This man was holding communications with King Alfonso, to whom he was inclined to surrender his estate in exchange for one in Naples. These negotiations coming to the knowledge of the Florentines, they sent envoys to Gherardo to learn his intentions. These gentlemen recalled to his recollection the obligations that both he and his ancestors were under to their republic, and the advantages to him of remaining in alliance with it. Gherardo expressed the greatest surprise at such a charge being made, and swore with great oaths that such wickedness had never come into his mind, and that he was willing to go in person to Florence as a pledge of his good intentions. Being however indisposed, he said he would send his son to fulfil what he could not accomplish himself, and he handed him over to the envoys to accompany them to Florence as a hostage. These words and actions induced the Florentines to believe that Gherardo spoke the truth and that his accusers were liars, and under this impression they remained quiet. But Gherardo pursued his negotiations with all the more energy with Alfonso and soon brought them to a conclusion. The king then sent into the Val di Bagno a knight of Jerusalem, named Frate Puccio, with a large body of troops to take possession of Gherardo's towns and fortresses. The people of Bagno, however, who were well disposed to Florence, only yielded a hesitating obedience to the king.

Frate Puccio having conquered almost the whole of the Val di Bagno, there only remained the fortress of Corzano of which to take possession, and he and Gherardo were actually carrying out the arrangements for its transference to their men when Antonio Gualandi, a Pisanian, young and bold, who despised the treachery of Gherardo, having considered the position of the fortress and its garrison, and seeing that his men were no better pleased than he, seized Gherardo, whom he found at the gate about to admit the

Aragonese, and taking him in both arms threw him outside, ordering the guard to close the gate upon such a traitor, and declared
himself for the Florentine Republic. The report of this deed
quickly spread through the Val di Bagno and neighbouring places,
and everywhere the people flew to arms against the Aragonese,
raised the banner of Florence, and drove out the invaders. When
these affairs became known in Florence, the authorities threw into
prison the boy whom Gherardo had left with them as a hostage,
and sent troops to the Val di Bagno to hold it for the republic; and
thus the state which had hitherto been administered as a princi-
pality was brought under the jurisdiction of a deputy. Gherardo
Gambacorti, traitor to his lord and to his son, escaped with difficulty, leaving wife, family, and all his possessions in the hands of
his enemies. This incident created a great impression in Florence,
because had the king succeeded in becoming master of the Val di
Bagno he would have been able at his leisure, and at little
expense, to harass the Val di Tevere and the Casentino, where he
could have done immense damage to the republic, who would
have been compelled to divide their forces had they still desired to
attack the Aragonese army which lay at Siena.

The Forentines had taken steps outside of Italy to combat the
hostile league by sending their ambassador, Messer Agnolo
Acciajuoli, to the King of France, entreating him to allow King
René of Anjou to come to the assistance of the duke and themselves; and should René come to the assistance of his friends, he
would then be able to consider if he should not attempt to regain
the kingdom of Naples, and for this purpose the Florentines were
ready to promise him men and money. Thus whilst the war was
being waged in Lombardy and Tuscany, as related above, the
Florentine ambassador had concluded a treaty with King René, by
which he agreed to arrive in Italy by the end of June with 2400
horsemen, and on his arrival at Alessandria the league agreed to
pay him 30,000 florins down and 10,000 florins each month as
long as the war lasted. King René therefore prepared to pass into
Italy, but was at once stopped by the Duke of Savoy and the

Marquis of Mantua, who would not permit him to pass through their country owing to their alliance with the Venetians. Whereupon the king was advised by the Florentine ambassador that, in order to maintain the integrity of the alliance, he must return to Provence and thence make the descent upon Italy by sea, whilst the King of France should use his influence with the Duke of Savoy for the rest of his men to pass through the duke's territory. This plan succeeded, and René reached Italy by sea, and his men were allowed to pass through Savoy out of compliment to the French king. King René was received with great honour by the Duke Francesco, and the union of the Italian and French armies being effected, they attacked the Venetians with such energy that all the towns which had been lost in Cremona were recovered. Not content with this they seized almost the whole of the Brescian territory, and the Venetian army, finding itself no longer secure in the open country, retired under the walls of Brescia.

The winter having now set in, the duke sent his troops into winter quarters, and Piacenza was assigned to King René. The winter of 1453 passed without any operations of war whatever, and when spring arrived, and it was thought that the duke would at once open the campaign and drive the Venetians into the sea, King René informed him that he must return to France. This strange and unexpected decision of the king greatly displeased the duke, and although he went in person to René to persuade him to remain, he could not move him either by prayers or promises; the utmost the king would do was to allow some of his men to remain and promise to send his son Jean to assist the league. This proceeding of King René did not affect the Florentines very much, because having now recovered their possessions they no longer had any fear of the King Alfonso, and on the other hand they had no particular desire that the duke should acquire any possessions in Lombardy beyond the few towns of his own. After King René left Italy, his son came as promised, and after a short stay in Lombardy passed on to Florence, where he was received with great honour.

The course adopted by King René turned the thoughts of the duke to peace, to which also the Venetians, Alfonso, and the Florentines were inclined, for all were utterly weary of the strife. The pope had always expressed his desire for peace, and it was now a matter of urgency with him, for Mahomet, the Grand Turk, had taken Constantinople and over-run the whole of Greece. This event alarmed the entire Christian world, especially the Venetians and the pope, because they had already felt the weight of his power in Italy. The pope, therefore, besought the Italian potentates to send envoys with full authority to arrange terms for a general peace; All consented, and the envoys met together to consider the terms upon which the proposed peace could be concluded, but many difficulties revealed themselves when details came to be discussed. King Alfonso insisted upon the reimbursement by the Florentines of his expenditure during the war; the Florentines made the same demand on him; the Venetians demanded Cremona from the duke, and it appeared impossible to reconcile these conflicting desires. Nevertheless, that which appeared very difficult of settlement among a number of people in Rome was easily accomplished at Milan and Venice by two gentlemen representing the duke and the Venetians; for whilst the envoys were debating in Rome over the terms of a general peace, these two met and concluded a treaty on April 9, 1454, by which each of the parties returned to the other all the towns of which they had been possessed before the war, and to the duke was further conceded permission to retake the towns of which the Princes of Monferrato and Savoy had dispossessed him. A month was allowed to the Other Italian powers within which to ratify this treaty. The pope, Florentines, and Sienese ratified it within the prescribed time. As if not content with this treaty of peace, the duke and the Florentines signed a further one for twenty-five years. King Alfonso was the only one among the princes of Italy who remained discontented with the turn affairs had taken, for it did not appear to him to be in accord with the dignity of his position, that he should be only a signatory to its ratification and not a principal to the treaty; he, therefore, took umbrage at this and would not declare his intentions. However, after several influential embassies had been sent him by the pope and other princes, he permitted himself to be persuaded, and chiefly at the instance of the pope he and his son agreed to enter into a treaty for thirty years. The duke and the king cemented this with the two marriages which were celebrated between the children of each. Yet, as if still to leave some seeds of further strife in Italy, the king would not consent to the peace unless his colleagues would first agree to his prosecuting a war against the Genoese, Gismondo Malatesti and Astorre, the Prince of Faenza. This was agreed, and his son, Ferrante, undertook it, but soon after returned to Naples, having acquired no territory but lost many men.

Having secured this general peace, the only anxiety that exercised men's minds was the dread lest Alfonso, owing to his hostility to the Genoese, should again disturb the peace of the world. This fear, however, was realised in other ways. Peace was broken, not indeed by the king openly, but by the ambition of the mercenary soldiers, as had so frequently happened before. The Venetians, according to their custom, on the conclusion of a peace, had discharged their condottiere, Jacopo Piccinino, who joining other condottieri had passed into Romagna, and thence into the Siena district. Here Jacopo commenced fighting and captured several towns from the Sienese. Pope Nicolo died in the year 1455, when this event happened, and Callisto III. was elected his successor. This pontiff at once sent his captain, Giovanni Ventimiglia, to stop this outburst of fighting so close to him, and Giovanni with as many men as he could collect, and with some forces of the Florentines and the duke, who had joined in the repression of the trouble, marched against Jacopo. They brought him to battle at Bolsena and, in spite of the fact that Ventimiglia was taken prisoner, Jacopo was defeated, and fled to Castiglione della Pescaia. Had not Jacopo been assisted by King Alfonso with money he would have been utterly ruined, and it was this which caused many people to believe that Jacopo's action had been instigated by the king. This belief gained such general credence that Alfonso, finding he could not deny it, compelled Jacopo to restore the towns in order that he might rehabilitate himself with his co-signatories to the treaty, having totally alienated them by such futile fighting. He, however, secured for Jacopo 20,000 florins from the Sienese, and when this had been received Jacopo and his men retired into the kingdom of Naples.

Although the pope had concerned himself with the attempt to curb Jacopo, he had not relaxed his efforts to relieve the Christian world of the Turkish oppression, and had sent envoys and preachers into every Christian country to stir up the people in defence of their religion. Great numbers of men came in person and many sent money to assist in the enterprise against their common enemy. Subscriptions were collected in Florence, where many men wore the red cross to show their readiness to go to the war; processions filled the streets, and no opportunity was lost of showing both in public and in private that the Florentines were desirous of being among the first Christians to support the crusade both with men, money, and counsel. But the eagerness for the crusade was considerably lessened by the news of the defeat of the Turks by the Hungarians, and the wounding of Mahomet whilst with his army besieging Belgrade, a castle on the Danube in Hungary. Thus the panic which had seized the pontificate and the Christian world ceased, and the preparations for war only proceeded slowly; whilst in Hungary, owing to the death of John Hunyadi, the captain in the recent victory, they ceased entirely.

But to return to Italian affairs, I must relate what happened in the year 1456, after the disturbance raised by Jacopo Piccinino had been quelled, when it appeared as if God had taken up the weapons which men had laid down, for there occurred a most dreadful storm, such as had never been known in Tuscany, and the effects of which were so wonderful and memorable as scarcely to be credited by posterity. This storm arose an hour before daybreak in the Adriatic Sea off the coast of Ancona, and sweeping across Italy re-entered the sea beyond Pisa—a whirlwind of cloud, thick

and black, which for the space of two miles wide overthrew everything in its course. This whirlwind, whether natural or supernatu-
ral, with enormous force, seized and whirled the clouds round
and round, breaking them up, flinging them first to heaven then
to earth; at one time dashing them together; then speeding them
along in circles with incredible swiftness; with these clouds moved
winds of raging impetuosity, whilst constant flames and brilliant
flashes appeared as though in combat among themselves. From
these confused and tearing clouds, and from these furious and
often flaming winds, there came a noise with the strength and
immensity of an earthquake or the sound of thunder, which so
appalled those who heard it they believed the end of the world
had come, and the earth, and water, and air were returning in one
confused ruin to their original chaos. Wherever this terrible whirlwind passed it left unprecedented and wonderful effects, but
those around the castle of San Casciano were the most marvellous.
This castle is situate about eight miles from Florence, beyond the
hills which divide the valleys of the Pesa and the Grieve. The hur-
ricane passed between the castle and the villages of Santa Andrea
situate on the same hill, and whilst San Andrea was not affected,
and San Casciano was only touched in such a manner that a few
pinnacles and chimneys were thrown to the ground, many houses
were ruined or levelled in the country which lies between these
two places. The roofs of the churches of San Martino at Bagnuolo
and of Santa Maria della Pace were carried more than a mile away,
just as they had been upon the churches. A carrier and his mules
were blown off the road into a neighbouring valley and picked up
dead. The great oaks and other large trees that would not bend
before the fury of the storm, were not only torn up by their roots,
but carried far away from where they had grown. When day broke
and the tempest had spent itself, men were stupefied by what was
around them. They saw the country desolated and ruined. They
could hear the lamentations of those who had witnessed the
destruction of all their possessions, whilst their relatives and cattle
lay dead under the ruins of the buildings; all of which sights and

sounds produced the greatest fear and pity in the survivors. It appeared as if God desired rather to threaten Tuscany than chastise her, for had such a tempest fallen upon a city, crowded with houses and inhabitants, instead of among trees and a few cottages, without doubt it would have caused such a scourge and ruin as no mind can contemplate. But God wished, with this trifling exhibition of his power, to restore among men the memory of Himself and His will.

Returning however to King Alfonso, who, as I have already written, was greatly dissatisfied with the peace, and who since the war which he incited Jacopo Piccinino to wage upon the Sienese had no important results, he wished to see if he could not obtain greater satisfaction from the war which, according to the terms of the convention, he was authorised to undertake. Therefore, in the year 1456, he declared war against the Genoese both by land and sea, with the intention of taking the government of Genoa from the Fregosi and handing it over to the Adorni. At the same time he sent Jacopo Piccinino across the Tronto to attack Gismondo Malatesti. Gismondo cared little for these attacks of Jacopo, for he had all his towns strongly fortified, so that this part of the king's adventure quite failed; whilst the other brought far more fighting than either he or his subjects desired. The Doge of Genoa at this time was Pietro Fregoso, and he, fearing that he could not possibly maintain his government against the king, decided to give away what he could not keep, and call in one who not only would defend him now but possibly reward him in the future for the benefits he was conferring upon him. He therefore sent envoys to Charles, King of France, and offered him the government of Genoa. Charles accepted the offer, and appointed Jean d'Anjou, son of King René, to take possession of the city. Jean was at this time in France, having returned there when he left Florence. King Charles had persuaded himself that Jean, having already acquired many Italian ideas, would be able to govern Genoa better than any other man; he also considered that Jean from that position would be able to direct his attention to the kingdom of Naples, from which his father, René, had been driven by Alfonso. So Jean went to Genoa, was received as its prince, and the government and all fortresses placed in his hands.

This move disturbed King Alfonso, for it appeared to him that he had brought down upon himself far too strong an adversary; yet he did not desist, but set about his undertaking with courage, and had already sent forth his fleet under Villamarina against Portofino, when he was suddenly taken ill and died. His death freed Jean and the Genoese from the immediate danger of war, because Ferrante, who succeeded his father Alfonso as king, was much alarmed at having so powerful an enemy as the King of France in Italy; besides he was doubtful of the loyalty of many of his barons, who in their desire for change might go over to the French. Ferrante had also some reason to fear the pope, whose ambition it was, he knew, to rob him of his kingdom before he could settle himself in it. Ferrante's only hope was in the Duke of Milan, who shared his anxieties regarding his own state, for he had no doubt that when the French had consolidated their position in Genoa they would not hesitate to seize Milan, for he knew they believed they could substantiate their claim to it. The duke, therefore, immediately on the death of Alfonso, sent letters and troops to Ferrante. The letters bade him to be of good courage, and assured him that the writer would in no case abandon him in his need, and that the forces sent would aid and increase his influence. The pontiff had intended at the death of Alfonso to give the kingdom to Pietro Lodovico Borgia, his nephew, but in order to gain the adherence of the princes of Italy he had concealed his real design, and merely expressed the desire that the kingdom should be brought once more under the sway of the Roman Church. With this view he had endeavoured to persuade the Duke of Milan not to show any favour to Ferrante, and in return for his compliance he offered the duke the towns which he already held in the kingdom. But in the midst of these new ideas and schemes Callisto died, and was succeeded in the pontificate by one of the Piccolomini family, a Sienese named Æneas, under the title of

Pio II. This pontiff sought only to benefit Christianity and to bring honour to the Church, he left out of consideration all private inducements, and at the request of the Duke of Milan crowned Ferrante King of Naples. The pope considered that to maintain Ferrante upon the throne of Naples would assist in the pacification of Italy far more than either to allow the French to seize the kingdom or to take it himself, as Callisto had intended doing. In consequence of the pope's action, Ferrante created his nephew Prince of Malfi and married him to his illegitimate daughter. He also restored Benevento and Teracina to the Church.

It now appearing as if peace were established in Italy, the pontiff was about to resume the campaign against the Turks, which had been commenced by Pope Callisto, when there arose dissensions between the Fregosi and Jean of Anjou in Genoa, which ended in a greater and more important conflict than any that had yet occurred. Pietrino Fregosi was residing at his castle in the Riviera, dissatisfied with the rewards Jean had given him for handing over the government of Genoa to him, and deciding that they were not in any way equal to the merits of either himself or his family, he broke out into open warfare against Jean. This incident met Ferrante's desires entirely in his present situation, and he looked upon it as a unique remedy for his difficulties and likely to bring him security, he therefore at once sent men and money to Pietrino, whom he hoped would drive Jean out of Genoa. Jean sent into France for men, and with them he marched against Pietrino who, by means of the assistance he had received, was making such considerable headway, that Jean was reduced to defending the city. Pietrino contrived to get into Genoa one night and secured a lodgment in it, but at break of day he was attacked by the forces of Jean and killed, all his men being made prisoners or slaughtered.

Jean was encouraged by this victory to make an attempt upon the kingdom, and in October 1459 he set sail with a powerful fleet from Genoa for Baia, landed there, and thence passed on to Sessa. Here he was received by the duke of that place, and the Princes of Taranto, Aquilani, and of many other cities came to meet him, and great disturbances arose through the whole kingdom. Ferrante had recourse to the pope and the Duke of Milan for assistance, and in order that he might have fewer foes to face he came to terms with Gismondo Malatesti, but this act so angered Jacopo Piccinino, who was the hereditary enemy of Gismondo, that he threw up Ferrante's service and joined Jean. Ferrante also sent money to Federigo, the lord of Urbino, and as soon as possible he assembled his army, a large one according to the ideas of those days, and confronted his enemy on the banks of the Sarni. Here a battle was fought and Ferrante was utterly routed with the loss of his best captains, who were taken prisoners. After this defeat only Naples and a few other cities remained faithful to Ferrante, the greater part of the kingdom surrendering to Jean. Jacopo Piccinino strongly advised Jean to at once attack Naples and thus master the head of the kingdom; but he would not do this, saying that he would first capture the territory and then attack the capital, thinking that Naples would be more easily captured after her territories were lost to her. The adoption of this course, against the advice of Jacopo, caused Jean to lose the fruits of his victory and his whole enterprise,—he did not realise that members follow the lead of the head more readily than the head follows that of the members.

Ferrante took refuge in Naples after his defeat, and thither came the refugees from other parts of his dominions, and with as little harshness as possible he collected money and gathered together a small army. He sent again to the pope and the Duke of Milan for assistance, and both responded far more quickly and freely than they did in the first instance, for they unmistakably recognised that he must not lose the kingdom. Ferrante showed great energy, drew his army out of Naples, recovered some of his towns, and thus retrieved in some measure his reputation. But whilst the struggle in the kingdom was opening in this manner, an incident occurred which deprived Jean of all his authority and chances of gaining the throne of Naples. The people of Genoa, who had become exasperated by the haughtiness and harshness of the Frenchmen, rose against the king's governor, and forced him to take refuge in the castelletto; the Fregosi and Adorni united their forces in this adventure, and were aided by men and money from the Duke of Milan, so that they were not only able to regain the city but hold it. René came with a fleet to the assistance of his son, hoping with the aid of the castelletto to retake Genoa, but his troops were utterly defeated in their attempts to land, and René was compelled to return beaten to Provence. When this news reached Jean it caused the greatest consternation in his councils, but encouraged by the barons, whose rebellion against Ferrante gave them no hopes of quarter from him, Jean would not abandon his efforts to keep the kingdom, and thus the fighting continued. Finally, after many skirmishes, the two royal armies came to battle near Troja in the year 1463, and Jean was defeated. This defeat did not injure him so much as the desertion of his cause by Jacopo Piccinino, who left him and joined Ferrante. After this Jean, having lost Piccinino's troops, retired into Istria, from whence he returned to France. This war of Jean's had lasted four years, and was entirely disastrous to him owing to his own negligence, although at one time the valour of his soldiers had gained him everything. The Florentines took no part in it although King Juan of Aragon, who had succeeded to the throne on the death of his father Alfonso, had sent ambassadors to Florence to remind the Florentines of their obligations under the treaty with his late father Alfonso, and to demand their assistance for his nephew Ferrante. The Florentines replied to this that the obligations of that treaty did not bind them to assist the son in a war which the father had commenced without either their knowledge or consent; therefore it would have to be continued and finished without their assistance. Whereupon the envoys of the king claimed the penalty for a breach of the obligation and payment for the damage, and left the city in anger. The Florentines were thus enabled to remain at peace as regards external affairs, but not so within the walls of their city, as will be shown in the following book.

SEVENTH BOOK

1459-1476

It may perhaps appear to some who have perused the former books that, as a writer of Florentine history, the author has dwelt too much upon events which happened in Lombardy and the kingdom of Naples. Nevertheless I have not, nor shall I in the future hesitate to do this, because however much I may have promised not to write of Italian affairs in general, it does not seem to me that I can leave out of my story the important events which happened in the above states. For should I not relate them, our history would be less intelligible and interesting; because it was from the actions of those princes and peoples that the wars frequently arose in which the people of Florence were compelled to interfere. As, for instance, out of the war between Jean d'Anjou and King Ferrante arose the terrible hatred and hostility of Ferrante against the Florentines — especially against the Medici family. For the king complained that not only was he refused assistance by the Florentines, but it was granted to his enemies, and his resentment was the cause of many of the calamities which this history will disclose. As I have brought my narration of foreign affairs up to 1463, it will be necessary for me in dealing with the internal affairs of Florence to go back some years. But I first wish to say, somewhat moralising as our custom is, that those people who expect a republic to remain without divisions deceive themselves very much; but it is also true that whilst some injure a republic, others do not. The divisions which injure are those accompanied by factions and feuds, whilst those which do not cause factions or feuds are of benefit to a republic. As therefore the founder of a republic cannot expect that no rivalries will arise in it, it is his duty to prevent them from degenerating into faction. He ought to understand that there are two ways in which citizens can secure popularity. It can be gained in public life either by winning a battle, capturing a town, carrying through a legation with diligence and prudence, or counselling the republic with wisdom and success. In private life it can be acquired by benefiting this or that citizen, defending him before the magistrates, assisting him with money, obtaining for him unmerited honours, and with public sports or donations indulging the people. From popularity thus gained factions and feuds are raised, and from renown thus acquired injury to the republic follows; whilst the renown which does not occasion faction benefits it, because it works for the common good and not for private ends. Again, it cannot be expected that no great rivalry will arise between citizens so disposed, yet having no partisans who will support them for their own advantage no great injury will happen to the republic. Indeed such divisions of opinion will benefit it, for in order to succeed, and demonstrate their value, they will closely watch each others doings, so that the obligations of the laws may not be transgressed. The rivalry which has arisen between the citizens of Florence has always degenerated into faction, and therefore has been a constant source of danger; nor has a successful faction ever remained united unless the faction opposing it has remained active and strong. But when the vanquished faction has been completely wiped out, its conqueror, not having the fear of others to keep its members united, soon splits up into minor factions. The party of Cosimo de' Medici rose superior to all others in 1434, and owing to the beaten party remaining numerous and powerful, the Mediceans maintained their position for many years—watchful and moderate. Inasmuch as they made no great mistakes, pursued no sinister methods, nor incurred the hatred of the people, when the time came for the renewal of their powers they always found the citizens disposed to concede all the authority they needed. Thus from 1434 until 1455, a period of twenty-one years, the authority of the balia fell into their hands by the usual courses.

There were in Florence two very powerful citizens, whom we have already named, Cosimo de' Medici and Neri Capponi. Neri was one of those men whose reputation had been gained in the public service, so that while he had many friends he had few partisans. Cosimo, on the other hand, owed his position to the sincere character of his public and private life, and had friends and partisans in abundance. Whilst these two men lived they were united, and always gained their objects with the people because there was so much urbanity mingled with their authority. However in 1455, when Neri died and the opposition had dwindled to nothing, the government met with some difficulty in renewing its term of office, and Cosimo's own party were the cause of it. Having no longer any fear of an opposition to keep them in order, certain members of the party conceived the idea of diminishing the personal power of Cosimo. This fancy of theirs was the commencement of the dissension which afterwards became acute in 1456, when the government party openly discussed in council the public administration, and recommended that, in the interest of the people, the balia should not be renewed, but that the city should recur to the ballot system, and by that system the magistrates should be elected. Cosimo had two courses open to him by which he could meet this idea, either to seize the government with the help of his personal friends, and snap his fingers at the rest of his party, or allow the proposal to go through and let his party discover that the government and authority had not been taken from him, but that it was they who had lost it. Of these two courses he chose the latter, because he knew that in such systems of election it was possible to get the ballot box filled with the names of his own friends, when he could take over the government from them at his pleasure without running any risks. Therefore the city reverted to the old practice in the election of magistrates, and to the generality of citizens it seemed as if they had recovered their liberty now the magistracy was no longer in the hands of a few powerful families, but was chosen by the people's free votes. Thus, first one then another member of the ruling party was beaten at the elections, and they who had been accustomed to have their houses full of suitors and presents found themselves neglected and deserted. They also found themselves on terms of equality with those whom they had long treated as inferiors, and those who had once been their equals were now their superiors. They were neither considered nor honoured, but rather laughed at and scorned, whilst the people spoke openly in the streets of them and the republic. By all this they soon learnt that it was not Cosimo but themselves who had lost control of the government. Cosimo appeared to take no notice of these events, and when any discussion arose concerning the improvement in the condition of the people, he was always the first to speak in favour of them. But what most alarmed the rich people, and gave Cosimo his first chance of returning to power, was the revival of the catasto of 1427, by which taxes were imposed according to law and not at the pleasure of men.

When this law was re-enacted, and the officers elected to put it into force, the rich citizens united and waited upon Cosimo and begged him to rescue them and himself from the hands of the plebeians and restore the government to that party which had made him powerful and themselves honoured. Cosimo replied that he was agreeable to this, but that the laws must be made in accordance with the will of the people. To this they would not consent, but attempted to pass through the council a law for a new balia; it however was thrown out. Upon this they returned to Cosimo, and with every expression of humility begged his consent to the summoning of a parliament. Cosimo refused the suggestion, because he desired to bring them to such a frame of mind as would compel them to confess their mistake. Besides this, Donato Cocchi, who was at this time the gonfaloniere of justice, had his own idea of calling a parliament without consulting with Cosimo; but Cosimo made the signori who sat in council with Donato ridicule him so much that the poor man lost his reason and had to be confined to his house as insane. Nevertheless, as it is not wise to allow things to get so far out of hand that it is difficult to bring them under control again, Cosimo decided to allow the matter to be dealt with by, Luca Pitti, a rash and somewhat headstrong man, who had recently been made gonfaloniere of justice, so that if the plan did not succeed the blame for its failure would fall on Luca and not on him. Luca at the commencement of his term of office had many times proposed to the people the election of a balia, but had never been able to secure one. As he did not succeed in this, he threatened the council with insulting and haughty language. From this he fell to deeds, and in August 1456, on the eve of the Vigil of San Lorenzo, he filled the palace with armed men, summoned the people into the Piazza, and by force of arms compelled them to do what they had previously refused to do. Having thus seized the government, created a balia, and elected their chief magistrate, they proceeded to inspire the people with some dread of them, and banished Messer Girolamo Machiavelli with several others, and deprived many of their offices. Thus the government begun in force was continued by terror, and because Messer Girolamo had not observed the terms of his banishment he was outlawed; he then wandered through Italy stirring up the princes against his country. In Lunigiana he was captured by the treachery of the signori and sent as a prisoner to Florence, where he died in captivity.

This government lasted eight years and was harsh, oppressive, and violent. This was owing largely to the fact that Cosimo, old and weary, and weakened also by sickness, could no longer give the necessary attention to public affairs, and a few strong men were allowed to prey upon the rest. Luca Pitti was rewarded with a knighthood for his service to the republic, and he not wishing to be behindhand in gratitude towards those who had honoured him, elevated those who had previously been called priors of trade to the dignity of priors of liberty, so that having lost the reality they should retain the name. He decreed also that, whereas the gonfaloniere had previously sat on the right hand of the governors, he should now sit in their midst. And as it appeared to Luca that God

had taken a large share in his enterprise, he ordained public processions and solemn ceremonies for the presentation of thanks to
God for the restoration of their honours. Messer Luca was richly
paid by both the signoria and Cosimo, and after these had given
him great presents, the city not to be outdone did the same, and it
was generally believed that these presents amounted to 20,000
ducats. By these means he rose to such a high reputation that it
was no longer Cosimo who governed Florence but Luca. This
inspired him with so much confidence that he began to build two
great houses, one in Florence and the other in Ruciano; situate
about a mile out of the city, both of them on a superb and regal
scale. He neglected no means however extraordinary to bring
these palaces to a completion, for not only did his friends and the
citizens bring him presents, and assist him with materials for the
buildings, but the municipality came to his aid. Beyond this, ban-
dits and other men who had incurred the penalties of the law for
murders, robberies, or other crimes, could always find a safe
refuge in those buildings, if they were persons who could be made
useful there. Other citizens who were not building as he was, were
no less violent in their methods, so that although Florence was not
desolated by war she was robbed by her own citizens. During this
period there was, as we have seen, fighting in the kingdom of
Naples and Romagna. Here the pontiff was endeavouring to rob
the Malatesti of Rimino and Cesena. With this enterprise, and
projects for a crusade against the Turks, Pope Pius occupied the
whole of his pontificate.

But Florence continued her broils and troubles. The break up of
the Medicean party in 1455 had been prevented by the wisdom of
Cosimo, but in the year 1464 his maladies greatly increased and he
passed out of this life. His death caused misgivings both among
friends and enemies, because those who, for reasons stated, had not
loved him, acknowledged that his authority had in some degree
restrained the rapacity of their rulers, and they much feared that
now he was removed by death the party who had opposed him
would be swept away. They had no confidence in his son Piero,

who, although a good man, was believed to be a weak one, and quite ignorant of affairs, consequently obliged to depend on others who would now be able to give full rein to their extortions. Thus the death of Cosimo caused much anxiety to the Florentines. He was among the most renowned of citizens who were not brought up in the profession of arms of which there is record either in Florence or elsewhere; not only was he superior to his contemporaries in influence and riches, but also in wisdom and generosity, and it was this generosity which distinguished him among the princes of his time. His liberality only became really known after his death, when his son, Piero, came to realise his estate, for it then appeared there was scarcely a citizen of any position in Florence on whom Cosimo had not bestowed large sums of money. He had frequently assisted noblemen whom he had learnt were in necessitous circumstances, without even being asked. He showed his magnificence in the buildings which he raised, for he not only restored but founded the convents and churches of San Marco and San Lorenzo and the monastery of Santa Verdiana in Florence, in the mountains of Fiesole San Girolamo and La Badia, and in Mugello a church of the Frate Minori. He also built splendid altars and chapels in Santa Croce, in the Servi, in the Agnoli, and in San Miniato. He furnished these churches and chapels with everything necessary for divine service. To these sacred edifices ought to be added his private houses, of which he had one in the city and four outside, in Careggi, Fiesole, Cafaggiulo, and in Trebbio, all palaces, more fit for a king than a private citizen. As if it were not sufficient for him to have the fame of these palaces throughout Italy, he built at Jerusalem an asylum for poor and infirm pilgrims. Immense sums of money must have been expended on these buildings, and although his other deeds were on an equally regal scale, and although he was the chief man in Florence, he never overstepped the bounds of prudence. In his way of living, in servants, equipages, and in all other lines of conduct, he never appeared anything but a simple citizen. His prescience told him that any immoderate display which people see day after day raises far more enmity against a man than when such is done under a cloak of modesty. Having to find wives for his sons he did not seek them among princesses, but he married Giovanni to Cornelia, the daughter of the Alessandri; and Piero married Lucrezia, daughter of the Tornabuoni. His granddaughter Bianca, the daughter of Piero, he married to Guglielmo de' Pazzi, and Nannina to Bernardo Rucellai. No one equalled him in knowledge of the position of princes and civil governments of those days, hence it happened that among the many changes of fortune, and amid such changeable and fickle citizens, he held the government for thirty-one years. Being a very far-seeing man he would recognise a trouble when it was only brewing, and he then had time either to prevent it coming to a head or prepare for it in such a way that when it came it failed to injure him. By this he not only withstood all domestic and civil ambition, but also the ambition of great princes, with such prudence and success that those who entered into an alliance with him or his country either overcame their enemies or at least did not lose. But if any one opposed him, then his opponent either lost his time, money, or estate. One can find no more forcible instance than that of the Venetians, who, when allied with Cosimo against the Duke Filippo, invariably won; but when they stood alone against Filippo, and later on against the French, in each case they were beaten. Again when they entered into an alliance with King Alfonso against the Florentines, Cosimo emptied Venice and Naples of money by his personal credit, and compelled both to accept such terms as he was willing to grant. Thus the difficulties which Cosimo encountered at home and abroad always concluded gloriously for him and disastrously for his enemies, for civil discords increased his influence in Florence and foreign wars his renown and authority abroad. He added to the Florentine territories the Borgo di San Sepolcro, Montedoglio, the Casentino, and the Val di Bagno. By his ability and good fortune he was able to overcome his enemies and strengthen his allies. Cosimo de' Medici was born in the year 1389, on San Cosimo's and San Damian's day, and his early years, in which he suffered imprisonment, exile, and peril of death, were full of trouble. He accompanied Pope John to the Council of Constance, from which he had to flee in disguise to save his life after the deposition of that pontiff. But his fortunes rose after he had passed his fortieth year, and all those who were associated with him shared in it, whether they were engaged with him in the administration of public affairs or in his business in distant parts of Europe. From this occurrence the enormous riches of many families in Florence took their rise, as in the case of the Tornabuoni, the Benci, the Portinari, and the Sassetti, and many others also who followed his advice and good fortune became rich. He would complain sometimes to his friends that, although he had continually spent his money on churches and given it away in charity, he could never do enough to the honour of God, and that he still found himself a debtor in His books. In person he was of middle height, of an olive complexion, and venerable in appearance. He was an eloquent man, full of a natural shrewdness though without much education. To his friends he was considerate, and to the poor charitable. He was instructive in his conversation, cautious in counsel, swift in the execution of his designs, in his sayings sharp and weighty. Messer Rinaldo degli Albizzi sent word to him at the beginning of his exile, "That the hen was hatching," to which Cosimo replied, "That she could not hatch out well outside the nest." To some rebels who complained they could not sleep he said that he believed it, he having taken their rest from them. When Pope Pius was urging the princes to a crusade against the Turks he said, "It is an old man taking on a young man's work." To the Venetian envoys who came to complain of the republic on behalf of King Alfonso he uncovered his head for them to see; he then asked them what colour the hair was, they said white, upon which he said, "There will not elapse a long time before the hair of your senators is as white as mine." Shortly before he died his wife asked him why he closed his eyes so much, he answered, "To accustom them to it." After his return from exile some citizens said that it did harm to a city, and was contrary to the will of God, to drive out so many honest citizens, to which he replied, "It was better a city should be harmed in that way than lost, for two ells of red cloth will make an honest citizen, and states are not governed with paternosters." These sayings, and others, gave his enemies the opportunity to calumniate him, as a man who loved himself better than his country, and this world better than the next one. Cosimo was also a friend and patron of men of letters. He invited Argyropolos, the Grecian, to Florence, one of the most learned men of the day; the Florentine youth and others who could appreciate his teaching flocked to his lectures. Cosimo also admitted to his own house Marsilio Ficino, the foster-father of the Platonic philosopher, a man whom he greatly loved and to whom he gave a house near to his own at Careggi, in order that Ficino might pursue his studies at his ease and be near when Cosimo wished to see him. Cosimo was not only loved and feared by the citizens of Florence and the princes of Italy, but he was wonderfully looked up to by the rulers of Europe for his wisdom, riches, conduct of affairs, and success. Such was the foundation which Cosimo laid for his posterity who, whilst equalling him in virtue, surpassed him in good fortune, and deserved to enjoy the same authority which he had wielded not only in Florence but throughout Christendom. Nevertheless in the last days of his life he suffered great anxiety because his son, Giovanni, upon whom he most relied, died, and Piero, who suffered bad health, was unfitted for either public or private affairs. Cosimo was carried through his house after the death of his son, and was heard to say with a sigh, "This is all too great a house for so small a family." It grieved his lofty spirit that he had not increased Florentine territory by some important conquest, and he complained that in this he was prevented by the deceit of Francesco Sforza, who when he was only a count had promised Cosimo that, as soon as he was master of Milan, he would invade Lucca on behalf of the Florentines. This he never did, for his mind changed with his fortune, and when he rose to the dukedom he had no intention but to enjoy in peace the state he had gained in war, and did not mean to engage in any war unless one was forced upon him. For these reasons the duke would not fulfil his obligations either to Cosimo or any one else. It was a source of great vexation to Cosimo that he should have endured immense trouble and expense to elevate a man who afterwards turned out both ungrateful and unfaithful. Owing to his increasing infirmities, Cosimo could no longer watch public and private affairs with his former diligence, thus the citizens wasted the resources of the commonwealth and his sons and servants his own estate. All these events brought him much anxiety in his latter days. Nevertheless he died great in name and fame, and the people and princes of Christendom sent their condolences to Piero on the death of his father. He was buried with solemn pomp in the church of San Lorenzo, and by public decree he was described on his tomb as PADRE DELLA PATRIA. If in writing as I have done the character of Cosimo, I have imitated those who write the lives of great men, not those who write general history, let none wonder at it, because he was one of the choicest spirits of our city, and I have been compelled to praise him as I have done.

Whilst the affairs of Florence and Italy were in this position, the King of France was engaged in a severe struggle with the barons of his kingdom, who were assisted by Francis, Duke of Brittany, and Charles, Duke of Burgandy; and the situation became so critical that Louis could send no assistance to Jean, Duke of Anjou, in his attempts against Genoa and the kingdom of Naples. But as the King of France considered that it was most important to obtain aid somewhere, he approached Francesco, the Duke of Milan, and won him over by the present of the lordship of Savona, which had remained in the hands of the French, and at the same time he let him understand that he had his permission to occupy Genoa. Francesco acceded to this, and with the prestige which his friendship with the French king gave, aided by the favour he enjoyed with the Adorni, he became master of Genoa. To show his gratitude to the king for these favours he sent 1500 horsemen into France under his eldest son, Galeazzo, to assist Louis. Thus Francesco Sforza became Duke of Lombardy and the master of Genoa, whilst Ferdinand became king of the entire realm of Naples, and having contracted a number of marriages between the members of their families, they believed they had established their power so securely that whilst they lived they would enjoy their governments in peace, and when they died they could hand them in safety to their successors. It became necessary, therefore, for the King of Naples to secure himself against those barons who had sided with Jean in his attempts upon the kingdom, and for the Duke of Milan to utterly destroy the Braccesci family, who were his personal enemies, and who under Jacopo Piccinino had risen to great power. Jacopo Piccinino, although at this time the most successful captain in Italy, had as yet no dominions. He was on this account to be feared, especially by the duke, whose own past made him dread that as long as Jacopo lived his possessions would not be secure, nor would he be able to hand them down to his son in security. The king made a point of coming to terms with his barons, in which he succeeded, because they realised that if they continued to oppose him their ruin would be certain, whereas if they made peace with him, and trusted to him, there was room for hope. As men invariably choose a course which avoids the more certain evil, it follows that princes can always deceive those who are not so powerful as themselves. In this case the barons made peace with their king seeing a certain danger in war; they threw themselves on his mercy, and by various methods, and under various pretences, were put out of the way. These events somewhat alarmed Jacopo Piccinino, who with his men was stationed at Sulmona, so in order to take away from the king a pretext for crushing him, he opened up negotiations through his friends for a reconciliation with the duke. This was effected, and the duke made Jacopo very liberal offers which induced him to return to his service, and accompanied by a hundred cavaliers he set out for Milan.

Jacopo and his brother had fought for many years under their own father, first for the Duke Filippo, and afterwards for the people of Milan, thus he had considerable acquaintance with the city and many friends and much goodwill there, all of which were increased under the present circumstances. The prosperity and power of the Sforzeschi had given rise to some envy, whilst the long adversity which Jacopo had endured had brought a feeling of commiseration for him in the minds of the people of Milan, and they longed to see him. They showed this in their welcome, for there were but few of the nobility who did not go out to meet him, and the streets through which he passed were thronged with those who wished to see him, whilst his name was on everybody's lips. This honour proved his ruin, for as the duke's fear of him increased so did his desire to destroy him. In order that this might be more thoroughly encompassed, the duke caused Jacopo's marriage to be celebrated with Drusina, his natural daughter, who had been long promised to Jacopo. Shortly afterwards the duke, in secret agreement with Ferrante, appointed Jacopo the head of his army with a grant of 100,000 florins. Having concluded this arrangement, Jacopo with Drusina and an ambassador were sent to Naples, where they were welcomed with great rejoicing and honour, and entertained with every description of entertainment for many days. On Jacopo asking permission to go to Sulmona, where his army lay, he was invited by the king to dine at the castle. After the banquet he and his son Francesco were thrown into prison and shortly after murdered. It was thus that our Italian princes destroyed in others that valour which they feared but did not possess, and exposed their country to that ruin which was soon to overtake it.

Pope Pio having settled by this time the affairs of Romagna, turned his attention once more to a crusade against the Turks, and renewed the proposals his predecessors had made, towards the carrying out of which all the princes promised either in men or money, and Matthias, King of Hungary, with Charles, Duke of Burgundy, undertook to go in person with the pope, who appointed them leaders of the crusade. The pontiff was so filled with enthusiasm that he left Rome and went to Ancona, whither he had summoned the whole army to meet him, and where the Venetians had promised to send a fleet to transport the force to Sclavonia. Within a few days of the arrival of the pope at Ancona there gathered such immense hosts that all the provisions of the place were exhausted as well as any supplies that could be brought from elsewhere, so that a great famine soon set in. Besides this there was no money, arms, or other provisions necessary for war; neither Matthias nor Charles put in an appearance, and the Venetians only sent one captain with a few galleys, rather as a pretence of keeping faith than for transporting an army. The old and infirm pope was overburdened by this mismanagement and trouble, and died, upon which everybody returned home. The pope died in 1465, and the Venetian, Paulo II., was elected to the pontificate. Other principalities in Italy also changed their rulers at this time, for in the following year Francesco Sforza, Duke of Milan, died after enjoying the dukedom seventeen years. He was succeeded by his son Galeazzo.

The death of Francesco caused the Florentine dissensions to become more acute and their effects to be shown more quickly. After the death of Cosimo, his son Piero succeeded to the wealth and estate of his father, and he called to his assistance Messer Diotisalvi Neroni, a gentleman of great authority and much respected by the citizens. Cosimo had confided so much in him that, when he was dying, he advised his son to consult with Messer Diotisalvi on all public or private affairs, and follow his advice. Piero therefore reposed the same trust in him as his father Cosimo had shown, and wishing to obey his father as implicitly in death as in life at once requested the assistance of Messer Diotisalvi in the management of his patrimony and the government of the city. In order that a commencement should be made with his private affairs, Piero caused a statement of them to be made; this he put into the hands of Messer Diotisalvi, in order that he might learn the true position of affairs and be able to advise him to the best of his ability. Messer Diotisalvi promised to use the utmost diligence and loyalty, but when he received the statement of affairs he saw at once they were in great confusion, and his ambition got the better of him and caused him to forget the benefits he had received from the father and his obligations to the son; for he believed that he could deprive Piero of the estate which his father had left him. He therefore went to Piero and offered him advice which appeared reasonable and honest, but the ruin of the Medici underlay it. Messer Diotisalvi pointed out the great disorder in which he found the estate, and that large sums of money were necessary if the credit of the family was to be maintained, and he proved to Piero that there was no possible way of doing this except by calling in the money that was due to his father's estate from both citizens and foreigners. It appeared that Cosimo, in order to obtain partisans in Florence and friends abroad, had been very liberal in supplying people with money from his own resources, and by this had become their creditor for very large sums. It seemed to Piero that if he wished to put his affairs in order the advice of Diotisalvi was sound and reasonable. But as soon as he carried this counsel into effect and demanded the money, his debtors resented it as deeply as if he had demanded their money and not his own. And without any hesitation they said all manner of evil of him, and called him an ungrateful and avaricious man.

When Messer Diotisalvi saw the universal disfavour in which Piero was involved by following this advice, he allied himself with Messer Luca Pitti, Messer Agnolo Acciajuoli, and Nicolo Soderini, and they decided to destroy the credit and authority of Piero. These men were influenced by various motives; Messer Luca desired to step into the shoes of Cosimo, because having risen to such a height he considered it beneath his dignity to bow to Piero. Messer Diotisalvi, who knew that Messer Luca had not the capability necessary for the head of a government, thought that if Piero were out of the way the government must in course of time devolve upon him. Nicolo Soderini only desired more liberty for the city and its subjection to the will of the magistrates. Messer Agnolo had a particular aversion to the Medici owing to the following circumstances. His son Raffaello had a short time back married Alessandra de Bardi, and received a very large dowry with her. This lady, either owing to her own shortcomings or the fault of others, was badly treated by her husband and father-in-law;

whereupon Lorenzo d'Ilarione, her relative, out of pity for the girl, went with armed men to the house of Messer Agnolo and took her away. The Acciajuoli complained of this injury committed against them by the Bardi, and the case was brought before Cosimo. He decided that the Acciajuoli must return the dowry to Alessandra, and the choice of returning to her husband must be left to the girl. Messer Agnolo did not consider that Cosimo, in giving the judgment, had treated him in a friendly way, and determined to take his revenge upon the son as he had been unable to effect anything against the father. Although the conspirators were actuated by so many different motives they published, as a reason for their dissatisfaction, the desire that the city should be governed by its magistrates and not by the will of a few men. The hatred against Piero increased owing to the failure of many merchants, who blamed him severely for so ill-advisedly calling in his money and causing widespread ruin in the city. The ferment increased against Piero when it was reported that negotiations were on foot for the marriage of his eldest son, Lorenzo, to Clarice, a daughter of the Orsini family. The cause of this complaint was the belief of the people that he would not consent to a Florentine connection in marriage for his son, because the city could no longer hold him as a citizen, and he was preparing to usurp it as a prince; that such men as are not willing to take their fellow-citizens as relations wish to have them as slaves, and therefore it is not reasonable to expect friendship in such quarters. Those who were at the head of this conspiracy thought they had victory in their hands, because the greater part of the citizens, deceived by the name of liberty, which was used to conceal the real design of the conspirators, were ready to follow them.

Whilst these feelings were agitating the city, it occurred to some of the leading citizens who disliked civil commotions, that they should endeavour to occupy the minds of the people with some new form of entertainment, because it has often happened that an idle people are mere tools in the hands of those who are seeking change. Therefore to employ this idleness, and give the people something to think of besides affairs of government, a year having already passed since the death of Cosimo, the opportunity was taken to indulge in merrymaking throughout the city, and two festivals were arranged, attended by all the gaieties of former times. One pageant was that of the three kings of the east following the star that pointed out the birthplace of the infant Christ, and it was carried out with such pomp and circumstance that the city was occupied many months in arranging and exhibiting it. The other was a tournament, as such spectacles are called, representing a fight between knights, in which the youth of the first families in Florence competed with the foremost knights of Italy. Among the most distinguished of the Florentine youths was Lorenzo, the eldest son of Piero, who gained the highest honours, not by favour, but by his own valour. But when all these spectacles were over the citizens returned to their former habits, and each one followed his own ideas as strongly as before. From these disagreements great troubles followed, and were increased by two events. One trouble was caused by the powers of the balia lapsing at this time, and the other by the death of Francesco, the Duke of Milan. Upon this latter event the new duke, Galeazzo, sent ambassadors to Florence to confirm the articles of the treaty his father Francesco had made with the city, by one of which articles Florence was to pay a certain sum of money each year to the duke. The principal people who were opposed to the Medici party took every opportunity, both in public and in the council chamber, to oppose this proposal, declaring that the alliance was with Francesco and not with Galeazzo, and that when Francesco died the obligation came to an end; nor was there any reason to revive it, for Galeazzo had not the abilities of Francesco, and consequently they could not expect the same advantages from an alliance with him as with his father; and, further, that if any citizen, for his own purposes, desired to subsidise the duke, then it was contrary to public policy and subversive of the liberties of the city. Piero urged against this that it was unwise to lose so necessary an alliance for the sake of a small sum of money, for there was nothing that had contributed so much to the safety of the republic and of the whole of Italy as this alliance with the duke, for as long as it lasted Venice had no hope, by either feigned friendship or open war, of getting the advantage of the Milan dukedom; but the moment it was known that the Florentines were alienated from the duke the Venetians would attack him, and the duke being young and inexperienced in government and without friends would fall, either by force or fraud, into the hands of the Venetians, and the destruction of the Florentine republic would follow.

This reasoning of Piero was not accepted, and hostility began to be manifested between the opposing parties and meetings were held every night. The friends of the Medici met in the Crocetta whilst their opponents met in the Pieta, and with the latter were enrolled many citizens who desired the ruin of Piero. A large party of these men met together one evening and discussed the steps that should be taken to lessen the power of the Medici, and although all agreed as to the desirability of doing it, all differed as to the means. One part of them, and that the more temperate and moderate, recommended deferring action until the present balia had expired, and then refusing to renew it, in order that the authority should lapse into the hands of the council and magistrates, a result everybody desired. Thus in a short time the authority of Piero would be destroyed, and his loss of commercial credit would follow the loss of official power, because his wealth being now limited it was believed that if he were unable to use public money he would be ruined. It was urged that if this course were followed they need fear no more trouble from Piero, and thus without bloodshed or exile their liberties would be restored, which was what every good citizen ought to desire. But, on the other hand, if force were adopted many dangers would be run, because such men as fall of themselves are allowed to fall, whilst many will run to help the man who is pushed over by others. Besides, if nothing beyond the usual operations of the law were enforced against Piero, he would have no excuse for arming or enlisting friends, and if he should arm them it would be so much to his prejudice and would make men suspicious of him; this would give others a chance of rising successfully against him and thus bring about his destruction. To many of the conspirators this delay was not satisfactory; they insisted that time was on the side of Piero and not on theirs, for if they were to be content with the ordinary process of the law Piero would incur no dangers, whilst they would run many risks, for the magistrates, although hostile to him, would allow him the rights of citizenship, and his friends would make him prince to their ruin, as they did in '58; that if the advice of the other friends was that of good men, this was the advice of wise men, and advantage ought to be taken of the angry feeling of the citizens against Piero to destroy him. Let them arm themselves within the city, and enlist the Marquis of Ferrara outside, and be ready to take action as soon as chance should give a signoria friendly disposed to their aims. Among the conspirators was one Ser Nicolo Fedini, who acted as secretary to them, and who tempted by the sure hope of reward revealed their proceedings to Piero, with a list of their names. Piero was alarmed at the number and rank of the citizens whose names he found inscribed against him, and acting on the advice of his friends he obtained a list of his supporters, also under their own signatures. He had entrusted this affair to his most faithful friends, and such was the vacillation and levity of the citizens, that he found many who had subscribed against him had also signed in his favour.

In due course the time arrived when the supreme magistrate was to be elected, and the choice fell upon Nicolo Soderini, and he was made the gonfaloniere of justice. It was wonderful to see with what a huge concourse of honourable citizens as well as rabble he was escorted to the palace, and how he was crowned on his way thither with a garland of olive leaves, to show that on him depended the safety and liberty of Florence. The fate of Soderini, as well as that of many others, is a warning that it is not desirable to take up a governorship or any office under a blaze of great expectations, because the holder not being able to realise all the hopes of those who put him there, disappointment and disgrace will surely follow in time. Messer Tommaso and Nicolo Soderini were brothers, and whilst Nicolo was the more bold and courageous, Tommaso was the wiser of the two. Tommaso was a great friend of Piero, and well understood the mind of his brother Nicolo, who desired only to secure the liberty of the city without injury to any one. Tommaso advised Nicolo to create a new ballot and take care that the boxes should only be filled with the names of citizens who wished that the city should obtain her freedom, and that when this was accomplished the government should be established on a sound basis, and the will of the people be made predominant without tumult or bloodshed, as Nicolo himself advocated. Nicolo was quite ready to accept the advice of his brother, and in the effort to accomplish these vain ideas he consumed all his magistracy. He was indeed allowed so to waste it by his friends, the heads of the conspiracy, for they were too jealous of him to allow the government to be established on his authority, because they were looking forward to the time when they would frame it to their own wishes under the ægis of another gonfaloniere. Thus Nicolo ended his governorship without having accomplished what he was appointed to carry through, and as he had entered upon office amid the applause of every one, so he left it followed by their curses.

This fiasco encouraged the Medici party to act with more vigour, to confirm the friends of Piero in their confidence in him, and to induce the neutrals to join him, so that affairs were now more equalised, and some months passed without any disturbances. The enemies of Piero at last realised that his adherents had vastly increased in number, therefore they met together and determined to accomplish by force what they had failed to do by lawful means—they decided to murder Piero, who was at this time lying ill at Careggi. The conspirators sent to the Marquis of Ferrara, and begged him to draw his army near to the city, in order that when Piero was killed he might enter the city, and take possession of the Piazza, when the conspirators would compel the signoria to form a government according to their wishes, for although they knew that some of the signori were not favourable to their views they hoped that all would yield from fear. Messer Diotisalvi, in order that he might conceal the part he was playing from Piero, would often visit and discuss with him the pacification of the city, upon which he had already advised. This treachery had now been revealed to Piero, and, further, Messer Domenico Martelli had informed him that he had been asked to join the conspirators by Francesco Neroni, the brother of Messer Diotisalvi, and that he had been assured by him of their certain success. Upon this Piero determined to be the first to strike; he took advantage of the negotiations his adversaries had been carrying on with the Marquis of Ferrara to pretend that he had received a letter from Messer Giovanni Bentivoglio, Prince of Bologna, intimating to him that the Marquis of Ferrara had reached the river Albo with his army, and had openly stated that he was bound for Florence. Upon this Piero resorted to arms, and accompanied by a large body of toops returned to Florence; whereupon the Medici party armed, as did their adversaries, but the Mediceans were the better prepared, the others not yet having decided upon a plan. Messer Diotisalvi, whose house was near to that of Piero, was much disturbed by what had occurred, and went to the palace to induce the signoria to insist upon Piero laying down his arms at once, and then he sought out Luca Pitti and begged him to hold firm to their party. But he who showed most vigour was Messer Nicolo Soderini, who flew to arms, and was followed by all the mob of his district. He also went to the house of Messer Luca, and prayed him mount his horse, come to the help of the signoria who were in their favour, and the victory was theirs, saying that surely he did not wish to remain at home to yield without a blow to his armed foes, or still worse to be cheated into some disgraceful surrender, when he would for ever repent leaving undone what he had now the chance of doing; that if he had desired the destruction of Piero by fighting now was the time to effect it; and if he had wished to effect this by peaceful means it was far better to be in the position of imposing terms than of accepting them. Messer Luca was not to be moved by these arguments because his mind was already made up, having been won over to Piero's party with promises of advantageous terms and marriages, having already married one of his nieces to Giovanni Tornabuoni. Messer Luca therefore advised Nicolo to go home and lay down his arms, thus gaining what he wished, namely, the government of the city by its own magistrates, and he urged all their party to do the same; and the signoria, in which they had a majority of their friends, would be the judge in the matter. Nicolo, finding himself unable to make any impression upon Messer Luca, returned to his house, but first said: "Alone, I cannot do much for my country, but I am still able to prophesy its evil destiny. The course you are now taking will lose our country its freedom, and you its government, me my possessions, and others their fatherland."

The signoria had closed the palace in the midst of the tumult, and with the magistrates had refused to show any favour to either party. The citizens, and chiefly those who adhered to the party of Messer Luca, finding Piero armed and Messer Luca unarmed, began to think they ought to take sides with Piero and not against him. Therefore the chief men among them were admitted into the palace, and in the presence of the signoria discussed the affairs of the city and the measures to be taken for its pacification. As the infirmities of Piero would not permit him to be present at the palace, a deputation of the citizens left the palace to wait upon him at his house. Nicolo Soderini would not go, but having recommended his children and affairs to the care of his brother, Messer Tommaso Soderini, he retired to his villa to await the end of the trouble, which he expected would be disastrous to his country. The deputation having reached the house of Piero, one of the number was appointed to speak. He complained of the disturbance that had arisen in the city, blamed the person who had first taken up arms as the cause of it, not knowing that Piero himself was the first who had recourse to them, wished to know what Piero desired should be done, and announced, if it were for the good of the city, their readiness to follow him. To this Piero answered it is not he who first takes up arms that causes trouble, but he who causes others to have recourse to them, and he added that if the citizens only knew what he had endured they would be far less surprised at what he had done for his own protection. They would then admit that it was the nightly secret meetings, the subscriptions, the plot to capture the city and to kill him which had driven him to arms. Yet he had never moved these arms from his house, thus showing that in resorting to them it was only in self-defence and not with the intention of injuring others. He had no object or desire but peace and quietness, nor had he ever expressed a wish for anything else. Although the authority of the balia had lapsed, he had never thought of re-creating it by any extraordinary means. He was quite content that the city should be governed in the usual way by its own magistrates, if that pleased them. They ought to remember that Cosimo and his sons had known how to live in Florence both with the balia and without it, and that in '58, when the balia was restored, it was not his family who restored it but the citizens. If they did not desire to have one now, neither did he. But it appeared as if this was not enough to satisfy them, for he had learnt that some considered it impossible to reside in Florence if he remained. Of a truth he would never have believed that the friends of himself and his father could ever have found it impossible to exist in Florence with him, for he had never shown himself anything but a peaceful and law-abiding citizen. He then turned and addressed himself to Messer Diotisalvi and his brother, who were present, and reproved them in grave and angry words, recalling to their memory the many benefits they had received from Cosimo, the trust he himself had reposed in them, and the base ingratitude with which they had repaid it all. Such was the force of his reproaches that some of those present moved threateningly against the brothers, and would have laid violent hands upon them had not Piero restrained them. Piero in conclusion said he was ready to accept whatever they and the signoria approved; all he desired was to be left in peace and security. After this many other matters were discussed but nothing decided, excepting that, generally speaking, the city required reforming and the government needed fresh authority.

Bernardo Lotti was acting at this time as gonfaloniere of justice, and as he was not trusted, Piero would not attempt any changes until his term of office expired. This was not of much importance seeing that Bernardo was nearly at the end of his term, but at the election for the position of gonfaloniere during September and October 1466, Roberto Lioni was elected chief magistrate. He at once took up the duties, being quite prepared, called the people into the Piazza, proclaimed a balìa entirely in the interests of the Medici party, and shortly after appointed magistrates devoted to the new government. This at once alarmed the heads of the hostile faction; Messer Agnolo Acciajuoli fled to Naples, Messer Diotisalvi and Messer Nicolo Soderini to Venice, whilst Messer Luca Pitti remained in Florence trusting in the promises of Piero and his new relatives. Those who fled were declared rebels, and all the family of the Neroni were scattered. Messer Giovanni di Nerone, the archbishop of Florence, chose a voluntary exile in order to avoid a greater trouble. Many other citizens fled suddenly or were banished. To complete the proceedings a procession was inaugurated in order that God might be thanked for having preserved the government and reunited the people; during the solemnisation of this many citizens were seized and thrown into prison, some of whom were tortured, others put to death, and the rest sent into exile. Among examples of the mutations of fortune there is no more notable instance than that of Messer Luca Pitti, who quickly discovered the difference between defeat and victory, honours and disgrace. He found a solitude in his house where previously there had been constant assemblies of citizens. His relatives and friends would not walk with him in the streets, and feared to salute him, because some had lost their positions, others their property, and all were threatened. The superb edifices he was building were deserted by the workmen; the benefits which had been showered upon him were converted into injuries, and honours into insults. Some who had made gifts to him, often of great value, for some act of grace, now demanded them back on the pretence that they had only been lent to him. Some who had been accustomed to praise him up to the skies now described him as a lawless and ungrateful fellow. Then he repented, too late, of not having lent an ear to Nicolo Soderini, and sought rather to die honourably, sword in hand, than to live dishonoured amid triumphant enemies.

Those conspirators who had been banished now began to consider the means by which they might regain those homes which they had not known how to keep. Messer Agnolo Acciajuoli, however, who still resided at Naples, desired to sound the mind of Piero before he attempted anything, and to see if there were any hopes of their becoming reconciled to each other, therefore he wrote Piero the following letter: "I laugh at the sport of fortune, who at her pleasure turns friends into enemies and enemies into friends. Thou canst recollect that during the exile of thy father, thinking more of his wrongs than I did of my own perils, I forfeited my country and nearly lost my life. Whilst Cosimo lived I was constantly honoured and advanced by your house, and since his death I have never injured thee. It is true that, owing to your indifferent health and the tender age of your sons, I have had many anxieties lest the country should be endangered if your death should occur, and I made some attempts to put the government in a shape to resist such dangers. Thus certain things were done, not against thee, but on behalf of our common country. This may have been an error on my part, yet my good intentions and my past services should earn me forgiveness. I cannot believe that your house having found me so faithful in times past will now show me no mercy, or that, with so many merits, I should be destroyed for one fault." Piero received this letter and answered it as follows: "That you laugh in Naples is the reason that I do not weep in Florence, because if you should laugh in Florence I might weep in Naples. I admit that you were a well-wisher to my father, and you must admit that you were rewarded. So much the more, therefore, ought you to have felt the obligation than we did, seeing that deeds are more weighty than words. And if you were duly recompensed in the past for your good deeds, it ought not to surprise you that you have now received a just reward for your misdeeds. Nor will your alleged love of country excuse you, for it will never be believed by the citizens of Florence that they have been less benefited and loved by the Medici than by the Acciajuoli. Live, therefore, far away in dishonour, since thou didst not know how to live here in honour."

Messer Agnolo, now despairing of obtaining his pardon from Piero, went to Rome, and having joined the archbishop there they used all the means in their power to ruin the business credit of the Medici in that city. Piero met this effort of theirs with some difficulty, but in the end his friends there enabled him to overcome it. Messer Diotisalvi and Nicolo Soderini endeavoured with the utmost art to induce the Venetian senate to attack Florence, urging that she could not possibly withstand it, seeing that the city had a new and hated government. At this time there was residing in Ferrara, Giovanni Francesco Strozzi, the son of Messer Palla Strozzi, who with his father had been driven from Florence in the revolution of '34. This gentleman had great credit, and was considered to be very rich by the trading world, and it was pointed out by these new rebels to Giovanni Francesco that he would easily regain his fatherland if the Venetians would support the enterprise, and it was believed they would do this if the exiles would bear some part of the expenses, otherwise it was feared they would not join. Giovanni Francesco, who thirsted for the revenge of his wrongs, readily believed all these men told him, and promised to assist them to the utmost of his ability. Having obtained this promise the exiles obtained an audience of the doge, and complained to him that they were suffering banishment for no other fault than wishing to live under the laws of their country, and to yield obedience to magistrates rather than to the will of a few men. Piero de' Medici, who with his following had ruled the city tyrannically, had deceitfully taken up arms and by stratagem had induced them to lay down theirs, and had then basely driven them out of the country. The Mediceans were not satisfied with this, but had even used the name of God to deceive many families, who under a sacred pledge had remained in the city; but at a public and holy ceremony and solemn supplication had been seized, thrown into prison, and put to death, so that God had became a participator in the Medicean treachery—a most wicked and impious act. To revenge this they knew not where to turn with more hope than to the Venetian people, who having always been free themselves would sympathise with those who had lost their freedom. They endeavoured, therefore, to raise the free man against the tyrant, the religious man against the impious, and they recalled to the memory of the Venetians that the Medici family had caused them to lose the empire of Lombardy, by Cosimo having rendered assistance to Francesco, in spite of the desire of the Florentines to help the Venetians. Thus, if the wrongs of the exiles did not move the Venetians, then their righteous indignation and their desire for revenge ought to do so.

These last suggestions stirred the senate to action, and they decided to instruct their captain, Bartolommeo Colleone, to attack the dominions of the Florentines. Colleone at once took the field and was joined by Ercole de' Esti, who was sent by Borso, the Marquis of Ferrara. The Florentines being unprepared for this attack, this general achieved some success, burnt the suburb of Dovadola and pillaged the country round. After driving out the faction hostile to the Medici rule, the Florentines had made new treaties with Galeazzo, the Duke of Milan, and with Ferdinand, the King of Naples, and engaged Federigo, Count of Urbino, as their captain. Thus prepared with allies and captain they had no fear of the Venetians. Ferdinand sent his eldest son, Alfonso, and Galeazzo came in person; each brought suitable forces and assembled at Castrecaro, a Florentine castle situated at the foot of the mountains which run between Tuscany and Romagna. Thus pressed the enemy retired towards Imola. Some slight skirmishes took place between the two armies, but as a rule they remained within their encampments, neither of them attacking or besieging towns, nor seeking to bring its enemy to battle, such was the custom of fighting in those days and the miserable pusillanimity which governed it. This state of affairs displeased the Florentines, who found themselves burdened with vast expense and obtaining no satisfaction. The magistrates complained to the men whom they had sent as commissioners to the army, and they replied that it was all the fault of the Duke Galeazzo, who had the chief authority and no ability, who knew not how to adopt a proper course, nor to trust those who did know, and that it would be impossible to do anything of advantage as long as he was with the army. The Florentines therefore let the duke understand that his coming to their aid had been of the greatest advantage to them, and that the mere knowledge of this had struck fear into their enemies, nevertheless they esteemed the safety of himself and his state of far more importance than their own concerns. Whilst he was safe all would prosper, but if he were not then any slight reverse was to be feared. But they did not consider him secure unless he returned to Milan where his government, still in its infancy, had powerful enemies who were to be feared, and whom he could easily manage if they attempted to plot against him. They advised him to return to his own government and leave part of his forces for their defence. This advice pleased Galeazzo, and without another thought he returned to Milan, leaving some of his men with the Florentines. Thus the Florentine captains got rid of their hindrance to action, and as if to show that it had been the true reason of their inaction they now pressed the enemy and brought him to a battle, which lasted the whole day without either side giving way. Yet nobody was killed, only some horses wounded and a few prisoners made on either side. With the arrival of winter both armies retired into winter quarters: Messer Bartolommeo went towards Ravenna, the Florentines into Tuscany, and the forces of the king and the duke into their respective states. No rising having taken place in Florence as the exiles had predicted, and the pay for the mercenaries not being forthcoming, the contending parties began to discuss terms of peace, and shortly after a treaty was signed, by which the exiles lost all hope and retired into various countries.

Messer Diotisalvi took refuge in Ferrara, where the marquis received him and took care of him; Nicolo Soderini went to Ravenna, where on a small annuity allowed him by the Venetians he lived and died. He was a valiant and honourable gentleman, but slow and irresolute in action; this caused him, when gonfaloniere of justice, to lose the opportunity of victory which afterwards as a private man he attempted to gain and failed.

As the peace which followed this treaty appeared to the ruling party in Florence to possess none of the emblems of victory, seeing they had inflicted no injuries upon their enemies or even upon their party opponents, they induced Bardo Altoviti, who sat as gonfaloniere of justice, to deprive many citizens of their honours and turn them out of the city. This action increased their power and filled the rest of the citizens with much anxiety, for this power was used without any consideration, as if God and Fortune had given the city into their hands as prey. Piero knew but little of what was done, and for that little he could find no remedy because of his infirmities, for he had lost the use of his limbs and his tongue alone remained to him as a weapon. Thus he could only admonish his party, and beg them to live in moderation, and enjoy their country in peace rather than destroy it. He also decided to distract the attention of the citizens from these affairs by celebrating the marriage of his son Lorenzo to Clarice, a daughter of the Orsini house, with great magnificence. It was therefore solemnised with all the pomp and splendour to be expected from such a wealthy man, and days were occupied with balls, banquets, and pageants of ancient deeds. As if to demonstrate the magnificence of the state and of the Medici two military tournaments were held, one for men on horseback representing a battle, the other the siege of a town. These were carried out with such precision and dash that it would be difficult to imagine anything nobler.

Whilst these events were happening in Florence, the other states of Italy were at peace, but in considerable apprehension of the Turkish power, which was following up its designs against the Christians, and had laid siege to Negroponte, to the standing disgrace of the Christian name. Several men of note died about this time, among whom was Borso, succeeded by his brother Ercole in the Marquisate of Ferrara; Gismondo di Rimini, the persistent enemy of the Church, succeeded by his natural son Roberto, who afterwards became one of the first captains in Italy. Pope Paulo also died, and was succeeded by Sisto IV. He was a man of low origin named Francesco da Savona, who by his abilities had risen to the position of General of the Order of St. Francis, and afterwards to that of cardinal. He was the first pontiff to show what a pontiff was capable of doing, and to demonstrate that many things which had formerly been considered sins were permissible under the cloak of pontifical sanction. He had in his family two young men, by name Piero and Girolamo, who according to common report were his sons, but whom he designated under a more discreet appellation. As Piero was a monk he was raised to the dignity of a cardinal, under the title of San Sisto; whilst to Girolamo was given the city of Furli, taken from Antonio Ordelaffi, whose ancestors had held the city for a very long period. These high-handed proceedings brought the pope into high repute with the princes of Italy, and they all sought his friendship. The Duke of Milan gave his natural daughter Caterina as wife to Girolamo, and dowered her with the city of Imola, which he took from Taddeo degli Alidosi. Between the Duke of Milan and King Ferdinand new relationships were made by the marriage of Elisabetta, the daughter of Alfonso, the king's eldest son, to Giovanni Galeazzo, the eldest son of the duke.

Italy was at this time enjoying a fair measure of tranquillity, and the princes were largely occupied in watching each other and strengthening themselves with fresh marriages, alliances, and leagues. Nevertheless, Florence did not share in this general peace, for she was grievously afflicted by her own citizens, and Piero de' Medici was prevented by his maladies from putting a stop to their exactions. Yet to relieve his conscience, and see if he could not shame his party into moderation, he called a number of them to his house and addressed them as follows: "I could never have believed that the time would come when the actions of my friends would cause me to turn in love to my enemies, and regret that my victory had not been a defeat, because I never expected to find such a boundless measure of greed in men, who after they had been revenged upon their enemies were not content to live in peace and security. But now I fear I am greatly deceived, and that I know little of the natural ambition of men, and less of yours. It is not enough for you to rank almost as princes in such a mighty city as this, and to hold in your hands all the honours, offices, and emoluments, which were formerly shared among many citizens. It is not enough for you to have divided among yourselves the possessions of your enemies; it is not enough for you to have laid upon other citizens all the public burdens and taken upon yourselves all the public honours, but you have afflicted them with every kind of indignity and injury. You have taken their possessions from your neighbours, you have sold justice, have disregarded the laws, have oppressed peaceful citizens, and encouraged the insolent. I do not believe there are in the whole of Italy any such examples of violence and robbery as are to be found in Florence. When we owe our lives to this city why should we seek to rob her of her life? She, who has given us so often the victory, why should we ruin her? She, who has conferred on us so many honours, why should we disgrace her? I promise you by that faith which good men pledge and keep that I shall not only repent of having gained the victory in our great struggle, if you continue to follow in these paths, but I will make you repent of having made such an evil use of that victory." The citizens answered Piero as it might be expected they would, in the circumstances in which they found themselves, but they continued their evil ways. Piero therefore secretly sent for Messer Agnolo Acciajuoli to come to Cafaggiolo, and consulted with him at great length upon the condition of the city. There is little doubt that, had not death interrupted Piero, he would have recalled many of the exiles in order that some curb should be placed upon the excesses within the city. But death put an end to such intentions, for worn out with bodily pain and mental anxiety he died in the fiftieth year of his age. His country did not so highly appreciate his virtues and abilities as it had done those of his father Cosimo, under whom he had always lived, and whom he only survived a few years, all of which were spent in civil turmoil and were troubled with bodily infirmities. Piero was interred in the church of San Lorenzo near to his father, and his obsequies were celebrated with the ceremonies so distinguished a citizen deserved. He left two sons, Lorenzo and Giuliano, who, although they gave every promise of becoming men most useful to the republic, caused much anxiety to the citizens owing to their youth.

Among the chief citizens who at that time ruled in Florence was Messer Tommaso Soderini, who towered above the others, and was not only in great repute with the people of Florence but also with the princes of Italy. Upon the death of Piero he at once became the most prominent man in the city, many citizens paid their court to him, and many princes wrote to him, as if he were the head of it. But he acted prudently, for he well appreciated the difference between his position and that of the house of Medici. He did not reply to his correspondents, and he clearly intimated to the citizens that it was not he but the Medici whom they should approach. To encourage them to do more effectively what he suggested he summoned the heads of all the noble families to meet him in the convent of San Antonio, at which meeting he also asked Lorenzo and Giuliano to be present. He delivered a long and weighty oration upon the affairs of the city and of Italy, and upon the several policies which the princes were pursuing; he concluded by expressing the wish that Florence should live in peace and harmony with herself and her neighbours, avoiding strife within her walls and war beyond them. Let them respect those young men, and stand by the reputation of their house, because men never make a trouble over what they are accustomed to do, whilst new things, although they may be quickly taken up, are as quickly dropped; and that it is always far easier to maintain an established power, the hatred to which has been extinguished by the lapse of time, than to establish a new one, which is vulnerable at so many points. After Messer Tommaso had spoken, the young man Lorenzo addressed a few words to the assembly, and he did it with such seriousness and modesty that he inspired all with those hopes which he afterwards fulfilled. Before the citizens left the hall they swore to look upon the young Medici as their own sons, and the youths upon them as fathers. Thus the affair ended by Lorenzo and Giuliano being honoured as heads of the state, in the government of which they followed the counsels of Messer Tommaso.

Whilst the people of Florence were thus living in quiet both within and without the city, for there was no war whatever to disturb the general peace, an unexpected disturbance arose presaging future trouble. Among the families who had fallen with Messer Luca Pitti was that of the Nardi, the heads of whom, Salvestro and his brothers, had been sent into exile and declared rebels after the war against Bartolommeo Colleone. One of these men was Bernardo, a ready and courageous young man, who could not endure the poverty of exile, and the general peace which now existed left him without hope of improving his position. He therefore determined to attempt something which might be a means of stirring up a new war, for it often happens that small beginnings are followed by great effects, as it is well known most men are more ready to follow than to commence an undertaking. Bernardo had a large number of acquaintances in Prado, and also many in the country round Pistoia, chiefly among the members of the Palandra family, who were country people, very numerous, and like all Pistolians inured to arms and bloodshed. Bernardo knew that these people were brooding over their discontent with the action of the Florentines in one of their recent quarrels; he knew also that the people of Prato considered that they were severely and selfishly governed by the Florentines, and that some spirits among them were hatching trouble against their rulers. These circumstances encouraged Bernardo in his hopes of setting the whole of Tuscany on fire by starting a rebellion in Prato, which would spread far beyond the control of those whose interest it would be to stamp it out. He communicated his schemes to Messer Diotisalvi, and asked what aid he might expect from him when he had succeeded in gaining Prato. The enterprise appeared a very hazardous one to Messer Diotisalvi—indeed almost impossible to accomplish—nevertheless he saw in it the opportunity of again tempting fortune at the expense of someone else, and he promised Bernardo help from Bologna and Ferrara if he could possibly hold Prato for fifteen days. Encouraged by this promise Bernardo secretly abtained admission into Prato and spoke of his plans to some whom he found ready to listen. He spoke also with the Palandra men and found in them the same desire and courage, and having thus completed his plans Bernardo communicated them to Messer Diotisalvi.

Cesare Petrucci was at this time the potesta of Prato for the Florentines, and it was the custom of officers holding such positions to keep the keys of the city gates always at their side; but in times of peace when there was no fear of danger this custom was somewhat relaxed, and people were allowed to go in and out of the gates by night. Bernardo was aware of this, and about daybreak he presented himself at the gate which opens towards Pistoia with the Palandra men and about one hundred others all armed. Those who were within the gate knew what was intended and armed themselves, whilst one of their number ran to the potesta for the key, pretending that one of the citizens desired entrance. The potesta having no suspicions of anything wrong sent a servitor with the keys, which were taken from him by the conspirators as soon as they were some distance from the palace. Directly the gate was opened, Bernardo and his armed men entered and divided themselves into two parties, one of which under the guidance of a Prato man named Salvestro seized the citadel, whilst the other lead by Bernardo captured the palace. Having left a party of men to guard Cesare Petrucci and his family, the conspirators spread themselves through the town, raising a great tumult and shouting the name of liberty. Day had now dawned and the people roused by the noise streamed into the Piazza, and to their astonishment found that the citadel and the palace had been seized and that the potesta was a prisoner. The council of eight who ruled the city met in their palace to consult upon what had better be done. Bernardo, having marched through the town without the citizens showing any disposition to join him or his following, went to the council when he heard it was sitting and informed them that he had come to give them liberty and to free their country from slavery. He spoke of the glory that would be theirs if they took up arms and joined him in this great enterprise from which they would reap everlasting fame and peace. He recalled to their memory their former freedom and contrasted it with their present condition; he pointed out the sure help which was coming, and that in a very few days they would obtain ample aid to sustain themselves against any forces the Florentines could send against them. He declared that he had an agreement with men in Florence that as soon as they heard that this city had joined him they would at once come to its help. The council of eight were not in the least moved by this enthusiasm, and replied that they did not know whether Florence was free or in slavery, as the matter did not concern them, but they knew well that the people of Prato did not wish to have any other liberty than that of obeying those magistrates who ruled in Florence, from whom they had never received any injuries that would justify them in taking up arms. Therefore the council advised Bernardo to give the potesta his liberty and get out of the town with his men as quickly as possible, and thus withdraw himself from the perilous position into which with great want of prudence he had plunged. Bernardo was not alarmed at these words, but determined to see, as prayers did not influence the Pratesians, whether fear would move them. Therefore in order to intimidate them he resolved to put Cesare to death, and with this intention took him out of prison and ordered him to be hanged from one of the windows of the palace. Cesare was already at the window with the halter round his neck, when he caught sight of Bernardo, and turning to him he said: "Bernardo, you are taking my life in the belief that the Pratesians will join you when you have done so. The very contrary will happen, because the reverence these people bear to the governors whom the Florentines send to them is so great that if you commit this wrong they will conceive so great a hatred against you that they will never rest until they have destroyed you. It is my life not my death that will help you, because when I command them to do what you wish they will obey me far more readily than they will you, and if I repeat your instructions you will gain your object." This appeared to Bernardo to be reasonable advice, and he commanded Cesare to mount upon a terrace which ran round the Piazza and tell the people to do whatever Bernardo should command. This was done, and Cesare was put back to prison.

These feeble efforts had demonstrated the weakness of the conspirators, and several Florentines who resided in the city met together, among whom was Messer Giorgio Ginori, a knight of Rhodes. This gentleman was the first to draw the sword, and he at once attacked Bernardo who was parading the Piazza, at one time appealing to the citizens and at another threatening them; Bernardo was wounded and taken prisoner by Messer Giorgio and his followers. When this happened it was easy enough to overthrow the other conspirators and liberate the potesta, because being few in number and divided into parties they were set upon and either taken or killed. The report of the affair had in the meantime reached Florence and been much exaggerated; it was reported that Prato had been seized, the potesta and his family murdered, the city overawed by hostile forces, and that Pistoia had risen and joined the rebellion; whereupon the citizens of Florence in great alarm flocked to the palace for consultation with the signoria. Roberto da San Severino, reputed one of the first captains of the day, happened to be at that moment in Florence, and it was decided to send him at once to Prato with such forces as he could get together. He was instructed to approach as close as possible to the city, and send back to Florence all particulars of the affair he could learn, and afterwards take such steps to put matters straight as his prudence suggested. Roberto had only passed the castle of Campi a short distance when he was met by a messenger from Cesare, who informed him that Bernardo was a prisoner, all his companions either dead or fled, and the disturbance quelled. Whereupon Roberto returned to Florence, and a short time afterwards Bernardo was brought thither. Questioned by the magistrates as to why he should have attempted such a hopeless enterprise, he replied that he had decided to die in Florence rather than live in exile, and that he wished to accomplish something worthy of record before his death.

Having crushed this rebellion as quickly as it arose, the citizens of Florence returned to their accustomed occupations, hoping to enjoy the government which had been established by themselves, but evils followed, such as are often generated in times of peace. The youth of the city were freer than their forefathers in dress and living, and spent more in other kinds of excesses, consuming their time and money in idleness, gaming, and women; their chief aim was to appear well dressed and to speak with wit and acuteness, whilst he who could wound the others most cleverly was thought the wisest. These habits were much increased by the presence of the courtiers of the Duke of Milan, who at this time, in fulfilment of a vow, as it is said, visited Florence with his wife and court. He was welcomed with all the pomp and ceremony due to so great a prince and good a friend. An event happened in the city such as had never been seen in Christian times. It being Lent, the Church had ordered a total abstention from eating flesh, but the court of Milan without any consideration for God or man ate it freely. Among the many fine spectacles which were given for the Milanese was one in the church of San Spirito, showing the descent of the Holy Ghost upon the Apostles, in the representation of which it was necessary to make a great display of fire, and the church was utterly destroyed by the flames. This was considered by many as evidence of the indignation of God for our sins. If the duke found our city full of courtesans, fine living, and extravagant display, he left it in a far worse condition. This state of affairs impelled some of the better class of citizens to put a curb upon such things; therefore, to bring them within proper bounds, sumptuary laws were passed regulating banquets, funerals, and clothing.

Amid this profound peace a new and unexpected trouble arose in Tuscany. Alum mines had been discovered in Volterra, the value of which was well known to some of the citizens of that place, who in order to raise money for the development of the same had taken partners who were to share with them the advantages arising from the mines. Such was the beginning of the affair, and as often happens in new enterprises the mines were little valued; but when time showed the advantages of them to the people of Volterra, they began to agitate for the possession of what they might have once had without any trouble. They brought the subject before the council, and stated that it was against public policy for an industry founded on public property to be worked for private advantage. The citizens also sent envoys to Florence to represent their views to the authorities there; by them it was referred to certain gentlemen for decision. Whether they were bribed by interested parties, or were only influenced by a desire for justice, it was adjudged that the people of Volterra had no right to deprive their citizens of the fruits of their foresight and industry, and therefore the alum mines belonged to private individuals and not to the public, but a certain payment should be made by the mines each year in recognition of the over-lordship of the state. This decision did not in any degree assuage but rather increased the animosities in Volterra, and the subject was violently discussed both in and out of the council chamber. The majority of the people urged the authorities to seize the mines, whilst it was only a few who had first acquired them who now desired them retained. When the judgment was confirmed a great disturbance was made in Volterra, in which a citizen of some repute, called Pecorino, and some others who supported him, were killed and their houses sacked and burnt; the Florentine governor was only saved from death with great difficulty.

The Volterrans, having flouted the people of Florence in this way, decided to send envoys to them informing the signori that, if the Florentines were willing to observe their ancient treaties, the Volterrans for their part were willing to be bound by their ancient obligations. The reply to this message was much debated by the signori. Messer Tommaso Soderini advised that the Volterrans should be received back in the spirit in which they desired to submit; he did not consider it a proper time to light a fire so near home, which might bum their own house down, for he feared both the intentions of the pope and the power of the king, and had found little reason to trust in the alliance with the Venetians or the duke, for he was not sure either of the loyalty of the one or the valour of the other; he recalled to them the old proverb, "Better a lean peace than a fat victory." On the other hand, Lorenzo de' Medici appeared desirous of seizing this opportunity in order that he might display his foresight and resolution, and was probably incited to this course by some who were envious of the authority of Messer Tommaso. Lorenzo spoke in favour of an expedition against the Volterrans to punish their arrogance with the sword; he argued that if an example were not made of them others would not hesitate on any trifling occasion to do the same without any fear of consequences. An expedition was therefore determined upon, and the Volterrans were informed they were not in a position to demand the observance of ancient treaties, seeing they themselves had broken them; they must either submit to the judgment of the signoria or prepare for war. Immediately the Volterrans received this message they prepared for war by fortifying the town and sending to several princes of Italy for assistance; but few listened to them, only the Sienese and the lord of Piombino gave any prospect of support. Knowing well that the effect of victory is enhanced by its swiftness, the Florentines sent 10,000 infantry and 2000 cavalry under the command of Federigo of Urbino into the districts round Volterra, which were quickly occupied. After this they approached the city, which being placed upon a hill could only be assaulted on the side near to the church of San Alessandro, the other sides being heavily fortified. The Volterrans had engaged about 1000 soldiers in their defence, who were quite overawed when they saw the vigour with which the Florentines were pressing on their preparations for the attack; but however backward the soldiers might be in fighting the Florentines they were very ready in plundering the Volterrans. Thus the poor citizens, harassed by their foes from the outside, plundered by their friends within, and despairing of safety, began to think of peace. No other course suggesting itself, they submitted to the commissioners; the gates were opened and the army admitted; The officers went direct to the palace where the signori were sitting and ordered them to return to their homes. On their way there one of the signori was set upon and robbed, and as men are always more ready for evil than for good this acted as a signal for the sack and destruction of the city. For a whole day it was overrun with riot, neither woman nor sacred place was spared, and the people were equally pillaged and wronged by the soldiery, whether of the attacking or defending army. The news of this victory was joyfully received in Florence, and as it had been the enterprise of Lorenzo he leapt at once into fame. One of his friends took upon himself to reprove Messer Tommaso Soderini for his advice, asking him, "What have you to say now that Volterra has been taken? " To which Messer Tommaso replied, "It appears to me to have been lost, because if you had received it in peace, it would have been secure and profitable to you; but seeing that you will have to hold it by force, you will find it a source of loss and expense in times of peace and of anxiety and weakness in war."

The pope during these events had decided to bring some of the towns of the Church into proper subjection, and with this aim had sacked Spoleto which had factiously rebelled; he had then laid siege to Citta di Castello, which had flaunted him in a similar manner. This city was held by Prince Nicolo Vitelli, a friend of Lorenzo, to whom was sent at once for help. Lorenzo de' Medici offered Nicolo little assistance, not sufficient to be of any use to him, but sufficient to sow those seeds of hatred between San Sisto and the Medici which afterwards bore such terrible fruit. This could not have been concealed very long had not Piero, the Cardinal of San Sisto, died about this time. This cardinal had been paying a series of visits to the Italian powers, and among others had visited Venice and Milan, ostensibly to celebrate the marriage of Ercole, the Marquis of Ferrara, but really to sound the minds of the rulers and to learn their disposition towards Florence. However, on his return to Rome, the' cardinal died suddenly, not without suspicion of having been poisoned by the Venetians, who feared the power of Sisto IV. when it was guided by the ability and courage of Piero. Notwithstanding that this cardinal was lowly born and brought up in a convent, he had no sooner reached the cardinalate, such was his pride and ambition, that neither it nor even the pontificate appeared to satisfy him. He had recently given a banquet in Rome which in its extravagance would have been considered ostentatious in a king, and could not have cost less than 20,000 florins. When Sisto found himself deprived of his minister his plans matured more slowly, and the Florentines renewed their conventions with the duke and the Venetians, and so arranged them that the pope and king could join at any time. The pope and the king did likewise so that others might ally with them if so disposed. Thus it came about that Italy was divided into two factions, between whom disputes soon arose that engendered mutual hatreds. One occurred over the island of Cyprus which King Ferrante wanted, but which the Venetians had seized. This contention caused the pope and the king to draw closer together. The most highly esteemed soldier at this time in Italy was Federigo, lord of Urbino, who generally led the Florentine armies. The pope and king determined therefore to win him over to themselves and deprive the league of his leadership. With this intention the king invited him to Naples and tile pope advised him to accept. To the surprise and displeasure of the Florentines, who expected that Federigo would share the fate of Jacopo Piccinino if he accepted, Federigo went to Naples. Nevertheless it happened otherwise, for Federigo returned from Naples and Rome in high honour, having accepted the captaincy of the league. The pope and king having succeeded in this case next attempted to gain the lords of Romagna and the Sienese to their party, and thus prepare themselves against their coming struggle with the Florentines. These intrigues were well known to the Florentines, who on their side took every opportunity of strengthening their position against the ambitions of their neighbours. Having lost the lord of Urbino they took Roberto da Rimini into their pay; they renewed their league with Perugia, and allied themselves with the lord of Faenza. The pope and the king alleged that the cause of their quarrel with the Florentines was a desire to break the alliance between Florence and Venice, for the pope did not consider that the Church could maintain its authority nor Count Girolamo his estates in the Romagna as long as Florence was allied with Venice and not with him. On the other hand, the Florentines feared that this attempt to bring them into hostility with the Venetians was not for love of them, but to get them into a false position in which the pope would be able to work them some injury. Thus for the space of two years Italy was filled with anxieties and contentions before any outbreak occurred; the first, although but a slight one, happened in Tuscany.

Di Braccio of Perugia, as we have already shown, a fine soldier, had died and left two sons, Odo and Carlo. The latter was of tender age when his brother, Odo, was killed by the men of the Val di Lamona, as related above, but when he became old enough to fight, out of respect for the memory of his father and the hopes they entertained of him, the Venetians admitted him among their condottieri. It was at about this time that Carlo's engagement with the Venetians had lapsed, but he had no wish to renew it with the senate, as he preferred to go out into the world and see if he could not with his own renown, and the reputation of his father, regain the state of Perugia. The Venetians raised no objections to this, for they had been long accustomed to increase their own dominions when changes took place around them. Carlo therefore entered Tuscany, and finding the capture of Perugia would be a difficult enterprise owing to its league with the Florentines, and being unwilling that nothing of importance should arise out of this enterprise, he turned his forces against the Sienese, upon the pretence that they were his debtors for the services of his father to their republic, and for which he now demanded satisfaction. Carlo attacked them with such impetuosity that nearly all their dominions fell into his hands. The citizens of Siena finding themselves thus outraged, and ready at all times to believe any evil of the Florentines, persuaded themselves that the attack was made with the connivance of the Florentines, and they overwhelmed the pope and the king with their complaints. They also sent envoys to Florence protesting against the invasion and clearly demonstrating that Carlo would not have dared to injure them without the permission of the Florentines. The Florentines excused themselves as best they could, and promised to use their utmost endeavours to compel Carlo to withdraw; accordingly they sent envoys to Carlo who commanded him to desist from his enterprise against the Sienese. Carlo was exceedingly angered by this order, and pointed out to the Florentines that not only were they causing him loss of honour, but they were themselves losing an opportunity of easily acquiring Siena, for he met with such feebleness among its defenders he had no doubt that he would capture it in a very short time. However Carlo could not help himself and had to take his departure. The Sienese, although they had been freed from their peril by the Florentines, retained all their anger against the people of Florence, and felt no obligations to those who in their opinion had only freed them from an evil they had themselves occasioned.

Whilst these events were occurring in the way we have mentioned between the pope and the king, and also in Tuscany, there happened in Lombardy an affair of far greater moment, that presaged still greater evils. A clever and ambitious man, named Cola Montano, was at this time teaching the Latin language to many youths of the first families in Milan. Whether moved by hatred of the character and habits of the duke, or by some other reason, Montano was always instilling into the minds of his pupils that it was detestable to live under a prince who was not a virtuous man, and that a people alone could be called happy and glorious whom nature and fortune had caused to be born under a republic, and not under a prince, because a republic nourishes virtuous men whilst princes destroy them; the one gains everything by the virtue of its citizens whilst the other dreads it. The youths with whom he was most intimate were Giovanni Andrea Lampognano, Carlo Visconti, and Girolamo Olgiato. Montano frequently spoke with these lads of the bad character of their prince, and of the misery of the people who were unfortunately governed by him, and with such hatred did he inspire the minds of the youth they swore that when they reached the age of manhood they would liberate their country from his tryanny. These principles thus instilled into the minds of these young men increased in strength as they grew older, as indeed did the misdeeds of the duke, until at last some particular injuries they suffered at his hands impelled them to carry into effect their early teachings. Galeazzo Sforza was licentious and cruel, and the many instances he had given of this had caused him to be much hated; it was not enough for him to violate the chastity of high born ladies, but he would delight in publishing their shame; and he was not content to kill men unless he could put them to death in some cruel manner. He even lived under the infamous suspicion of having murdered his mother, for he considered that as long as she in some measure shared the government he was not in reality a prince, therefore he ordered her to retire to her dower-house at Cremona, on the way to which she was suddenly taken ill and died. Many persons believed she had been poisoned by her son. The duke had dishonoured the young men Carlo and Girolamo in one of his affairs with women, and had also offended Giovanni Andrea by refusing the abbey of Miramondo to a relative of his after it had been conceded to him by the pontiff. These private injuries had increased the longing of these young men to rid their country of such a monster, and at the same time to avenge themselves; they believed that when they had succeeded in killing the duke, not only the nobility but the people would rise in their support. Having decided to murder the duke they were often to be seen consulting together, but their long standing friendship prevented any suspicions being aroused. They discussed the subject continually among themselves, and in order to increase their proficiency they would stab at each other with the sheaths of their daggers in the way they intended to carry out their designs. They also discussed the time and place. In the castle, did not appear to them sure enough; when hunting, doubtful and dangerous; when out walking, difficult and perhaps unsuccessful; at a banquet, uncertain. Therefore they decided to assassinate him at some public ceremony, when it was certain he would be present, and where it would be possible under various pretences to assemble their friends. They also arranged that if by any chance one of their number should be held back by the cortege of the duke, then the others with their armed companions should kill Galeazzo with their daggers.

The great festival of the Nativity, 1476, was approaching when the duke was accustomed to attend the church of the Martyr with great pomp on the morning of San Stefano, and the conspirators resolved that the time and opportunity had arrived for them to carry their plans into execution. On the morning of the saint's day they armed themselves and their most faithful friends and servants, and gave out that they were going to the assistance of Giovanni Andrea who desired to obtain the possession of an aqueduct in opposition to some competitors of his. They led these armed men to the church under the pretext of taking leave of the duke before they departed; they also caused many other friends and relatives on one pretence or another to attend the church, hoping that when the deed was done they would all give their assistance in the trouble which would follow. Their further intention was, having killed the duke, to make a call to arms and immediately pass on to a part of the city where they believed themselves able to raise the plebeians, and then fall upon the duchess and the heads of the government. The conspirators expected that the people would rally to them because of the famine that was raging at the time, and had decided to give up the houses of Messer Cecco Simonetta, Giovanni Botti, Francesco Lucani, and other heads of the government to the mob for plunder, and by these means secure its goodwill and restore its liberty. Having made all their arrangements and sworn to each other to carry them through, Giovanni Andrea with the others went at an early hour to the church, where they all heard mass together. After which Giovanni Andrea turned himself to the statue of Santo Ambrogio and said, "O patron saint of our city, thou knowest our intentions, and the end we desire to accomplish amid so many dangers. Help us in our enterprise, and show that injustice is hateful to you by favouring justice." The duke, on his part, had many presages of his approaching fate before he went to the church. At break of day he put on the cuirass he was accustomed to wear, but which he afterwards took off, either because it did not fit or he did not like its appearance. He had a strong desire to hear mass in the castle, but he found that his chaplain had left for San Stefano with his requisites for the chapel. He then, in place of his chaplain, desired the Bishop of Como to celebrate the mass, but he gave some good reason against it, and thus as it were by necessity the duke was compelled to attend the church of San Stefano. Before he left the castle he many times embraced and kissed his two sons, Giovanni Galeazzo and Ermes, and seemed scarcely able to tear himself away from them. He, however, summoned sufficient resolution in the end to leave the castle, and in company with the envoys of Ferrara and Mantua made his way to the church. In the meanwhile the conspirators had retired to a chamber of the head priest who was a friend of theirs, in order that they might avoid the cold, which was severe, and give no cause for suspicion. But when they heard that the duke was arriving they re-entered the church, and Giovanni Andrea and Girolamo placed themselves on the right and Carlo on the left hand side of the porch. The men who marched in front of the duke were already within the church, and he, surrounded by a great number of persons as might be expected in a ducal ceremony, followed. The first to make any movement against the duke were Giovanni Andrea and Girolamo. These young men, pretending to make way for the duke, drew close up to him and stabbed him with the short sharp daggers they had concealed in their sleeves; Giovanni gave him two wounds, one in the stomach the other in the throat; Girolamo also pierced him in the throat and breast. Carlo Visconti, who was posted nearer to the doors, was not able to attack the duke in the front as his companions had done, but finding the duke passing before him gave him two blows which transfixed his shoulder and spine. These six wounds were inflicted so rapidly that the duke had sunk to the ground before any one perceived what had happened; nor was he able to do or say anything, save to call upon the name of Our Lady to help him. When it was seen that the duke had fallen, a great shout was raised and many swords were drawn; and, as happens in all unexpected events, many people rushed out of the church, whilst others surged towards the centre of disturbance without knowing what had occurred. Nevertheless those who were immediately close to the duke, and saw him killed, recognised the murderers and pursued them. Giovanni Andrea made for the door of the church, fell among some women who were there in great numbers, kneeling as usual upon the ground, became entangled in their long dresses, was over-taken and killed by a Moor, one of the duke's serving men. Carlo Visconti was killed by the bystanders. But Girolamo Olgiato escaped with the crowd out of the church, and seeing his companions killed knew not where to fly except to his home. Here his father and brothers would not admit him, but his mother, out of compassion for her son, sent him to a priest, an old friend of the family, who took him to his own house and disguised him in his own clothes. Here he stayed several days in the hopes that some tumult would arise in Milan to save him, but nothing of the sort happened; fearing then that he might be discovered he fled in disguise. He was, however, recognised and taken before the potesta of justice, when he revealed the whole conspiracy. Giralamo, who was in his twenty-third year, was no less courageous in his hour of death than he had been in his life, for when he stood naked before the executioner, who with his knife in his hand was ready to kill him, he repeated these words in the Latin language, for he was highly educated: —

Mors acerba, fama perpetua, stabit vetus memoria facti.

The deed of these unfortunate young men, although secretly planned and courageously executed, produced no effect, because those upon whom they had relied for defence and support neither defended nor supported them. Therefore let princes live and carry themselves in such a way that they are loved and honoured, then no one can hope in killing them to escape himself, and let conspirators remember that all thoughts of relying upon the multitude are utterly vain, because although the people may be discontented they will never join or support you in danger. This incident terrified all Italy, but the events which followed in Florence did far more than this to break up the peace which had lasted twelve years, as the following book will show, and as it will have its commencement in blood and terror, so its end will be in tears and sorrow.

EIGHTH BOOK

1476-1492

IF we followed our usual custom the present would appear to be a suitable opportunity for discussing the subject of conspiracies, their importance and their many varieties, seeing that the events which are spoken of in the beginning of this book occurred between two great conspiracies—the recent one at Milan already described, and the one which followed at Florence, and is now to be related. I would willingly have written of them if I had not done so in another place, or if the subject only required a brief glance in passing. But seeing that they are events requiring very careful consideration, and have already received it elsewhere, we will leave them, and passing on to other matters we will describe the methods of government adopted by the Medici. This family having overcome all the hostility which had been openly directed against it desired now to exercise the sole power in Florence; to accomplish their wish it became necessary to deprive other families of the protection of the constitution, and to carry this into effect it would be necessary to destroy them, otherwise they would have recourse to plotting in secret. In the beginning, and as long as the Medici were opposed by families of equal power and authority to themselves, the citizens who might be jealous of them were able to oppose them openly, and had no reason to fear them seeing that magistrates were independent; but things were different after a serious defeat. For instance, after the great victory of

1476, which placed the entire government in the hands of the Medici, this family acquired so much power that those who were discontented had either to endure things patiently or resort to secret conspiracy if they wished to alter them. And since success in conspiracy is so difficult to attain, it follows that destruction overtakes those who participate in it, whilst increased aggrandisement often results to those against whom the plot is directed. A conspiracy against the head of a city nearly always brings increased power to him, unless like the Duke of Milan he is killed, and, further, constant plotting against a good prince tends to turn him into a bad one. Conspiracies give rise to fear, fear forces a prince to seek security, and to secure himself he injures others; from this follows hatred, and in many cases his destruction. Thus conspiracies destroy those who enter into them and those against whom they are planned, and their final end is ruin to all.

As we have already seen, Italy was divided at this time into two parties, the pope and the king being on one side, and the Duke of Milan with the Venetians and the Florentines on the other. Although no hostilites had as yet broken out between them each day brought some fresh incitement, and the pontiff directed his energies towards schemes which would injure the government of Florence. When Filippo de' Medici, the Archbishop of Pisa, died, the pope, knowing that Francesco Salviati was hostile to the Medicis, invested him with that dignity. This appointment was also in opposition to the wishes of the signoria of Florence, who refused to give up possession, and fresh cause of offence arose between them and the pope in the settlement of this affair. Beyond this the pope had conferred many honours upon members of the Pazzi family who resided in Rome, whilst he had in a most marked manner shown a want of consideration for the Medici. In Florence the Pazzi excelled all others in the splendour of their establishments, in their wealth, and in the nobility of their lineage. The head of the family was Messer Jacopo, who for his riches and generosity had been knighted at the request of the people. He had only one natural son but many nephews, sons of his brothers Piero and Antonio, among whom were Guglielmo, Francesco, Rinalto, and Giovanni, the sons of the elder, whilst Andrea, Nicolo, and Galeotto were of the younger. Cosimo de' Medici, recognising the high birth and wealth of this family, had married his niece Bianca to Guglielmo Pazzi, hoping thus to bind the families together and allay the envy and hatred which mutual fear so often engenders. Nevertheless, so vain are our hopes, it fell out far otherwise, because those persons who advised Lorenzo pointed out to him that it was a matter of the gravest danger to his authority to permit so much wealth and power to be united in the person of one citizen. Thus it came about that positions of honour, which in the opinion of many citizens were due to Messer Jacopo and his nephews, were not given to them. Hence arose the first feelings of distrust among the Medici and of resentment among the Pazzi; for as the fear increased on one side so did the hatred on the other, and on those occasions on which the citizens were accustomed to meet together the Pazzi were refused proper consideration by the magistrates. The council of eight once summoned Francesco de' Pazzi for some trifling reason to come from Rome to Florence, thus displaying a total want of respect due to so great a personage. The Pazzi complained with scornful and angry words of this treatment, which increased the fears of the Medici and brought down more wrongs upon the Pazzi family. Giovanni Pazzi had married a daughter of Giovanni Buonromeo, a very rich man, whose possessions devolved at his death upon his daughter, his only child. His nephew Carlo, however, seized part of the possessions and threw the estate into litigation. The decision of the court deprived Giovanni's wife of her father's wealth and gave it to Carlo. The Pazzi attributed this decision to the influence of the Medici. Giuliano de' Medici complained of this award many times to his brother, telling him he feared that he who desired so much was in danger of losing everything.

Nevertheless Lorenzo, in the hey-day of his youth and power, wished to have the decision of everything, and desired that the people should recognise his hand in everything; but the Pazzi, with all their wealth and pride of race, would not sit still under such injuries, and began to think of revenge. The first to make any move against the Medici was Francesco. This gentleman was very sensitive and high spirited, and he determined either to regain the position of which he had been deprived or to lose all he had in the attempt. As he was on bad terms with the government of Florence he resided in Rome, and having plenty of means, traded from there after the manner of Florentine merchants. He was very friendly with the Count Girolamo, and together they often discussed the Medici. After having deplored the situation of affairs they came to the conclusion that the only way in which the one could enjoy his government and the other be restored to his country was to overturn the government of Florence, and this they considered they were unable to accomplish without the death of Lorenzo and Giuliano. They believed also that the pope and the King of Naples would assent when it was proved how easily the murders could be perpetrated. Having come to this determination they communicated their plans to Francesco Salviati, the Archbishop of Pisa, who being an ambitious man, and having been only a short time previously injured by the Medici, willingly agreed. They debated between themselves how to accomplish it, and decided to draw Messer Jacopo Pazzi into their schemes in order to ensure success, as without it they feared they would fail. Francesco de' Pazzi went to Florence with a view to securing this aid, whilst the count and the archbishop remained in Rome to secure the pope to their side, when the time should arrive for communicating their designs to him. Francesco found Messer Jacopo very cautious, and far more difficult than was expected; he therefore let the friends in Rome know that more influence would be needed to bring Jacopo into their plans. Whereupon the archbishop and count communicated the whole affair to Giovanni Batista da Montesecco, the condottiere of the pope. This soldier was highly esteemed and under many obligations to the pope and the count, but he at once pointed out that the affair was one of extreme difficulty and danger; the archbishop strove to minimise these difficulties, and to assure him of the aid which the pope and king would give to the enterprise, of the hatred which the people of Florence bore to the Medici, of the number of relatives which the Salviati and Pazzi would influence, of the ease with which the two Medici could be killed when walking with their companions in the city and quite unconscious of danger, and of the ease with which the government could be changed when they were killed. Giovanni Batista did not place much faith in these assurances, because he had heard something entirely different from other Florentines.

Whilst affairs stood thus it happened that the Signor Carlo of Faenza fell ill and was near to death. This occurrence appeared to the archbishop and the count to be a good opportunity for regaining certain towns which Carlo had seized, and for sending Giovanni Batista to Florence and thence into Romagna for that purpose. Giovanni was accordingly despatched by the count to Florence under the pretence of discussing this affair with Lorenzo, but really to speak with Messer Jacopo with a view to inducing him to support their conspiracy. As it was necessary to make use of the authority of the pope with Messer Jacopo, the plot was revealed to the pontiff before Giovanni left Rome, and full assistance was promised. Having reached Florence Giovanni had an interview with Lorenzo, at which he was most graciously received, and in the advice which he asked he was so wisely and courteously counselled that Giovanni Bastista was struck with admiration. Lorenzo appeared to be a very different person to what he had been led to expect; he found him to be a very genial man of the world, and quite friendly to the count. It was, however, necessary for him to speak with Francesco Pazzi, but he failed to meet him as he was absent in Lucca; he then approached Messer Jacopo Pazzi, whom he found at first quite averse to the affair, but before Giovanni left him he appeared somewhat influenced by the countenance the pope gave to it. Messer Jacopo advised Giovanni to pass on to Romagna, and by the time he returned to Florence Francesco would be back from Lucca, and the matter could then be discussed at greater length. Giovanni Batista completed his business in Romagna and returned thence to Florence. He again pretended to discuss with Lorenzo the affairs of the count, but was afterwards closeted with Messer Jacopo and Francesco de' Pazzi. Giovanni, and Francesco so wrought upon Messer Jacopo that he finally agreed to join the conspiracy; they then discussed the methods by which it could be carried into effect. To Messer Jacopo this did not appear feasible whilst the two brothers were in Florence together, and he counselled waiting until Lorenzo went to Rome, where common report said he was going, and then carrying it out there. It would, of course, have been perfectly satisfactory if Lorenzo did go to Rome, but supposing he did not, then it was decided that the two brothers should be killed either at a wedding, or the play, or at church. With regard to assistance from outside, Francesco proposed that the pope should assemble forces for the purpose of attacking the castle of Montone, of which he had just cause for depriving Count Carlo, for his action in the Sienese and Perugian country some time back, of which we have spoken. Nevertheless no decision was reached excepting that Francesco de' Pazzi and Giovanni Batista should return to Rome and fix everything up with the pope. At Rome their plans were carried still further, and in prosecution of the Montone enterprise it was decided that Giovanni Batista should again go to Florence in order that he might provide all that was necessary for the undertaking, towards which King Ferdinand, through his envoys, promised assistance. Francesco de' Pazzi and the archbishop also came to Florence and brought into their conspiracy Jacopo, the son of Messer Poggio, a clever and ambitious youth, always desirous of novelty; they induced also the two Jacopo Salviati to join them, one was the brother and the other a distant relative of the archbishop; also Bernardo Bandini and Napoleone Franzezi, two ardent youths, both under obligations to the Pazzi; two foreigners also joined, Messer Antonio da Volterra and one Stefano Sacerdote, who taught Latin to a daughter of Messer Jacopo. Rinato de' Pazzi, a grave and prudent man, who far better than the others knew the evil of such deeds, would not join the conspiracy; nay, he detested it and took all the steps that he honestly could to put a stop to it.

For the purpose of studying pontifical literature, the pope had sent to the Pisan Academy a nephew of Count Girolamo, named Raffaello di Riaro, and had afterwards elevated him to the dignity of a cardinal. It now occurred to the conspirators that they should take him with them to Florence, in order that his appearance there might enable them to conceal their designs, and with his assistance find an opportunity of executing their plans, besides this it was possible to conceal in his suite those men of whom they had need. The cardinal therefore set out for Florence, and was received by Messer Jacopo de' Pazzi at his villa Montughi, near to Florence. The conspirators intended to avail themselves of the first opportunity to bring Lorenzo and Giuliano together and then kill them. They managed matters so that the Medici invited the cardinal to their villa at Fiesole, but either by chance or design Giuliano did not attend, and that plan was in vain. They then arranged that the cardinal should be invited by the Medici to Florence, where of necessity both brothers would have to meet him. The banquet was fixed for Sunday, April 26, 1478, at which the conspirators determined to kill the two brothers, and they met together on Saturday night and arranged everything for the following morning. Francesco, however, learnt the first thing on Sunday morning that Giuliano would not be at the banquet, so that the chiefs of the conspiracy had again to make fresh plans; but it was evident to them that as the conspiracy was now known to so many persons the chance of discovery had multiplied, therefore its execution should no longer be delayed, and it was decided to murder the Medici in the cathedral church of Santa Reparata where the cardinal was going, and where the two brothers would be as usual. They requested Giovanni Batista to take in hand the killing of Lorenzo, whilst Francesco de' Pazzi and Bernardo Bandini would kill Giuliano. Giovanni Batista begged to be excused, either because his recent intimacy with Lorenzo caused him to relent, or some other reason influenced him; he alleged that he had not sufficient courage to commit such a desperate deed in a church, and that sacrilege ought not to be added to treason. With this defection commenced the ruin of the conspiracy, for as time pressed the conspirators were compelled to entrust the murder of Lorenzo to Messer Antonio da Volterra and Stefano Sacerdote, two men who by nature and training were quite unfit for such a deed. If ever such a business is to succeed it must be entrusted to minds fixed and resolute, hardened amid many scenes of life and death, for it has often been found that even men expert in the use of arms and accustomed to bloodshed have failed in resolution on such occasions. The conspirators having now completed their arrangements the design was communicated to the priest who was to celebrate High Mass, and their plans were also completed for the seizure of the palace by the archbishop and his men, who with Messer Jacopo Poggio were to compel the signoria to declare in their favour, either willingly or by force, as soon as the two brothers were killed.

Everything being now prepared the conspirators repaired to the church, where the cardinal and Lorenzo had already arrived. The church was crowded with people, and the sacred office had already commenced although Giuliano had not arrived. Whereupon Francesco de' Pazzi and Bernardo, who had been told off to kill him, ran to his house to find him and by prayer and guile brought him to the church. It is indeed to be noted that Francesco and Bernardo were inspired by such feelings of hatred and the lust of murder, and pursued their object with such callousness and resolution, that as they led Giuliano to the church, and even within it, they amused him with droll and jovial stories. Francesco even, under pretence of embracing him, took him in his arms and pressed him with his hands, to see if he were wearing a cuirass or other defensive armour. Although both Lorenzo and Giuliano were perfectly well aware of the resentment of the Pazzi and their desire to deprive them of the government, they had never gone in fear of their lives, as they always believed that when anything was attempted against them it would be by civil process and not by violence; so having no fears for their personal safety the Medici had always appeared friendly to the Pazzi. The murderers being now quite ready, those at the side of Lorenzo, having approached with ease owing to the crowd, and the others having reached their destination with Giuliano, Bernardo Bandini struck Giuliano in the stomach with a short dagger. Giuliano fell to the ground and Francesco covered him with wounds whilst he lay there, indeed with such rage did he strike that he wounded himself seriously in the thigh. Lorenzo was at the same time attacked by Messer Antonio and Stefano Sacerdote, who made many strokes at him, but only slightly wounded him in the throat. Either by their own lack of ability, or the courage of Lorenzo, who, finding himself attacked, defended himself with his sword, or by the aid of those around him, the efforts of his assailants were in vain. They becoming alarmed fled and endeavoured to hide themselves, but being discovered were killed and their bodies dragged through the city. Lorenzo and his friends retreated to the sanctuary, and shut themselves up. Bernardo Bandini, finding that he had killed Giuliano, turned on Francesco Neri, a great friend of the Medici, and killed him, either because of some old feud or because he had tried to save Giuliano. Nor was Bernardo content with these two murders, but he ran in search of Lorenzo, that with his own courage and swiftness he might make amends for the slowness and cowardice of others. But he found Lorenzo had taken refuge in the sanctuary and defied his attempts. In the midst of these terrible deeds it seemed as if the church would fall in upon the people; the cardinal clung to the altar, and with difficulty was saved by the priests; when the tumult was appeased he was taken by the signori to the palace where he remained until his liberation.

At this time there were residing in Florence some men of Perugia, who had been driven out of that city by the dominant faction, and whom the Pazzi had induced to join their conspiracy by promising to restore them to their city. When the archbishop with Jacopo, the son of Messer Poggio, and their friends and relations reached the palace which they were to seize, the archbishop left a number of his followers below, with instructions that when they heard a disturbance upstairs they were to hold the door. The archbishop and the greater number of the Perugians then mounted the stairs and found the signori at dinner as it was now getting late. However, after a short time he was admitted by Cesare Petrucci, the gonfaloniere of justice. When the archbishop had entered with a few of his company, the greater number of his followers who were left outside shut themselves up in the Record room, the door of which was constructed in such a way that it could be opened neither from the inside nor the outside without a key. The archbishop had been admitted by the gonfaloniere into the council chamber under the pretence that he had something of importance from the pope to communicate; but when he commenced to speak in a hesitating manner, and to show some excitement, the suspicions of the gonfaloniere were aroused, and in a moment with a great shout he thrust him out of the chamber; at the same time he seized Jacopo Poggio by the hair and handed him over to the serjeants. He then raised the alarm among the signori, who seizing such arms as they could find fell upon the followers of the archbishop who had come upstairs, all of whom were either killed and thrown from the windows of the palace or locked up; whilst the archbishop, the two Jacopo Salviatis, and Jacopo Poggio were hanged. Those men who had been left downstairs had overpowered the guard, forced the doors of the palace, and occupied the lower part of the palace, so that those citizens who heard the tumult and came running to the defence of the palace could render no assistance whatever.

Francesco de' Pazzi and Bernardo Bandini lost heart when they found that Lorenzo had escaped them, and that one of themselves, and he the mainstay of the enterprise, was very grievously wounded. Thereupon, seeing that all was lost, Bernardo devoted himself to his own safety with the same ardour he had shown in his attack upon the Medici, and fled; Francesco de' Pazzi returned to his house, where he found that his wound would not allow him to mount his horse. The arrangement had been that he should ride through the city with armed men and call the people to arms and to liberty, but this he was unable to do because of his terrible wound and loss of blood. He undressed and threw himself naked upon his bed, and prayed Messer Jacopo to take his place, and do what he was to have done. Although Messer Jacopo was old and quite unaccustomed to such tumultuous scenes, he mounted his horse and made a last bid for success. With about 100 armed men who had been prepared for this service he sallied out in the direction of the Piazza of the palace calling the people to liberty and to his standard. But he obtained no response, for the liberality and success of the Medici caused the people to turn a deaf ear to him, besides which the name of liberty was hardly known in Florence. The signori, who were masters of the upper part of the palace, saluted him with stones and menaced him with threats. Whilst Messer Jacopo was hesitating what to do he encountered his relative, Giovanni Serristori, who reproached him for all the trouble which had arisen and advised him to go home, for the care of the people and of liberty was dose to the hearts of many other citizens besides himself. Thus Messer Jacopo lost courage, for he found the palace hostile to him, Lorenzo still alive, Francesco disabled, and the people indifferent. Not knowing what else to do he determined to save his life if that were still possible by flight, and with some friends who had followed him to the Piazza he left Florence for Romagna.

By this time the city was thoroughly aroused, and Lorenzo de' Medici accompanied by a great escort of armed men had returned to his house. The palace had been recaptured by the people, and most of the rebels either killed or taken prisoners. Already the streets were re-echoing with the name of Medici, and the limbs of the dead were being borne aloft on pikes, or dragged along the ground, and all who bore the name of Pazzi were persecuted with rage and cruelty. Their houses were in possession of the mob, and Francesco, all naked, was dragged from his bed and led to the palace where he was hanged by the side of the archbishop and the others. Neither on the way to the palace, nor elsewhere, was it possible by word or deed to make him speak a word, but keeping a fixed look he breathed his last in silence. Guglielmo de' Pazzi, the brother-in-law of Lorenzo, because of his innocence, was saved by the aid of his wife in the house of his relative. In this emergency there was not a citizen who, whether armed or unarmed, did not go to the house of Lorenzo and place himself and his substance at the disposal of the Medici, such was the goodwill which this family had won by its prudence and liberality. Rinato de' Pazzi had retired to his villa before the above events happened, but when he heard of them he attempted to escape; he was, however, recognised, captured and led back to Florence. Messer Jacopo was also taken when crossing the mountains by the mountaineers who, noticing the speed with which he was travelling, and having heard of the events in Florence, arrested him and sent him back to the city. Although he entreated them to kill him rather than take him back to Florence, he could not induce them to do so. After a trial lasting four days, Messer Jacopo and Rinato were condemned to death. Among the many persons who were put to death during that time, and there were so many that the streets were strewn with their limbs, none excited any compassion but that of Rinato dei Pazzi, for he had none of the haughtiness of the other members of the family, but was considered a wise and honest man. In order that an extraordinary example should be made of the fate of these conspirators, Messer Jacopo was first buried in the sepulchre of his ancestors, afterwards he was treated as one excommunicated, taken thence and reburied under the walls of the city; he was dug up from there and dragged naked round the city by the halter with which he was hanged; then, as if earth was not to be allowed to give him a resting-place, those who had dragged him round cast him into the river Arno, which was then in great flood. To see a man so rich and powerful fall to such depths of misery amid ruin and disgrace was indeed a signal example of the mutability of fortune. Some men have spoken of his vices, among which were gambling and cursing, more fitting to a damned soul than to any other; but such vices were overbalanced by his countless charities to all in need, as well as to sacred places. One can also say this good thing of Messer Jacopo, on the Saturday previous to the Sunday chosen for the assassination he paid all his creditors and most scrupulously handed over to its owners all merchandise which happened to lie in his house or warehouses belonging to them, in order that Others should not be involved in any reverse of his fortunes. Giovanni Batista da Montesecco was beheaded after a long trial. Napoleone Franzezi escaped punishment by flight. Guglielmo de' Pazzi was banished to Volterra, where with such of his cousins who were alive he was confined in the dungeons beneath the fortress. The tumults being now quieted and the conspirators punished, the obsequies of Giuliano were celebrated, accompanied by the lamentations of the whole city, for he was a man of more gentleness and liberality than is usually found in one of his position. He had one natural son, named Giulio, who, however, was born a few months after the death of his father. He possessed those virtues and acquired that high fortune by which he is known to-day to all the world, and which shall be set forth at length when I come to deal with the present events, if God only spares me for the task. The armies under Lorenzo da Castello in the Val da Trevere, and under Giovanni Francesco da Tolentino in Romagna, had united and were moving on Florence to the assistance of the Pazzi when they learned that the rebellion had failed, and at once turned back.

Seeing that no change of government had followed these disturbances in Florence, as had been desired by the pope and king, they determined to effect by open war what they had failed to accomplish by treachery, and both assembled their forces with the utmost despatch in order to attack the government of Florence, at the same time declaring they had no intentions against the city itself but the removal of Lorenzo, who alone of all Florentines was their enemy. When the army of the king had passed the Tronto, and that of the pope had reached Perugia, the pope desiring to give the Florentines a taste of the spiritual power as well as the temporal, excommunicated them and laid them under a malediction. The Florentines, finding that armies were gathering against them, began to prepare for defence with great vigour. As common report gave it out that the war was only against Lorenzo, he assembled the signori with many of the leading citizens at the palace and addressed to them the following words: —

"I cannot say, my lords and gentlemen, whether I should rejoice or mourn with you over what has occurred. When I call to mind the treachery and ferocity with which my brother has been slain and myself wounded, I cannot fail to be saddened and to grieve with my whole soul. But when I remember, on the other hand, with what readiness and earnestness, and with what sympathy and unity, the whole city has risen to avenge my brother and defend me, I am disposed not only to rejoice, but to feel honoured and exalted. And if my experience has now taught me that I had more enemies in this city than I supposed, it has also proved to me that I have far more fervent friends than I could have believed possible. I am therefore compelled to condole with you upon the wickedness of some, whilst I can congratulate myself upon your wonderful kindness to me; yet I am constrained to remember our wrongs, inasmuch as they are unparalleled, and totally undeserved by us. Let us for a moment, gentlemen, consider the evil fortune which has overtaken our family, that even among friends and relatives, nay in the very church itself, we are not safe. Those who fear murder are accustomed to fly for protection to their friends and relatives, but it was these whom we found armed for our destruction; whilst those who are persecuted for public or private reasons fly to the church for safety. Thus the Medici are killed by those who should have defended them, and where parricides and assassins find sanctuary the Medici found murderers. But God, who has never abandoned our family, has once more saved us, and has taken upon Himself our just defence. What injuries have we done to anyone to inspire such a thirst for vengeance? But in truth these men, who have shown such hostility against us, have never been injured by us in private life, for had we wronged them, we should have taken care to have put it beyond their power to retaliate. If on the other hand they attribute public injuries to us, by saying that you by our means have injured citizens,—and I do not know of any who have been wronged,—then they insult you, and the majesty of this palace of justice and the government of this city, rather than our family. But this statement is far from the truth, for we would not have done so had we had the power, and you would not have permitted us had we had the will. The man who seeks to find the truth of this matter will find that our family have always been held in the highest estimation by you for no other reason but that we have gained the goodwill of all by our kindliness and liberality. If we have conferred benefits upon strangers, is it likely that we should have reserved injuries for those who are nearer to us? But if our enemies have been incited to this crime by a thirst for dominion, as it would appear they have been by their seizure of the palace and the invasion of the Piazza with an armed force, then such a cause is ambitious, reprehensible, and brutal, and as soon as its object was discovered it was universally condemned. If they have entered upon this course out of envy and hatred of our authority, they have passed a censure upon you, because it was you who conferred all such authority upon us. Of a truth, for power to deserve hatred it must be usurped, not conferred for public spirit, generosity, and goodwill. You know well that this family has never assumed any authority but that which has been conferred upon it by the united voice of this council. My grandfather Cosimo did not return from exile by force and violence, but by the call of the whole people. My father, old and infirm, did not defend the government by himself against so many enemies, but it was you, who with your power and loyalty defended it. After the death of my father, whilst a mere child, so to speak, I could not have maintained the position of my house if it had not been for your help and counsel. Therefore I cannot say what is the reasonable cause of the hatred or envy they have displayed against us. Let them rather execrate the memory of their ancestors who by their arrogance and avarice lost that reputation which ours by far different conduct knew how to gain. But let us concede that the injuries they received from us were very great, and demanded nothing less than our destruction, why then should they seize the palace? Why should they make a league with the pope and the king against the liberties of this republic? Why should they break the peace which has prevailed for so long in Italy? To these charges they have no reply, for they ought to have punished those who injured them, and not have confused private enmity with public injury. Although our enemies may have been destroyed the evil they committed still lives, because for their sake the pope and the king are advancing with their armies against us, declaring that the war is only upon me and my family. Would to God this were the truth, for then the remedy should be swift and certain, because I am not such a bad citizen as to value my own safety more than your peril, and willingly would I put an end to your troubles by my own destruction. But the injuries which the powerful inflict are always disguised under some specious pretence. Should you, however, believe otherwise, I am in your hands. You have to support me or abandon me. You, my fathers! You, my defenders! You have only to command me and I will obey. I will not refuse, nay I will do it willingly, if you will but say one word, and as this war was commenced with the death of my brother, so it shall be ended with mine."

Lorenzo was listened to with so much sympathy by the citizens they could not keep back their tears whilst he was speaking, and when he had finished one of them was commissioned to speak for the rest. He bade Lorenzo be of good courage, that the citizens recognised in him and his family such merit that they would defend his life with the same readiness they had shown in revenging the murder of his brother, and that they would fight for him and his government, and before he should lose either they would lose their country. In order that their deeds should correspond with their words, they committed the care of his person to a body of armed men to defend him against domestic enemies.

After this they prepared for war, enlisting as many men as possible and, in virtue of their treaties, sending for aid to the Duke of Milan and the Venetians. As the pope had proved himself a wolf rather than a shepherd, the Florentines filled all Italy with the story of the treatment their government had received, and they took all means in their power to justify themselves, so that it should not be as a guilty people the pope should destroy them. They pointed out the impiety and iniquity of the pope, the frauds he had practised in obtaining the pontificate, and that he had wickedly abused his power. He had sent those whom he had elevated to the prelacy in company with murderers and traitors to commit perfidious deeds during the celebration of the sacrament in the midst of divine service. And afterwards, when he could not succeed in killing their citizens, or overturning their government, or putting the city to the sack, as he had wished, he had laid them under the pontifical malediction. But if God is a just God, and if violence is hateful to him, then He must be angry with His Vicar here on earth, and anxious that injured men, who can no longer find a place of refuge here, should have recourse to Him. The Florentines would not accept the interdict, but disobeyed it and compelled the priests to celebrate divine service. They also called a meeting of all Tuscan prelates who owed obedience to them, and appealed against the wrongs the pope had committed to the forthcoming general council. Neither did the pope fail to attempt his justification by maintaining that it was the duty of a pope to drive out tyrants, to punish wicked men, and to reward the good, and this he ought to do on every occasion; that it did not appertain to secular princes to put cardinals under restraint, to hang archbishops, to put to death and dismember priests, and drag them through the streets, or to kill without distinction the innocent and the guilty.

Nevertheless, in spite of so much discord and injury, the Florentines restored the cardinal whom they had in their hands to the pope, but neither he nor the king paid any regard to this concession, but continued their preparations for invasion, with their two armies, the one under Federigo, the Duke of Urbino, and the other under Alfonso, Duke of Calabria, the eldest son of Ferdinand, entered Chianti by the way of Siena, which had declared itself against the Florentines. They seized Radda and many other castles, and laid waste the surrounding country; they afterwards besieged Castellina. This caused the Florentines great anxiety, for they had no army ready and the aid of friends came in very slowly. The Duke of Milan had sent them some assistance, but the Venetians had denied that they were bound to assist them in private quarrels, and seeing that the war was declared to be against a private individual they were not bound to help; they added that private hostilities ought not to be encouraged by governments. The Florentines therefore sent Messer Tommaso Soderini as an envoy to the Venetian senate with the object of bringing them to take a more reasonable view of affairs; in the meantime more soldiers were engaged, and Ercole, the Marquis of Ferrara, was made leader of the Florentine army. Whilst these preparations were being pressed forward the invaders had held Castellina so closely invested that the garrison, despairing of relief, had surrendered after forty days' siege. The invaders had then turned towards Arezzo and laid siege to Monte San Savino. The Florentine army was now in order and was at once sent against the enemy, whom it so seriously threatened when within three miles that the Duke of Urbino asked for a truce of three days. This was conceded to the great surprise of the duke and to the prejudice of the Florentines, for had it not been granted the enemy would have been obliged to retreat in disorder. But the duke used these three days to strengthen his position and to seize the castle under the eyes of the Florentines. The winter had now come and the enemy retired into quarters within the territory of the Sienese. The Florentines also sought out suitable quarters, whilst the Marquis of Ferrara, having accomplished so little either to his own credit or that of others, returned to his own state.

It was about this time that Genoa rebelled against the Duke of Milan for the following reasons. After Galeazzo was killed his infant son was proclaimed his successor, but grave dissensions arose between his three uncles, Lodovico, Ottaviano, and Ascanio Sforza, and his mother, Madonna Bona, because both parties wished to obtain the custody of the little duke. Madonna Bona, the duchess, acting under the advice of Messer Tommaso Soderini, the Florentine envoy, and of Messer Cecco Simonetta, the secretary of Galeazzo, succeeded in this struggle, and the Sforzas fled from Milan. Ottaviano was drowned when crossing the Adda, and the others, including Signor Roberto da San Severino, who had deserted the duchess in the midst of her troubles and joined her enemies, were banished to several places. When the disturbances arose in Tuscany these princes hoped that something would happen to enable them to restore their fortunes. They broke out of their places of exile, and each of them attempted something to better his fortunes. King Ferrante saw that the Florentines had only the Milanese upon whom to rely, and determined to give such trouble to the duchess as would prevent her from sending any aid to Florence. With this intention, Prospero Adorno with Signor Roberto and the rebel Sforzas stirred up a rebellion in Genoa against Milan until there remained only the castle in the hands of the Milanese. To support this the duchess sent an army to Genoa, but it was defeated, and she then saw the peril in which she and her son stood if she became further involved in this trouble. Affairs in Tuscany had also fallen into great disorder, and the Florentines upon whom she entirely relied were hard pressed to hold their own; the duchess therefore decided that, since she could no longer retain the Genoese as subjects, she would secure them as friends. She stipulated with Battisto Fregoso, the enemy of Prospero Adorno, to give up the castle to him, on the understanding that he should drive out the Adorni and give no countenance to the Sforzas. When this was agreed, Battisto took possession of the castle, and with the help of his party, drove the Adorni out of Genoa and became master; according to custom he was created doge. Thus the Sforzas and the Signor Roberto were driven put of Genoa, and with such men as followed them went to Lunigiano. When the pope and king found that the troubles they had hoped to raise in Lombardy were settled, they turned for assistance to the men who were driven out of Genoa to disturb Tuscany in the direction of Pisa, and thus weaken the forces of Florence by diverting them elsewhere. The winter being now ended Signor Roberto left Lunigiano with his men and invaded the country round Pisa. He raised a great disturbance in the district, took many castles, sacked several towns, and even approached the walls of Pisa.

The Emperor and the kings of France and Hungary were sending envoys to the pope, and reaching Florence about this time persuaded her to join in the mission with a view to putting an end to the war. To avoid being accused of not desiring peace the Florentines agreed, and sent envoys, who, however, returned without achieving anything. As the Florentines had been abandoned by one half of Italy and warred upon by the other, they determined to send an envoy to the King of France to render him that homage which they considered was his due. They chose Donato Acciajuoli, a gentleman learned in the Latin and Greek languages, whose ancestors had always been held in high repute by the citizens of Florence, but unfortunately he had only reached Milan, on his way to France, when he died. To honour his memory the city celebrated his funeral at the public expense, and to recompense those whom he had left behind his sons received advancement and his daughters marriage portions. In Donato's place there was sent as envoy to the king Messer Guido Antonio Vespucci, a highly skilled man in pontificial and imperial matters. The attack of the Signor Roberto upon the Pisan territory had caused much anxiety to the Florentines, as all unexpected occurrences will do, and having on the Siena side a very severe struggle in progress they did not see how they could succour Pisa. However, they succeeded in throwing some levies and supplies into the city. In order that the Lucchese might be kept loyal to the Florentines, Piero di Gino, the son of Neri Capponi, was sent to Lucca as an ambassador, but he was received with so much hostility—the result of years of distrust and wrong—that he experienced many escapes from death at the hands of the populace, and his mission caused fresh resentments rather than promoted union. The Florentines now recalled the Marquis of Ferrara, they also engaged the Marquis of Mantua, and succeeded by great insistance, and only after great cavilling on the part of the Venetians, in obtaining the services of Count Carlo, the son of Braccio, and Deifebo, the son of Count Jacopo. The Venetians only yielded these men because, having come to terms with the Turks, they had no longer any excuse whatever for not observing the terms of the league. Count Carlo and Deifebo now joined the Florentines with a good number of men-at-arms, and together with such men as could be spared from the army under the Marquis of Ferrara, who was operating against the Duke of Calabria, moved towards Pisa against Signor Roberto, who was posted on the banks of the Serchio. Although Signor Roberto made some pretence of awaiting the Florentine attack he retired on Lunigiano, where his quarters were before he had entered the Pisan territory. Upon his retreat Count Carlo recovered all the towns which had been taken from the Pisans.

The Florentines having now rid themselves of danger on the Pisan side, turned all their forces in the direction of Colle and San Giminiano. When Count Carlo joined the main body of the Florentine army, it was found that all the old hostility between the Braccescan and Sforzescan soldiery was revived, owing to there being large numbers of both in the army. It was feared that if the two parties remained long together it would come to a fight, therefore it was decided, as a lesser evil, to divide the forces, and send one part under Count Carlo to Perugia and the other to Poggibonzi, where it would form an entrenched camp strong enough to prevent the enemy entering Florentine territory. It was believed also that this plan would compel the enemy to divide his forces, because either Count Carlo would occupy Perugia, where the Florentines had many partisans, or the pope would detach a number of men to defend it. Beyond this arrangement they determined to bring further pressure to bear upon the pope by assisting Messer Nicolo Vitelli to recover Citta di Castello from his enemy Messer Lorenzo, who had expelled Nicolo from that city. It appeared at

first as if fortune would favour the Florentines, for Count Carlo
made the greatest progress in the Perugian country, whilst
Messer Nicolo Vitelli, although he did not succeed in capturing
Citta di Castello, was paramount in the field and wasted the surrounding district without check; and the other wing of the army
at Poggibonzi harried the country up to the walls of Siena.
Nevertheless, all these hopes were vain, for the count died
before he could realise his promise of victory, and his death
might even have proved of service to the Florentines had they
known how to avail themselves of the victory which followed.
When the pope learnt of Count Carlo's death, he took the field
at once with his army, which was assembled near Perugia, with
revived hopes of now overcoming the Florentines, and drew
them up in battle array near the lake, about three miles distant
from the enemy. Jacopo Guicciardini, who was the commissioner
to the Florentine army, accepted the advice of Signor Roberto,
who, now that Count Carlo was dead, had the highest reputation
with the army, and determined to await the attack, for he divined
the cause of the enemy's new confidence. Thus the two armies
came to an engagement on the same spot where Hannibal the
Carthaginian inflicted his memorable defeat upon the Romans,
and the army of the Church was utterly routed. This victory was
received in Florence with the greatest joy by the people, and
brought great renown to the leaders; it would have proved of the
utmost advantage, as well as honour, to their cause if the disorder
which broke out in the army stationed at Poggibonzi had not upset
all their plans. Thus the benefits which were gained by one army
were lost by the other. The trouble arose through the Poggibonzi
army having taken a quantity of booty from the Sienese and the
Marquises of Ferrara and Mantua quarrelled as to its division.
They came to blows and attacked each other fiercely; the
Florentines came to the conclusion they could not employ both,
and it was agreed that the Marquis of Ferrara should return
home with his men.

The army weakened in this manner, and having no leader, fell into every kind of disorder, and the Duke of Calabria, who lay with his army at Siena, was encouraged to attack it. The Florentine army, seeing the approaching enemy, and trusting neither in its own arms, nor numbers, which were both superior to the adversary, nor to the position, which was one of the strongest, and without waiting even for a sight of the enemy's forces, but only on the appearance of the dust they raised, fled, leaving their transport, artillery, and all their munitions of war to the duke. The cowardice and want of discipline in the armies of those days was such that it only needed a horse to turn his head or his tail to the enemy to decide whether an enterprise should meet with victory or defeat. This victory gave the King of Naples immense quantities of spoil, and caused the Florentines terrible anxiety, for Florence was inflicted, not only with the terrors of war, but also with those of the plague, which had broken out so severely that many of the citizens had fled to the country. This defeat was the more disastrous because those citizens whose estates were in the Val di Pesa and the Val d'Elsa were compelled to fly back to Florence for fear of a worse fate, not only with their families and household goods, but also with their work people. Everybody feared the enemy would soon appear at the gates of the city. The council to whom the prosecution of the war had been committed at once ordered the army which had been victorious in Perugia to abandon the campaign against the Perugians and occupy the Val d'Elsa and drive back the enemy who were plundering the country without hindrance. Although the Florentines were so closely pressing the city of Perugia that its capture might be looked for any day, yet they would not wait for this event, preferring to defend their own city rather than conquer another. However, the army, which was thus taken away from the scene of its successes, marched to San Casciano, a castle situate about eight miles from Florence, but refused to go further before it had collected some of the men from the recently defeated army. On the other hand, the liberated garrison from Perugia became very bold on the retirement of the Florentines and committed depredations every day in the Aretino and Cortona districts. Under Alfonso, Duke of Calabria, the remainder of the enemy's army became masters of Poggibonzi, and afterwards of Vico, the sack of Certaldo followed, and having committed many depredations laid siege to the castle of Colle. This place was considered very strong in those days, and being held by men faithful to the government of Florence, it was expected to hold the enemy at bay until the Florentines had collected their forces. These being now in order at San Casciano, and the enemy pushing the castle of Colle very hard, the Florentines decided to march towards it in order to encourage the garrison to persist in its defence and to deter the enemy from storming it. In accordance with this decision the Florentines broke up their camp at San Casciano and moved to San Giminiano, about five miles from Colle; from here they harassed the duke daily with light cavalry and skirmishers. This, however, was of little use to the defenders of Colle, because they were in the utmost need of provisions, and on November 13, they surrendered, to the great joy of the enemy and regret of the Florentines. The men from Siena were greatly delighted with this victory, because however much they hated the Florentines they had a particular hatred of the men of Colle.

It was already mid-winter, and the weather very much against all operations of war, therefore the pope and the king, influenced either by a desire to enjoy their victories or a sincere wish for peace, proposed a three months' truce to the Florentines, and gave them ten days in which to reply. This offer was accepted at once, but, as always happens, wounds hurt more when the blood grows cold than when first received, so this brief breathing space gave the Florentines an opportunity of realising their many troubles. The citizens accused one another freely without respect of persons, pointed out the mistakes made in the war, showed how the vast expense had been made in vain, and complained of the heavy burden of taxation. They did not speak of these things only in their private circles, but courageously in the public council. One man was bold enough to turn on Lorenzo de' Medici and say to him: "The city is sick of war, and it is necessary for you to think of peace." Lorenzo recognised the necessity of this as strongly as any one, and assembled a few of his friends, whom he considered the most devoted to him and the most capable, and their main decision was that, seeing the Venetians were lukewarm and faithless and the duke a minor and embroiled in civil discord, it was time for the Florentines to seek fresh fortunes with new friends. But they were doubtful into whose arms they should throw themselves, whether the pope's or the king's. Having weighed the matter carefully they decided in favour of an alliance with the king as likely to be more stable and reliable. The short life of the popes, the uncertainty in the succession, the scanty respect shown by rulers to the Church, the few inducements it has to adopt a decisive course, are all considerations which prevent a secular prince putting entire reliance in a pontiff, or placing his fortune on equal terms with that of the Church. The prince who enters into a defensive or offensive alliance with the pope will have to share with him the spoils of victory, whilst in defeat he will have to stand alone, seeing that the pope is sustained and defended by spiritual powers. Lorenzo and his friends for these reasons determined to make an effort to gain over the king, and came to the conclusion there was no better or surer way of doing this than by sending Lorenzo to him, because they felt that the more completely they threw themselves upon the generosity of the king, the more likely they would be to disarm his hostility. Lorenzo having decided to accept the mission handed over the government of Florence to Tommaso Soderini, who was at that time gonfaloniere of justice, and left Florence early in December. Upon his arrival at Pisa he wrote a letter to the signori explaining the reasons of his departure, and they, in order to honour him and increase his dignity in treating with the king, conferred upon him the title of envoy from the Florentine people, and gave him authority to make such alliances as might seem best to him in the interests of the republic.

Whilst the above events were occurring Signor Roberto da San Severino, together with Lodovico and Ascanio Sforza, the other brother being dead, again attacked the government of Milan by seizing Tortona. Milan was greatly disturbed by this, and the Duchess Bona was advised, that in order to put an end to all civil discord, the Sforzas should be recalled and admitted to the government. The author of this advice was Antonio Tassino, a Ferrarese, who, although he was of very humble extraction, had attracted the notice of Duke Galeazzo and his duchess and been raised to the position of chamberlain. Either by reason of personal beauty or secret influence he mounted high in the confidence of the duchess after the death of the duke, until he almost ruled the state. This caused the gravest displeasure to Messer Cecco, a prudent and experienced man, who strove to his utmost, both with the duchess and the other ministers, to lessen the authority of Antonio. It was to obtain revenge for this attempt to supplant him, and to have some one at hand to defend him against Messer Cecco, that Tassino, as soon as he learnt what was preparing for him, advised the duchess to repatriate the Sforzas. The duchess accepted this advice without informing Messer Cecco, and the Sforzas returned. Upon this Messer Cecco remarked to the duchess: "The course thou hast taken will lose me my life and thou thy state." This was verified shortly afterwards by Lodovico killing Messer Cecco and driving Tassino out of Milan; upon this happening the duchess was greatly incensed and left Milan and the wardship of her son to Lodovico. Thus Lodovico became the sole ruler of Milan, and was the cause, as will be shown, of the ruin of Italy.

During the journey of Lorenzo de' Medici to Naples, and whilst the truce was still in force, Lodovico Fregoso came to an understanding with certain Serezanese, and without any warning took possession of Serezana with an armed force, and held all the Florentines found within prisoners. This occurrence gave great anxiety to the rulers of Florence, for they were persuaded it was done with the connivance of King Ferrante, and they complained to the Duke of Calabria, who lay with his army at Siena, of this attack upon them during the truce. He assured them by every sort of proof, by letter and by ambassador, that the act was committed without the knowledge of either him or his father. Nevertheless the Florentines were greatly depressed by the state of their affairs: their treasury was empty; the head of the republic was in the hands of the King of Naples; they had an old-standing war with the pope and the king, a new one pending with the Genoese, and no allies; they had nothing to hope for from the Venetians, and affairs in Milan were so unstable and changeable they had to fear rather than hope from them. There remained only to the people of Florence the hope of what Lorenzo de' Medici would accomplish with the king.

On Lorenzo's arrival at Naples by sea he was received not only most honourably by the king and the whole city, but also with great curiosity, because the mightiness of his enemies and the severe character of the war which had been waged solely against him had invested him with a personal grandeur. Being conducted into the presence of the king he discussed with him the position of affairs in Italy, and the aspirations of its princes and peoples, what was to be hoped from peace and what was to be feared from war. Now that the king had heard Lorenzo speak he was more impressed by him, and by the breadth of his views, the rapidity of his thought, and the gravity of his judgment, than he had previously been aston-ished at his ability to sustain the weight of so vast a war. The king began to think that he would rather have Lorenzo for a friend than an enemy and to press many honours upon him, at the same time he would not allow him to depart, but kept him in Naples from December to March, possibly to gain a further insight into his char-acter, possibly to see how affairs in Florence would shape them-selves. It is to be noted that the enemies whom Lorenzo had left behind him in Florence would have been quite willing for the king to detain him and treat him as Jacopo Piccinino had been treated; under pretence of grieving for him they would suggest this fate throughout the city, at the same time they would raise opposition in public assemblies against those who supported Lorenzo. By these means they spread the report that if the king should detain him much longer in Naples a change would take place in the government of Florence. This was one of the reasons which induced the king to detain Lorenzo so long, in order to see if any disturbance should break out in Florence. But nothing of the sort happened, and Lorenzo was permitted to leave Naples on March 6, 1479. This he did loaded with honours and with every demonstration of regard from the king, with whom he had fixed a treaty by which each undertook to assist the other in maintaining his state. Thus, if Lorenzo left Florence a great man, he returned far greater, and was received by the citizens with the enthusiastic affection which his high qualities and achievements deserved, having exposed his own life to secure peace for his country. Two days after his return the treaty of peace between the King of Naples and the republic of Florence was published, by which each party was compelled to support the other in the maintenance of their respective states; the towns taken from the Florentines were to be restored at the discretion of the king; the Pazzi were to be liberated from the dungeons of Volterra; and the Duke of Calabria was to receive a certain sum of money for a few years.

The pope and the Venetians were extremely annoyed when the terms of the treaty became known to them, because the pope considered the king had treated him with scant respect in concluding it, and the Venetians held the same views of the Florentines — seeing that both had assisted in the war, both complained they had not been made parties to the peace. These feelings caused some alarm in Florence lest a greater war than ever should grow out of the treaty, therefore the rulers determined to make certain changes in the government which should restrict the power of those who might wish to take advantage of such trouble; the number of governors was lessened, and a council of seventy was created with full authority to deal with all important affairs. This new council at once assumed importance by ratifying the treaty made between Lorenzo and the king and sending envoys to the pope, for which purpose Messer Antonio Ridolfi and Piero Nasi were chosen. In spite of the peace Alfonso, the Duke of Calabria, had not yet evacuated Siena, being detained there by the disturbance which had broken out among the citizens, as he alleged. This discord had indeed been so considerable that, when the duke had been encamped outside, the citizens had made him the arbitrator of their differences and admitted him within the walls. Many of the citizens were put to death, many thrown into prison, many fined, and many sent into exile. This alarmed not only the Sienese but also the Florentines with the dread that the duke meant to make himself Prince of Siena, and seeing they were in alliance with the king, and at enmity with the pope and Venetians, they saw no way of preventing it. Not only were these apprehensions held to be real by the populace of Florence—those subtle interpreters of every event—but the rulers of the state were impressed by them, and the city seemed again about to be overwhelmed by her troubles and lose her liberty. But God, who always had our city under His care, caused an unhoped-for event to occur, which gave the king, the pope and the Venetians something far more important to deal with than the affairs of Tuscany.

The Grand Turk, Mahomet, had laid siege to Rhodes, and although the attack had lasted many months with incessant fierceness and the employment of enormous forces, the garrison had defended itself with such valour that it had proved stronger than the Turk, and compelled him to raise the siege in disgrace and sail away. He left Rhodes, and part of his fleet under Jacometto Bascia and went towards Velona. As he passed along the coast of Italy, either because the ease of the enterprise tempted him or his master had ordered it, he suddenly threw 4000 soldiers on shore and attacked Otranto. He quickly captured it, sacked it, and slew all the inhabitants, and afterwards, with such means as he had at hand, fortified the city and port; he also ordered to be sent to him some good cavalry, and with it harassed and plundered the surrounding country. The King of Naples hearing of this attack, and

knowing with what a powerful enemy he had to deal, at once notified the invasion by messengers in every direction, demanding
help against the common enemy, and with great insistence he
recalled the Duke of Calabria and his army from Siena.

This invasion of the Turk which disturbed the duke and the
rest of Italy so much, was a matter for congratulation to Siena and
Florence, for it relieved the one from its dangers and gave back its
liberties to the other, which it appeared to be on the point of losing. It was this consideration which increased the chagrin of the
duke in releasing his hold upon Siena, and he railed at fortune for
depriving him of the empire of Tuscany by such an unexpected
and unreasonable occurrence. This same event also caused the
pope to alter his plans, and whereas before he had refused to
entertain the Florentine envoys, he now became much more reasonable, and even listened to their overtures for a general peace.
The envoys were also informed that when they were ready to ask
the pope's pardon it would be granted. It appeared to the Florentines they ought not to allow this opportunity to pass, therefore
they sent twelve ambassadors to the pope, who upon their arrival
at Rome were received with the usual ceremonies, and afterwards
were given audience by the pope. Their future relationships with
each other were finally determined, together with the amount of
money to be contributed by each in times of peace and war. After
this the ambassadors were permitted to kiss the feet of the pontiff
seated in the midst of his cardinals. The ambassadors apologised
for all that had happened in the past, excusing themselves at one
time on the plea of necessity, at another because of the evil dispo-
sitions of men; then it was the rage of the populace and its menaces, and then as being in the miserable position of men who had
been forced to fight or die. And as anything ought to be endured
rather than death, so they had suffered war, the interdict, and every
kind of affliction which had troubled them of late, in order that
their republic might avoid the slavery which threatened their free
city. Nevertheless, if they had been compelled to commit faults,
they were determined to make amends, and threw themselves

upon the pope's clemency, trusting that he would receive them into his merciful arms after the example of the great Redeemer. The pope replied to these excuses with angry and haughty words; he reproved them for all they had done against the Church in past times, but in order that he might observe the commandments of God he granted them the pardon they begged, but they must clearly understand they must obey him in future; if, however, they disobeyed him, then the liberty which they were now in danger of losing would be taken away from them entirely, and justly so, because it is only those who do right that deserve liberty, not those who do evil, for when liberty is abused it is injurious to everybody; to respect God indifferently and the Church not at all is the act of wicked men not of free men; and as more are inclined to wickedness than to good, so their correction belongs not only to princes but to all Christian people. Among their recent misdeeds of which he had to complain was their having occasioned the war by their wickedness, and having prolonged it by their contumacy; this war was now to be concluded, but it was owing more to the clemency of others than to their own merits. After the terms of the treaty and of the benediction had been read, the pope added to what had been agreed upon and ratified that if the Florentines wished to enjoy the benefits of the benediction they must support with their money fifteen armed galleys during the whole of the time the war lasted between the Turks and the kingdom of Naples. The envoys loudly complained of this heavy imposition being added to the signed treaty, but they were unable by either prayers or favour to get rid of it. Upon their return to Florence the signori sent Messer Guidantonio Vespucci as an envoy to the pope to conclude with him the peace. Messer Vespucci had only recently returned from France, and by his prudence brought affairs in Rome to a satisfactory conclusion, and obtained many concessions from the pope in token of the great reconciliation.

The Florentines having made their peace with the pope, and the Sienese having regained their liberty, and both parties being relieved of their anxieties regarding the king by reason of the departure of the Duke of Calabria to the Turkish war, the Florentines pressed the king to restore the castles which the duke on his departure had left in the hands of the Sienese. The king was in some fear lest the Florentines should take these castles by main force from him in his necessity, and thus precipitate a fresh war with the Sienese, and throw obstacles in the way of his obtaining the aid of which he was in need from the pope and other Italian princes. Therefore he consented to the restitution of the castles and thus bound the Florentines to him by fresh obligations. But this is one more proof that only force and necessity, not writings and treaties, will compel princes to keep faith. Having recovered the castles and confirmed the new confederation, Lorenzo de' Medici entirely regained the prestige which he had lost during the war and whilst the action of the king was in doubt, for there were many in Florence who calumniated him during those days by saying openly that he had sold his country to save himself, and that they had lost their territory in war and were going to lose their liberty in peace. But when the lost territory was recovered, and an honourable peace concluded with the king, and splendour once more reigned in Florence, Florence—that city of reckless chatter, so prone to judge events by their success and not by the judgment which dictated them—now changed its tune and praised Lorenzo to the skies, saying that his wisdom had known the way to recover all that bad fortune had caused them to lose in war, and that he had accomplished with his tact and wisdom more than the arms and power of the enemy.

The invasion of Italy by the Turks had only postponed the outbreak of the war which the resentment of the pope and Venetians at the recent treaty was to bring forth, and as the occasion of that invasion was unexpected, and in reality effected much good, so the end of it came as a surprise and wrought much evil. Contrary to all expectations the death of the Grand Turk, Mahomet, was followed by a great conflict among his sons, and the Turks who were in Puglia, finding themselves abandoned by their lord, came to terms with the King of Naples and surrendered Otranto. On the removal of this menace, which had hitherto exercised a restraining influence upon the pope and the Venetians, fresh troubles were expected by every one. On the one side there was the King of Naples, the Duke of Milan, the Florentines, the Bolognese, and many Italian lords. On the other side there was the pope and his allies the Venetians, and with them the Genoese, Sienese, and other minor powers. The Venetians had long had a desire to possess Ferrara, and it now appeared to them they had every chance of success and a reasonable pretext for seizing it. The pretext which they put forward was that the marquis had stated that he was no longer, either bound to receive their deputies or to buy their salt, as the convention between them stated that Ferrara was to be free from both after a period of seventy years. The Venetians replied that as long as the marquis retained the Polesine he was bound to receive the deputies and take the salt. The marquis would not consent to this, and consequently the Venetians believed they had a reasonable cause for taking up arms against him, and further the present appeared a very opportune time, seeing that the pope was bitterly enraged against the King of Naples and the Florentines. Count Girolamo happened to be in Venice at that time, and in order to gain him to their side the signori entertained him most honourably and conferred upon him a patent of Venetian nobility, which was the highest honour they could give. They also raised new taxes for the purpose of this war, and appointed Lord Roberto da San Severino one of their captains. The count had fallen out with Signor Lodovico, the governor of Milan, and fled to Tortona; having caused some disturbance there he passed on to Genoa, and whilst there was sent for by the Venetians and made the head of their army.

These preparations for a new struggle becoming known to the opposite party they also prepared for war. The Duke of Milan chose Federigo, lord of Urbino, for his captain, and the Florentines appointed Costanza, lord of Pesaro. In order to discover the intentions of the pope, and to ascertain if it were with his consent that the Venetians were entering into this war against the Ferrarese,

King Ferrante sent Alfonso, the Duke of Calabria, to ask permission of the pope to pass into Lombardy to the assistance of the Marquis of Ferrara. This the pope utterly refused to allow, and consequently the king and the Florentines considered they had a good indication of his intentions, and they determined to bring sufficient pressure to bear upon him to compel him to ally himself with them, or at least to raise such obstacles as would prevent him assisting the Venetians. Already the Venetians had taken the field against the marquis and had harassed his country far and wide, besides laying siege to Figarolo, a castle of considerable importance in his territory. This determined the king and the Florentines to attack the pope, and Alfonso was ordered to advance against Rome; this he did with the aid of the Colonna party who joined him, whilst the Orsini opposed him on behalf of the pope; nevertheless he committed great damage in the country districts. The Florentines, on their side, attacked Citta di Castello with the help of Messer Nicolo Vitelli, captured it, drove out Messer Lorenzo, who held it for the pope, and left Messer Nicolo in possession.

The pope found himself reduced to great distress by these measures, for not only was the country round Rome harassed by his enemy but the citizens within were much disturbed. Nevertheless, being a man of courage, he would not yield but determined to fight his enemy; he made his Magnificence Roberto da Rimini his chief captain and sent for him to Rome, where his forces were assembled; The pope described to Roberto the great honour which would accrue to him if he overcame the army of the king and liberated the Church from her enemies; that this would not only lay the pope under the greatest obligations, but also his successors; and that not only men but God would recompense him. His Magnificence immediately reviewed the pope's men-at-arms and the munitions, and advised him to get together as much infantry as was possible; effect was given to this advice with the utmost diligence and rapidity. As the Duke of Calabria lay with his army near to Rome he could harass the country freely up to the very city gates, and this so enraged the citizens that they willingly

enrolled themselves under his Magnificence for the liberation of
their city, and were gladly received by him. When the duke heard
of what was happening within the city he withdrew some distance,
thinking that his Magnificence would not have the courage to
attack him when he found he had retired; the duke also desired to
await the arrival of his brother, Federigo, who was coming to his
assistance with fresh troops. His Magnificence Roberto finding
himself almost equal to the duke in cavalry, and superior to him in
infantry, drew his army out of Rome and pitched his camp within
about two miles of his enemy. The duke seeing that his adversary,
contrary to expectations, had come outside the city, concluded
that it would be necessary to fight or seek safety in flight. Thus to
avoid acting a part unworthy of the son of a king the duke was
compelled to fight; he therefore turned his front to the enemy,
who also put his forces into battle array, and led them to the
fight, which lasted almost the entire day. This engagement was
fought with more valour than had been shown in any battle in
Italy for the last fifty years, and more than one thousand men
were killed on one side or the other. The result was a glorious
victory for the army of the Church, which with its superiority in
infantry was more than a match for the ducal cavalry. The duke
himself would have been taken prisoner had he not been rescued by the Turks, who formerly held Otranto and were now
fighting for him. His Magnificence returned to Rome in triumph, which unhappily he enjoyed but a short time, for having
drunk large quantities of water during the heat of the battle, he
succumbed in a very few days to an attack of dysentery, and his
body was interred with all honour by the pope. The pope having
gained this great victory at once sent the Count Girolamo against
the Citta di Castello to rescue it from the hands of Messer Nicolo
Vitelli, and also to make an attempt upon the city of Rimino.
This city had remained, after the death of his Magnificence
Roberto, in the care of his wife, who had been left with one little
son. It appeared to the pope that he would easily gain possession
of the city, and in this he would doubtless have succeeded had

not the lady received, as did Citta di Castello, assistance from the Florentines, who defended them both with such energy that the pope effected nothing against either.

Whilst these events were occurring in Rome and Romagna, the Venetians had captured Figarola and crossed the Po with their forces, while the forces of the Duke of Milan and the Marquis of Ferrara had fallen into some disorder owing to the death of Federigo, Count of Urbino, who finding himself ill had been carried to Bologna, where he died. Thus the affairs of the marquis were in a dangerous position, whilst the hopes of the Venetians of seizing Ferrara were brightening. At the same time the king and the Florentines were doing their best to bring the pope over to their views, and having failed to do this by force of arms they were now threatening him with a general council, which had been proposed by the emperor to meet at Basle. By means of envoys whom the Florentines had sent to Rome, and of some leading cardinals who desired peace, the pope was induced by their persuasions to consider the pacification and unification of Italy; further he was brought to recognise and to fear that the greatness of the Venetians meant ruin to the Church and Italy, therefore he came into agreement with the league. He thereupon sent his nuncios to Naples, where a treaty was signed for five years between himself, the king, the Duke of Milan, and the Florentines, and a place reserved in it for the Venetians. When the treaty was executed the pope informed the Venetians that their war upon Ferrara must cease; to this they would not consent, but pushed on their operations with greater energy. Having routed the army of the duke and the marquis at Argenta, they approached Ferrara and took up a position in the park of the marquis.

It was now quite evident to the league they must no longer defer sending to the assistance of the marquis, and they moved forward the armies of the Duke of Calabria and the pope to Ferrara; the Florentines also sent their forces. In order that the business of the war might be conducted to greater advantage, a diet was summoned by the league to assemble at Cremona; it was attended by the pope's legate, Count Girolamo, the Duke of Calabria, the Signor Lodovico, Lorenzo de' Medici, and many other Italian rulers; at this meeting all matters connected with the war were discussed, and it was decided that no better way could be devised of assisting Ferrara than by creating a vigorous diversion, and the diet requested Signor Lodovico to declare war against the Venetians in the name of the Duke of Milan. Lodovico would not consent to this course, as he feared it would bring a struggle upon his own shoulders which he could not sustain. In consequence of this refusal it was determined to march the entire army to Ferrara, and with 4000 cavalry and 8000 infantry they moved against the Venetians, who had only 2200 cavalry and 6000 infantry. The league decided that the first thing to do was to attack the Venetian fleet assembled on the Po, and this they did near to Bondeno, defeating it and destroying more than two hundred vessels. Messer Antonio Justiniano, the Venetian contractor, was captured. When the Venetians found the whole of Italy against them, they engaged the Duke dello Reno, with two hundred men-at-arms, and sent him when the naval disaster occurred, with part of their army, to hold the enemy at bay, whilst Signor Roberto crossed the Adda with the rest of their army to fall upon Milan and proclaim the young duke and his mother, the Duchess Bona. The Venetians, who belived that Signor Lodovico and his government were hated, thought a revolution would be sure to follow. Although this attack raised great alarm, and threw the whole city into a turmoil, its results were entirely opposite to the expectations of the Venetians, for whereas Lodovico had previously abstained from declaring war upon them, this insult now moved him to do it. The Duke of Calabria, leaving 4000 cavalry and 2000 infantry at the disposal of the Marquis of Ferrara, passed on with 12,000 horsemen and 5000 footmen into Bergamasco, and from there into the districts round Brescia and Verona. These cities and the surrounding country quickly fell into his hands, the Venetians under Signor Roberto being unable to save them. The Marquis of Ferrara, on his side, recovered the chief part of his possessions, for the Duke dello Reno, who had been appointed to oppose him, could make no headway against him with only 2000 cavalry and 1000 infantry. Thus matters had fallen out very successfully for the league during the summer of the year 1483.

The winter passed quietly, and as soon as the spring opened both armies took the field. The league had gathered the whole of their forces together, in order that they might bring overwhelming numbers to bear upon the Venetians, and had they conducted their operations with the same resolution as in the previous year, the league would have deprived the Venetians of all their possessions in Lombardy. For the army of the Venetians was reduced to 6000 cavalry and 5000 infantry, whilst opposing it were 13,000 cavalry and 6000 infantry. The year of service of the Duke dello Reno had expired and he had gone home, when, as often happens where several leaders possess equal authority, disunion worked more harm than the valour of the enemy. Federigo Gonzaga, the Marquis of Mantua, had died, and he whilst living had been able by his personal authority to keep in check the animosities of the Duke of Calabria and Signor Lodovico. Thus disagreements began to arise among the leaders, and from disagreements hatreds. Another event which raised trouble was the coming of age of Giovan Galeazzo, Duke of Milan, who took up the reins of government, and having married a daughter of the Duke of Calabria, he desired that his father-in-law should assist him in his state rather than Signor Lodovico. Lodovico was quite aware of the intentions of his nephew, and determined not to give him the opportunity of carrying them into effect. The views of Lodovico were also well known to the Venetians, and in this fact they believed they saw a chance to do as they always had done, gain more out of the terms of peace than they had lost by the fortune of war. Therefore they set on foot negotiations with him, and in August 1484 they concluded a treaty with him. When this came to the knowledge of the confederates they were extremely annoyed, especially when they found that the Venetians were to receive back all the territories they had lost in the war, to retain Rovigo and Polesine, which they had captured from the Marquis of Ferrara, and to have restored to them the suzerain rights which they had formerly enjoyed over the city of Ferrara. It appeared to the confederates they had borne all the fatigues of the war, earned all the honours, and were fooled at the end of it, because the towns they had captured were restored to their enemy without any compensation to them. But they were compelled to accept these terms, because wearied with the heavy charges of the war they refused any longer to stake their lives and fortunes upon the necessities and ambitions of others.

Whilst affairs in Lombardy were thus shaping themselves, the pope was once more laying siege to Citta di Castello, in order to restore Messer Lorenzo and drive out Nicolo Vitelli, whom the league had abandoned as soon as they had come to terms with the pope. But during the siege the garrison sallied out and inflicted a severe defeat upon the assailants, whereupon the pope recalled the Count Girolamo from Lombardy in order that he might reorganise the army of the Church and carry on the enterprise against Nicolo Vitelli. The pope, however, changed his mind, and concluded that it would be better to make peace with Nicolo and reconcile him with his old enemy, Messer Lorenzo, as best he could; this he succeeded in doing. The pope was forced into this course, not so much by a love of peace, as by the troubles which he saw arising between the Colonnesi and Orsini. These quarrels were due to the King of Naples, when at war with the pope, taking from the Orsini the country districts of Tagliacozzo and bestowing them on the Colonnesi, who had supported him. When peace was restored between the king and the pope, the Orsini, by virtue of the terms of peace, claimed a return of the territory. Although often notified by the pope that it ought to be restored, the Colonnesi would never consent, and neither the prayers of the Orsini nor the threats of the pope had any effect beyond drawing down insults. The pope, no longer able to endure this, got his forces together and, assisted by the Orsini, sacked the Colonnesi houses in Rome, killing or taking prisoners all who resisted, and destroying the greater number of their castles. Thus the trouble was not settled peacefully, but by the infliction of punishment on one of the parties.

Affairs were not yet composed either in Genoa or Tuscany, because the Florentines kept the Count da Marciano with an army on the frontiers of Serezana, and whilst the war lasted they harassed the Serezanesi with skirmishes and forays. In Genoa the Doge Battistino Fregoso, who had put his trust in the archbishop, Pagolo Fregoso, had been with his wife and children thrown into prison, and the archbishop had made himself doge. The Venetians had attacked the kingdom of Naples with their fleet, and made themselves master of Gallipoli and the surrounding country. All these troubles were settled by the peace, excepting those in Rome and Tuscany, because five days after peace was signed the pope died, either because the term of his natural life was reached or because of chagrin at the conclusion of this peace to which he was greatly opposed. He thus left his pontificate with Italy at peace, which during all his term of office he had kept at strife. Upon his death becoming known the people of Rome sprang to arms, drove the Count Girolamo with his men to the castle, and the Colonnesi threatened revenge for their recent injuries. They demanded back their castles, and murders, robberies, and fires occurred in many parts of the city. The cardinals persuaded the count to restore the castle into the hands of the Sacred College and free Rome of his army by retiring to his own state; desiring to propitiate the future pontiff, he consented, restored the castle and retired to Imola. When the cardinals were liberated from this danger and the barons had no further prospect of assistance from the count in their dissensions, the election of a new pontiff was proceeded with, and after some dispute Giovan Battista Cibo, a Genoese, Cardinal of Malfetta, was chosen. He took the title of Innocent VIII., and being a courteous and amiable man induced the people of Rome to lay down their arms, and the city was once more at peace.

After the Lombardian peace the Florentines could not rest, for it appeared to them undignified to submit to the loss of the castle of Zerezana without making an attempt to regain it, for it had been one of the terms of the treaty that they should not only be able to demand what they had lost, but to levy war upon those who should oppose them, and they at once prepared for the enterprise. Whereupon Agostino Fregoso, who had seized the castle, fearing that he would not be able to hold his acquisition, handed it over to San Giorgio. As the affairs of the Genoese and San Giorgio have often been mentioned, it does not seem to me improper to describe in some detail the constitution and course of events in Genoa, for she is one of the principal cities of Italy. After the severe war between the people of Genoa and Venice the government of Genoa had not been able to repay the vast sums which it had raised among its citizens, and had therefore handed over to its creditors the customs revenue, with the stipulation that such creditors were to share in the revenue according to the amounts of their loans until the indebtedness was entirely wiped out by the commune. As it was necessary for the creditors to meet together from time to time, the palace devoted to the customs business was handed over to them. The creditors arranged amongst themselves a system of management, and formed a council of one hundred members to discuss all matters of general interest, with a magistracy of eight as an executive. The amounts due to the creditors were divided into parts called shares, and the entire body was called San Giorgio. The society of San Giorgio being thus instituted, circumstances arose out of which the city had fresh needs, and it again had recourse to San Giorgio, which being well managed had grown very rich. As the commune had in the first instance pledged its revenue from the customs, so now it put its lands in pawn, and to such an extent did this occur, owing to the increasing needs of the commune and the ready help of San Giorgio, that the greater part of the lands and subject towns of the Genoese government came under the administration of San Giorgio and were managed and protected by it; governors of the towns were chosen each year by open voting, and sent out without the commune having a voice in the matter. Hence it has happened that many citizens have transferred their interest from the commune, as being a mere matter of tyrants, to San Giorgio, as being well and consistently governed; from this it has followed that changes in the government of the city have been made with ease and frequency, and first one citizen and then another, even foreigners, have ruled, because it has been the commune which has made the change, whilst San Giorgio has taken no part in it. Thus when conflicts arose between the Adorni and Fregosi for the position of doge the greater number of the citizens took no part in the struggle, and left the spoils to the victors, for it was only the rule of the commune which was the object of their contention. San Giorgio only concerned itself, when one of the combatants had seized the government, by compelling him to respect its privileges, which up to this time have remained untouched, because, possessing a constitution, revenues, and armies, the society could not be tampered with except at the risk of revolution. It is an example that may have been pictured in the imagined republics of philosophers, but rarely realised, of a state of affairs whereby, within the same circle and amid the same citizens, liberty and tyranny, civic virtues and corruption, justice and absolutism, have existed side by side. Thus San Giorgio alone in the city of Genoa maintains its ancient and venerable institutions, and if it should happen that in some way or other the whole city merges into San Giorgio, then the republic of Genoa will become more famous than even the republic of Venice.

Agostino having turned over Zerezana to San Giorgio it was willingly received and its defence readily undertaken. A fleet at once put to sea and an army was sent to Pietrasanta, where it threatened the camp of the Florentines, who had already approached Zerezana. The Florentines found it now necessary to capture Pietrasanta, otherwise there would be no advantage in the possession of Zerezana, seeing that the former town was situate between them and Pisa. Having, however, no just cause for seizing it unless the Pietrasantese or its garrison should interfere with their operations against Zerezana, they determined to precipitate a struggle. Accordingly they despatched from Pisa to their encampment a large convoy of stores and provisions under the charge of a weak escort, in the hope that the men of Pietrasanta, tempted by the weak escort, would endeavour to capture the convoy. The plan succeeded; the men of Pietrasanta seeing so much booty passing under their eyes at once seized it. This gave the Florentines a legitimate reason for declaring war against them, and at once leaving Zerezana they laid siege to Pietrasanta, which possessed a strong garrison and made a vigorous defence. The Florentines posted their artillery in the plains and closely invested the town on the hillside by a wall. Whilst Jacopo Guicciardini was fighting at Pietrasanta the Genoese fleet captured and burnt the fortress of Vada, landed an army, and ravaged the surrounding country. To restrain this the Florentines sent horse and foot under Messer Bongianni Gianfigliazzi, who in some measure succeeded in checking the foray, but the fleet continued to harass the Florentines. It attacked Leghorn, and with pontoons and other means approached the tower, battered it with artillery for a few days but made no impression upon it, and soon sailed away.

In the meanwhile the siege of Pietrasanta had been conducted with such little spirit that the garrison were encouraged to attack the bastion, and were able to capture it. This inspired the defenders with much ardour; they forced the Florentines to withdraw four miles from the town, and almost compelled them to retreat; The month of October having arrived, the leaders determined to go into winter quarters and postpone the further siege until the spring. When this disaster became known in Florence the heads of the state were extremely angry, and took measures at once to restore the discipline and courage of their troops by sending new commissioners, Antonio Pucci and Bernardo del Neri, with large sums of money; These commissioners informed the captains of the indignation of the whole city and government at their not having returned to the walls of Pietrasanta, and of the infamy to a great army, with so many captains, being unable to capture so weak and paltry a town, with nothing to oppose them but a trumpery garrison; they promised them an immediate advantage and future rewards if they captured it. The army, being inspired with fresh courage, returned to the siege, determined to capture in the first place the bastions it had recently lost; In this attack was shown the influence of affability and courtesy upon soldiers, for Antonio Pucci, by taking one man by the hand, embracing others, and encouraging all with promises, inspired them with such dash that in a moment the fortification was captured; but it was not recovered without loss, for the Count Antonio da Marciano was killed by a cannon ball. The loss of this bastion brought despair to the garrison and it began to consider a surrender. In order that more distinction should be conferred upon the siege Lorenzo de' Medici took the field, and a few days after his arrival the castle was captured in his presence. The winter was now at hand, and it seemed best to the captains that they should not proceed further with the enterprise but await the spring. They were led to this decision chiefly because the autumn air had infected the army with much sickness, and many of the officers were seriously ill or dead. Among the latter were Antonio Pucci and Bongianni Gianfigliazzi, and because of his deeds before Pietrasanta Antonio was greatly mourned. Shortly after the Florentines had captured Pietrasanta the Lucchese sent to demand it, alleging that, by one of the articles of the treaty, all towns thus recovered should be returned to those to whom they had primarily belonged, and this town had first belonged to their republic. The Florentines could not deny the stipulation, but replied that they did not understand that it would apply to such towns as Pietrasanta, which was under a treaty made between themselves and the Genoese, therefore they were not in a position to decide the question at once. However, when it was to be restored, it would be necessary for the Lucchese to state in what way they were prepared to satisfy the expenses incurred in its recovery and recompense them for the loss of so many Florentine citizens; when this was done the Lucchese might hope to have the town surrendered to them. The winter was occupied with a discussion of the terms for a peace between the Genoese and Florentines, and the question was finally referred to Rome for the mediation of the pope. Nothing having been concluded by the arrival of spring, the Florentines would have proceeded to the attack upon Zerezana had it not been for the war which broke out between the pope and King Ferrante, and also for the illness of Lorenzo de' Medici. Lorenzo not only suffered from the gout, which he had inherited from his father, but also from severe stomachic troubles which necessitated his going to the baths for the cure.

The most important of these two causes was the war, the origin of which was as follows. The city of Aquila was in some measure under the jurisdiction of the King of Naples, but was allowed its freedom under the Count di Montorio, who enjoyed a great reputation with its citizens. The Duke of Calabria was lying with his army near to Trento, and under pretence of quelling some slight disturbance which had occurred among the peasantry in those parts, but with the real intention of bringing Aquila entirely under the sway of the king, had sent for the Count di Montorio under the pretext of consulting with him concerning the trouble which had arisen. The count obeyed the summons without any suspicion, but when he reached the duke's quarters he was made prisoner and sent to Naples. When the news of this reached Aquila the whole city was enraged; the people flew to arms and slew Antonio Cencinello, the king's commissioner, with several citizens who were known to be supporters of his Majesty. In order to obtain recruits to support their rebellion the Aquilegians raised the banner of the Church, sent envoys to the pope, and placed themselves and their city under his protection. The pope courageously took up their defence, as for some reason, public or private, he disliked the king very much, and Signor Roberto da San Severino, being at the moment hostile to the state of Milan and without employment, was taken into the pope's service and summoned to Rome in great haste. The pope also took into his pay those friends and relatives of the Count di Montorio who had rebelled against the king. The king, finding himself thus suddenly attacked, had recourse to the Duke of Milan and the Florentines. The Florentines were in great doubt what to do, for it seemed hard to have to leave their own business and undertake that of others, and to again take up arms against the Church seemed also dangerous. Nevertheless, as they were members of the league, they once more preferred to keep faith rather than consider their own interests or perils. They took the Orsini into their pay, and sent their army under the Count di Pitigliano towards Rome to the assistance of the king. The king divided his forces into two camps; one under the Duke of Calabria was directed against Rome; it joined the army of the Florentines and was opposed by the army of the Church; with the other army, under his own command, he opposed the barons. This war was waged with varying success on one part or another, but in the end the king remained generally successful, and in August 1486 peace was concluded through the mediation of the King of Spain; the pope was quite ready to assent, for having been beaten he had no further desire to tempt fortune. All the potentates of Italy joined in this convention, excepting the Geneose, who as rebels to the rule of Milan and usurpers of Florentine towns were left outside of it. When peace was concluded Signor Roberto da San Severino, who had been neither loyal to the pope nor dangerous to his enemies, was driven out of Rome by the pope, pursued by the armies of the duke and the Florentines. When passing Cesena he found himself on the point of being overtaken, so pressed on to Ravenna with less than a hundred horsemen; the rest of his men either surrendered to the duke or were dispersed by the peasantry. The king, having concluded peace and become reconciled to his barons, put to death Jacopo Coppola and Antonello d'Aversa, with their sons, for having revealed his secrets to the pontiff during the war.

During this war the pope had learnt with what loyalty and readiness the Florentines observed their obligations to others, and whereas he had resented their action at its commencement, because of their assistance to the king and of his alliance with the Genoese, he now began to love them and to show greater attention to their envoys than he had previously done. This predilection was early recognised by Lorenzo de' Medici, who strove to increase it by all the means at his disposal, for he saw that it would increase his own power if, to the friendship which he enjoyed with the king, he could add that of the pope. The pope had a son named Francesco Cibo, whom he desired to endow with estates and friends, in order that he should be provided with both after his father's death, and he knew not to whom he could turn with greater confidence than to Lorenzo. He succeeded in his desires completely; Lorenzo even gave Francesco one of his daughters to wife. When this relationship was secured, the pope expressed a strong wish to the Genoese that Zerezana should be surrendered to the Florentines. He pointed out to them that Agostino had not the power to give Zerezana to them for it was not his to give, neither should they keep it although he had sold it to them; but the pope could make no impression upon them. Even whilst they were discussing the matter the Genoese were arming their ships, and before Florence knew what was happening they had thrown 3000 men on shore and attacked the fortress of Zerezanello, which was situate above Zerezana and held by the Florentines. They plundered and burnt the few houses near to it, and posting their artillery against the fortress incessantly battered it. Upon this new and quite unexpected attack the Florentines at once assembled their army under Virginio Orsini at Pisa, and complained to the pope that, whilst he was treating for peace with the Genoese, they had renewed the war against them. They sent Pietro Corsini to Lucca to hold that city to its loyalty. Pagolantonio Soderini also went to Venice to keep that republic steadfast to its engagements. They demanded assistance from the king and Signor Lodovico, but received none from either, for the king alleged he was in fear of the Turkish fleet and Signor Lodovico cavilled about terms. Thus the Florentines always had to stand alone in their own troubles, and found none to assist them in the spirit in which they had often assisted others. Although once more abandoned by their allies they did not lose courage, but raised a great army under Jacopo Guicciardini and Piero Vettori. They sent this army against the enemy who had encamped upon the banks of the Magra, and had closely invested Zerezanello, and with mines and other engines of war were pressing it very hard. The Florentines determined to relieve it, nor did the Genoese refuse the fight; coming to blows the latter were routed and lost a great number of men and prisoners, among whom were Messer Lodovico del Fiesco and several captains. This victory of the Florentines did not terrify the Zerezana garrison into surrender, but rather hardened it for sterner defence, and in defence and attack both sides behaved valiantly. The siege having continued for a length of time, Lorenzo de' Medici determined once more to take the field; his coming inspired his soldiers with fresh courage whilst it depressed the defenders of Zerezana, for they contrasted the energy of the Florentines in pressing them with the coldness of the Genoese in supporting them; therefore they threw themselves on the mercy of Lorenzo, freely and without conditions, and came under the dominion of the Florentines, by whom all but a few of the authors of the rebellion were generously treated. Signor Lodovico had sent some cavalry to Pontremoli during the siege, merely as a demonstration in favour of the Florentines, but having partisans in Genoa he incited a rebellion in that city against its rulers, and by the aid of his friends there the city was surrendered to the Duke of Milan.

About this time the Germans were involved in a war with the Venetians, and Boccolino da Osimo had incited the town of Osimo in La Marca to rebel against the pope, and declared himself its tyrant. This man allowed himself to be persuaded into surrendering the town again to the pope, and relying after all that had happened upon the word of Lorenzo went to reside in Florence, where he remained for many years in security. But going afterwards to Milan he did not meet there with the same good faith, and was put to death by Signor Lodovico. The Venetians were attacked by the Germans near to the city of Trento, defeated, and Signor Roberto da San Severino killed. After this disaster the Venetians made peace with the Germans, and in accordance with their usual good fortune did not come out of the war as losers but as victors, because the peace was an advantageous one for their republic.

There arose at this time considerable trouble in Romagna owing to Francesco di Orso, an inhabitant of Forli, in great reputation with the citizens, falling under the suspicions of Count Girolamo, and being threatened by him on several occasions. Francesco, who lived in daily fear for his life, was advised by his friends and relatives to be beforehand with the count, because if death is to be feared at the hands of a man, that man should be killed, then all danger would vanish with his death. When they had come to this decision and had resolved to make the attempt, market day at Forli was chosen, because it was expected that many of their friends amongst the country people would be in the town on that day, without having been summoned to assist in the deed; It was during the month of May, when the custom of many Italians is to take their supper by daylight, and it was considered a good opportunity for the conspirators to kill the count when his family had left him after the meal, and whilst he rested. The hour chosen by the conspirators having come, Francesco went to the door of the count's house, and leaving his companions on the ground floor sought the chamber where Girolamo was, and told the chamberlain that he desired to speak to the count. Francesco was admitted and, after a few words with the count upon his pretended mission, killed him, and called to his confederates who slew the chamberlain; there chanced also to arrive at the house at that moment on business the captain of the town, and him also the murderers immediately killed. This done they raised great shouts, and hanging the body of the count from the window, cried for Church and Liberty, and called the people to arms. The people who hated the count for his avarice and cruelty speedily sacked his house and took the Countess Caterina and her children prisoners. The fortress, which the castellan refused to give up, remained to be captured before the enterprise was entirely successful, and the people demanded of the countess that she should order the castellan to yield. She promised to do this if they would permit her to enter the fortress, and as hostages for her good faith they might keep her children. The rebels relying upon her word permitted her to enter the fortress, but as soon as she was within she threatened them from the walls with torture and death in revenge for the murder of her husband. They replied by threatening to take the lives of her children, to which she replied that she could still bring forth others. When the rebels learnt that the pope refused to assist them, and that Signor Lodovico, the uncle of the countess, was sending men to her assistance, they gathered such booty as they could carry with them and fled to the Citta di Castello. As soon as the countess recovered the government of the town, she avenged the death of her husband with every kind of cruelty. When the Florentines heard of the death of the count they took the opportunity to seize the fortress of Piancaldoli, of which the count had deprived them, and sent forces which accomplished the capture with the death of one man only—the famous architect Cecca.

To the above trouble has to be added one of no less importance which happened also in that country. Galeotto, the lord of Faenza, had married the daughter of Messer Giovanni Bentivogli, the Prince of Bologna. This lady hated her husband, either because she was badly treated by him, or she was jealous, or it may have been her own evil disposition, until unable to contain herself any longer she determined to take his life and appropriate his state. Simulating sickness she took to her bed, intending that some of her confidants whom she would secrete in her chamber should kill her husband when he visited her as usual. She had made her father a participator in her crime, for he hoped to become the lord of Faenza after the death of his son-in-law. At the time appointed for the murder, when Galeotto was in his wife's room as expected, the murderers rushed from their hiding place and killed him before he could make any resistance. Immediately he was killed a great disturbance broke out in the town, the people flew to arms, and the lady with her little son Astorre fled to the fortress. Messer Giovanni Bentivogli, together with a man from Bergamo, a condottiere of the Duke of Milan, entered Faenza with a body of soldiers. Antonio Boscolo, the Florentine commissioner, was also there, and the future government of the city was discussed between them amid great tumult. Whilst this was occurring the men from the Val di Lamona, who had gathered into the city at the first report of the murder, fell upon Messer Giovanni and the man from Bergamo, killed the latter and took the former prisoner; then they handed over the city to the commissioner amid great shouts for Astorre and the Florentines. Upon the report of these deeds being carried to Florence all the city was greatly displeased with it, nevertheless they set Messer Giovanni and his daughter free, and took the city and the young Astorre under their protection, to which the people of Faenza assented. Romagna, La Marca, and Siena continued, however, in a very unsettled state long after the conclusion of the great wars between the leading states in Italy, but being of small importance I do not further allude to it. It is true that the disturbance was very persistent in Siena after the departure of the Duke of Calabria to the war in 1478, until firstly the domination of the people and then that of the nobles was finally settled. Among these latter Pandolfo and Jacopo Petrucci held the chief power, the one by his courage and the other by his prudence.

From the conclusion of the siege of Zerezana, until the death of Lorenzo de' Medici in the year 1492, the Florentines lived in the height of prosperity, for Lorenzo, having by his good sense and authority secured peace in Italy, turned his attention to the aggrandisement of himself and his city. He married his eldest son, Piero, to Alfonsina, the daughter of the chevalier Orsini. He afterwards obtained the dignity of cardinal for his second son, Giovanni. The elevation of a youth who was scarcely fourteen years of age to so high an honour was very remarkable, and had never occurred before. These were the steps by which the Medici family were to mount to the highest positions, as after events showed. Lorenzo was unable to provide any extraordinary advancement for his third son, Giuliano, because of his extreme youth at the time of his own early death. He married his eldest daughter to Jacopo Salviati, his second to Francesco Cibo, and his third to Piero Ridofi; his fourth daughter died after she had been betrothed to Giovanni de' Medici, by which alliance he had hoped to maintain the unity of the family. In his private affairs as a merchant he was very unfortunate, owing to the misconduct of his servants, who would not administer his affairs as private people, but as if they were princes; thus his possessions were dissipated in every direction, and his country had to come to his assistance with immense sums of money. In order that he should not be the sport of such vicissitudes of fortune in future he abandoned mercantile pursuits in the later years of his life, and turned his attention to acquiring land, as likely to bring him more stable riches. In the Pratesian and Pisan districts he bought large estates, as also in the Val di Pesa, which in their extent and value, and the magnificence of the buildings upon them, ranked rather with those of a king than with those of a private citizen. It was after this that he turned to the beautifying of Florence, and finding many parts of it quite bare of buildings he laid out new streets, and ordered new houses to be built there, so that the city greatly increased and became far more beautiful. He increased the security of his State by fortifying the castle of Firenzuola in the mountains towards Bologna, and had commenced strengthening Poggio Imperiale in the direction of Siena, in order to diminish the risk of invasion by fighting and keeping his enemies at a distance, whilst the acquisition of Pietrasanta and Zerezana had closed the way to hostile armies approaching from Genoa. He retained the friendship of the Baglioni in Perugia and the Vitelli in Citta di Castello by pensions and subsidies, and he took Faenza under his protection, all of which acted as bulwarks to his city. During times of peace he entertained the city with festivals, at which were displayed tournaments and representations of ancient deeds and triumphs. It was throughout his aim to make the city prosperous, the people united, and the nobles honoured. He loved exceedingly all who excelled in the arts, and he showered favours on the learned, of which Messer Agnolo Montepulciano, Messer Cristofano Landini, and Messer Demetrio Greco are able to bear abundant testimony. It was for this reason that Count Giovanni della Mirandola, a man of almost divine genius, turned his back on all other parts of Europe, where he would have been welcome, in order that he might reside in Florence, whither he had been attracted by the magnificence of Lorenzo. Lorenzo delighted in architecture, music, and poetry, and many of his own compositions in poetry are extant, as well as many upon which he had written commentaries. To give the youth of Florence an opportunity of studying letters he founded a college at Pisa, to which he had appointed the most excellent professors that Italy could produce. He built a monastery near to Florence for Brother Mariano de Chinazano of the Order of San Agostino, because of his great powers as a preacher. Lorenzo had been highly favoured by both God and fortune, inasmuch as in all his enterprises he had been successful, whilst those in which his enemies had engaged against him were failures. Besides the conspiracy of the Pazzi, there was one in the Carmine by Battista Frescobaldi and one at his villa by Baldinotto of Pistoia, all designed to put an end to him, yet not only did their authors suffer just punishment for their evil intentions, but also those who were privy to them. His character, prudence, and good fortune were such that he was known and esteemed, not only by the princes of Italy, but by many others in distant lands. Mattia, the King of Hungary, gave him many proofs of his regard. The soldan sent him envoys and gifts. The Grand Turk gave into his hands Bernardo Bandini, the murderer of his brother. All of these great qualities filled Italy with his renown, which his prudence increased day by day. In his conversation he was ready and eloquent, in his resolutions wise, in action swift and courageous. There was nothing in his conduct, although inclined to excessive gallantry, which in any way impaired his many virtues; it is possible he found more pleasure in the company of droll and witty men than became a man of his position; and he would often be found playing among his children as if he were still a child. To see him at one time in his grave moments and at another in his gay was to see in him two personalities, joined as it were with invisible bonds. During his last days he suffered great agony owing to the malady with which he was afflicted—oppressed by some deadly stomach trouble—which terminated fatally in April 1492. There had never died in Florence—nor yet in Italy—one for whom his country mourned so much, or who left behind him so wide a reputation for wisdom. Heaven gave many unmistakable signs that ruin would follow his decease, among such signs was the destruction of the highest pinnacle of San Reparata by lightning. He was mourned by all his people and by the princes of Italy, none of whom failed to send envoys to express their sympathy with the citizens. All had indeed just reasons for deploring his loss, for Italy deprived of his counsel could not find among the men who were left one who could fill his place or curb the ambitions of Lodovico Sforza, the governor of the dukedom of Milan. For as soon as Lorenzo de' Medici was dead there sprung up those fatal seeds, which soon accomplished the downfall of Italy, and which, none knowing how to destroy, will perpetuate her ruin.

INDEX

SUGGESTED READING

BOCCACCIO, GIOVANNI. *The Decameron.* New York: Penguin, 1996.

HALE, J.R. *Florence and the Medici.* London: Phoenix, 2001.

HIBBERT, CHRISTOPHER. *The House of Medici: Its Rise and Fall.* New York: HarperCollins, 1982.

MACHIAVELLI, NICCOLÒ. *Art of War.* Trans. Ellis Farneworth. Cambridge, MA: Da Capo, 2001.

---. *Discourses.* Trans. Nathan Tarcov and H.C. Mansfield. Chicago: University of Chicago Press, 1998.

---. *The Portable Machiavelli.* Trans. and Ed. Peter E. Bondanella and Mark Musa. New York: Penguin, 1979.

---. *The Prince and Other Writings.* Trans. Wayne A. Rebhorn. New York: Barnes & Noble, 2003.

MARTINES, LAURO. *April Blood: Florence and the Plot Against the Medici.* New York: Oxford University Press, 2003.

MASTERS, ROGER D. *Fortune Is a River: Leonardo Da Vinci and Niccolo Machiavelli's Magnificent Dream to Change the Course of Florentine History.* New York: Plume, 1999.

MCCARTHY, MARY. *The Stones of Florence.* New York: Harcourt Brace, 2003.

SKINNER, QUENTIN. *Machiavelli: A Very Short Introduction.* New York: Oxford University Press, 2000.

STRATHERN, PAUL. *Machiavelli in 90 Minutes.* Chicago: Ivan R. Dee, 1998.

STRAUSS, LEO. *Thoughts on Machiavelli.* Chicago: University of Chicago Press, 1995.

TREXLER, RICHARD C. *Public Life in Renaissance Florence.* Ithaca, NY: Cornell University Press, 1991.

VIROLI, MAURIZIO. *Niccolo's Smile.* Trans. Antony Shugaar. New York: Farrar, Straus and Giroux, 2001.